DISCARDED BY
FREEPORT
MEMORIAL LIBRARY

HOME GROWN

DENYS DE SAULLES

Consulting Editor
JIM WILSON

HOUGHTON MIFFLIN COMPANY
BOSTON 1988

7-8-88

6̇35
D

B4y- 29.85 334 4768

A Marshall Edition
Conceived, edited, and designed by
Marshall Editions Ltd, 170 Piccadilly,
London W1V 9DD

Copyright © 1988 by Marshall Editions
Limited

Editor   Carole McGlynn
American editor   Elizabeth Duvall
Art editor   Daphne Mattingly
Managing editor   Ruth Binney
Design assistant   Rachel Mozley
Research   Jazz Wilson

Production   Barry Baker
Production secretary   Nikki Ingram

Color plates   Kate Osborne
Herb color plates   Lynn Chadwick
Line illustrations   Liz Pepperel
                            Jim Robins

Typeset by Servis Filmsetting Limited,
Manchester, UK
Originated by Newsele Riproduzioni
Fotolitografiche, Milan, Italy
Printed and bound in Spain by
Printer Industria Gráfica S.A., Barcelona
D.L.: B. 39215-1987

1 2 3 4 5 92 91 90 89 88

All rights reserved. No part of this work may
be reproduced or transmitted in any form or
by any means, electronic or mechanical,
including photocopying and recording, or by
any information storage or retrieval system,
except as may be expressly permitted by the
1976 Copyright Act or in writing from the
copyright owner. For information about
permission to reproduce selections from this
book, write to Houghton Mifflin Company, 2
Park Street, Boston, Massachusetts 02108,
USA.

Library of Congress Cataloging-in-Publication Data

De Saulles, Denys.
Home grown/

Includes index.
1. Vegetable gardening. 2. Organic gardening.
3. Fruit-culture. 4. Vegetables—Preservation.
5. Fruit—Preservation. I. Wilson, James W. (James
Wesley), date II. Title.
SB324.3.D4 1988   635   87-22625
ISBN 0-395-45686-X

First published in the USA 1988 by
Houghton Mifflin Company, 2 Park Street,
Boston, Massachusetts 02108

CONTENTS

Growing your own fruit and vegetables is a source of real pleasure in every season of the year, whether you're planning or planting, sowing or harvesting – or enjoying the culinary delights home-grown produce provides. And those delights are considerable, especially in flavor and freshness. Add to them the relaxation and satisfaction of making and tending a food garden and you have a leisure activity second to none.

With a food garden, whether it's a plot that spans an acre or a collection of pots and tubs on your patio, you can bring fruit and vegetables to your table within minutes of the moment they are picked. Their color will be superb, their taste unmatched by anything you can buy from a supermarket. As a consumer, you can be sure, too, that the produce from your garden is free from potentially harmful pesticides and preservatives, and that its health-giving vitamins and minerals have not been destroyed or diminished by careless handling or storage.

As more and more people travel abroad, so tastes in food have come to express the spirit of adventure. This is reflected in the vast range of fruits and vegetables now eaten by the average American. The quest for a healthful diet, lower in fat, preservatives and salt and higher in fiber than processed foods, has also had a strong influence in broadening the spectrum of varieties available to today's gardeners. These newcomers may be selections from familiar themes – purple lettuces, white radishes, yellow tomatoes, and golden beets – or exotic, imported additions to the scene, such as Chinese vegetables and herbs from Latin America and the Middle East.

Advances made by plant breeders and nurserymen have created new hybrids such as the tayberry and boysenberry, and the relatively hardy kiwi. They have also led to consistent improvements in the disease resistance of garden fruit and vegetables, to compact forms ideal for small, modern gardens, and to better yields. All these are important considerations when space is at a premium.

With so many different kinds of fruits and vegetables to choose from, you should have no trouble in enjoying food from your garden all year round. But even with good planning, there are bound to be times of the year when you'll have produce to spare. This is when you can stock your pantry with chutneys and preserves, fill the freezer, and make welcome presents of home-grown fare to friends and neighbors.

As the following pages prove, the food garden can be as pretty as it is practical. We hope that *Home Grown* will be both a help and an inspiration, a reference book that you'll turn to again and again.

Jim Wilson

PLANNING TO GROW YOUR OWN

Growing vegetables and fruit successfully demands, as many beginners can testify, more than merely having "green fingers." It actually depends on the fundamentals of gardening—choosing the right plants for your site, growing and caring for plants according to simple instructions, and, most important of all, being prepared to improve and care for the soil. It is poor, neglected soil that accounts for most crop failures and disappointments.

If you are establishing a plot from scratch, or replanning a garden, the first step is to decide where the food garden is going to be. It is worth taking some trouble over this, for no amount of effort at the growing stage will compensate for an unsuitable site.

Before consigning food crops to the far end of the garden, like outcasts, consider whether they might form part of the decorative area—particularly if this will provide them with the most favorable growing conditions. A well-kept fruit and vegetable plot looks attractive in its own right, and trained fruit trees and bushes are both decorative and productive.

Study the needs of the crops you plan to grow (details of the preferences of individual fruits and vegetables are given later in the book) and give careful thought to what you can grow where. Some crops, such as tomatoes and onions, need plenty of sun, whereas others, such as lettuce and raspberries, will grow well in partial shade. Many low-growing plants will withstand a considerable amount of wind, whereas plants that are taller or more tender need protection and/or support.

Obviously, a small area will yield less than a large one, but worthwhile crops can be grown in relatively cramped surroundings. When space is limited, it is particularly important to study a variety of possibilities and establish your priorities before deciding what, and how much, to grow. Garden size will also be a factor in determining layout, but remember to plan for paths. Harvesting vegetables and fruit, moving compost, pruning fruit trees, and doing a number of other garden jobs means that you need easy access to your plants all year round.

Before buying seeds or plants, take time to study the selections of fruit and vegetables included in this book and to thumb through suppliers' catalogues to see what appeals. Also, work out what tools and equipment you will need.

If you are a beginner, there is much to be said for starting in a fairly small way— for example, by growing salad vegetables or herbs, or some quick-maturing vegetables such as zucchini. A lot will depend on the condition of your soil and your personal tastes and preferences.

When planning a food-growing plot, you may be concerned about how much time you need. There is really no absolute answer, but in most temperate climates plants will need attention and jobs will need to be done in the garden during most spring, summer, and autumn weekends. It partly depends on what you grow—celery takes up a lot more time than cabbage, for example—as well as on the condition of your soil.

As a guide, you can assume that tending a greenhouse and a plot measuring about 150 square yards will demand around half a day's attention a week. You might well need to spend more hours in the garden and greenhouse during the spring and early summer months, but if you find gardening a pleasurable pursuit, you will want to spend as much of your spare time as possible tending your plants and your plot.

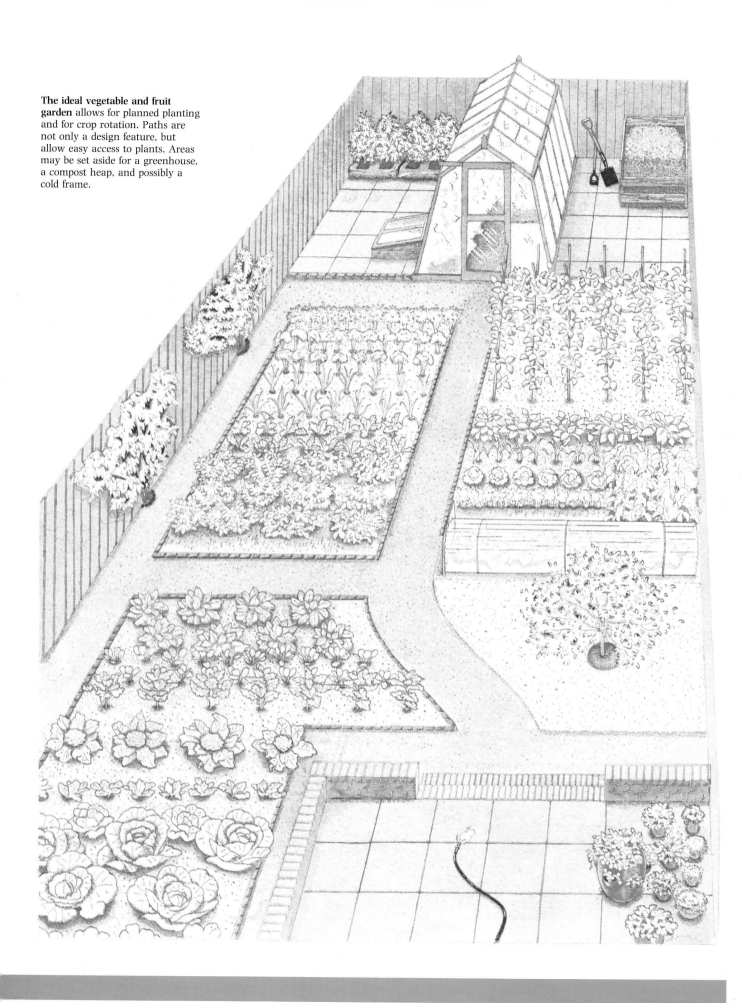

The ideal vegetable and fruit garden allows for planned planting and for crop rotation. Paths are not only a design feature, but allow easy access to plants. Areas may be set aside for a greenhouse, a compost heap, and possibly a cold frame.

Food crops need a favored position in your garden if they are to produce a worthwhile harvest, not least because they often have to grow quite a lot in a short time. A cabbage grows from a tiny seed to a plant the size of a soccer ball in only four months, for example, and a single seed potato planted in spring should give a twentyfold increase by autumn. Fruit trees produce over a longer time, but an established apple tree, for instance, can be expected to produce a hundred pounds of fruit per year—every year—for a lifetime.

SUN AND SOIL

The ideal spot for most crops is generally well drained and open to the sky so it receives plenty of sunshine. You will probably have to compromise, but avoid at all costs a patch shaded by an overhanging tree and starved by its roots. Neither vegetables nor fruit will prosper there.

You cannot do anything to increase the average number of hours of sunshine your area receives each year. But what you can do is site your food crops so that they receive the maximum your garden can offer. For example, if you live in the North, you can grow fruit trees against a south-facing wall so that they get all the sunshine going and benefit from the extra heat stored by the wall. On the other hand, too much sun is a problem where temperatures zoom into the nineties for much of the growing season. Shelter vulnerable crops under translucent row covers or nets.

If your soil is poorly drained, it is essential to improve it, as explained on page 26, since very few vegetables or fruits thrive in soggy ground. If the soil remains damp and sticky for long periods, you have a drainage problem on your hands.

The type of soil—sand, clay, or somewhere in between—is less critical. Though each type has its merits and drawbacks (see pp.24–25), all are capable of growing crops, especially if you take steps to improve their texture and fertility. It is a question of making the best of what you have. All soils can be improved.

WIND AND FROST

Whether your garden faces north or south and its degree of exposure to winds are as significant as the average amount of sunshine or rainfall.

Shelter from wind is a bonus in any garden, and almost essential on an exposed site. A living windbreak formed by a hedge causes less turbulence than a wall or solid fence, and can be productive if it is, say, a double row of raspberry canes. Restricted forms of fruit trees, such as espaliers or fans, can also be trained against barriers.

Frost can be a particular hazard in low-lying gardens, since cold air flows downhill. A frost pocket can also be formed when a barrier checks the movement of air down a slope. Other than avoiding a vulnerable site, the solutions are to plant later in spring and to make full use of cloches and frames. It is also a simple matter to choose late-flowering varieties of fruit trees and to delay spring pruning in order to retard new shoots, if you expect spring frosts.

Another protective measure against frost is the use of mulches—in the form of compost, straw, plastic, leaves, or newspapers. These are laid on the ground around plants to protect their roots until the soil warms up in spring.

MAKING THE MOST OF THE SPACE

If you are short of space, you will need to think carefully about what to grow as well as where to plant it. There are no set rules, since much depends on personal taste. Even so, some crops do give better value than others for the space they occupy, and provided they are crops you enjoy, these are the ones to grow. Crops that can be grown vertically are a particularly good choice.

Planting vegetables in beds or patches makes the most of a small plot. The closer spacing between plants in a bed, as opposed to a row, enables you to grow many more plants in a given area. Details of bed systems are given on p.132.

MINIMUM-SPACE CROPS

Salad vegetables, including lettuce, spring onions, and radishes, are all compact, rapid growers and much tastier when freshly gathered. A few well-chosen herbs can be successfully grown in pots or an odd corner: select the ones you use most, such as chives, mint, thyme, parsley, and basil.

Plants that grow vertically, such as pole beans, cucumbers, or even cantaloupes, increase the output of any given area. They may be grown against a fence or on a trellis. If there is enough space for one or two growing bags, tomatoes will crop heavily on a sheltered patio. You may also like to experiment with peppers or eggplants, which can be grown in the same way—as can many garden vegetables.

Most root crops are ruled out if your space is restricted, but try to find room for a few early carrots, which are delicious when freshly pulled. Likewise, most brassicas— cauliflowers, Brussels sprouts, and the like —take up a lot of space, but the small, plump heads of 'Golden Cross Hybrid' cabbage are a worthy exception, as are several kinds of Chinese cabbage.

For an ongoing supply of tender leaves from just two or three plants, consider growing perpetual spinach. And bear in mind that both globe artichokes and rhubarb chard, though large, are attractive plants for the flower garden. A row of beets makes an effective edging to a flowerbed, as do alpine strawberries, the red varieties of lettuce, and several decorative herbs.

PLANTS IN CONTAINERS

A windowbox garden is a practical and decorative possibility. Among suitable herbs are sage, chives, mint, and marjoram. The restricted space will help to keep the plants small. Pots or hanging baskets can be used for the same purpose.

If you have a sizable patio, it is perfectly feasible to grow zucchini, cucumbers, and even melons in tubs or other substantial containers. Some of the plants may need to be supported with stakes, however.

Strawberries grown in barrels or tall terra-cotta pots bear well. Once covered with foliage, blossoms, and fruit, the container makes an attractive feature in its own right, on a patio or elsewhere. With all container-grown plants, however, you must water regularly and generously.

TRAINED FRUIT TREES

Nearly all gardens have space for a fruit tree, although you might want to choose one of the trained forms—fan, espalier, or cordon—and a self-fertile variety instead of planting and tending an entire orchard. Such trees can be grown against a wall or fence; they take up very little room but are capable of substantial yields.

Alternatively, cordons and espaliers can be planted as dividers or screens within the garden. The trees look neat and decorative, even during the dormant season.

USING A GREENHOUSE, pages 12–13
MULCHING, page 43

THE FRUIT GARDEN, page 65
GROWING TREE FRUITS, pages 87–89

SPACE-SAVING METHODS, pages 132–133

The climate map shown below is divided into zones based on the average annual minimum temperatures. All gardeners need to be aware of the anticipated degree of cold in their area, since this is one of the most significant considerations in choosing which crops to grow and what protective measures to adopt.

However, such a map can give only the broadest categories of temperatures, and you should also take local factors, both within your area and within your garden, into consideration. The altitude of your garden, whether it is in an open, rural place or a built-up urban location, and whether it is exposed to coastal winds or nestling in a sheltered valley will all influence your choice of crops and varieties and your method of cultivation. The orientation of your garden and the microclimate within it will also govern what you can grow.

Although you cannot change the weather patterns of the area in which you live, there are many ways in which to minimize the drawbacks and maximize the potential of a particular site. There are

usually sheltered corners within the garden that will give half-hardy plants extra protection, or walls that will shelter fruit trees. Crops can be protected from the extremely high temperatures of midsummer by temporary shading and from frosts by mulches.

If you have a greenhouse, you can extend the growing season for several weeks or even grow crops in winter, provided you are prepared to heat it. Tender crops such as grapes and melons can be grown indoors in the far North.

Frames and cloches can be put to good use in the same way—to give extra protection as well as to sow and raise early crops. Cloches also help to warm up the soil ready for seeds or seedlings.

Bear in mind that it is always more important to garden by the weather than by the book. In most climates the weather is variable and unpredictable from year to year. Whatever it says on the seed packet, do not sow seeds outdoors in midspring if the ground is still cold. Trust your judgment, provide protection where necessary, and you will grow successful crops.

THE EFFECTS OF MICROCLIMATE

- **Type of soil** A light soil heats up in spring and cools down in fall more rapidly than a heavy soil.
- **Orientation** A south-facing garden receives the most sunshine.
- **Slope** A south-facing slope is warmest and will encourage spring growth. Avoid planting in a hollow, since cold air flows downhill.
- **Walls** A wall gives shelter and stores heat, which it will radiate at night. This benefits fruit trees.
- **Proximity of buildings** A garden surrounded by buildings is likely to be warmer than an open one, but buildings can cut out light.
- **Proximity of trees** Beware of planting crops too near a large tree. Its extensive roots may starve your crops of food and moisture.
- **Exposure** Erect fences and hedges to reduce the force of the wind and to shelter your plants.

Approximate range of average annual minimum temperatures

Below − 50°F	Zone 1
− 50° to − 40°F	Zone 2
− 40° to − 30°F	Zone 3
− 30° to − 20°F	Zone 4
− 20° to − 10°F	Zone 5
− 10° to 0°F	Zone 6
0° to 10°F	Zone 7
10° to 20°F	Zone 8
20° to 30°F	Zone 9
30° to 40°F	Zone 10

The protected environment of a greenhouse offers the food gardener many advantages. If you live in a temperate or cooler climate zone, it enables you to grow crops that need winter protection and that can be grown outdoors only in warmer or frost-free areas. By lengthening the gardening year, it allows you the satisfaction of growing out-of-season crops, if only by means of early seed-starting under glass. It also lets you enjoy particular crops over an extended period. Not only can you make early sowings, before the garden soil has warmed up, but you can extend the fruiting period of crops such as tomatoes, at the other end of the growing season.

A greenhouse also protects tender plants against weather hazards such as frost, rain, and chilling winds, to which they are vulnerable outdoors. At the same time it offers all plants protection against pests, including birds and certain insects.

SPRING SOWINGS
Early salads are a considerable bonus for all food growers. Even in an unheated greenhouse, radishes, lettuces, and spring onions will germinate and grow long before the soil outside has started to warm up.

Several half-hardy vegetables and fruits can be started inside—under glass—for planting out after the last spring frosts. This category includes melons, cucumbers, tomatoes, pumpkins, and both summer and winter squash.

You can give pole beans and sweet corn an early start by sowing them in the greenhouse. Established plants can then be transplanted to outdoor positions. There is no need to raise all of each crop in this way. Start enough plants to provide some early pickings before the main outdoor-sown crop matures.

SUMMER CROPS
After spring plant-raising, you can plant the summer crops that will grow to maturity inside the greenhouse. Most important of these are tomatoes, which provide a supply of ripening fruit both earlier and later than garden tomatoes.

Cucumbers are another worthwhile greenhouse crop. Because they can be grown vertically, right up to the greenhouse roof, both cucumbers and tomatoes provide excellent returns for the ground space they occupy.

You can also grow a number of tender crops in a greenhouse, including eggplants, peppers, chiles, and okra, as well as fruits such as grapes, kiwi fruit, and melons. Any of these will grow successfully outdoors, but a northern gardener's chances are considerably improved indoors.

COLD OR HEATED?
Artificial heating brings a further advantage to the greenhouse gardener; in particular, it allows earlier sowing and planting. To grow food crops, however, it is by no means essential to heat the whole greenhouse. Localized warmth, in the form of soil-warming cables or a propagator (see p.38), is sufficient to give seedlings a good start; it is also much cheaper.

Your aim in using a partially or wholly heated greenhouse must be to time your sowings to suit the conditions that will prevail after the seedling stage. If a small propagator is your only heat source, you will have to sow later than in a heated greenhouse. But the lengthening spring days will soon help delayed sowings to catch up.

GROWING BAGS AND CONTAINERS
An alternative to planting directly in the ground is to grow crops in containers. This is less trouble, and cuts down on the disease problems that arise in greenhouse soil. Disease organisms multiply and the soil becomes exhausted in greenhouse beds that are used for years in succession; this often happens with tomatoes, for instance. Instead of simply replacing the soil in the beds with fresh soil, you might prefer to grow the plants in plastic bags or in pots.

Miniature lean-to Designed for small gardens, these structures serve the dual function of greenhouse and cold frame. The plants, grown on shelving, are tended from outside. Small volume makes it more difficult to maintain a stable temperature in these structures, so extra attention is needed during frosty or hot weather.

Lean-to (above) These are warmer than freestanding greenhouses. The reduced area of glass results in lower heat loss by day, and the backing wall serves to some extent as a heat bank at night. A wall facing between southeast and southwest is needed.

Plastic (right) The advantages of low capital outlay must be weighed against the cost of replacing the cover regularly—perhaps every two years.

SOWING UNDER GLASS, pages 38–39
GREENHOUSE EQUIPMENT, pages 14–15

Growing bags, which are laid flat and have slits cut in the top for plants, are about a yard long, which is large enough for a couple of cucumbers or three tomato plants. Water the mature plants once or twice daily, and start using liquid fertilizer at an early stage.

CHOOSING A GREENHOUSE

Shape, size, and structural material are the chief points to consider when choosing a greenhouse. Once you have a broad idea of your requirements, send for makers' catalogues to compare specifications and prices.

Size A ground area of as little as five square yards will suffice if your object is simply to start half-hardy plants in spring and to leave enough space during the summer for a few tomatoes and cucumbers. If you also wish to grow salad crops during the spring, followed by a greater range of summer crops, you will need a base of about nine square yards.

It is best, if you have enough space and money, not to start small, if only because you will quickly become aware of the many uses and possibilities of the greenhouse.

Shape Although most greenhouses are rectangular and freestanding, there are a number of permutations and other possibilities (see illustrations). Consider the practical pros and cons for your site and your preferences, rather than judging by appearances alone.

Materials The principal choice is between wood (unpainted) and aluminum frames. Given occasional treatment with a nontoxic preservative, a good wooden greenhouse will last several decades.

Cedar and redwood have natural resistance to rot. It is easy to fit shelves, insulating sheeting, and vine eyes for plant support and training in a wooden greenhouse.

Aluminum is strong and needs no maintenance. Though less convenient for attaching sheeting and screws, most systems include clamps and fittings for securing shelves to the glazing bars. A metal greenhouse lets in more light than a wooden one, and glazing takes less time, since the panes are simply clipped into place. Condensation is heavier than in a wooden greenhouse.

Plastic greenhouses Plastic tunnels are widely used by commercial growers, and are sold in smaller form for amateurs. Polyethylene, which deteriorates in sunlight, needs replacing every year or two. Vinyl has a longer life but costs more.

A disadvantage of plastic-covered greenhouses is their rapid heat loss, with accompanying condensation. Because the main tunnel section is formed by a continuous skin, ventilation may also prove to be a problem.

SITING CHECKLIST
You may have little choice about where to site your greenhouse, but if there is more than one possibility, consider the following points:

Light Choose the sunniest position available. Remember that trees and buildings cast longer shadows early in the year, when good light is particularly important for plant growth, than in high summer. In hot climates, however, shade can be beneficial.

Shelter Make sure your greenhouse is not in an exposed position, where the wind can chill the walls and significantly reduce the inside temperature. Position the door on the side least affected by cold winds.

Access As a rule, the nearer a greenhouse is to the house, the more convenient it will be. However, it should not be so close, and in such a position, that the house shades it. Access by a well-drained path is essential.

Services A water faucet in or near the greenhouse is valuable—the alternative is a hose and water barrel. Consider, too, the distance from the electricity supply.

Span-roof Inside this conventionally shaped greenhouse, the usual arrangement is to have a central path with a soil border on each side and across the far end. One side border may be covered with benches, for raising plants at least part of the year. Some span-roof greenhouses have partially boarded side walls; others are glazed to ground level. The fully glazed type is preferable for food growing, since the crops receive maximum light. However, the structure itself gets colder.

Geodesic Along with the distinctive appeal of their futuristic shape, these greenhouses make good use of available space. Though they do not have vertical walls, you can fit multiple layers of benches and you can grow tall plants such as tomatoes in them.

Control of the greenhouse environment is entirely in the hands of the gardener. The inside temperature, the degree of ventilation or insulation, the provision of shade, and the amount of watering are all your responsibility; they can be adjusted according to the time of year and to suit the crops you are starting or growing inside. Technology has come to the aid of the greenhouse gardener, however, and many of these routine tasks, which were once so time-consuming, are now automatically controlled. But although modern equipment will make your tasks easier, it cannot replace your personal care and judgment.

STAGING

You need some form of work surface on which to stand seed trays and pots at a convenient working height. Most greenhouse manufacturers offer staging—semipermanent benches—to fit their structures, along with the necessary fittings.

Simplest of all are the wooden supporting frames with slatted tops generally supplied for wooden greenhouses. Good air circulation and free drainage are two of their major advantages.

A metal frame supporting a mesh top provides similar conditions. These devices are supplied by the makers of aluminum greenhouses, and may also be fitted with metal trays about an inch deep. The trays make good supports for a capillary watering system (see below) or, turned upside down, provide a firm working surface.

Staging must be removable if you plan to use the greenhouse border for summer crops. Dismantle it in late spring when the last of the seedlings or tender plants have been moved outside. Some greenhouse owners choose to have permanent staging on one side of the house, leaving the other side open for crop-growing. It is possible to grow salad crops beneath the staging if it is on the sunny side, but the legs of the staging must stand on bricks or metal plates so they do not settle into the soil in the border. Shelves fixed at a higher level will provide space for pots and small trays.

HEATING

Several worthwhile crops can be grown in an unheated greenhouse, especially if you wait until the end of winter to make the first sowings. However, you must sow the seeds of some tender fruits, such as melons, and certain vegetables, such as peppers, in a warm environment. If you wish to grow any of these plants, you might consider providing local heat in the form of an electric propagator or soil-warming cables (see p.38). These are an economical alternative to heating the whole greenhouse.

The biggest drawback to providing heat is, of course, its cost. But if you do decide to extend the scope of your greenhouse by heating it, you will have a choice between various sources of artificial heat.

The chief advantage of electricity is that it emits a dry heat, so does not cause extra condensation. Electric fan heaters are particularly good, since they help to avoid a stagnant atmosphere, which encourages disease. Tubular heaters, secured to the walls, take up little room. The main drawback of electric heating is its relatively high running cost.

Gas provides reasonably economical heating, and the carbon dioxide given off by natural gas is beneficial to green plants. Running costs are relatively low for both gas-fired piped hot water systems and natural-gas heaters. Heavier condensation is a drawback to consider. Bottled gas is substantially more expensive as a fuel, but there is no installation cost.

Kerosene heating also gives rise to condensation, but it provides a convenient means of heating during the early spring when weather conditions are not too severe, and it is inexpensive.

INSULATION

Only a few costly greenhouses are double-glazed. Heat lost through the glass in the majority of greenhouses is considerable, and this significantly increases the fuel costs during winter and early spring.

Improved insulation is the answer to heat preservation and lower heating bills. The best method of insulation is to secure plastic sheeting to the inside, which traps air between the plastic and the glass.

VENTILATION

Efficient greenhouse ventilation is essential throughout the year. In summer it provides a necessary means of temperature control; without adequate ventilation plants wilt and rapidly die. In winter, some ventilation is needed to prevent the development of a stagnant atmosphere in which disease-causing organisms can flourish. Winter ventilation is very important in greenhouses with heavy condensation.

Roof ventilators are the most efficient type, but many small greenhouses are inadequately supplied with these. The ideal is to have two ventilators six feet apart on opposite sides. Side ventilators—sliding, hinged, or louvered—help to increase the flow of air, and you can always leave the greenhouse door open.

Automatic vent openers, which are sensitive to heat and thermostatically controlled, are a boon. They keep hinged louvers adjusted to suit the temperature, so you can leave a greenhouse all day without worrying about your plants.

Electric ventilator fans, similar to those used in kitchens but thermostatically controlled, provide another means of automatic ventilation. Small circulating fans, which help to maintain an even and oxygen-rich atmosphere, are also available.

SHADING

Sun that strikes plants directly through the glass can overheat and scorch them, even in a well-ventilated greenhouse. Some form of shading is needed to counter this.

The simplest and cheapest form of shading is a prepared shading liquid that you can paint directly onto the outside of the glass or plastic. It is resistant to rain, but you can rub it off at the end of the season. Some are formulated to turn opaque in bright sunlight and remain transparent on dull days.

Roller blinds provide a more expensive but more satisfactory solution. Those fitted to the outside of the greenhouse are best, since they keep both the glass and the interior of the greenhouse cool. Inside blinds, which are less at risk from the weather, shade the plants effectively but have less effect on the overall temperature.

WATERING

Hand watering of greenhouse plants is time-consuming but allows accurate control. Because your aim should be to act before plants begin to show signs of distress, you will need to water greenhouse plants at least once a day during the main growing season. Use the weight of trays and pots, as well as the feel of the soil itself, as a guide to moisture content. Use a trowel to check the state of the border soil a short way down.

A number of automatic watering systems are available. You can run a drip system directly from the tap, using a pressure regulator control, or else from a container mounted at a higher level inside the greenhouse. The drip nozzle can be positioned above the capillary matting or over individual pots or growing bags.

The simpler capillary system is based on capillary matting, a highly absorbent material from which soil in pots draws up moisture by capillary action. This is most suitable for small plants in pots.

To set up a capillary system, check that the staging is perfectly level, then lay the matting on a sheet of plastic. Turn one end of the matting over into a water-filled tray; make sure that the water level is lower than the matting. Or use a narrow strip of matting to link the soil to the water.

Regular treatment with an algicide is needed to prevent the matting from becoming clogged up with green growth.

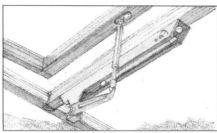

Automatic vent openers depend on heat-sensitive mineral wax in a cylinder exerting pressure on a piston, which in turn is linked to the vent. The device can be adjusted to make the vent open when the inside temperature reaches more than about 55°F. The weight of greenhouse vents varies, so be sure to buy an opener suitable for your vents.

Exterior blinds (above) keep the glass and interior of the greenhouse cool. Though formerly made from slats or natural reeds, they are now made in weather-resistant plastic. Pleated interior shading (right) slides up and down on guide cords. A cheaper, but less flexible, alternative is to fasten material directly to the glazing bars.

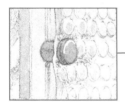

Bubble insulation is particularly effective in reducing heat loss. If draped over taut strings at ridge and eaves, the material can be secured with double-sided adhesive tape, thumbtacks, or—for aluminum greenhouses—a variety of attachments.

Electric tubular heaters, mounted here beneath the staging, are an efficient form of greenhouse heating. At the far end is a small kerosene heater for use when conditions are not too severe. Small fan heaters and gas heaters (left) can be controlled thermostatically.

Capillary matting will absorb water from a tray or similar container with a maximum lift of up to four inches from the surface of the water. The soil in the pots will take up moisture from the matting, provided that you don't use drainage pebbles when you are potting up plants.

USING A GREENHOUSE, pages 12–13
CLOCHES AND FRAMES, pages 16–18

SOWING UNDER GLASS, pages 38–39

In a cold or less than temperate climate, cloches serve as unheated miniature greenhouses to protect a variety of crops from cold and wind. Their great advantage, compared with greenhouses, is that they are easily moved about. As one crop matures or ceases to need shelter, you can shift the cloches to another. In a carefully planned cropping program, cloches are in use in both spring and fall.

Because the air and soil inside a cloche are warmer than outside, you can sow or plant crops earlier in the season. Subsequent growth is then much faster, so that you can harvest crops started under cloches well ahead of their usual season. Lettuce, for example, matures up to three weeks sooner than it does in open ground.

Tender plants, such as snap beans, can be protected under cloches and sown or planted before the last of the spring frosts. Strawberries cloched from early spring onward will be ready for picking from late spring. In the North, melons planted during the spring will benefit from cloche protection into the summer.

Used in this way, cloches add up to a mini-revolution in garden food growing for those who live in cooler climates.

TYPES OF CLOCHE

Cloches are constructed from glass or from a variety of plastic materials to provide a translucent covering for a row of plants. The ends must be closable to prevent a wind-tunnel effect.

Cloches were designed originally as solitary, bell-shaped units: hence their name, from the French for bell, *la cloche*. Although the common aim of gardeners is now to form a continuous shelter, this is still, in most cases, made up of separate units (which can vary in height and width) placed end to end in a row. One exception is the tunnel cloche (see below).

Glass Glass cloches are expensive, but they provide particularly good conditions in northern gardens. They let in more light and conserve more heat than their plastic counterparts. Occasional breakages are inevitable, but glass cloches stand up well to heavy winds.

There are two basic shapes. Tent cloches, formed from two sheets of glass secured by wires or fixed together at the top with a galvanized iron clip, are designed for compact crops such as lettuce. Barn cloches, made from four sheets of glass with a pitched roof, are designed for multiple rows and for larger plants, such as peas. Besides the one-foot-high barn cloche, there is a higher-sided version, about twenty inches, for protecting tomatoes, eggplants, and peppers until they are well grown. The panes are secured either with wire supports or with metal clips.

Since glass is expensive both to make and to transport, you can make your own cloches using old pieces of glass, or have glass cut to size. Old windows make good cloches for larger plants.

Corrugated plastic Cloches made from this material are light and strong and give good protection. Because they weigh so little, they need to be well anchored in the soil; always choose supporting frames that have spikes to serve as ground anchors.

Polyethylene Various types of individual polyethylene cloches are marketed, in dif-

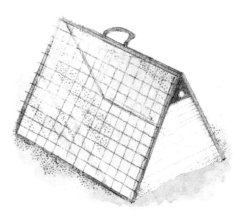

At least one design of tent cloche has netting secured under the plastic cover, giving it a dual function. With the cover in place, it serves as a normal cloche. Without it, the netting gives protection against birds.

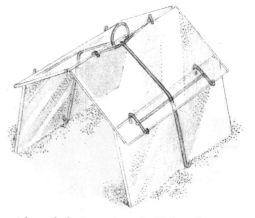

A barn cloche is constructed with four sheets of glass and supported by a thick wire frame. There is a carrying handle at the top, and one side of the roof can be opened to increase the amount of ventilation.

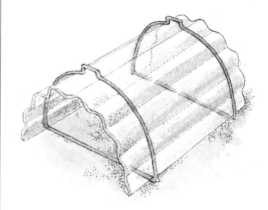

Corrugated plastic combines strength and lightness. The wire or plastic frames that hold this type of cloche in place have spikes that you push into the soil. For ventilation, simply move adjacent cloches apart.

PLANTING WITH CLOCHES
Fava beans Sow direct as early as possible in spring, or in the fall on the West Coast. Cover until midspring.

Snap and pole beans Sow in early spring, either direct or indoors for planting out. Cover until early summer.

Beets Sow direct in fall in the South, in early spring elsewhere. Cover until late spring unless it is too hot.

Brassicas Start early cabbages and broccoli under cloches in early spring. Remove when they outgrow the cloches.

Carrots Sow direct from early spring onward. Cover until mid- to late spring.

Cucumbers Sow indoors; plant out when cloches will protect from frost. Cover until it is warm both day and night.

Lettuce Sow direct in fall, winter, or early spring. Cover until mature, unless the weather turns warm.

Melons Sow indoors in early spring, or direct if you live in the South. Cover until the weather is consistently hot.

Peas Sow direct in early spring, or in late fall or winter in the South. Cover until warm weather arrives.

Peppers Sow indoors in early spring and protect until it is hot.

Squash Sow indoors in early spring and plant out when frost protection is sure. Remove cloches in early summer.

Sweet corn Sow direct or indoors in early spring. Cover until early summer.

Tomatoes Sow indoors in late winter or early spring. Protect until it is hot.

Tunnel cloches provide an inexpensive means of covering rows of any length. They are easy to erect and to ventilate; their chief drawback is that the polyethylene has to be replaced fairly frequently.

Cone-shaped plastic cloches give protection to single plants. Individual cloches can also be improvised. For example, use a transparent plastic umbrella, with its handle cut off and glued to the end spike. Empty plastic bottles cut off at the base may also be used.

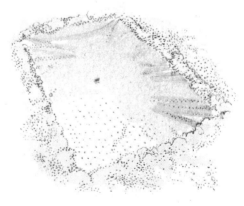

A floating row cover is so called because the plants raise it clear of the ground. It gives moderate protection while allowing moisture to penetrate. The edges are held in place by a covering of soil or stones.

ferent thicknesses. They are less expensive than fiberglass cloches, but check that the cover is easy to replace. This will become necessary every year or two. Some cloches have a secondary covering of netting to prevent birds from damaging the crop when the plastic is removed.

Condensation can be a problem with plastic-covered cloches, and this is to be avoided, since such conditions encourage the spread of fungus diseases. It is important to make sure that such cloches are well ventilated.

Fiberglass Cloches made of this material cost more than both polyethylene and corrugated versions. Though not always fully translucent, which means that they transmit less sunlight, they combine lightness with strength. They also have good insulating properties, and give satisfactory results for many years.

Polyethylene tunnels Tunnel cloches can be bought as kits and are easy to erect. The tunnel is formed by stretching a sheet of plastic over wire hoops anchored in the ground, then securing the plastic. They are a particularly good choice for fairly long rows—upward of about twenty feet. You can simply slide back one side of the cover for access to seedlings or plants.

The plastic will probably need replacing every two years or so, since it deteriorates in sunlight and is liable to be easily ripped or damaged. It also gets very dirty, so wash and dry it before storing it.

Individual cloches Rigid plastic box- or cone-shaped cloches are ideal for covering individual plants, such as tomatoes, peppers, and eggplants. They protect the plants against frost and wind, as well as against insects and birds, until they are well established. These cloches are semitransparent, so they let in enough light without allowing heat to build up. They are sturdy enough to last for several years.

Another individual cloche is the Wall O'Water, in which plastic tubes filled with water absorb heat by day and release it at night, protecting plants from too much heat and from frost.

MAKING THE BEST USE OF CLOCHES
Although cloches are fairly sturdy, you should avoid using them in the most exposed positions in the garden. Increase the anchorage if there is any danger that they will be blown away.

Place the cloches in position two weeks or so before early sowings or plantings, so that the soil can warm up. Secure the end panels in place with canes driven into the ground,

CONSTRUCTING A TUNNEL CLOCHE
Insert the supporting wires at intervals. Stretch the plastic cover over the top and tie its ends to pegs driven into the soil. Hold the cover down and stretch it with thin wires, then hook them into loops at the base of the main supporting wires.

if necessary. Be ready to sow or to plant once the ground is sufficiently warm. For a single row, position the seeds or plants along the center of the cloche, where plants will have most headroom. Position double rows at equal distances from the sides.

Ventilation is needed, especially with polyethylene, but you may find that there are enough gaps where individual units are joined to provide sufficient ventilation early in the season, and many tunnel systems are designed with ventilation slits or holes. As the weather warms up, raise one side of the tunnel cloche or space individual cloches a little further apart.

Remove the cloches before watering seedlings or small plants. Use a watering can with a rose attached. In good soil, there should be no need to remove cloches before watering established crops during a dry spell. Water percolating from the edges of the cloche generally supplies sufficient moisture. If in any doubt, check the soil a little way down in the center of the cloche.

FLOATING ROW COVERS
These are not cloches in the true sense, but consist of a rectangular sheet of polyester, polypropylene, or acrylic laid loosely over the seedbed or plants to speed up their growth. Row covers are either slitted or made with an open weave, both for ventilation and to allow rainwater to penetrate. Secure the edges of the sheet by covering them with soil or stones. Because the material is very lightweight and porous, it is lifted or "floated" by the developing crop.

Some row covers can be used throughout the season to protect plants from frost, sun, wind, and pests. Most last at least two or three years.

A cold frame is a low, glass- or plastic-covered box that has many uses in the food garden. It is more permanent than a cloche, and usually remains in a fixed position. Since it can be heated by means of electric soil-warming cables, it is a small version of a greenhouse in some respects, and widens the gardener's scope even further. Cold frames can be bought or made at home.

An unheated cold frame can provide an invaluable halfway house for plants started in a greenhouse or on a windowsill indoors. A spell in the frame, during which the ventilation is gradually increased, will acclimatize seedlings before they are planted out in the garden (see p.39).

A cold frame is a good place, too, for sowing seeds of cabbages, cauliflowers, and other brassica plants for growing outside. It can also be used for lettuce and such tender plants as lima beans and sweet corn. Brassicas, in particular, tend to grow more sturdily in a frame than when started in a greenhouse.

You can also use a cold frame for growing salad crops to maturity. Lettuce sown in late summer is ready early in the winter when grown in a frame. Radishes, spring onions, beets, and carrots can all be sown and harvested well before outdoor crops.

Even in summer, the frame need not be left vacant. Cucumbers and melons fruit more reliably with this form of protection in cold northern gardens, and in more temperate regions you can use the frame for hardening off seedlings that you will plant late in the season.

If you use electric soil-warming cables, the timing of crops is brought forward even further. The cables are easy to install if you follow the manufacturer's instructions.

TYPES OF COLD FRAME

A traditional cold frame is a shallow wooden box, with walls that slope down to the front and a glass top that slides or is lifted to open. You can construct this type of frame at home quite easily, using spare pieces of wood and old windows or doors. Make sure the sides are not so high that they exclude a lot of light.

Most ready-made frames have a metal framework (generally aluminum) and glass or plastic sides and roof; they are both lightweight and maintenance-free. The walls can be higher without affecting plants adversely, though more heat is lost through them than through wooden sides. A deeper frame provides more space for cucumbers, peppers, and other tender plants.

The frame's cover might be hinged or sliding, single or multiple. The most important consideration is that it is sturdily made, and will not come off in windy weather.

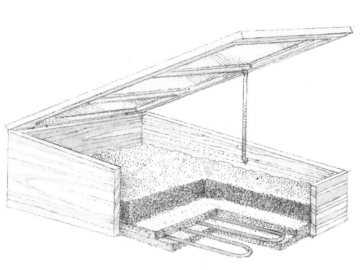

A homemade cold frame constructed of wood will give long service if treated with a preservative safe to plants. Use glass or rigid plastic for the top, and hinge this at the back. Soil-warming cables may be installed.

SITING AND USING A COLD FRAME

The ideal position for a cold frame is a sheltered spot in the garden, so you can ventilate plants without creating cold drafts. A sunny position is essential, especially with wooden frames; a single, sloping cover should face south. If you can meet these criteria and place the cold frame close to the greenhouse, this is desirable, since you will want to move plants from greenhouse to frame quite often.

If the frame has a sliding cover, make sure there is sufficient space at the sides or rear to accommodate it. You also need a firm place to stand in front of the frame.

Before growing crops in a cold frame, improve the soil inside it, if necessary. The soil should drain well and contain plenty of organic matter; you may have to buy potting soil or bring soil from another part of the garden. The addition of manure and peat will insure that the ground is sufficiently moist for overwintering plants, which should not be watered until they start to develop in spring. Add sterile sand to improve drainage if necessary.

Keep the glass or plastic clean at all times to admit maximum light. When necessary, cover the frame at night with old carpet or burlap to help retain warmth.

A little daytime ventilation is required at most times; this need increases rapidly as spring advances. Remove the cover altogether during hot weather.

Ready-made cold frames are often made of cedar, an attractive and durable wood. Some designs, based on a commercial system, have low sloping sides and large, single-sheet glass tops—ideal for early crops.

Aluminum frames, with glass or plastic sides and ends, admit maximum light and are immune to rot. They come in many shapes and sizes, the largest offering a growing area comparable with a small greenhouse.

Every food gardener has to make a decision about whether or not to stick to natural, or "organic," means of nourishing crops and of preventing and combating pests and diseases. Indeed, the main reason that some people decide to grow their own crops is in order to have some control over how many chemicals are applied to the fruit and vegetables that they eat.

Organic means derived from living organisms, and has a number of connotations in gardening. First and foremost, it concerns the materials that are added to the soil to promote growth. (Organic methods of pest and disease control are discussed below and in more detail on the next page.)

Organic soil additions include bulky materials such as manure, leaves, and garden compost, and also concentrated fertilizers of plant or animal origin, such as bonemeal and fishmeal (see pp.28–29). In contrast, inorganic fertilizers are the product of chemical manufacture and have no direct origins in plant or animal life. Two common examples of these are superphosphate and sodium nitrate.

So, is there anything wrong with these chemical products? Whether or not they do significant harm to humans is open to debate. Some chemical products are, of course, more toxic than others, but many people dislike the idea that their food has been tainted with chemicals of any description, since they will ingest those chemicals when they eat the food.

As experienced gardeners have discovered, inorganic fertilizers can give crops a considerable boost, if used with care. Their effect can be quite dramatic when plants have been undernourished. But there are two major drawbacks. One is that the effect is generally short-lived. The other, more serious drawback is that chemical fertilizers do nothing for the long-term fertility and structure of the soil, both of which are vital for the continuing healthy growth of plants. This is because plants are able to make immediate use of chemical fertilizers, without the soil itself gaining any benefit.

ORGANIC SOIL ADDITIONS
The nourishment provided by organic manures and fertilizers has to be "unlocked" by the complex action of bacteria and fungi residing in the soil. Since this is a relatively slow process, most organic soil additions have a long-lasting effect.

The benefit is cyclical, too, since the vast army of microscopic workers depends on adequate amounts of organic material for maintaining soil fertility and a soil structure that is favorable both to plant growth and to easy working. Their action in turn results in the fine, dark material known as humus,

which aids both drainage and moisture retention and serves as a storage reservoir for plant foods.

The benefits of organic soil additions are therefore incontrovertible. Without manure, compost, or other organic substances, it is impossible to grow good crops year after year on the same ground.

In addition, more concentrated applications will be needed from time to time, particularly on sandy soil, where nutrients quickly leach out. Truly organic gardeners will use only those fertilizers derived from plant or animal materials. Some will use a judicious mixture of organic and chemical fertilizers. Either course can bring good results, but only if the soil is maintained with organic additions.

PESTS AND DISEASES
The longer and more widely any crop has been growing in a particular area, the more firmly established are the pests and diseases associated with it. Several of the newer and less well-known fruits and vegetables, such as Florence fennel, scorzonera, and mildew-resistant snap peas, are relatively free of pests and diseases, and it is worth trying at least one or two of these.

Chemical sprays and dusts may be the easiest and most direct method of preventing or eradicating known pests and diseases, but their use is shunned by organic gardeners. The more toxic chemicals are not only of potential danger to humans, but they kill beneficial insects, including bees, and other wildlife in the garden in addition to the pests they are designed to eradicate.

If you choose to employ chemical sprays, be sure to time your spraying to minimize the possible damage to other forms of life. Rotenone, for example, is relatively safe because it is not persistent. If plants are sprayed in the evening, when bees are back in the hive, the rotenone will have lost its toxicity by the following morning.

An alternative solution is to use safer

sprays, such as the ones mentioned on p. 21. There is also some scope for preventing unwanted damage by taking alternative forms of preventive action.

For instance, if you interplant cucumbers with tomatoes and onions and sow them on a staggered schedule, cucumber beetles may be less likely to take much of your crop. To attract hoverflies, whose larvae decimate aphid colonies, plant a patch of the annual *Convolvulus tricolor* as a food source.

Rather than spreading poisonous slug pellets, you can lure slugs and snails to their death in shallow pans filled with diluted, sweetened beer, or you can place cabbage leaves or other large leaves around the garden and simply collect the slugs and snails that shelter under them during the heat of the day.

The sections on Pests and Diseases of Fruits (pp.108–111) and Pests and Diseases of Vegetables (pp.172–175) give further details of such methods.

You must expect minor damage to some crops if you do not use chemical sprays at all. It is a price that organic gardeners are prepared to pay. The compromise is to use such sprays when all else fails, but always with consideration for other creatures.

WEEDS
Chemical weedkillers exist in a wide variety of forms. Managing without these is not a great problem in most gardens, provided you eradicate perennial weeds at the outset. You can dig out others by hand as they appear, and regular hoeing or mulching will take care of annual weeds. Further advice is given on pp. 45–47, together with information on weedkillers for those with a persistent problem to overcome.

ORGANIC METHODS OF CULTIVATION: A SUMMARY
- Improve the texture and fertility of your soil by adding organic matter.
- Where hand weeding is difficult, such as around berry bushes, weeds can be effectively controlled by mulching (see p.43).
- Practice a rigid rotation of vegetable crops to control soil-borne pests and diseases (see p.25).
- Encourage natural predators. Dig over the vegetable plot in late fall to enable birds to eat the pupae of cabbage moths and onion flies, and fork around raspberry canes to turn up the larvae of raspberry beetles. Have a pond for frogs and toads, which feed on slugs.
- Choose disease-resistant strains of vegetables and buy certified virus-free fruit trees.
- Use safer organic pesticides and fungicides such as pyrethrum and rotenone, which are nonpersistent and nonsystemic.

FEEDING THE SOIL, pages 28–29
MAKING GARDEN COMPOST, pages 30–31

DEALING WITH WEEDS, pages 45–47
PESTS AND DISEASES OF FRUITS, pages 108–111

PESTS AND DISEASES OF VEGETABLES, pages 172–175

Many gardeners, as well as scientists and concerned laymen, are uneasy about the widespread use of chemical sprays and powders for the control of pests and diseases. Some contain highly toxic substances that are slow to break down in the soil and potentially dangerous to humans and wildlife. Furthermore, several of them kill beneficial insects, such as bees, that are responsible for pollination and others that prey on the insects regarded as pests. In this respect, and because resistant strains eventually develop, chemical means of pest control are to some extent self-defeating. They are also quite expensive.

Yet there is no denying their effectiveness. Without them it is almost impossible to keep crops free of pests and diseases, particularly during the first year or two of organic gardening. Many gardeners settle for a compromise, using commercial sprays only when less drastic measures (see below) have failed, and always with care. They resign themselves to accepting a certain amount of damage to crops rather than expecting everything to be blemish-free.

Well before the spraying stage, though, there is plenty that you can do to reduce the risk of attack from pests and diseases. Plant diseases in particular are much easier to prevent than to cure. Of prime importance as a preventive measure is building up soil fertility.

PREVENTING PESTS AND DISEASES
Well-nourished crops are less likely to develop ailments. When plants grow sturdily and rapidly, they are better able to cope with attacks by insect pests. Humus-rich soil, the result of plenty of organic additions (see p.28), provides the surest basis for such growth.

It is important, too, that you pay attention to soil and weather conditions as well as the calendar when sowing and planting. Plants recovering from a slow start caused by cold, wet soil are particularly susceptible to disease and pests.

Overcrowding is another hazard, especially where diseases are concerned. Sow seeds thinly, and remove surplus seedlings as soon as they are large enough to handle. Allow sufficient space for plants to develop; if they are jammed together, they are more prone to fungus troubles.

Crop rotation (see p.25) helps to counter the buildup of pests and diseases associated with particular classes of crops. Club root, a fungus that affects the cabbage family, is an example. Growing brassicas on the same piece of land only one year in three reduces the risk of the spores infecting the soil permanently.

Slugs and snails are much more trouble-some on a weed-grown plot or where there are weeds and dense grass around the edges. These night feeders must have cover during the day, so regular weeding will deter them. Similarly, many pests and diseases either breed or find sanctuary in the neglected corners to be found in many gardens, among the refuse and rotting wood. A cleanup can do a great deal to keep them at bay, as well as to improve appearances.

Make use of disease-resistant strains of vegetables when you can. 'Bountiful Stringless' green beans, for example, are highly resistant to rust and mildew. 'Grand Slam Hybrid' midseason cabbages are fungus-resistant, and 'Earliglow' strawberries seldom suffer from root rot or verticillium wilt. Both 'Champion' and 'Celebrity' tomatoes are especially resistant to fungus diseases and tobacco mosaic virus.

THE GARDENER'S FRIENDS
The garden is a jungle, where one species depends on another for its living. Among ground-dwelling insects, the fast-moving kinds are often the predators, consuming the slower, plant-eating kinds. Study the illustrations on this page so that you know, at least, which to spare.

Remember that birds have insatiable appetites for insect pests, from greenflies to cutworms. Attract birds to the garden with food in winter and nesting boxes from late winter on. Any damage the birds themselves may do is relatively easy to control (see p.44).

Frogs, toads, turtles, and snakes are also to be encouraged, since they consume large quantities of grubs and insects. Frogs and toads prefer cool, damp conditions, and will happily live in clay flowerpots that have been turned over and chipped to provide an entrance. Box turtles, too, are content with shelter and a supply of water.

SAFER FUNGICIDES
Organic gardening enthusiasts are reluctant to recommend any sprays or dusts as completely safe. The following, though, are some of the types given tentative approval by the Henry Doubleday Research Association, a leading British organic group, and by several American organizations. Control may not always be as decisive as it is with some chemicals, but disease is unlikely to develop resistance to them.

Bordeaux mixture, obtainable as a powder or liquid, is a general-purpose, copper-based fungicide and a long-established preventive spray against potato blight.

Burgundy mixture, which is more powerful, is recommended as a winter wash for fruit trees and bushes. To make your own,

Lacewing
The adult and its grubs have an impressive appetite for aphids and red spider mites.

Centipede
This fast-moving creature, with a flattened orange body, eats insects and small slugs.

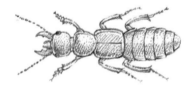

Devil's coach horse
This active European predator, easily distinguished by the way it turns its tail up, eats soil insects.

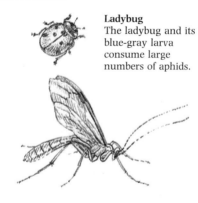

Ladybug
The ladybug and its blue-gray larva consume large numbers of aphids.

Ichneumon
As well as consuming aphids, this insect lays its eggs in the bodies of caterpillars.

Hoverfly
The adult is a useful pollinator; the larva devours aphids.

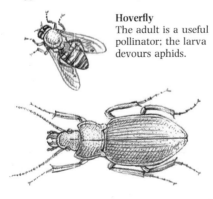

Ground beetle
Both the adult and the larva of this common creature live on insects, grubs, and slugs.

stir three ounces of copper sulfate into a gallon of hot water in a plastic bucket. In a similar container, dissolve four ounces of washing soda in a gallon of cold water. Wait for a few hours for the copper sulfate to dissolve thoroughly, then mix the two liquids and use at once.

Copper dust and **liquid copper** control anthracnose and leaf spot in tomatoes, potato blight, and mildew and other funguses in vine crops. The former is easier to use as a dust, whereas the liquid form makes a good spray.

Washing soda controls downy mildew, including American gooseberry mildew. Dissolve three ounces of washing soda in a gallon of hot water and stir in an ounce of soap flakes. Allow to cool before use.

Elderberry leaves Another fungicidal spray, claimed to be effective against mildew, is prepared by placing one pound of elderberry leaves and young, smooth-barked shoots into an old saucepan with six pints of water. Bring to the boil and simmer for thirty minutes, topping up as necessary. When cold, strain through cheesecloth and use undiluted.

Micronized sulfur is useful as a spray to prevent rust, black spot, mildew, and scab, particularly on fruit trees. Use before blossoms form for best results.

SAFER PESTICIDES

Rotenone is particularly useful, since it is harmless to animals and humans, ladybugs, and hoverfly larvae. It kills bees, however, and is poisonous to fish. Both liquid and powder preparations are available. Use it in spray form to kill aphids and caterpillars; as a dust to control flea beetles.

Pyrethrum is harmless to humans and animals but kills insect predators along with the pests. If it is sprayed at dusk, plants will be safe for bees by the following morning. This pesticide is moderately effective against aphids and caterpillars. Crops can be treated right up until harvest time.

Nicotine is extremely poisonous to both humans and bees, but it is said to break down in the soil within four days and to have no effect on plants a few hours after application. It is harmless to ladybugs and several other predators, but gives good control of caterpillars, leafhoppers, and red spider mites. It is advisable to wash your hands after using it, to keep it off your skin as much as possible, and to stick a prominent POISON label on bottles containing it.

To make a spray solution, simmer four ounces of filter-tip cigarette ends or chewing tobacco in a quart of water for half an hour. Strain the liquid and dilute it with four times as much water before spraying. Reduce the dilution if pests prove persistent,

and add an ounce of soap flakes to each quart when spraying in the fall against cabbage worms.

Rhubarb leaves can be made into a safe and reasonably effective spray against aphids. Simmer one pound of sliced rhubarb leaves in a quart of water for half an hour. Dilute the liquid with two quarts of cold water and use within twenty-four hours.

Insecticidal soap, made from cellular fats and oils, is biodegradable and leaves no residue, so it does not harm humans, bees, or ladybugs. It is useful for control of soft-bodied insects such as aphids, thrips, and mealybugs, and can be applied to most vegetable and fruit crops.

Ryania is a plant-derived insecticide that is particularly effective against codling moths and corn borers. It does not usually kill these pests, but poisons them so that they are unable to feed on plants.

Sabadilla dust is fairly nontoxic and controls adult pests such as squash bugs, harlequin bugs, and beetles particularly well.

ALTERNATIVE METHODS

Sprays and dusts apart, there are other biological controls that you can use to discourage the pests that attack crops. Most of them are commercially available. The following are a few examples:

Bacillus thuringiensis is a disease that attacks pests and it is available in powder form. It is useful against cabbage loopers and other caterpillars.

Ladybugs are predators of aphids on most vegetables and fruits.

Praying mantids feed at night, and are thus particularly useful in controlling adult moths and the notorious Colorado potato beetle.

Trichogramma wasps, which are also commercially available, are parasites of the eggs of various moths, including corn earworms, cucumber beetles, European corn borers, and tomato hornworms.

Diatomaceous earth is a talclike powder that is said to be effective against slugs and most soft-bodied insects.

CARE WITH CHEMICALS

Even when you follow the best growing methods, there is still some risk of invasion by pests or diseases. If "safe" sprays or dusts do not give adequate control, you will have to decide whether to accept a degree of damage or to use a chemical product.

Details of which products to use against particular pests or diseases are given on pp.108–111 (for fruits) and pp.172–175 (for vegetables).

If you decide to use a chemical spray, try to minimize the possible side effects by taking a few sensible precautions. In addition to using the environmental safeguards listed below, make sure you keep all chemicals where children cannot reach them. Store liquids, whether diluted or not, only in the manufacturers' clearly labeled bottles.

- ■ Follow every detail of the manufacturer's instructions.

- ■ Use at the safest time of day. Try to spray during the late evening, when bees and other pollinating insects have stopped flying. They are also less active during dull weather. Do not spray when it is raining, or while you have a sprinkler watering the garden.

- ■ Avoid spraying during windy weather, when the droplets will drift over a wider area.

- ■ Keep the spray well away from ponds and other water.

- ■ Spray as lightly as possible from underneath the leaves. A fine misting of all the foliage is more effective than a drenching.

DOWN TO EARTH

The returns you get from your food garden depend to a large extent on the amount of care and attention you devote to your soil. Other aspects of gardening, including sowing, planting, pruning, and weeding, are important, but without good soil your results are bound to be disappointing, however conscientious you are.

The section that follows treats the basics of gardening in the order in which they should be tackled. It starts by explaining what soil is and how it can be improved—by composting, digging, draining, and feeding. Details of sowing, planting, watering, crop protection, and weeding then follow each other in logical progression, and you will quickly discover that most techniques of crop growing are both straightforward and easily mastered, even if you are a complete beginner.

Gardening activity follows a pattern that is repeated from year to year. As you work and get to know your soil, and become attuned to the ways of the weather, you will gradually learn which crops do best in your garden and which respond best to the climatic conditions to which your garden is exposed.

In the first few seasons, make a real effort to link cause and effect. If you do this, you may be able to conclude that your soil responds well to a specific treatment, that a particular pest can be thwarted by a certain strategy, or that the prevailing climate in your area makes your plot earlier or later as regards sowing, planting, and harvesting than the averages that are generally quoted.

To keep track of your progress, and to help you work out what influences your garden from year to year, you may find it helpful—and entertaining—to keep a gardening diary. Note in it the work you do on the soil, such as digging and fertilizing, the most troublesome pests, weeds, and diseases, and, of course, the weather, including temperature and rainfall. After a few years you will see a definite pattern emerging, which will be a great help in improving your efforts and your output. Above all, it will help you learn by your mistakes.

As you become more experienced, you will learn which garden practices work best for you. The same is true of equipment. A nucleus of a few good tools, each of which performs well for you, has the correct weight and balance, and is easy and comfortable to use, is far better than a plethora of expensive gadgets.

Care of the soil in your garden is critical to all aspects of starting and growing crops, and the tools and other equipment you choose will be devoted to this end. All soil needs to be dug, enriched with organic matter, weeded, watered, and, in cooler climates, protected with cloches or mulches.

Soil consists mainly of fragmented rock, ground down over centuries by weathering agents such as rain, frost, and sunshine into minute particles. Each particle is surrounded by a film of moisture in which plant nutrients are dissolved, and the juxtaposition of the particles helps to force water, and therefore food, up to the plant roots. It is the size of these particles that determines the nature of the soil. Only by understanding your soil can you get the best out of it.

TOPSOIL AND SUBSOIL
Each type of soil contains organic matter in addition to the rock particles. This is concentrated in the shallow layer of surface soil on which all plant and human life depends. Termed the topsoil, it may vary from trowel depth to below that of a spade.

Beneath this, and distinguishable by its paler color, is the generally infertile subsoil. Its depth varies according to the hardness of the underlying rock and the amount of erosion and leaching it has suffered. Though the subsoil may contain some nutrients useful to deep-rooting plants, most of your efforts to improve the soil should be concentrated on the fertile upper layer.

It is essential, especially when leveling uneven ground, to maintain a consistent depth of topsoil and not to mix it with the subsoil. The only way to do this is to remove all the topsoil first, then level the subsoil before replacing it. If you are correcting uneven ground, aim to have a layer of topsoil of at least a spade's depth (about ten inches deep).

SOIL TYPES
Sandy soil is a light soil made up of coarse particles. It feels gritty when rubbed between finger and thumb and does not readily form lumps. It remains crumbly and workable even after rain.

Light soils warm up early in the spring, because of the easy flow of air between the large particles, and they are easy and rewarding to cultivate. They dry out rapidly, though, and are "hungry" in the sense that plant foods soon wash through them.

Clay soil, at the other extreme, consists of minute, finely ground particles that stick together in a puttylike mass. Water drains only slowly through this type of soil, air is excluded, and the soil remains cold until well into spring. Clay soils, which are difficult to work, are termed heavy—with good reason.

Clay soils are sometimes well supplied with nutrients; since there are a greater number of particles to a given area, more water adheres to them. But these nutrients are not always available to the plants, since in a compacted soil they may be blocked from reaching the plant roots. And some clay soils are too acid and thus deficient in important elements. However, supplied with plenty of organic matter to improve their texture, clay soils will usually grow fine crops.

Loams, which include the best of garden soils, consist of a mixture of sand and clay. The proportions may vary—hence the terms *light loam* and *heavy loam*—with a medium loam being the elusive ideal.

Limestone soils, gray in color, are alkaline and free-draining, though they may be sticky after rain. Some are very shallow, presenting a considerable challenge to the gardener to increase the depth of the topsoil by creating humus. The deeper soils are easier to cultivate, so long as you avoid acid-loving plants.

Peat is derived from plant materials. When it is found in a marshy area, peaty soil is rich in nutrients and easy to work. Naturally occurring peat, like limestone, is relatively rare in the United States, and gardeners who want to reap its benefits must usually buy packaged peat moss.

ACID OR ALKALINE?
Soils vary in their degree of acidity or alkalinity. Most vegetables and fruits have a broad measure of tolerance, but it is sensible to avoid extremes. Some plants, however, have definite preferences for, or an aversion to, acid or alkaline conditions.

Simple kits are sold for home soil testing. These indicate the soil's pH value; pH is the standard scale for measuring acidity. A reading of pH 7.0 denotes a neutral soil. Above this the soil is alkaline, and below this it is acid.

Most crops grow best in slightly acid soil, with a pH reading of about 6.5. You can reduce excessive acidity by spreading lime (see p.29), and excessive alkalinity by adding sulfur.

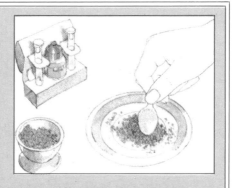

1 To test the pH level of your soil with a simple kit, first gather a small sample from two to three inches beneath the surface. Do not touch it with your hands. If the soil is wet, let it dry naturally. When it is reasonably dry, crumble it finely on a plate and remove any stones or other debris.

2 Fill a test tube about a quarter full with some crumbled soil. Use a spoon to avoid touching it with your hands. Next, pour in the lime-test solution until the tube is half full. With the stopper inserted, shake the tube thoroughly to mix liquid and soil. Allow the soil to settle to the bottom.

3 You can now check the pH level of the soil by comparing the color of the liquid with the bands on a gradated shade chart. A simple table in the instruction booklet explains what to add to your soil, and in what quantity, to raise or lower the pH level in one-point stages to meet the needs of your crops.

There are several ways in which you can improve the texture and condition of your soil, apart from feeding it (for details see pp.28–29) and watering it when necessary (see p.42). The principal means are by digging and at the same time adding various soil improvers, and by growing your crops in such a way that the soil benefits from crop rotation. (The techniques of digging are covered in detail on pp.34–35.)

Certain soils have special needs, but all soils are improved by the addition of organic matter, usually in the form of compost (see pp.30–31). Eventually reduced by microorganisms to humus, compost helps light soils to retain moisture as well as nutrients by giving more bulk to the soil.

Digging in organic matter not only improves the fertility but also opens up heavy soils, making them more crumbly and less sticky. You can also dig in shredded newspaper, or bury it in a trench, to help break up a clay soil. Similarly, repeated additions will add precious depth and alkalinity to the topsoil on acid ground.

IMPROVING A HEAVY SOIL
Waterlogging is a common problem on uncultivated clay soils. If water lies on the surface after rain or collects in a trench during digging, the soil is waterlogged and crops are unlikely to thrive. Waterlogged soil is cold and airless, the opposite conditions of those needed for healthy root growth. Clay soil also sets hard when it dries and has a tendency to crack, subjecting plant roots to another danger.

Leave a clay soil alone while it is wet and sticky: you will damage the structure if you attempt to cultivate it. Late autumn is usually the best time to dig a heavy soil; add organic material at the same time. Leave it in rough clods for the frost to work on; then, as the ground dries in spring, rake it into a crumbly, seed-sowing tilth.

You can further open up heavy soils, and thereby improve drainage, by adding grit or sterile sand while digging. This will remain in the topsoil indefinitely. Where a hard subsoil is preventing water from draining away, artificial drainage is the only answer (see p.26), and other attempts at soil improvement will be wasted without it.

IMPROVING A LIGHT SOIL
Late winter or early spring is the time to dig organic matter into light soil. Autumn digging inevitably results in some nutrients being washed away during the winter.

Mulching (see p.43) helps to keep light soils moist during dry weather. Be prepared to feed plants generously with fertilizers (see p.28): nitrogen, in particular, is often in short supply.

CROP ROTATION
Maintaining the soil's fertility is one of the reasons for growing a given crop in a different part of the plot in successive years. This is because certain crops make special demands on available nutrients, which may become depleted if there is no movement, or rotation. Legumes, one of the three vegetable groups, take little out of the soil and may in fact put back some nitrogen from their root nodules.

Grouping crops with similar needs facilitates their cultivation and enables them to use organic material, often in short supply, to best advantage. All root vegetables, for example, need a deep tilth.

The other benefit of moving plants around the plot is that it helps to break pest and disease chains, such as club root, to which all brassicas are prone.

For all of these reasons it is helpful to group vegetables into three broad categories (below), and to devote a section of the garden to each one in turn for a year.

A LEGUMES (peas and beans)
B BRASSICAS (cabbages, sprouts, etc.)
C ROOT VEGETABLES, and potatoes.

This grouping omits all the salad crops, onions, sweet corn, tomatoes, and other vegetables that have no particular problems or advantages and whose positioning is therefore not critical. Add them to whichever group you wish, aiming to fill about a third of the total area with each basic group. Unless you grow a great many legumes, this will probably mean adding most of the remaining vegetables to Group A.

You will want to find a more or less permanent position for perennial vegetables, such as asparagus, and for fruit.

To put this scheme into action, divide the plot into three equal parts. Each year, follow the same manuring/liming program. For Group A crops (legumes), dig in as much manure or compost as you can spare. For Group B (brassicas), spread lime after digging, then fertilize at sowing or planting time. On an alkaline soil, you should omit the lime dressing and apply manure or compost instead, if available. For Group C (roots), use fertilizer only.

Year by year, rotate the crops in the same order. That is, in the second year of the cycle plant brassicas on what had been the legume patch, sow roots where brassicas had been, and grow legumes in place of the roots—and so on, through successive years on a three-year cycle.

Year 1	A. Legumes	B. Brassicas	C. Roots
Year 2	B. Brassicas	C. Roots	A. Legumes
Year 3	C. Roots	A. Legumes	B. Brassicas

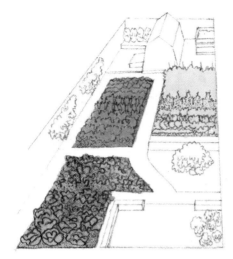

First year Brassicas are in the foreground, roots behind them, and legumes on the right.

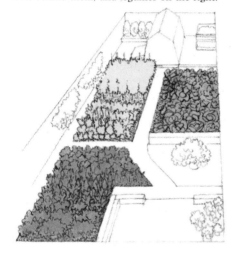

Second year Brassicas are now in the plot heavily manured a year ago for legumes.

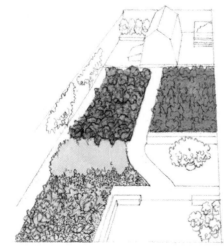

Third year Roots are always grown in land not manured recently, as this could cause them to fork in their search for nourishment.

USING WEEDKILLERS, pages 46–47
FEEDING THE SOIL AND PLANTS, pages 28–29

Good drainage is essential to the condition of your plot and the health of your crops. Not only is waterlogged soil hard to cultivate, but it is cold and airless, which makes the plant roots cold and unhealthy. There may be several ways in which you can improve the drainage of your plot without going to the trouble and expense of installing a full drainage system.

A compacted surface alone will prevent water draining from heavy soil, for example, but digging will be enough to cure this. As mentioned earlier (see p.24), digging organic material into a heavy clay topsoil will help to open it up and improve natural drainage.

If the land remains waterlogged, check that there is not an impervious layer of compacted subsoil or rock just below spade depth—something that is by no means uncommon. The solution in this case is to loosen the bottom of each trench as you dig, using a fork, crowbar, or pickax.

A quite different approach to a badly drained soil is to grow at least some of your vegetables—preferably shallow-rooted ones —in beds raised above ground level, with a brick, stone, or wood edging. A good example would be one about three feet off the ground on a free-draining base, with gravel added to the soil; the problem would thus be largely circumvented. You will, of course, have to find additional soil for raising the level of the bed.

If all else fails, however, you will need to lay some form of pipework in the soil. On a small scale, a rubble-filled trench could serve instead of pipes, but this would be almost as much trouble and might soon become clogged with soil. It is the outlet that creates the chief difficulty in laying a system of drainage pipes, for few gardens have drainage ditches. The answer is to dig a dry well at the lower end of the drainage system. A capacious dry well should prevent or reduce waterlogging for much of the year, though it is likely to fill up during wet spells.

DRAINAGE SYSTEMS

Until recently, almost the only method of draining soil has been to lay plastic or terra-cotta pipes in trenches and surround the pipes with gravel. The trenches need to be deep enough for the pipes to lie below spade depth. The joints between pipes are uncemented, allowing water to percolate through. They are laid at a gentle but even angle to provide a flow toward the outlet (see below).

This method is still very common, but an alternative is now available in the form of a continuous plastic core surrounded by a tough but porous fabric. This is easier to lay and does not require the normal backfilling of gravel. Nevertheless, on clay you should mix sand and peat with the soil when refilling the trench to improve the flow toward the drain.

PLANNING THE LAYOUT

The layout of the drains can take much the same form whichever system you choose. On a small, narrow plot, a single drain will suffice. Otherwise, lay a main drain down the center, with well-spaced side drains leading into it from each side. Set the side drains at an angle to the main run, giving the drainage layout its distinctive herring-bone pattern.

The spacing between the side drains depends on the nature of the soil. It varies from about fifteen feet on clay to forty feet on sandy soil. Suggested spacings for the plastic patent system are provided in an instruction booklet. Both forms of drainage must be laid with a fall toward the outlet. Take advantage of a natural fall if there is one; otherwise, a slope of 1 in 90 is the minimum.

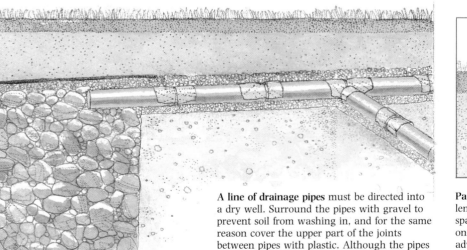

A line of drainage pipes must be directed into a dry well. Surround the pipes with gravel to prevent soil from washing in, and for the same reason cover the upper part of the joints between pipes with plastic. Although the pipes fit closely, there is sufficient pressure for water to force its way in.

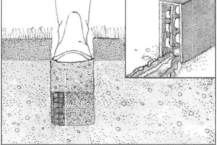

Patent drainage tubing, supplied in continuous lengths many feet long, is easy to lay. Dig a spade-width trench and lay the tubing along one side of the base. On heavy soil it is an advantage to add free-draining sand or gravel immediately around it. Direct the outlet into a ditch or dry well.

If you are starting with a long-neglected, weed-grown jungle, it may take a year or two to achieve a productive garden. Shorter-term neglect may be remedied more quickly. Assess the nature of the problem first and then work according to a well-thought-out plan.

CLEARING THE WEEDS

Before you clear weeds, determine what kind they are. If your plot is knee-high with weeds, it may be worth using a string trimmer first; this will take off the top of the growth so that you can at least see what you are doing at ground level.

A short period of neglect, resulting in a covering of annual weeds, is hardly a problem at all, since digging will destroy them. A fresh batch of seedlings will probably follow, but hoeing will take care of this problem.

Perennial weeds are more serious: digging will multiply them by chopping their roots; a new plant will grow from a very short piece of root. If there are just a few, dig them out individually with a fork or trowel, removing all the roots. If the weeds are numerous, and especially if the ground is overgrown with persistent types such as quack grass, Bermuda grass, or convolvulus, this is a good reason for using a systemic weedkiller or a rototiller.

During spring or summer, when the weeds are in active growth, a weedkiller based on glyphosate would be suitable. This will work right through the plant systems without affecting the soil. A number of weedkillers are designed to be used quite early in the season, before growth has really got under way. Do not use them indiscriminately, however, because many of them remain in the soil and can even damage shrub and tree roots, and they may be absorbed into the crops you will eventually harvest.

An alternative to weedkillers is to cut down and remove the weeds, then cultivate the ground at frequent intervals throughout the first spring and summer with a rototiller, which you can buy or hire. As long as the weather remains dry, this will kill most of the perennial weeds, as well as successive batches of germinating annuals.

Another alternative, if you live in a warm climate and the area covered by weeds is not too extensive, is to "solarize" the soil under clear plastic for a month or so.

You should burn the roots and woody stems of perennial weeds cut and gathered before the soil is cultivated rather than compost them. Only the hottest of fermenting heaps can be relied on to kill all their seeds and roots. Weeds destroyed with a weedkiller should also be burned.

AFTER THE WEEDS

Builders' rubble, stones, or other debris may have to be removed from the ground in a new or neglected garden. If you have the space, store it: you can recycle it eventually for foundations, drainage trenches, and other purposes.

Once the ground is clear, dig some random holes to check the depth of the topsoil (see p.24). This is often inadequate where a builder has been at work. It is even possible that you will find a substantial area of topsoil buried under the subsoil. If the soil has been subjected to drastic upheaval, the subsoil as well as the topsoil may have to be leveled in order to produce an even depth of topsoil. This will involve a lot of digging and wheelbarrowing. In extreme cases, bought-in topsoil may be needed.

Once the ground is relatively smooth and level, you will need to dig in plenty of bulky organic matter before you can consider growing even a few crops.

THE FIRST GROWING SEASON

The soil in a hitherto neglected garden is unlikely to be in very good condition. You will need to use fertilizers, preferably organic ones, during the early days of growing crops to build up soil fertility. Lime, too, may be needed (see p.24); if so, apply it as soon as practicable, but do not use fertilizers for a few weeks afterward.

Potatoes are an excellent crop to grow on a reclaimed plot during the first year; their wide-spreading foliage will discourage weed growth, as will the hilling-up process. If you do decide to grow potatoes, do not add lime to the soil. Alternatively, make a border in which to plant some radishes, lettuces, or other short-term crops that do not need a permanent position.

USING A ROTOTILLER

Use a rototiller to turn over neglected ground from spring on or to make a seedbed on land left untouched since the previous year. When you are using it as a way of killing perennial weeds, which may take some months, frequent cultivation is the key to preventing regrowth. By the end of summer the roots will have died from starvation.

On most domestic tillers the rotating tines serve the dual purpose of breaking the soil and drawing the machine forward. Forward speed is controlled by pressure on the handlebars; this also controls the depth of cultivation. When first using a tiller, set the depth skid quite low to insure that it does not run away with you. Allow it to move forward only a short distance at a time while the blades dig down to the depth required.

A **hood** attached to the end of a sprayer will prevent the droplets from drifting.

A **gas-powered brushcutter** can cut back even dense and woody growth.

A **rototiller** will turn undug ground and keep germinating weeds under control.

GETTING TO KNOW YOUR SOIL, page 24
DEALING WITH WEEDS, pages 45–47

POTATOES, pages 150–151

The fertility of your soil has a direct bearing on the quantity and quality of the crops grown in it. Because all plants derive nutrients from the soil, the soil's food reserves need to be replenished regularly. All soils need annual treatment with organic additions such as compost and farm manure, and with both chemical and organic fertilizers. Through their combined use, you will create a well-fed soil that will in turn nourish the crops you choose to grow in it.

The three main requirements for the nutrition of plants are nitrogen, phosphate, and potash. They are absorbed through the plant roots in a diluted form and are essential to all plant growth.

Nitrogen is the principal growth promoter, stimulating the development of stems and leaves. A shortage of it in your soil is revealed by yellow leaves and stunted plant growth, as well as by small fruits or tubers. Nitrogen is readily washed out of the soil and needs to be replaced every year.

Phosphate contains phosphorus, which aids root growth and is especially valuable for root vegetables such as carrots and turnips. A lack of it results in stunted, discolored foliage, small or misshapen flower buds, and sour-tasting fruit.

Potash contains potassium. This chemical helps to build up resistance to stress and disease. It is also valuable for the development and ripening of berries and tomatoes, as well as for building up starches and sugars in vegetables such as potatoes, beets, and sweet corn. A deficiency manifests itself as stunted growth, brown-edged or blotched leaves, curling foliage, or early fruit drop.

Potash and phosphates remain in the soil for longer than nitrogen when applied in an organic form—generally for two or three years or more.

Organic substances such as compost and manure can provide a good proportion of the nutrients that plants need. On a heavily cropped vegetable plot, though—and especially on light soil—fairly massive amounts would be needed to provide enough nutrients by this means alone. For continuing heavy yields, you will probably need additional plant foods, in the form of concentrated fertilizers in either organic or inorganic forms. Guidelines for how much to apply are given under the entries for specific crops when a particular fertilizer is needed. Otherwise follow the manufacturer's instructions.

ORGANIC ADDITIONS

The virtues of organic soil additions are many (see pp.24–25), but finding enough material may appear to be the main difficulty, especially in town gardens. Even in cities, though, there are sources from which you can obtain suitable organic material at very little cost, if not free.

First and foremost is garden compost, which can be made from garden waste such as grass clippings and annual weeds supplemented by vegetable waste from the kitchen. Shredded newspaper can also be added in small amounts. You should always return all used compost from containers and seedboxes to the soil, as long as the plants grown in it were disease-free.

Farm manures

If you live in or near the country, animal manures are the most obvious choice. There are also riding stables in many towns which will gladly give or sell you sacks of horse manure. Check the yellow pages for addresses.

Horse manure is the richest, followed by that from pigs and cattle. All animal manures need to be stacked and rotted down in a heap for several weeks or months before use. They are too concentrated when fresh and would provide an excess of nutrients which would damage plants. Unless they already contain a lot of straw, add some more to increase the bulk. Pig manure especially needs this treatment, as it is particularly strong and caustic on its own.

Fresh poultry manure is also highly concentrated and initially smells rather unpleasant, so it is best to stack it well away from the house. Once composted with plenty of straw, it provides a rich addition to the soil, and when dried it forms a nitrogen-rich, concentrated fertilizer. You may beneficially mix it with peat moss.

This stacking and rotting process applies to every kind of animal manure, including goat, rabbit, and sheep. Try to turn the heap at least once while it decomposes, shifting the outside to the inside.

Garden compost

This valuable source of organic matter is available to all gardeners. Made and used sensibly, it is a prime source of improved soil condition and garden fertility. For further details see pp.30–31.

Mushroom compost

The used compost on which mushrooms have been grown is excellent for the soil as well as being easy to handle. It contains ground limestone, which makes it of particular value on acid soils. Check in the yellow pages to see whether there is a mushroom farm near you; share with a neighbor if the farm's smallest load is too much for you. You can also buy mushroom compost in sacks from a garden center, though it is more expensive this way.

Seaweed

Once it has rotted down, which it does quite readily, seaweed improves the soil structure and is a rich source of plant foods, especially nitrogen and potash. Collect as much as you can if you live near the sea, and either stack it separately or mix it with garden compost. Leave it for a month, or until the rain washes the salt out, before you use it. If you do not do this, the salt will disrupt the internal chemical balance of plants.

Leafmold

To supplement your own raked leaves, ask the local park manager if you may collect some of the park's leaves, or visit a local forest after the leaves have fallen, provided you have the space to stack them. Taken home in plastic bags, the leaves provide a rich source of humus after they have been stacked for a couple of years. They need this long period to rot thoroughly.

Peat

Though rather expensive, peat provides a ready source of humus and is especially useful for small town gardens. It may be dug into the topsoil or spread as a weed-suppressing mulch (see p.43).

Other possibilities

Depending on where you live, a number of other organic substances to enrich your soil might be available. Hop waste, which you might find at a local brewery, is good; so are cider mill and winery pomace, which are created as the fruit is crushed. Most sawmills are happy to give you sawdust, and many lumberyards can supply wood chips, both of which make useful mulches.

ORGANIC FERTILIZERS

True organic fertilizers are concentrated plant foods made of processed materials such as bonemeal and dried blood. Just like bulky organic additions, organic fertilizers depend on the action of microorganisms in the soil to convert them into sources of plant food. By stimulating this activity they aid soil fertility, as well as feed the plants, though they do little toward creating humus.

The majority of organic fertilizers are a good deal more expensive than their inorganic counterparts. Though they act more slowly, their effects are longer-lasting, so they need to be applied less often.

Most organic fertilizers come in powder form. The main types are

Bonemeal Animal bones, coarsely or finely ground, make a long-lasting phosphatic fertilizer, usefully applied when planting fruit trees or bushes as well as vegetables. Its effects last about three years.

Cottonseed meal is a good source of nitrogen and makes an especially good fertilizer for acid-loving plants. It is also cheap and easy to find.

Fishmeal contains nitrogen and phosphorus and is effective for two years. An inorganic form of potash is usually added to make a balanced fertilizer, so you could end up paying a high price for a product that is not truly organic.

Dried blood provides a fast-acting nitrogenous tonic for plants. It comes in the form of powder or liquid food.

INORGANIC FERTILIZERS

The value of inorganic fertilizers is that they can be absorbed immediately by plants and can quickly remedy known deficiencies. However, they make no lasting contribution to the soil's fertility.

If you suspect, from the symptoms of your plants, that your soil is deficient in one of the main nutrients, you can confirm this with the aid of a testing kit like the kit that measures the pH level in the soil. Instructions with the kit will also tell you how to remedy a specific deficiency in order to create a more balanced soil. Potash, for instance, is often in short supply in light soils. A "straight" or single chemical fertilizer will remedy a particular shortage.

Unless you know that your soil is deficient in a particular chemical, a general or "complete" fertilizer is the best choice. That is, you want an inorganic formulation (NKP) containing a balanced mixture of the three main nutrients—sulfate of ammonia, superphosphate of lime, and sulfate of potash—in the proportions needed by most soils, as well as traces of minerals such as iron.

The complete fertilizer may take the form of granules, liquid, or powder. You can apply granular fertilizers, the most common form, either to bare ground about two weeks before sowing or planting, or to the soil around growing plants. Many quick-maturing crops, such as radishes, benefit from the former, called a *base dressing. Top dressings*, as the latter are called, are particularly useful as a boost for crops that remain in the soil for a number of months, such as Brussels sprouts. Work both dressings into the soil, using a rake on unplanted ground and a hoe between plants.

Liquid formulations, both balanced and single-purpose, need to be diluted before use. They are applied as a top dressing watered into the soil and are quickly absorbed by the plants.

Foliar foods are those that are applied directly to the foliage of plants by spraying; the leaves are able to absorb the nutrients immediately. During a dry spell these foods give quicker results than soil dressings. Some foliar foods are designed to correct a shortage of one or more trace elements, essential chemicals that plants need in only minute quantities. Soils that are low in organic matter are most likely to lack them, with the result of stunted plant growth or oddly colored leaves.

A range of "straight" or single-purpose fertilizers are also sold for garden use. These one-chemical inorganic fertilizers act faster than their organic equivalents but are readily washed out of the soil, leaving no enduring benefits. Phosphatic fertilizers are an exception; the phosphate is fixed on iron and aluminum and thus remains in the ground.

Sulfate of ammonia, a major source of nitrogen, is very fast-acting, but it has an acidifying effect on the soil. You can rake it in prior to sowing or use it as a top dressing for growing crops, especially brassicas and salad vegetables.

Nitrate of soda, also fast-acting, tends to make clay soils more intractable.

Superphosphate is the most popular inorganic source of phosphate. Used before sowing or planting, it remains effective for a season or two.

Sulfate of potash is a safe source of potash for all plants. Use it as a top dressing, especially for fruit trees and bushes and for tomatoes.

Muriate of potash is a more concentrated high-potash liquid fertilizer than sulfate of potash. It may damage berries and tomatoes.

LIME LORE

Most vegetables grow best in a slightly acid soil, so an application of lime is the answer if your soil is too acid. Lime is good for certain crops, too: onions, brassicas, and lettuces in particular.

Lime is available in two forms: ground limestone and dolomitic lime. An average dressing of ground limestone for a light soil is about eight ounces per square yard, and double this amount on clay. If you use dolomitic lime, reduce the amounts by a third.

■ Spread lime on the soil surface after digging. Do not dig it in. Try not to spread lime after manuring the soil.

■ Excessive alkalinity, produced by too much lime in the soil, is less likely to be a problem but can be reduced by the liberal use of peat. A dressing of sulfate of ammonia, at one ounce per square yard, also helps.

Compost is a term loosely used to describe any bulky organic additions made from animal or vegetable waste. You can buy some forms ready-made or make garden compost yourself. The value of organic additions is indisputable; they are fundamental to the soil's well-being. Many gardeners, however, have a problem finding enough material to make their own compost: those with access to plenty of farm manure are in a minority. Possible alternatives, such as peat-based planting mixtures, can be costly. Organic fertilizers are particularly expensive.

Garden compost, in contrast, is free, and despite a certain mystique surrounding it, it is not difficult to make. Most vegetation will rot down of its own accord without assistance. What the gardener can do is speed up the process and make sure that the finished product—the compost—is evenly and thoroughly decomposed.

Making good compost rapidly is all about keeping bacteria happy. These microorganisms convert garden waste into the rich, moist, crumbly material that greatly enriches the soil. To do this they must have sufficient—but not too much—air, water, and (at least initially) warmth.

COMPOST MATERIALS

A wide variety of waste is suitable for composting. Most leafy waste from the garden or the kitchen can be used. Avoid diseased garden material, though, and any weeds that are full of seeds. You should also avoid perennial weeds with tough, persistent roots. Though the heat in the center of a well-made heap will destroy the leafy part of such weeds, you should burn the rest, because the woody stems will not rot down and the roots may survive. Take care also not to include plants suffering from club root. Burn them instead.

Vegetable peelings and trimmings provide good compost material, but avoid any waste that might attract rats, such as meat scraps; bones will not decompose. You can place tough, fibrous material such as cabbage stalks near the center of the heap if you are confident that it will heat well, but it is essential to chop or hammer them thoroughly first in order to start the breaking-down process. Better still, with long-term compost making in mind, invest in a garden shredder to process these and other tough materials. An average family does not usually generate enough vegetable waste to provide sufficient compost for a sizable plot. One answer is to collect vegetable trimmings from a supermarket or from neighbors.

Another invaluable supplement is grass clippings, easily the most plentiful garden "waste" for at least half the year. Mixed with plenty of straw, which both prevents their compaction and increases their bulk, they rot down beautifully. But added to the heap on their own, they will form a dense mass, the very opposite of good compost.

COMPOSTING: THE ESSENTIALS

The compost heap itself—that is, the vegetation—needs to be contained in some form of structure, known as the bin (see the illustrations on this and the facing page).

The right conditions are most easily provided in a compost heap that has upright sides and adequate depth (minimum of three to five feet). Compared with a sprawling mound, this shape prevents excessive wetting and drying and, most important, aids the heating process that results from bacterial action. It does not matter whether the heap is square or circular, but you must contain the mound of rotting vegetation in some way.

A ready-made compost bin looks neat and, if made from metal or plastic, will not rot. But get the largest size you can: many bins on the market are too small to allow the contents to heat and decompose rapidly or to contain all you have to put in them. They work, but the process takes longer than it needs to. Inadequate ventilation, depriving the bacteria of air, is another disadvantage with some models. If this looks like being a problem, stand the bin on bricks and leave the top uncovered.

A homemade wooden compost bin, with slatted sides and front, can be as large as you wish and will have adequate ventilation. Make it with sides at least four feet long and wide, and of a similar height. A bigger bin is an advantage if you are likely to have plenty of material. Design is not critical; the main

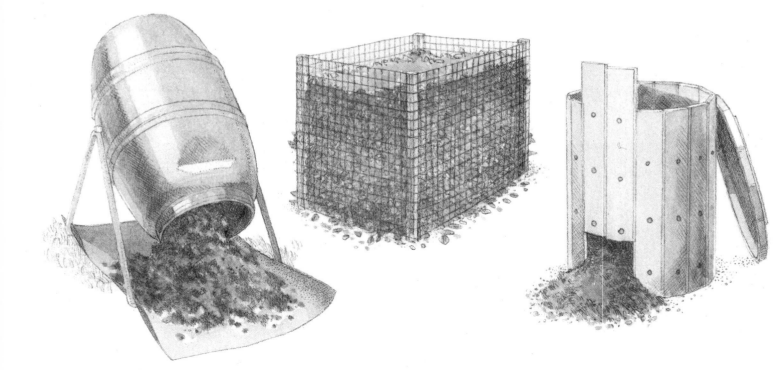

feature is a front that you can fit or remove in stages during filling and emptying. You could line a slatted bin with fine-mesh plastic netting to prevent material from falling through the spaces.

The price of new lumber means that a homemade bin can cost almost as much as one bought at a garden center. Broken pallets are a possible cheap source of wood, as are offcuts from a lumberyard. Treat the wood with a nonpoisonous preservative before you use it.

It is a great advantage to have at least two compost bins so that you can leave one to mature while you are filling the second. If you become really compost-minded, you will find that you need three or more.

BUILDING THE HEAP
Some gardeners build their compost heap on a base of open, stemmy material, with or without bricks beneath, to help aerate it. This is a good idea if the bin containing it has fully closed sides, but is less important if there are gaps for ventilation.

Bacteria thrive on a mixed diet, so fill the bin accordingly. In particular, mix soft and fibrous material together, rather than adding unmixed layers of either. Spread the stuff evenly, leaving it loose. It will soon consolidate on its own.

Mix in a little manure at intervals, if it is available. Failing this, use a ready-made compost activator. The purpose is to stimulate bacterial action, which is often slow to get going in winter or in a heap where soft, leafy material is in short supply.

Water the heap, and then keep it covered with plastic if it shows signs of drying out during warm weather. There is no need to water it during changeable weather. If you wish, empty the compost from the completed bin after a few weeks and put it back in so that the outer, slow-to-rot material is on the inside. Alternatively, simply add it to another bin when using the material. Rotting down takes about three months in the summer and twice as long in winter.

Keep the bin covered once the compost is ready for use. Even in winter, try to have a fresh heap of compost on the go at all times to make use of every scrap of waste.

Far left Tumbler bins, turned daily to assist aeration, are designed to speed up the process of compost making.
Center Wire-mesh bins are relatively inexpensive, but the compost may be slow to generate heat and to decompose.
Left Sliding panels allow you to take small amounts of rotted compost from the base of this metal bin before the rest is ready.

MAKING YOUR OWN COMPOST BIN
The available space in your garden will dictate the size of compost bin to a large extent. But bear in mind that bins smaller than about four square feet do not heat up as readily as large ones. You may be able to use cheap offcuts from your local lumberyard; even if they are a little shorter than this, they will still make a serviceable bin.

Planks about three quarters of an inch thick and four inches wide will make a reasonably strong bin. Of course, they may be thicker or broader. The corner uprights should be at least two inches square, or somewhat thicker. Buy them long enough to bury the bottom one foot in the soil. Pressure-treated fenceposts are ideal.

Old railroad ties are another possibility. They will make extremely strong and stable bins, though they cannot be joined by nailing. Use angle-iron stakes, driven into the ground at the corners on the inside and the outside, instead.

Protect untreated lumber with wood preservative, painting this on liberally after cutting the wood but before construction. Choose a preservative that is not based on tar oil, if possible; creosote will have little effect on the compost but can kill plants.

Use galvanized nails throughout for fastening the slatted sides.

1 First construct two sides of the bin, nailing the slats to the corner uprights. Then stand the sides on end and connect them with the slats that will form the back.

2 Stand the three sides of the bin in position, with the foot of each corner upright set one foot into the soil. Now

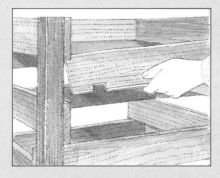

position the removable front slats, cutting a notch in each to hold it secure.

3 A pair of bins, built side by side, is a great advantage. You can fill one while the other is maturing. Alternatively, you can turn the first heap, partly decomposed, into the second one to complete the process.

Well-made tools are a good investment, since they should last you a lifetime. It is therefore worth spending time choosing them carefully. Their cost is not the only consideration. Apart from the design, and the quality and suitability of the materials used, the weight and balance of all tools should be checked carefully before you buy. If they are too heavy and cumbersome for you, even simple chores may prove a trial.

Those illustrated here are the basic tools required by all gardeners who are growing their own fruit and vegetables. If both you and your partner garden, you may find that you need to duplicate some of the essential tools. Other, more specialized tools are available to help with specific tasks, such as long-handled shears for pruning tall fruit trees, but these will clearly depend on the particular crops you grow.

SPADES

Consider whether you are strong enough, or your soil is light enough, for a full-size blade, which is about a foot long and seven inches wide. A smaller one, called a border spade (nine inches by five and a half inches), may be more suitable, particularly if you have heavy soil. A spade with a flat tread is less tiring to use if you are digging for a long time, and it will not damage your footwear. If you are carrying out a single task, such as planting an apple tree, the nontreaded spade is fine.

Choose a model with a smooth, slightly angled shaft and a D-shaped handle, preferably made from polypropylene, which is lighter and stronger than wood. The shaft should be long enough to enable you to drive the blade into the soil without much bending.

Stainless steel blades retain their mirrorlike finish; this makes for easier digging, especially on heavy soil, since soil does not cling to them. They are relatively expensive, though, and an ordinary forged steel blade can always be kept rust-free by cleaning and greasing. (Treaded stainless steel blades are not generally available.)

FORKS

Choose a fork with square tines and overall dimensions about the same as those of a spade, or even slightly larger. Forks with flat tines are intended mainly for digging potatoes. Stainless steel forks are available, though their advantages are less marked than those of spades.

Among their several uses, forks are invaluable for breaking up lumpy soil, for breaking up the subsoil layer in double digging, for loosening a compacted surface between plants, and for moving manure, piles of weeds, and garden rubbish.

RAKES

A rake is an essential tool for seedbed preparation and leveling. It is used to break the soil into a fine tilth after digging. Choose the kind with a one-piece forged head and about a dozen gently curved teeth.

Lightness is an advantage, since part of the weight should be supported by the lower hand. If it is not, you will pull the soil into ridges instead of forming a level bed.

HOES

Regular hoeing is the key to controlling annual weeds, provided that you act as soon as there is a hint of green throughout the garden. That way, minimum effort is needed, because weeds never get a chance to become established. There are several other gardening tasks for which a hoe of one kind or another is suitable.

A draw hoe, with its blade set almost at right angles to a long handle, is used with a scraping or chopping action. It is suitable for dealing with heavy weed growth, but small weeds tend to get buried and may continue to grow. Two other important uses are for drawing soil up around potatoes and for forming seed furrows.

A Dutch or "action" hoe has one main purpose. When pushed forward in a series of short, jabbing motions, its flat blade severs annual weeds without burying them.

An onion hoe is a short-handled draw hoe. It is effective for thinning out rows of seedlings and for close, accurate hoeing around small plants. The gardener has to bend low, however, so it is tiring to use.

In addition, a number of patent hoes, for the most part based on the Dutch hoe principle, are available. Some, with flattened blades sharpened at front and rear, are used with a push-pull action.

CULTIVATORS

A tool with three or five hooked tines, a cultivator is invaluable for breaking up lumps on heavy soil. If your land was dug in late autumn, one or two passes with a

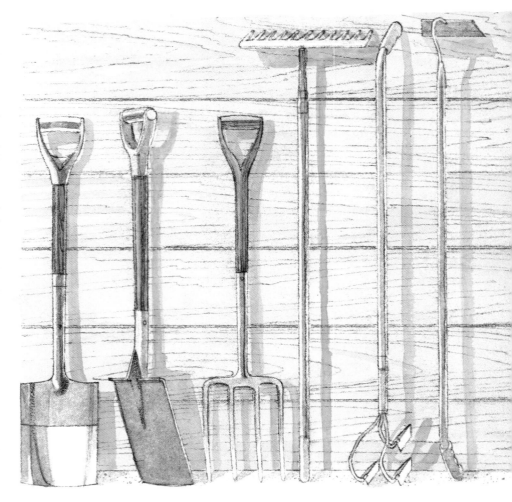

cultivator in spring, followed by a light raking, provides a splendid seedbed.

Cultivators are also useful for loosening compacted soil at any time of year. When drawn through the soil in a series of parallel passes, the curve of the tines helps the cultivator to penetrate densely compacted earth and thus allow air and moisture to reach plant roots more easily.

MEASURING BOARD AND LINE

A flat piece of wood about three feet long is useful for accurate spacing between rows and plants. Paint thick lines across or cut notches in the planting board at about one-foot intervals, with smaller notches or lines every six inches.

A cord mounted on a reel is a more accurate and convenient way of marking seed rows than making do with sticks and string. If the free end is secured to a steel pin, the line should be strong enough and remain taut enough to guide the hoe when you are making furrows.

DIBBERS

Some plants, brassicas in particular, require firm planting. A dibber is the ideal tool; you can use its pointed end first to form the planting hole, and then, inserting it again alongside the plant, to press the soil hard against its roots.

Purpose-made European dibbers have a steel tip to reduce friction. But if you have a broken spade, you can cut off the top six inches of the shaft and trim it to a point to make a dibber.

TROWELS

A trowel's main use is for planting. For plants with little or no stem, such as lettuces, a trowel is the only tool to use. If you don't have a dibber, a trowel is also quite effective for planting brassicas. The knack is to form a slit just wide enough to take the roots, without removing any soil.

Trowels are also essential for removing perennial weeds individually, and for any close work around plants.

CLIPPERS

You will need garden clippers or shears if you are growing fruit, but they are also useful for a variety of tidying-up jobs in the garden. There is little to choose between the two basic designs, those that cut with a scissor action and those with a single blade that cuts against an anvil. Make sure the blades cut cleanly and keep them sharp.

WHEELBARROWS

Unless the garden is very small, buy a substantial barrow or garden cart, preferably one with a pneumatic tire. Throughout the year it will make your work much easier, particularly in tasks that involve moving soil, manure, compost materials, or rubbish. A flimsy barrow with a small wheel may have to be replaced within a short time.

Apart from the garden tools listed above, each with a specific use, there is a miscellany of small, general-purpose items that you will find invaluable in the vegetable garden. Keep a penknife on hand for general trimming jobs and a sharp knife especially for trimming vegetable crops such as brassicas.

Have a supply of bamboo canes in assorted sizes to use as stakes and supports. You will need a ball of string and a supply of plant ties (lengths of plastic-covered wire) for tying plants to their supports or against a wall. Plastic markers are useful for identifying rows of seeds or individual plants; write on them with a special waterproof pen.

It is worth keeping a supply of empty yogurt cartons and plastic margarine tubs to supplement flowerpots and trays. Empty food containers are perfectly satisfactory for seed-sowing and for pricked-out seedlings.

From left to right: untreaded spade; spade with a tread; garden fork; rake; cultivator; draw hoe; Dutch hoe; patent hoe (Swoe); push-pull weeder; onion hoe; anvil-type clippers; reel and line; dibber; trowel; planting board; pneumatic-tired wheelbarrow.

CARING FOR TOOLS

■ Clean all tools after use; in particular, remove earth.
■ Either smear blades with grease or spray them with an antirust aerosol.
■ Store tools in a dry shed or garage; never leave them outdoors.
■ Remember to oil bearings and pivots.
■ Use a coarse file to sharpen hoe blades.

It may seem odd that you need to turn your garden upside down at regular intervals; wild plants manage well enough without such an upheaval. So is digging really necessary?

The answer, unfortunately, is yes, unless your soil is already in a superb state of rich, crumbly fertility. The fruit and vegetable gardener asks a great deal of the soil in terms of returns, and digging enables you to put something back—to mix in plenty of organic matter, bury weeds, let in life-giving air, and relieve the compaction caused by stepping on the beds. Heavy soil in particular benefits from digging at the right time of year.

For the most part, digging applies only to the topsoil, that precious fertile layer that supports plant life. "Single digging," by far the most common practice, involves loosening and turning this layer without disturbing the inorganic subsoil beneath. From time to time, though—and particularly if you are aware of an extra-hard pan below the topsoil—it is worth loosening the subsoil as well.

WHEN TO DIG
Full-scale digging is not practicable until the end of the growing season, when only a few late-season vegetables remain. If you need to loosen the soil between harvesting one crop and planting another, this is best done with a fork.

Autumn and early winter are the easiest times to dig heavy soil, which may be too dry and hard earlier in the year. At the same time, however, you should aim to finish digging heavy soil before it becomes saturated with winter rains or frozen. Left too late, the work will be twice as hard or impossible, and the structure of the soil may be harmed or fail to improve.

The exception is light soil, for which early digging is less important. Indeed, if you are going to dig in manure or compost, the job is better left until late winter, to reduce the risk that plant foods will be washed away. It is easy enough to get a fine tilth on light soil, with or without the help of frost.

If you leave dug soil in unbroken lumps, the combination of rain and frost during the winter will yield a crumbled surface by spring, creating a manageable soil more effectively than any amount of hard labor. In spring, you simply need to rake or lightly fork the surface to prepare it for sowing or planting.

Always avoid digging ground that has a frozen crust or a covering of snow, especially toward the end of the digging season. Either will chill the soil unnecessarily, and sometimes remain unmelted until well after the surface has thawed.

PREPARING TO DIG
Annual weeds should be dug into the soil and buried, and this will happen automatically as you dig your plot. If the same treatment is given to perennial weeds, though, many will survive to grow again the following year. Some will actually be increased by the chopping action of the spade. If you are unsure about distinguishing perennial weeds from annual ones, turn to pp.45–46 for help in identifying them.

The solution is either to dig out the perennial weeds individually, roots and all, or to kill them with a weedkiller before digging (see pp.46–47). Persistence does eventually pay off with perennial weeds: if you are meticulous about removing their roots, they do come back less quickly. Once they are dead, rake long-rooted perennial weeds into a pile and burn them.

HOW TO DIG
Assuming that you are digging in some organic matter, first wheel this to the plot in your barrow and empty it out into evenly spaced heaps. Spread it over the ground but leave bare a narrow strip along one edge where you will begin.

Dig out a fairly broad trench about the depth of a spade along the edge of the plot (the strip you left bare). Throw the soil from it into the wheelbarrow, then take this soil

SINGLE DIGGING
1 The first task is to dig out a trench at one end of the plot. This will provide space for you to throw soil forward as digging proceeds. In this way you maintain an open trench to the far end of the plot. Move the soil from the first trench to just beyond the end, ready for filling in at the final stage of the operation.

2 With the soil out of the way, move to one end of the trench and start on the first row of actual digging. Chop the spade in at right angles to the trench, marking and loosening a spade's width of soil. Now press the blade in with your foot about four inches from the edge, lift the soil just clear of the ground, and throw it forward.

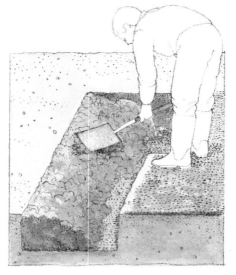

3 As you throw the soil forward, twist the shaft of the spade with your upper hand so that the earth, and any manure or compost on it, is inverted. This will also bury annual weeds, but you must take care to remove the roots of perennial weeds. Scrape manure from near the edge of the trench onto the newly turned trench, then dig the next row.

to a spot just beyond the far end of the plot, where you will need it for filling in the final trench.

Carry on with digging, trench by trench, keeping the spade as vertical as possible. Throw the soil forward to fill the previous trench; try to keep an open trench all the time. Either turn the manure under with each spadeful of soil, or flick it forward across the face of the previous spadeful.

In a new or recently replanned and altered garden you may have to dig up a turfed area. In this case, make the first and subsequent trenches a little wider, so that you can place turf stripped from the surface upside down on the bottom of the trench. Cut and invert a spade-wide strip of turf at a time, chopping it into easily lifted pieces. If you have recently cleared a piece of ground and have a pile of annual weeds, you can also put these into the trench.

DIGGING WITHOUT STRAIN

If you are unused to digging or if you have had a long break from gardening, take it in easy stages and do not try to hurry. The risk of back strain is increased by attempting too much too soon. Half an hour a day may prove long enough until your spine and back muscles are used to the unfamiliar movements.

Buy a good spade, and make sure that it is not too heavy for you to use comfortably. Lift small amounts of soil at a time rather than the maximum that the blade will carry. Avoid digging when the soil is wet or frozen.

Let the weight and momentum of the spade, and your own weight pressing on the blade, do most of the work. Free each spadeful by driving the blade in at right angles to the trench. Lift the soil just clear of the ground, tilting the blade with a rhythmic action.

An automatic spade can be a good investment if you have a weak back. This works with a lever action, virtually eliminating lifting and bending. The blade is hinged to a footplate, so that a

pull on the handlebars throws the soil forward into the trench, inverting it at the same time. An alternative is to hire or buy a rototiller (see p.27); these machines are especially effective on light and medium soils. However, though they avoid the strain of lifting and bending, handling them calls for quite a lot of strength on heavy, hard, or stone-filled soil.

DOUBLE DIGGING

"Double digging" involves penetrating the subsoil: the compacted and generally infertile layer immediately below the topsoil. It is coarser in texture and paler in color than the topsoil itself. Double digging will improve overall drainage and gradually increase the depth of the upper, fertile layer. Plants benefit from the moisture, and sometimes from the few nutrients to be found at a lower level.

Double digging is slow, hard work. The best plan is to tackle only a limited area at a time, marking the point to which you have double dug as a guide for the following season. When double digging, you must be careful not to mix the upper, fertile layer of topsoil with the subsoil beneath. It is especially useful to double dig an area where you intend to plant deep-rooted vegetables, such as parsnips or pole beans.

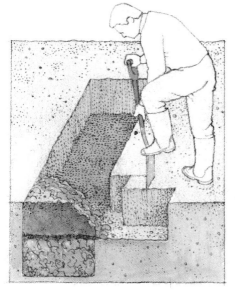

DOUBLE DIGGING

1 First dig a spade-depth trench, about two feet from front to back, across one end of the plot. Move the topsoil you have just removed to just beyond the end of the plot. After loosening the bottom of the trench by forking, add some manure or compost. This may be left as a layer or forked lightly into the surface of the subsoil.

2 Fill the trench by throwing the soil forward from the next two-foot strip. This will create a new trench, ready for loosening and manuring in the same way as the first one. Double digging is of most value when the lower layer is compacted.

GETTING TO KNOW YOUR SOIL, pages 24–25
DEALING WITH WEEDS, pages 45–47

Most vegetables and some herbs are grown as annuals and raised from seed each year. To germinate successfully, seeds need warmth, moisture, and air, so they should be sown in soil that is warm and damp, and they should not be planted too deeply.

Most vegetables *can* be sown directly in the ground. But whether you sow your seeds outdoors or indoors will depend on the climate zone in which you live and on how early a start you wish them to have. Some tender vegetables, such as eggplants, peppers, lima beans, and tomatoes, need fairly high temperatures to germinate and must therefore be sown in a greenhouse (see pp. 38–39) or a warm room indoors; they can either be grown permanently in the greenhouse or else be moved outside once the weather has become milder.

SELECTING SEEDS
Study the seed catalogues and make your selection of plants and varieties. Buy seeds well ahead of the sowing season in case sought-after varieties become scarce.

When choosing the varieties to grow, you will see that some are termed F_1 hybrids. These are the result of crossing two carefully selected parent strains and produce very vigorous, uniform plants.

Another designation that you will see is "All-America Winner," which means that the plant has been selected as the best variety in its class for a particular year. All-America Winners are usually the result of intensive research, and they can be relied on to produce especially fine crops.

You may find pelleted seeds, which are individual seeds coated with soluble clay,

which makes them easier to sow at regular spacings. They reduce the need for thinning and are an excellent idea for crops that are difficult to thin after germination.

Each year brings a crop of new vegetable varieties announced in the seed catalogues; some of them are illustrated in the color catalogues, pages 112–128 and 176–192. You must decide whether to try these or to stick to old favorites that have been recommended by books, fellow gardeners, or the Cooperative Extension Service.

On balance, it probably pays to stay with known good performers for most of your crops. However, it is always interesting to try something new, and it is a good idea to experiment with at least one or two interesting newcomers each year. Some may well become your long-term choices.

PREPARING FOR MAIN SOWINGS
Many plants, particularly root crops such as carrots and potatoes, should be sown in the place where they are to grow and mature, because they are difficult to transplant successfully.

Getting the soil ready for sowing and planting is one of the main spring jobs in the food garden. Whatever the time of sowing indicated on the seed packet, you should pay as much attention to the condition of the soil as to the calendar. Never make a start while the land is still sticky, but wait until it is dry enough to walk on without having the soil stick to your shoes. Also be sure it has had time to warm up enough to foster seed germination.

If you have already dug over the soil the previous fall, light soil will need no more than raking. This is the time to spread compost and fertilizer (see p.29) if the soil, or the crop, requires it. Heavy soil that has been dug should crumble if it is lightly forked or stirred with a cultivator first; you can then use a rake. Disturb only the loose surface soil.

If you did not dig the plot the previous fall, light and medium soil will respond to being turned with a fork, preferably with the addition of well-rotted manure. You may need to work at heavy soil repeatedly with a fork and/or a cultivator to coax a tilth. It is important to start work on clay soil when it has dried out but before it sets hard. A rototiller can be a considerable help in preparing heavy soils for planting (see p.27); several passes will loosen the soil to a depth of six or eight inches.

If the ground is very dry at sowing time, soak the bottom of the furrow with a hose immediately before distributing the seeds of your chosen crops.

SOWING IN SEEDBEDS
Some vegetables, notably brassicas and leeks, are often sown in a seedbed and moved to their final positions when partly grown. The plants tend to be leggy if they are sown where they are to grow.

The seedbed can be in any sunny, well-drained corner of the plot. First prepare the ground and form the furrows as described for main sowing, and as shown in the illustrations. However, instead of using a line and pegs, use a planting board as a guide for the hoe. Space the rows six inches apart and label each one as you sow the seeds in it.

You can give some crops, such as early-maturing cabbages, an earlier start by preparing the seedbed in a cold frame, in a plastic tunnel, or under cloches. The

method is the same, but you need to put cloches in position two weeks before sowing to warm up the soil. Remember to ventilate the frame if the weather turns warm.

When the soil is loosened, use a rake to complete the preparation of a fine seedbed (above). Once you have raked in one direction, finish by raking across the seedbed.

A cultivator (left), with three or five prongs, is invaluable for loosening compacted soil, either between rows of plants or as the first stage in seedbed preparation. Drawn behind in a series of passes, it causes a minimum of back strain.

THE LIFE OF SEEDS

As long as they are carefully stored, many vegetable seeds remain viable for several years. Seal the opened packets with adhesive tape and keep them in a dark, cool place in a closed tin or jar; the refrigerator or freezer is ideal. Write the year of purchase on the packet if it is not printed on it. Two exceptions are onions and parsnips, which will probably fail to germinate if they are kept for a year or longer.

Seeds gathered from the previous year's crop are often a risky proposition. Many vegetables, notably brassicas, will cross-pollinate, with unpredictable and disastrous results. Hybrids are unlikely to reproduce true to type, too, so it is safer to buy seeds from a reputable supplier, unless you are trying to save an heirloom variety.

SOWING THE SEEDS

Vegetables may be grown either in well-spaced rows or, with closer spacing, in beds (see below and p.132). The sowing method is essentially the same in each case, though a planting board placed crosswise is sufficient guide for drawing the furrows in a bed. The line method, described here, is for well-spaced rows on a conventional plot.

Measure the correct spacing between rows with a planting board, then insert a peg at each end of a row to hold the line taut. Form the seed-sowing furrow, called a drill, with the corner of a hoe; rest the blade lightly against the line as you draw it backward in short, easy movements. Make the drill as deep as indicated for the particular plant; this will vary from about half an inch for the smallest seeds, such as carrots, to two inches for the largest seeds, such as beans. Peas are one exception: they require a flat trench, formed with the whole blade.

Take a pinch of seeds between finger and thumb and sow them thinly along the drill as you walk forward. As you finish each pinch of seeds, make a mark in the soil alongside the drill as a guide to where to start sowing again. Never sow seeds too thickly. If you prefer, you can use one of the seed sowers that simply need pushing along the drill; they save a little time.

Cover the seeds by walking backward from the far end of the drill, brushing soil into it from each side with your hands, or use the upturned head of a rake. Finish by walking forward once more, firming the replaced soil lightly with one foot, or, on a seedbed, with the back of your hand.

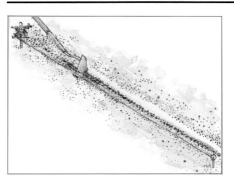

To form a seed drill, first fasten the line and make sure that it is taut. Holding a hoe at an angle against the line, pull it toward you in a series of movements to form a V-shaped groove. As a rough guideline, the larger the seed is, the deeper it needs to be sown.

Empty some seeds from a packet into the palm of one hand, and distribute them between thumb and forefinger to sow sparingly along the drill. Ready-made sowing aids (inset) are simply pushed along a preformed drill. Check their accuracy on a plain surface first, such as a path or floor.

After sowing, use an inverted rake head, or your hands, to draw some soil back gently into the drill. Firm the replaced soil, either by tapping with the rake head or by pressing gently with your foot. Mark one end of the row with a stick and the other with a label before removing the line.

PROTECTION

Seedbeds are a sure attraction for birds and cats. If your experience suggests extreme caution, cover the rows with wire or plastic netting stretched over wire arches. Otherwise, crisscross black cotton thread over the rows between short sticks.

THINNING

With a few exceptions, such as spring onions, beets, and sparsely sown radishes, all vegetable crops need thinning to prevent overcrowding. This applies to plants raised in seedbeds as well as to those sown in the open ground. Failure to thin inevitably leads to weak, spindly growth, as plants compete with each other for nutrients, moisture, and sunlight.

Plants that were sown too thickly suffer unduly from being overcrowded at the seedling stage. Thinning very overcrowded seedlings can also disturb the roots of those that are left.

Start to thin as soon as the plants are large enough to handle, but leave a surplus at the early stage in case of losses from pests or disease. Thin once or twice again later on. For example, you might thin first so that the seedlings are an inch apart, then later to two inches apart, and finally to the distance recommended for that vegetable. In a seedbed, however, thin only once before transplanting the seedlings to their permanent position.

Try not to disturb the plants that are left: thin when the soil is damp to reduce the risk of damage to their roots, and firm the soil around them if it is loose after thinning.

SOWING UNDER GLASS, pages 38–39
CROP PROTECTION, page 44

SPACE-SAVING METHODS, page 132

In cool climates, tender crops, such as peppers, eggplants, and tomatoes, need a warm start in life and should be sown under glass—that is, indoors. Many, of course, can be planted outdoors once all danger of frost is past. With some crops it is a matter of variety. There are types of cucumber and melon, for instance, that are bred to be grown in a greenhouse. But others, with a hardier constitution, grow better outdoors. All squashes and pumpkins fall into this category, as do tender beans.

Indoor sowing is also valuable for giving an earlier start to crops normally sown outdoors, such as lettuce and sweet corn. You can stagger the harvesting of some of your crops by sowing a proportion of their seeds inside a few weeks earlier than the rest, which you sow outdoors.

If you do not have a greenhouse, a cold frame with soil-warming cables provides good conditions for germination and growth (see p.18), as does an electric propagator. If you are using a soil-warmed bed, press the seed trays or pans well into the soil. Pack moist peat around them to help conserve the warmth.

PROVIDING WARMTH
During late winter and early spring, it is a good idea to use soil-warming cables or a propagator even for seeds started in a greenhouse. (Install the cable exactly as you would in a frame.) Either method will cost less than heating the whole greenhouse to the relatively high temperature needed for germination. After germination, a soil-warmed bed will keep the seedlings growing, but you will need some form of air heating for plants moved from a propagator fairly early in the season.

The need for artificial heat lessens as the season advances. Sowings delayed until midspring need only gentle supplementary warmth by night and perhaps none by day. Later still, seeds will germinate successfully and seedlings will prosper in an unheated greenhouse or cold frame.

The precise time of sowing depends partly on the amount of heat available, partly on what you are growing, and partly on where the plants are to grow. For instance, if you can maintain a minimum temperature of 60°F, even on chilly nights, you can sow celery seeds in a propagator during late winter. It is better to wait until spring, however, if you prefer to economize on fuel. A midspring sowing is quite early enough for plants such as zucchini, which will be moved outside in late spring. If they are sown earlier than this, they may outgrow their pots before it is warm enough to move them outdoors, and they will suffer after they have been transplanted.

Seeds may be sown in an electrically heated propagator and the seedlings grown on in a greenhouse or indoors on a sunny windowsill. The one-directional light on a sill makes for lanky growth, so the sooner you can move seedlings outdoors, the better.

CONTAINERS FOR GROWING PLANTS
Small seeds, such as lettuces, are sown by being sprinkled on a pan or tray of potting soil; the seedlings are then moved individually (pricked out) soon after germination. Larger seeds, such as those of squash or sweet corn, are sown in small pots where they will remain until planting time.

Plastic seed trays are often used for seed-sowing, but shallow seed pans, which require less potting soil than a pot, are even better. Seedlings can also be grown in a plastic seed tray and left in this rectangular container until they are ready for planting out. A pot measuring about three inches across is big enough for planting individual larger seeds.

You can also use disinfected plastic margarine tubs for sowing small seeds, or yogurt cartons for individual seeds, but rectangular trays and pans are most economical of space on greenhouse staging.

Pans and pots are made of plastic or clay, and both are satisfactory. The plastic ones have the advantage, however, since they are cheaper, lighter in weight, and easier to clean; they also need watering less often. It is worth soaking clay pots in water before using them; otherwise they absorb too much moisture from the potting soil. Cover drainage holes with a piece of broken pot or a small stone first, to stop soil from being washed through.

You can also use compressed peat pots and peat blocks for sowing large seeds or for planting pricked-out seedlings. At planting time the whole pot or block, complete with its plant, is set in the soil. The compressed peat disintegrates and the plant roots grow through. Peat pots must be damp when planted, or else the peat will form a hard case and the plant will die.

POTTING SOILS AND MIXES
Ordinary garden soil is unsuitable for starting seeds. Used in pots and seed pans, it becomes muddy or hard, both of which discourage root growth. It also contains weed seeds and disease organisms.

To germinate seeds, you might want to use a mixture of perlite and/or vermiculite, milled sphagnum moss or peat moss, ground limestone, and a little fertilizer. Such a soilless mix holds moisture well, allows plenty of air to circulate around the seedlings' roots, and is sterile—and if you make it yourself, it is not expensive. Once the seedlings are well established, however, they need plenty of fertilizer to thrive, since the growing medium itself contains no available nutrients.

Ready-made seed-starting and potting soils are the ideal growing medium for seeds, since they are sterilized and specially formulated to meet the needs of young plants. They are, of course, quite distinct from garden soil, which is made of decomposed vegetation, minerals, and microorganisms.

Seed-starting and potting soils are either peat-based, with added plant foods, or made from a mixture of pulverized pine bark, sand, peat, limestone, and fertilizers. Peat-based potting soils are more likely to be all-purpose mixes—that is, they suit plants of all ages, provided that additional fertilizer is given within six weeks or so of the plants being potted.

SOWING THE SEEDS

Fill the container with moist potting soil and level it off; remove any surplus. Firm the soil with the base of another pot or seed pan. Distribute the seeds evenly over the growing medium. After sowing, sprinkle just enough potting soil or sphagnum moss over the seeds to cover them.

When sowing in pots, press two large seeds a half-inch deep into the soil; place them slightly apart. Cover the pots with glass or plastic and paper. Remove the weaker seedling if both germinate.

Check the trays, pans, or pots daily after the first few days for signs of germination. Remove the cover, or, if you are using a propagator, remove the tray, at the first sign of the seedlings. Most seeds will germinate within one to two weeks; some, such as parsley, take longer.

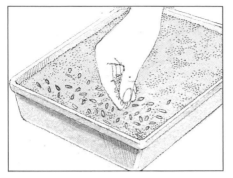

With your finger and thumb, sprinkle small seeds thinly and evenly over the surface of the potting soil. Leave more space between seeds of intermediate size, such as tomatoes, or set them in equally spaced rows about a half-inch apart. Leave about half an inch between pelleted seeds.

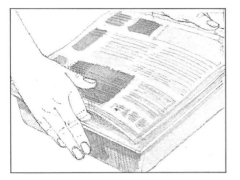

Water the soil lightly, then cover the container, first with glass to prevent drying out, then with folded newspaper to exclude light. Label the tray with the name of the seeds and the date of sowing. Turn the glass daily to dry any condensation.

PRICKING OUT

Seedlings raised from scattered seeds need thinning to prevent overcrowding. Prick them out as soon as they are large enough to handle, before they become tall, spindly, and intertwined. Space lettuces, celeriac, and other small plants about one and a half inches apart in a tray. Allow two inches for celery. Pot tomatoes and squashes individually into three-inch pots.

Water the seedlings with a fine spray and try to keep a constant temperature while they form new roots. They are best kept out of direct sunlight for the first day or two.

Peat-based potting soils and peat pots need regular and careful watering, since it is difficult for them to absorb water again after they have dried out.

Pricking out consists of transplanting very small seedlings to another container in order to give them more space. Lift each seedling by one of its leaves to avoid damaging its stem. Use a pencil, a plant label, or a small knife to help ease it out of the soil.

Use the same tool to make the new planting holes, and cover the seedlings with soil to just below their first seed leaves. Firm the soil back in place around their roots. Water the seedlings in with a fine-holed rose and place them in a well-lit position.

HARDENING OFF

Gradually acclimatize seedlings grown indoors before planting them outdoors, so they do not suffer a check in their development. If possible, stand them in a cold frame for up to two weeks, and gradually increase the ventilation. Cloches or row covers can be used instead, provided the temperature is not too low or the weather too severe.

Alternatively, stand the plants outside in a sheltered spot by day, and move them back indoors or into the greenhouse for at least the first week or ten days.

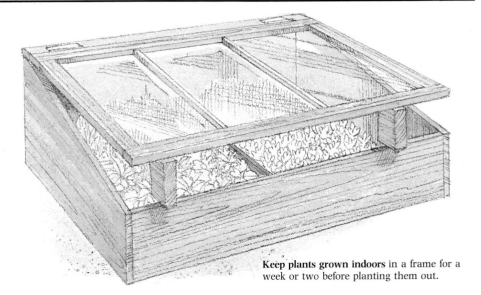

Keep plants grown indoors in a frame for a week or two before planting them out.

USING A GREENHOUSE, pages 12–13
CLOCHES AND ROW COVERS, pages 16–17

COLD FRAMES, page 18
SOWING SEEDS OUTDOORS, pages 36–37

Wait until after the last spring frosts before moving tender, greenhouse-raised seedlings outdoors. Acclimatize them to outdoor conditions first in a cold frame, if possible (see p.39). Certain tender plants, such as eggplants, tomatoes, melons, cucumbers, and peppers, should not be transplanted outdoors until you are confident that the soil and the air are quite warm and all risk of frost has passed.

Hardy plants started in a seedbed can be moved to their final growing positions when their size indicates that they are ready. Plant cabbages and other brassicas when they are about four inches high.

Choose compact, sturdy plants with healthy green leaves for transplanting. Discard any that look weak or lanky—perhaps because of insufficient thinning—and any that are discolored or stunted. Check also that brassicas are not "blind"—that is, without a growing point.

PREPARATION OF THE SITE
Ground that was dug over the previous fall is best for transplanted vegetables. If you did not dig over your plot in the fall, dig or till the site at least two or three weeks before planting to give the ground time to settle. Add a generous helping of general fertilizer if this is needed, then rake the soil over to level the surface.

The ideal conditions for planting are provided by a spell of mild but damp, still weather. Otherwise, plant during the late afternoon or evening and take steps to reduce dehydration, as outlined below.

Use a line and a planting board to mark the rows when planting, and be sure to follow the recommended spacings, even if they seem excessive at this early stage. If, however, you are using the bed system, you can reduce the spacing (see p.132).

Water the seedbed, or pot-grown plants, several hours before planting. Dig up seedbed plants immediately before transplanting. If the soil is very dry, you should fill the planting holes with water before planting. In any case, water it immediately after the plants have been set in.

PLANTING
Take brassicas and leeks from the seedbed bare-rooted, and take care not to damage the roots. When removing lettuces from a seed tray, retain as much potting soil as you can around the roots.

As a rule, make a planting hole of the suitable size with a trowel first. Plant brassicas firmly, and slightly deeper than they were previously, preferably using a dibber. After planting, it should not be possible to dislodge a plant by pulling one of its leaves. Plant leeks by dropping each one

into a separate hole made with a dibber or the handle of a hoe; then pour in a little water to wash some soil over the roots.

For pot-grown plants, use a trowel to dig a hole large enough to take the root ball. Hold the pot upside down and tap the side of it against something hard to loosen the plant. Support the plant gently with your hand. Firm the soil around the root ball after planting. Do not remove plants grown in peat pots; plant the pots just as they are, but tear off any rim above the soil.

If the soil is dry, puddle the young plants in by watering gently around their stems.

If you are planting more than one row of a particular vegetable, you can stagger the plants in adjacent rows to give them more room to grow. But remember to allow aisle space for hoeing and so on.

AFTERCARE
During hot, dry weather, cover the plants with newspaper for a few days: use stones or bricks to support the sheets like tents. Another means of combating loss of moisture is to spray plants with clear water several times a day.

Plants that were started in a peat-based potting soil or in individual peat pots are at greater risk if they are allowed to become dry. Their roots will not extend into the surrounding soil, and insufficient watering will result in stunted growth or dead plants. To avoid this, cut slits in peat pots before planting them.

It may be necessary to protect a newly planted bed against birds (see p.44).

Brassicas require especially firm planting. Once you have formed the hole, insert the plant's roots and lower stem into the soil, then push the trowel or dibber in again alongside, to press soil against the roots. The plant should remain firm when pulled by one of its leaves.

Use a trowel to form the planting hole for seedlings grown in a peat pot or taken from a flowerpot. It is important to prevent the bed from drying out afterward; otherwise the plant's roots may remain confined to the soil ball.

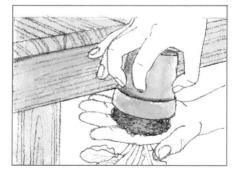

Water pot-grown seedlings an hour or so before you plant them. To extract a young plant from its pot, place your fingers on each side of the stem, turn the pot over, and tap its rim on a firm edge to loosen the soil. Lift the pot clear of the plant and the root ball.

Immediately after planting, be prepared to protect seedlings from slugs, sun, and birds. A wire-mesh guard will keep birds off, and metaldehyde pellets are the surest deterrent to slugs. It is worthwhile erecting temporary shading during hot weather.

SOWING SEEDS OUTDOORS, pages 36–37
SOWING UNDER GLASS, pages 38–39
CROP PROTECTION, page 44
SPACE-SAVING METHODS, pages 132–133

Herbs are both highly ornamental and excellent value for space. There is a great variety of leaf shapes and forms, from feathery fennel and dill to the spikes of rosemary and the smaller-leaved thymes. Many herbs have unusual leaf colors too: there are golden- and silver-leaved varieties of thyme and marjoram, as well as bronze or purple forms of fennel, sage, and basil. Several herb species have attractive gray foliage. You might consider growing some herbs for their scent and others for their flowers as well as growing some for their culinary uses.

Herbs take up very little room in the food garden and can always be grown near the house (see below). Several species can be grown in even a small bed, and will add piquancy and variety to home-cooked meals. Most herbs are extremely adaptable: given sunlight and good drainage, they need a minimum of attention, and they seem immune to most pests and diseases.

WHERE TO GROW HERBS
Choose a well-drained spot that gets the sun. The soil needs to be of average fertility; many herbs grow leggy in extremely rich soil. A few, including mint, parsley, chervil, and sorrel, will grow in partial shade.

A small bed near the kitchen is convenient for picking. Alternatively, you can grow herbs in beds or borders among the garden flowers. The taller herbs, such as rosemary, dill, and fennel, can go at the back of a border. Smaller, more compact herbs, such as marjoram, summer and winter savory, and the ornamental thymes, make attractive edging plants.

There are annual, biennial, and perennial species of herbs, and one or two of them, notably mint, are fairly invasive. You will need to restrict mint, either by planting it in an old, bottomless bucket flush with the soil surface, or else by inserting metal or plastic barriers a foot or more into the soil around it (see p.221).

Herbs were once planted in miniature knot gardens, edged with dwarf box hedging, and these are still occasionally seen. Although they make a charming feature in a garden, a great deal of work is involved.

A much more practical solution is to grow herbs in pots, tubs, and other containers. Since many herbs are decorative and some are scented, they make a good choice for patios. Pots of perennial and biennial herbs, such as chives, parsley, and marjoram, can be brought in for the winter.

A sunny windowbox is another suitable place to grow some of the lower-growing, more compact species of herbs, such as thyme, parsley, marjoram, and winter savory. Keep all containers well watered.

MAKING A START
If you want to create an instant herb garden, you will have to buy plants from a nursery or garden center. Many herbs can be raised from seed, however, which is less expensive and more interesting.

The herbs you choose to grow should be those you like to use most in cooking. The basics, which most gardeners and cooks grow in quantity, include parsley, mint, chives, thyme, and sage. But it is worth growing a few of the more unusual herbs too, either to try out new and subtle flavors, or just to enjoy their decorative qualities. Experiment with such herbs as angelica, lemon balm, burnet, chervil, and rue.

PROPAGATING HERBS
Perennial herb species can be increased, or replaced as they get old and straggly. Either divide them or root cuttings in a mixture of peat and sand or in vermiculite.

Herbs to increase by division include balm, chives, fennel, marjoram, mint, hyssop, winter savory, tarragon, and thyme. Cuttings are the best means of increasing bay, rosemary, and lavender.

HARVESTING AND PRESERVING
As well as using herbs while fresh, which assures the best flavor, you can dry or freeze them for winter use (see p.236). The time of harvesting depends on whether they are being grown for their leaves, flowers, or seeds. Details are given under the individual herb entries, starting on p.219.

Some herbs are easily propagated by removing nonflowering shoots during the summer. Trim just below a leaf joint and remove the lowest leaves. Root in free-draining soil in a cold frame. To help promote rapid rooting, dip cuttings in hormone powder.

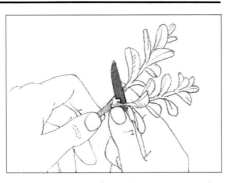

Semiripe cuttings, taken in late summer with a small "heel" of wood from the parent stem, are the best method for rosemary and lavender. Use a sharp knife to cut just above and below the joint. Pot and root in the same way as for tip cuttings.

A cartwheel herb garden not only looks attractive but also provides a means of separating the different plants.

Water is crucial to the life of your crops: not only do plants need moisture, but their nutrients have to be dissolved in water so that they can be taken up by the plant roots. A parched soil means that plants are starved of both water and food, since their roots cannot assimilate nutrients in a dry form. Regular and adequate watering is essential during dry weather, especially during summer, when lower rainfall is likely to coincide with a high evaporation rate.

Soils vary in the amount of water they can hold: clay soils retain far more than sandy soils. The more any soil is improved with organic matter, however, the greater becomes its capacity to store water. The need for watering is therefore greatest on soils low in humus, especially those with a light, sandy structure.

Certain crops are particularly thirsty and therefore especially vulnerable to lack of water; these include tomatoes, cucumbers, corn, squashes, pumpkins, and beans. Melons need a lot of watering in the early stages. Leafy vegetables such as broccoli and spinach also need ample moisture if they are to crop consistently well.

There are a few crops, however, that are at risk from excessive moisture around maturity. Too much water may split ripening melons, or induce the growth of molds on onions nearly ready for harvesting.

WHEN TO WATER
As soil dries out, plants find it increasingly hard to draw up water, and they will eventually reach wilting point. Aim to water all your plants *before* they show signs of distress. Although it may be possible to revive them, wilting checks their growth and slows development. In some cases they will flower prematurely, or "bolt."

The appearance of the surface soil is not a good guide to its moisture content, except while plants are still small and have short roots. During that period the top layer must never be allowed to dry out. As the plants grow, you need to use a trowel to check the state of the soil further down—nine to ten inches for well-developed plants.

Thorough applications of water, scheduled well apart, are the most beneficial to plants. A policy of "little and often" can do more harm than good, since you may be supplying too little water to reach the plant roots. It is better to supply enough water to soak right through the topsoil, which means applying about five gallons per square yard if the soil shows signs of drying out. Water during the evening in summer.

Large-capacity watering can

Hose and storage reel

Pulsating sprinkler

Rotating sprinkler

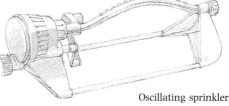

Oscillating sprinkler

Basic watering equipment consists of a hose—preferably the reinforced type that will not kink and is unlikely to split—and a long-spouted can. A reel for storing the hose can also be considered a necessity. There are various forms of sprinklers; the choice is dictated partly by cost and partly by the size of the area needing to be irrigated.

Since they cover a rectangular area, soaker hoses are particularly useful for watering rows of vegetables and berries. The water is ejected as a mistlike spray on either side.

Pulsating sprinklers have a long throw, which makes them a good choice for the larger vegetable plot. Some are mounted on stands to cover an even greater area, regardless of the height of nearby crops.

MULCHING

Mulching consists simply of spreading organic matter over the surface around plants, including berry bushes as well as vegetables. Suitable materials include well-rotted manure, garden compost, peat, grass clippings, leaves, and bark or wood chips.

The object of mulching is to reduce the amount of evaporation from the soil and to suppress weeds. Mulching is also, in the longer term, an aid to soil fertility, since it will eventually be dug into the soil and will break down to form humus.

A suitable depth of mulch is about two inches for most materials, though less than this for grass clippings. Leave a space around the trunks of grafted fruit trees: if the mulch comes into contact with the union between rootstock and scion, new roots might try to form.

Black plastic is an even more effective way of conserving moisture and smothering weeds, though it does nothing for soil fertility. It is especially useful for strawberry plants and melons, since it prevents the fruit from touching the soil. If you do use it, you might want to lay drip hoses underneath first. Cut slits for well-spaced plants, such as brassicas; lay the plastic along each side of closely spaced plants.

Wait until the soil has warmed up before spreading the first spring mulch; otherwise it will act as an insulator, keeping the ground cold and blocking out the sun. Water the ground well before mulching.

WATERING AIDS

Hand watering with water drawn from a tap takes too long for most of the food garden, apart from containers. The least you can do is rig up a hose to save having to walk between the tap and the plants.

When you are watering with a can, it is easy to judge how much you are supplying. If you are using a hose, check how long it takes to fill a can of known size, then relate this to the area being watered, keeping the tap on at a constant pressure.

Once you have a hose, it is a logical step to buy a sprinkler attachment for it, or some other automatic dispenser. The cost is low but the time saved is considerable.

The most basic of sprinkler attachments, with no moving parts, dispenses a circular curtain of water around it. Those that are a little more sophisticated are adjustable to allow a square spray pattern. This helps to prevent gaps and overlaps.

Rotating sprinklers, which have a wider throw, sometimes have adjustable nozzles for varying the size of the spray droplets.

Pulsating sprinklers work with a circular action too. They emit the spray in fine bursts and cover a substantially greater area than the ordinary rotating kinds.

Oscillating sprinklers sweep from side to side instead of in a circle, and can be adjusted to cover square or rectangular patterns. The area watered is about the same as with the larger rotating sprinklers. The droplet size is rather heavy for seedlings and for very small plants.

Irrigation or **drip hoses** are one of the most labor-saving and efficient watering devices. They consist of plastic tubing with multiple perforations. When you lay one along a row, a steady trickle of water along the length of the tube saturates the soil.

Sprinkler or **soaker hoses** are flat in section, and release the water as a mistlike spray over the crops on either side. They are excellent for watering vegetable crops at all stages of growth, and the spray is gentle enough not to damage young plants.

GREENHOUSE WATERING

A piped water supply to the greenhouse is a great time-saver. A good alternative is a water barrel, which can be replenished from a hose and/or from the greenhouse guttering. If it can be placed inside the greenhouse, the temperature of the water will be closer to that of the soil and planting media in which plants are growing. However, lack of space in a small greenhouse may make this impossible.

A long-spouted watering can is the most common watering aid, but it should have a fine rose for use with seedlings. A one-gallon can is large enough for bench watering, but you need one twice this size for plants grown in borders.

A capillary bench (see p.15) provides a simple means of semiautomatic watering for seedlings and other plants growing on staging. Plants growing in the border or in pots can be supplied by one of the drip emitter systems, as described under Watering Containers, below.

WATERING CONTAINERS

Salad crops, tomatoes, and herbs grown in containers need frequent watering—often twice daily during a warm, dry spell. Do not allow peat-based potting soil, in particular, to dry out, since it can be difficult to saturate it again. Reduce the evaporation from growing bags by cutting only small holes for the plant stems.

Limit the heavy moisture loss from absorbent containers, such as wooden plant tubs and clay pots, by lining them with plastic before planting. Be sure to leave the drainage hole uncovered.

As an alternative to hand watering, consider one of the manufactured systems that make use of drip emitters and timers; the flow can be regulated to keep the soil consistently moist. Such a system is especially useful at vacation time.

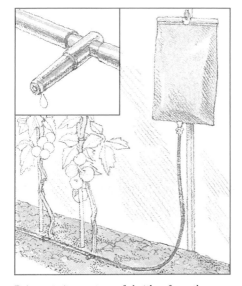

Drip watering systems, fed either from the faucet or, as here, from a reservoir bag, supply water to individual containers and plants. Fertilizer can be added if required.

Apart from the numerous pests and diseases that attack specific plants, your crops need protection from the birds and animals that roam gardens looking for sources of food. The nature of the problem will vary according to where you live. Sparrows and squirrels are the bane of many suburban gardeners, whereas deer and starlings may be more of a nuisance in the country.

Whatever the particular hazard, your aim is to protect your crops and deter the pests without harming the wild creatures and pets with which you share your garden.

BIRDS Large and small birds are an obvious source of damage, although they also help to control insect pests. Berries and tree fruits are particularly at risk from birds, which will spoil ripening fruit in summer and damage fruit buds in winter. You must either protect your crops in some way or frighten the birds off by unsettling them.

Deterrence has to be a fairly short-term policy, since bird scarers lose their effectiveness once they become familiar objects. For this reason it is a good idea to change your strategy at frequent intervals. However, only a formidable deterrent will keep crows away from corn seed.

The alternative is to net crops securely, preferably using a ready-made cage that gives easy access and comfortable headroom. You may not have space in your garden for a permanent cage, however, or you may feel that you don't grow enough berries to make one worthwhile. It is worth protecting individual bushes, canes, strawberry plants, and dwarf trees by draping lightweight netting over them.

Large fruit trees are more of a problem. Black cotton thread wound between branches will deter birds, but it is a time-consuming task to put it there.

CATS Seedbeds are irresistible to cats for use as lavatories. Protect the bed until the crops are established by laying chicken wire or plastic mesh on the ground after sowing.

RODENTS Rabbits, mice, squirrels, woodchucks, and gophers love garden vegetables, and can harm fruit trees as well. A fence is the answer; you'll need one at least two feet high to keep rabbits out, and be sure to bury the bottom edge. Inflatable snakes laid between the crops frighten rodents as well as birds. To protect trees, erect guards and keep mulch away from the trunks, especially in winter.

DEER A slanted fence four or five feet high is more effective than a vertical one, which would have to be at least eight feet tall to prevent deer from jumping over.

Black thread crisscrossed between short sticks two or three inches above the soil will protect a seedbed or small seedlings from sparrows and other small birds. Though the birds can pass through the spaces between the strands, contact with the almost invisible threads alarms them.

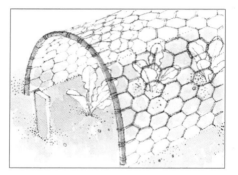

Cloches formed by bending a length of narrow-mesh wire netting or chicken wire are self-supporting. Alternatively, support plastic netting on wire hoops.

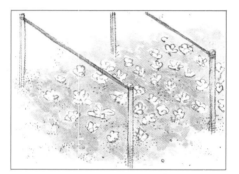

A humming line, a plastic tape that vibrates and hums even in a light wind, is an effective bird scarer for a short time. Fix the tape at intervals, stretching it between sticks.

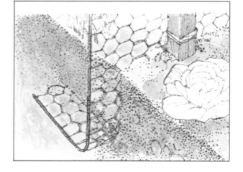

Wire mesh will keep rabbits from the plot if the bottom edge is buried in the ground and the final six inches turned outward to prevent burrowing beneath. To allow for this concealed edge, buy the mesh in a roll not less than four feet wide.

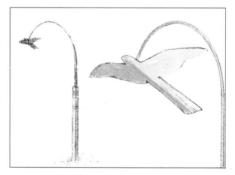

Cut-out birds of prey, bought or homemade, act as short-term deterrents. Almost any suspended object that swings in the breeze will serve the same purpose.

FURTHER PRECAUTIONS

- Growing seedlings in a greenhouse or a frame or under cloches will offer a reasonable degree of protection against larger pests.
- Never put food scraps or any animal matter on a compost heap; they will attract rats to the garden. Always keep the compost heap covered.
- Grow fruit bushes close to the house if you possibly can; the presence of people is some deterrent to birds.
- Chemical deterrents for discouraging animals of all sorts as well as birds are available. Most are applied in liquid form, with a sprayer or a watering can.

All weeds are a threat to your crops, since they compete with the plants for water and nutrients and can harbor pests and diseases. They therefore must be controlled.

The annual species of weeds can be destroyed relatively easily, by severing their stems with a hoe at any stage of growth. Perennial weeds are more of a problem; they have to be removed from the ground, complete with their roots, or treated with a weedkiller. Otherwise, many will grow again from even small pieces left in the soil.

IDENTIFYING THE WEEDS
It is important to be able to differentiate among the different kinds of weed so that you can adopt the best treatment to destroy them. The illustrations below show some of the most common annual weeds to invade the garden. Common perennial weeds are illustrated on p.47.

Apart from identification, there are other clues to help you distinguish one type of weed from another. Their growing habits differ, for a start. Annual weeds tend to grow densely in cultivated soil—in a vegetable plot, for instance—and often in large patches of a single species. There may be some perennial weeds mixed with them.

Annual weeds will also be found in untilled soil, but perennial species, such as quack grass, are more likely to dominate there. When establishing a food garden, you absolutely must clear such weeds from the site first (see p.27).

PREVENTING WEEDS
Provided the site was thoroughly cleared at the outset, weed control should not be too difficult. Many gardeners find that a combination of regular hoeing and annual digging prior to planting, removing all perennial weeds and their roots at the same time, is sufficient to keep the weeds at bay. However, you may wish to adopt other means of checking annual weed growth.

Mulching (see p.43) is one of the main preventive steps. This inhibits the germination and growth of annual weeds, of which millions of seeds are always present in the soil. Dig out any perennial weeds and hoe existing annual weeds before spreading a mulch. A two-inch layer of organic material is an effective weed suppressant.

Close planting provides another method of controlling weed growth. This is practical if you adopt the bed system of vegetable growing (see p.132). You will need to hoe in the early stages, but once the crop is well established, reduced light and greater competition for moisture combine to the detriment of the weeds.

Chemical weedkillers (see p.46) Annual weeds may be treated with a contact weedkiller, as used for perennial weeds. Pre-emergence weedkillers will kill newly germinating seedlings and can be used to control weeds around berries and some kinds of vegetables.

DEALING WITH ANNUAL WEEDS
Some gardeners take pleasure in weeding by hand, but unless you have time to spare, it is sensible to limit hand weeding to the area immediately around the tender stems of young plants, as in a seedbed. Elsewhere, a sharpened hoe is a fast, accurate, and deadly means of eradicating annual weeds.

It is essential to hoe frequently, and as soon as possible after the weed seeds have germinated; if they are left until they are well grown, their removal will disturb other plant roots. The other requirement is to wait for a dry day, so that you can leave the weeds to shrivel on the soil. If they remain in damp soil, perhaps partially covered, some of them may grow again. In showery weather, you will need to rake up the weeds and put them on the compost heap.

The best tool for the job is a draw hoe (see p.33) or else a hoe with a push-pull action. A short-handled hoe is useful for working close to plant stems.

Shepherd's purse
A common annual weed.

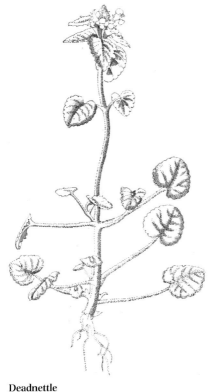

Deadnettle
Easily controlled by hoeing.

Knotweed
A ground-hugging annual weed.

GROWING PLANTS NATURALLY, pages 20–21
TOOLS FOR THE VEGETABLE GARDEN, pages 32–33

MULCHING, page 43
PERENNIAL WEEDS: USING WEEDKILLERS, pages 46–47

SPACE-SAVING METHODS, pages 132–133

Because seeds are carried by birds or on the wind, no garden is ever completely free of perennial weeds. To keep perennial weed problems to a minimum, it is vital to clear the plot effectively before you plant it.

A chemical weedkiller provides the easiest means of killing persistent weeds that have established themselves in a neglected garden. The hardest types to get rid of are those that are multiplied by creeping rhizomes. These rootlike structures spread underground from the parent plant and throw up vigorous shoots that form new plants. Rhizomatous weeds, which include bindweed and quack grass, are actually multiplied by digging. Digging the pieces out is another possible approach, but it is almost impossible to remove every piece from heavily infested land.

A mass clearance of persistent weeds will save endless work and frustration in the long term. After that the chief means of control is to dig out individual perennial weeds as they appear. If they are removed before they get established, there is no risk of a buildup of roots in the soil. Even quack grass and goutweed, two of the most persistent species, will not have a chance to form an extensive underground network.

Digging in late fall provides one of the best opportunities for the removal of perennial weeds. Always stop to pick out stems and roots rather than turn them under. Either burn them or leave them to shrivel and die before you add them to the compost heap. An alternative is to smother the weeds under heavy plastic for a season; the summer heat should destroy the roots.

Take particular care not to let perennial weeds encroach on the plot from uncultivated ground alongside your land. Cut a definite edge if one does not exist, and maintain this either by sinking metal strips or bricks into the soil or by regular mowing and hoeing. A fence may also help.

TYPES OF WEEDKILLER

You can, if you wish, use weedkillers to kill isolated perennial weeds, as well as to clear an uncultivated site completely. Before you adopt this approach, however, bear in mind that digging the weeds out is really just as easy. Also, it costs nothing and does not expose your crops to unwanted chemical contamination. You will be able to harvest your crops knowing that they are as free from manmade pollutants as is possible.

If you decide to use a weedkiller, be sure to choose the right kind. There are three basic kinds, and each works in a different way. Before use, check the ingredients, which should be listed on the label, since a product that is excellent for one purpose may be useless for another.

Contact weedkillers These kill the foliage to which they are applied but have little or no effect on the plant roots. A single application will kill annual weeds successfully, but several may be needed to destroy the more persistent perennials.

Some contact weedkillers become harmless once they reach the soil and cause only local damage if a few drops touch a cultivated plant by accident.

One of the most effective new contact weedkillers is a relatively safe herbicidal soap, sold under the trade name *Top Gun*. Like most contact weedkillers, it can be used on lawns as well as garden plots.

Translocated weedkillers These move to all parts of the plant, from leaves to roots or the other way around. This makes them a valuable weapon against deep-rooted perennial weeds such as bindweed, dandelion, broad-leaved and curly dock, and common pokeberry.

Glyphosate is a most effective translocated weedkiller that will destroy weeds and grasses of all types. It is inactivated on contact with the soil. *Dalapon* controls perennial grasses, including the ubiquitous quack grass as well as Bermuda grass, which grows in the South, but will also kill many other plants. It needs careful application. These two are often sold in formulations that contain other chemicals to give a wider measure of weed control.

Pre-emergence weedkillers These are applied to the soil and kill germinating weed seedlings; they will keep the ground weed-free for an extended period by inhibiting the germination of new seedlings. A useful version for the vegetable and fruit garden is *Dacthal*, which destroys grass seeds and prevents annual weeds from appearing for up to eight weeks, and therefore gives new food plants a better start. It is suitable for strawberries and a number of vegetable crops, including beans, brassicas, and members of the onion family.

Simazine gives even longer control—up to a year; it kills existing small weeds too. It is useful for paths, but since it remains in suspension in the top layer of soil, in the food garden it should be used only around deep-rooted vegetables, such as asparagus and sweet corn, or between deeper-rooted fruit bushes.

If you want to clear prepared ground of all weeds, you might consider using a soil fumigant such as *Vapam*, which kills most seeds before they germinate. Fumigants must be used very carefully, as the vapor can be poisonous. They take between one and three weeks to dissipate from the soil, depending on the weather, but will eliminate all annual and some perennial weeds in the garden plot.

APPLYING WEEDKILLERS

Spraying is the easiest and most efficient way to treat foliage, but with it comes the risk that spray may drift to and harm other plants. Even small amounts of a translocated weedkiller can do a great deal of damage to all plant life.

As a precautionary measure, spray only during still weather and when it is not too hot. Early morning and evening are the best times. Fit a cone to the sprayer to help direct the droplets (see p.27) and keep the nozzle low. When you are working between or close to plants, use a wand-type spray attachment with an adjustable nozzle. Be sure to use a sprayer that is easy to carry and the right size for your garden.

Use a large sprayer or an ordinary watering can fitted with a rose to apply a chemical such as Dacthal to a large area of uncropped ground.

To achieve even distribution of a pre-emergence weedkiller, which is often in granular form, divide the area into yard squares and sprinkle a measured amount of the chemical over each.

USING WEEDKILLERS SAFELY
- Read and follow manufacturer's instructions, which relate to safety as well as results.
- Stick to the recommended concentration. Adding "a little extra" is a waste of money and seldom helps. Do not mix with other chemicals unless you are advised to do so.
- Store weedkillers out of the reach of children and pets.
- Wash utensils and sprayers before and after use. Some chemicals leave a residue in spite of washing, so use a separate sprayer for each of these weedkillers.
- Do not store diluted weedkiller in bottles. Label each container clearly, and dispose of surplus chemicals immediately.

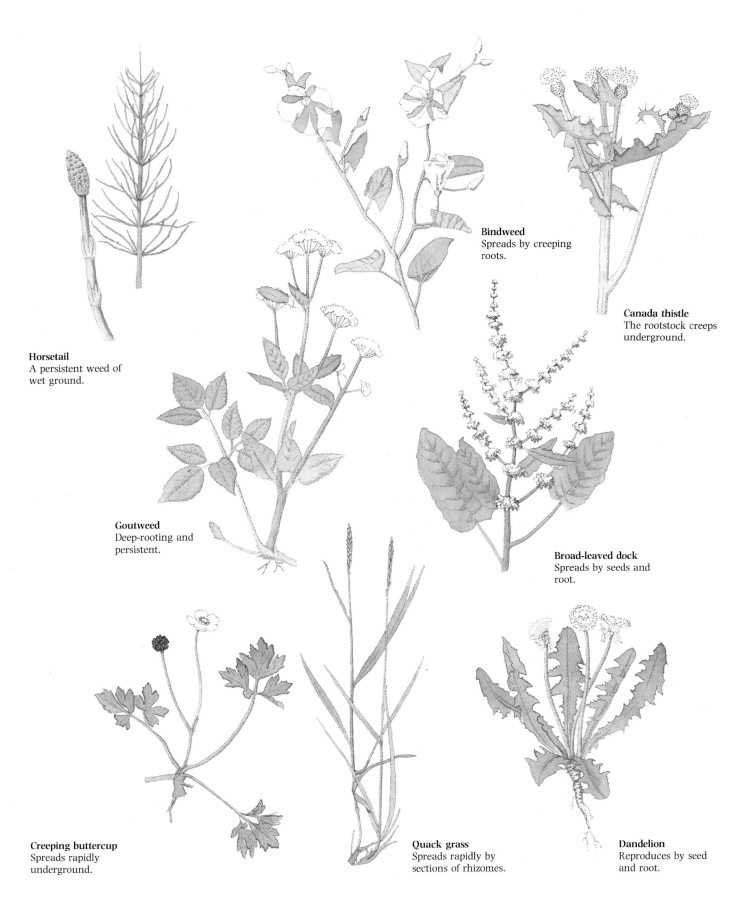

Bindweed
Spreads by creeping roots.

Canada thistle
The rootstock creeps underground.

Horsetail
A persistent weed of wet ground.

Goutweed
Deep-rooting and persistent.

Broad-leaved dock
Spreads by seeds and root.

Creeping buttercup
Spreads rapidly underground.

Quack grass
Spreads rapidly by sections of rhizomes.

Dandelion
Reproduces by seed and root.

The
FRUIT COLOR CATALOGUE

The color plates that follow show the wide range of berries and tree fruits suitable for growing in the food garden. Although they certainly are not totally comprehensive, their aim is to suggest the scope available to home growers; many of the varieties shown are not grown by commercial fruit producers. A specialist nursery may offer fifty or more apples alone, each to be considered for its vigor, frost tolerance, and season, as well as its use, flavor, appearance, keeping qualities, and resistance to pests and diseases.

The separate fruit entries, on pages 68–107, give specific details about individual cultivation requirements as well as recommendations for varieties other than those selected for illustration.

STRAWBERRIES Selected varieties

ALPINE STRAWBERRY
'Alexandria'
'Fraises des Bois'
'Ruegen Improved'

STRAWBERRY
'Cardinal'

STRAWBERRY
'Ogallala'
'Surecrop'

STRAWBERRY
'Sequoia'
'Ozark Beauty'

STRAWBERRY
'Shortcake'

CULTIVATION DETAILS SEE PAGES 68–69

BERRIES Selected varieties

RED RASPBERRY
'Latham'
'Canby'
'Dorman Red'
'September'
'Heritage'

PURPLE RASPBERRY
'Royalty'
'Brandywine'

YELLOW RASPBERRY
'Fallgold'

BLACK RASPBERRY
'Bristol'
'Blackhawk'
'John Robertson'
'Cumberland'

THORNLESS BLACKBERRY
'Black Satin'
'Hull'

BLACKBERRY
'Darrow'
'Rosborough'

50

CULTIVATED BERRY
Dewberry

HYBRID BERRY
Boysenberry

HYBRID BERRY
Marionberry

HYBRID BERRY
Loganberry

CULTIVATED BERRY
Japanese Wineberry

HYBRID BERRY
Tayberry

CULTIVATION DETAILS SEE PAGES 70–74

CURRANTS AND BERRIES Selected varieties

CRANBERRY

HIGHBUSH BLUEBERRY
'Berkeley'
'Earliblue'
'Jersey'
'Northblue'
'Northland'

WHITE CURRANT
'White Imperial'

BLACK CURRANT
'Boskoop Giant'

CHINESE GOOSEBERRY

RED CURRANT
'Red Lake'
'Wilder'

GOOSEBERRY
'Pixwell'

YELLOW GOOSEBERRY

GOOSEBERRY
'Poorman'
'Fredonia'

GOOSEBERRY
'Welcome'

HYBRID BERRY
Worcesterberry

CULTIVATION DETAILS SEE PAGES 74–80

53

MELONS Selected varieties

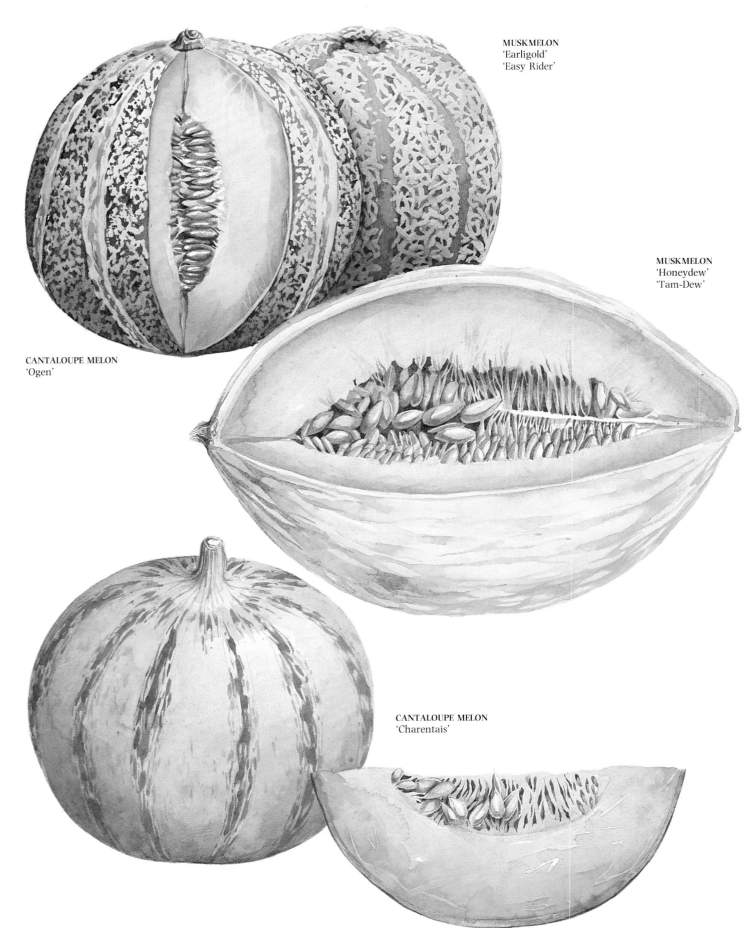

MUSKMELON
'Earligold'
'Easy Rider'

MUSKMELON
'Honeydew'
'Tam-Dew'

CANTALOUPE MELON
'Ogen'

CANTALOUPE MELON
'Charentais'

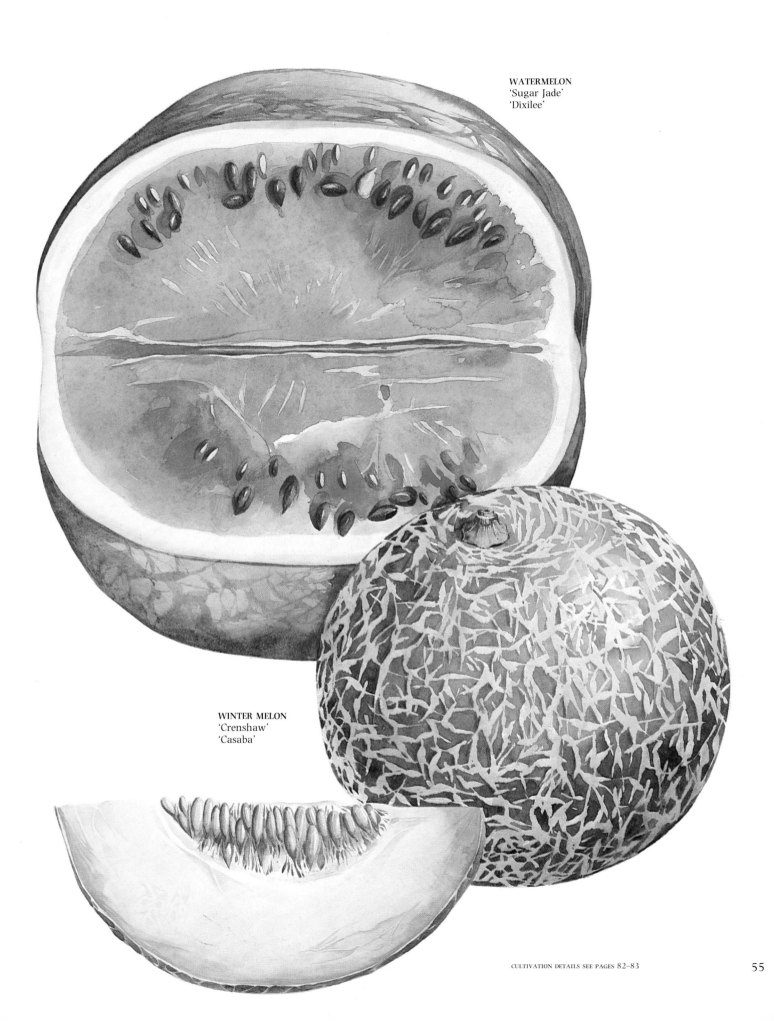

WATERMELON
'Sugar Jade'
'Dixilee'

WINTER MELON
'Crenshaw'
'Casaba'

CULTIVATION DETAILS SEE PAGES 82–83

55

GRAPES AND KIWI FRUITS Selected varieties

RED GRAPE
'Zinfandel'
'Tokay'

BLACK GRAPE
'Black Monukka'
'Concord'
'Fredonia'

MUSCADINE GRAPE
'Summit'
'Scuppernong'

KIWI FRUIT
'Hayward'
'Miller's Northern'

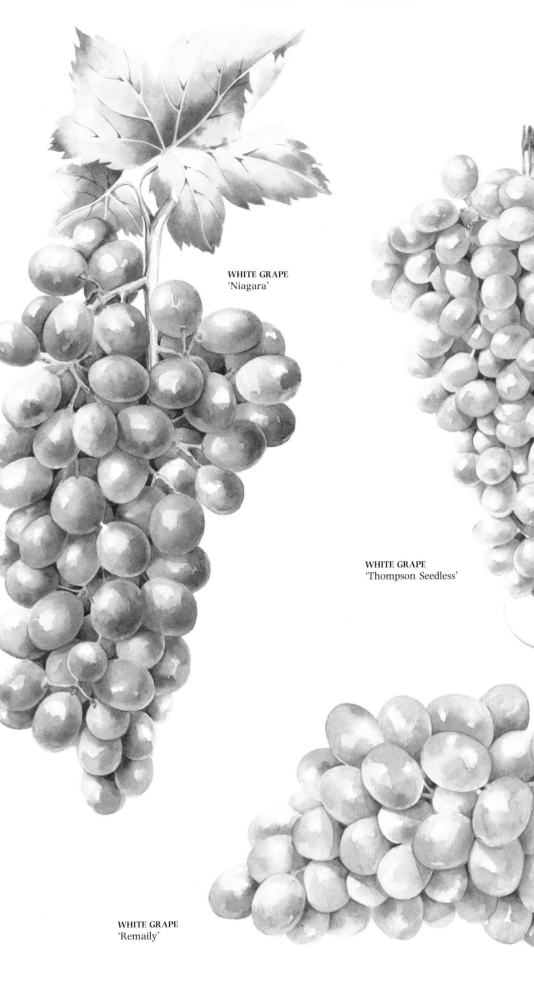

WHITE GRAPE
'Niagara'

WHITE GRAPE
'Thompson Seedless'

WHITE GRAPE
'Remaily'

APPLES Selected varieties

RED APPLE
'Cox's Orange Pippin'

YELLOW APPLE
'Golden Delicious'
'Ein Sheimer'
'Dorsett Golden'

GREEN APPLE
'Granny Smith'
'Summer Granny'
'Newton Pippin'

GREEN APPLE
'Bramley's Seedling'

RUSSET APPLE
'Golden Russet'
'Roxbury Russet'

CRABAPPLE
'Dolgo'
'Whitney'
'Hyslop'

RED APPLE
'Red Delicious'
'Starkrimson'

RED APPLE
'Freedom'
'Carefree Liberty'

RED APPLE
'Baldwin'
'Red Rome'

YELLOW APPLE
'Jonagold'

RED APPLE
'Wealthy'
'Northern Spy'

CULTIVATION DETAILS SEE PAGES 90–95

PEAR
'Beurre d'Anjou'

PEAR
'Bartlett'
'Lincoln'

PEAR
'Bosc'

PEAR
'Baldwin'

PEAR
'Maxine'
'California'

PEAR
'Fan Stil'

PEAR
'Seckel'
'Stark Honeysweet'

ASIAN PEAR
'Shinseiki'
'Twentieth Century'

FIG
'Celeste'
'Brown Turkey'

FIG
'Conadria'

MULBERRY

QUINCE
'Cooke's Jumbo'
'Pineapple'
'Champion'

ELDERBERRY

61

TREE FRUITS Selected varieties

JAPANESE PLUM
'Ember'

JAPANESE PLUM
'Tecumseh'

JAPANESE PLUM
'Santa Rosa'

EUROPEAN PLUM
'Stark Blue Ribbon'
'French Improved'

DAMSON
'Blue Damson'

EUROPEAN PRUNE PLUM
'Stanley'

CHERRY PLUM
'Delight'

APRICOT
'Stark Sweetheart'
'Moorpark'
'Gold Kist'

YELLOW PLUM
'Shiro'
'Gold'

EUROPEAN PLUM
'European Green Gage'

FREESTONE PEACH
'Red Haven'
'Sun Haven'
'Reliance'

NECTARINE
'Stark Sunglo'
'Mericrest'
'Desert Dawn'

FREESTONE PEACH
'Belle of Georgia'
'Polly'

CLINGSTONE PEACH
'Strawberry Cling'
'White Heath'

CULTIVATION DETAILS SEE PAGES 102–106

CHERRIES Selected varieties

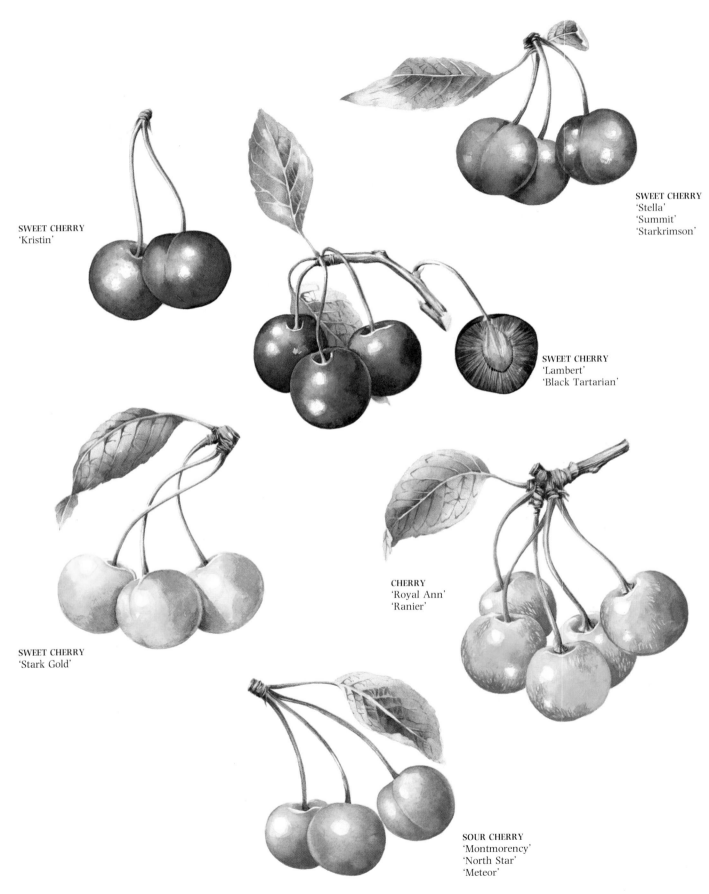

SWEET CHERRY
'Kristin'

SWEET CHERRY
'Stella'
'Summit'
'Starkrimson'

SWEET CHERRY
'Lambert'
'Black Tartarian'

SWEET CHERRY
'Stark Gold'

CHERRY
'Royal Ann'
'Ranier'

SOUR CHERRY
'Montmorency'
'North Star'
'Meteor'

The FRUIT GARDEN

One of the gardener's greatest pleasures is to pick and eat home-grown, sun-ripened fruit. Apart from the satisfactions successful cultivation brings, the taste of garden-grown fruit is vastly superior to that offered by commercial producers. Certainly it should be sufficient to convince you that it is worth making room for fruit in your garden, however limited your space.

If you study the pages that follow, you will be able to choose a selection of fruit to suit your palate and your size and style of garden. The modern trend toward growing fruit trees such as apples, pears, and peaches on small or dwarfing rootstocks, which restricts their growth but not their fruitfulness, makes them eminently suitable for smaller gardens. And by training fruit trees into neat and conveniently shaped cordons you can maximize your use of garden space.

Some of the newest types of fruit trees are small and adaptable enough to be suitable for container cultivation. Another good candidate for containers is strawberries, which do well in tubs, pots, or barrels on balconies or patios. Both strawberries and melons will also thrive in growing bags. The latter may need the protection of a greenhouse, however, in areas with short, cool summers.

A place can be found in any ornamental garden for fruit trees or bushes. Apart from their display of spring blossoms, they have appealing shapes and foliage that can be used to great effect in a landscaped area. Many, notably figs, blueberries, grapes, and some varieties of apples, pears, and cherries, also add to the autumn colors of the garden.

Any fruit-bearing plant that has a natural inclination to climb, or that can be trained upward or sideways, has great potential in garden design. You might try making a low hedge of gooseberries or blueberries, for example, or planting a grapevine or kiwi fruit so that it can be trained over a pergola. Instead of planting an ordinary, nonfruiting flowering cherry, why not grow a *real* cherry instead? Or you might consider adding a fruit tree such as a mulberry to your collection, which your children and grandchildren can enjoy in years to come.

For the gardener who is already familiar with the basics of fruit gardening, this section offers some suggestions for novel or more adventurous projects. The new types of hybrid berries, such as boysenberries or tayberries, make an interesting choice of less well-known fruit, or you can try everbearing raspberries, cranberries, alpine strawberries, or black currants.

Finally, do not forget the potential offered by the walls of your home when planning your fruit garden. They not only provide a means of support for trained fruit trees, but also give valuable shelter to tender fruits such as peaches, apricots, and nectarines.

Berry, or soft, fruits are produced either on canes, such as raspberries, blackberries, and other hybrid fruits, or on bushes, such as currants, gooseberries, and blueberries; strawberries are produced on low-growing individual plants.

On average, berries provide rather better value for space then tree fruits. They bear a worthwhile crop more quickly after planting, and there is a better chance of consistently good yields. Berries are also easy to grow, and pruning is more straightforward than it is for some tree fruits. These broad generalizations, to which there are inevitably a few exceptions, suggest that berries are well able to earn their keep in a small garden.

Compared with tree fruits, berries do need more protection, however. Some berry crops —notably strawberries and raspberries— may be devastated by birds unless they are covered by netting.

WHERE TO GROW BERRIES

A sunny, sheltered site is best for berries. Avoid planting them under trees or in a frost pocket. If planted alongside vegetables, fruit bushes and canes should be positioned where they will not shade low-growing crops. Raspberries in particular cast considerable shade during late winter and spring. If possible, plant the rows to run north and south, so the fruits on each side receive an equal amount of sun. If you are planting on a slope, plant them in line with it—that is, plant them up and down the slope, not across it.

Shelter is a considerable advantage, both for the growth of the plants and to assist pollinating insects. A hedge or a plastic windbreak is best; both of these filter the wind without causing backdrafts.

Any well-drained, averagely fertile soil is suitable. Most berries need a pH of about 6 to 6.5, the exceptions being blueberries and cranberries. These require a moisture-holding, acid soil that has a pH reading as low as 4.5.

BUYING CANES AND BUSHES

It is most important to be sure that the canes and bushes you buy are not infected with any of the virus diseases associated with berries. These are widespread, incurable, and have a serious effect on both growth and cropping. Infected canes and bushes are therefore simply not worth growing. If you are buying new plants, deal only with well-established nurseries and insist on stock officially certified as healthy and true to type, if such a scheme exists for the particular fruit you are buying. Such plants should bear satisfactorily for a number of years before they gradually succumb to virus infections. Raspberry canes, for example, can be expected to last for about eight or nine years.

Obviously, it is unwise to accept gifts of berry plants or cuttings from friends or neighbors, as they may well be virus-infected. The same applies to old, neglected bushes and canes in your own garden. Dig them out, buy new stock, and plant in fresh ground.

Berries can be purchased as bare-rooted or container-grown plants. The main advantage of container-grown plants, which are more expensive, is that they can be planted at any time of year, provided the soil is neither frozen nor waterlogged.

SOIL PREPARATION

Overall, check that the planting area has an adequate depth of soil, and remember that the root systems of most berries are more extensive than those of vegetables. In particular, make sure that there is not a layer of stone or compressed soil beneath the topsoil. Double dig the ground and remove any pieces of rock if there is.

Dig or cultivate the site well in advance of planting, and add some well-rotted organic material. Other, more particular needs are outlined with the growing instructions for each type of fruit, starting with strawberries on page 68.

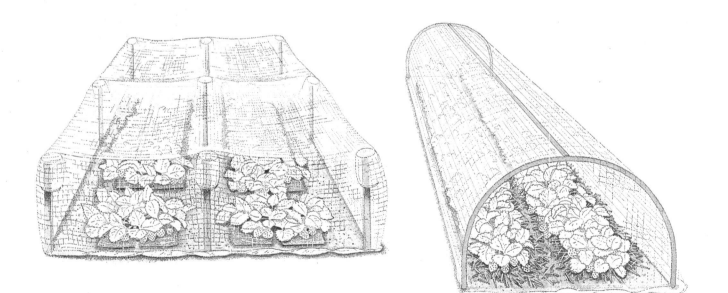

To protect strawberries, you can easily provide low-level support by hammering in short stakes at intervals, their tops about a foot and a half above the soil. Place an inverted jar over each, then cover with small-mesh plastic netting. Draw the netting away from one side before picking; replace it afterward and secure it with bricks.

As an alternative (right), you can support the netting with wire hoops.

WHAT TO GROW?

Provided you have a freezer, there is every incentive to grow more of your favorite berries than you can eat fresh. Many freeze extremely well, though some are better than others; one major exception is strawberries, which become mushy when thawed, though they are excellent frozen as a purée.

It makes sense to grow the fruits you most enjoy eating, and that give a good return for the space if that is at a premium. Gooseberries and blackberries are among the most prolific berries, with yields of eight to ten pounds per bush. An exceptionally successful blackberry may double these amounts, but it takes up a lot of space and needs training.

If you want to grow something more unusual, most hybrid berries give good returns, with perhaps twelve pounds per bush; examples include loganberries, tayberries, and boysenberries. Main-crop raspberries should yield up to two pounds per plant. With eighteen inches between plants, a couple of twelve-foot rows will often yield more than thirty pounds of delicious fruit.

When planting your berry plot, study the spacings advised for each type and also consider how large an area you are prepared to cover with a fruit cage or netting.

Raspberries and strawberries are the most vulnerable to bird damage. The former need a full-height cage, with standing headroom, but a structure just clearing the tops of strawberries will suffice.

Total losses from birds appear to remain the same whether you grow few or many bushes. Some gardeners prefer to take account of this by planting a few extra canes or bushes for the neighboring blackbirds. This might be a rather extreme measure for strawberries, however.

PLANTING

Late winter and early spring are the best times to plant bare-rooted canes and bushes, though autumn may be a preferable choice where winters are mild. Plant container-grown bushes at any time when the soil is neither frozen nor waterlogged.

Plant bare-rooted bushes in a hole wide enough to take the spread-out roots and deep enough to bring the soil mark on the stem level with the surrounding ground. Cut back any damaged roots, then cover the remainder with a mixture of soil and either peat or a prepared planting mixture. Shake the stem to settle the mixture around the roots, firm the covering gently with your feet, then replace the remaining soil mix and firm again.

Plant container-grown bushes by digging a hole a little larger than the root ball and filling in the space with a blend of soil and planting mixture.

AFTERCARE

Make sure that the soil around spring-planted bushes and strawberry runners remains moist. Water thoroughly if a check made a short way below ground level suggests that the soil is drying out. Mature bushes also require watering during prolonged dry spells, especially on light soil. Hoe regularly to keep weeds from becoming established. Avoid deep hoeing around shallow-rooted plants such as raspberries.

Keep a watchful eye for pests and diseases so that you can take appropriate action in good time, before the trouble becomes too firmly established.

A full-height fruit cage provides the most effective form of protection for berries. To avoid damage to the structure from a heavy snowfall, replace the small-mesh roof netting with four-inch mesh for the winter.

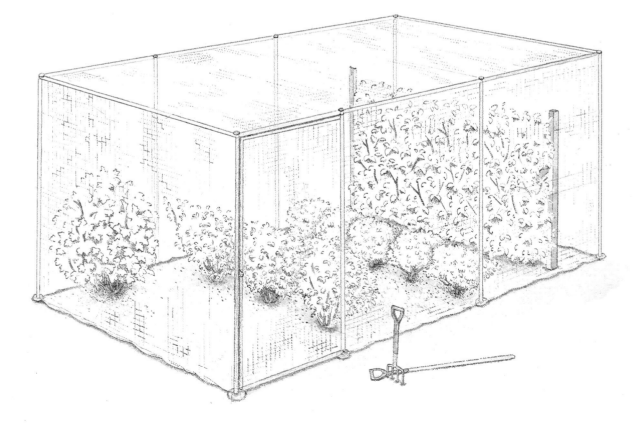

Rapid returns and delectable flavor are two sound reasons for growing strawberries (*Fragaria* sp.). Planted in high summer, the plants will first crop less than a year later. They are also easy to grow, in beds or containers, and the berries are suitable for preserves as well as for eating fresh.

There are three types. The first two are grown from purchased plants which can remain in place for several years. The third is usually grown from seed.

Single-crop strawberries produce their fruits over a two- to three-week period during early or midsummer. There are many varieties, the main difference being in size, flavor, and precise time of ripening.

Perpetual varieties bear successive flushes of smaller fruit over a longer period between summer and fall. Their flavor may not be quite up to the best of the single croppers, and they are less hardy.

Alpine strawberries (*Fragaria vesca*), with tiny berries, are both delicious and decorative; they have a unique fragrance and an unusual taste. Raised from seed, they crop during the second half of summer. Their compact growth makes them particularly suitable for growing in containers or as an edging to flower borders. The small size of the fruits, produced in modest quantities over an extended period, means that you need at least twenty-five plants to get a worthwhile picking at any one time.

Plant ordinary strawberries in well-drained but moisture-retentive soil, in an open position. They do best in slightly acid ground containing plenty of organic matter.

If you have a low-lying garden that is subject to late spring frosts, be prepared to cover the plants to protect the blossoms. The other essential precaution, wherever you live, is to buy plants that are certified free from virus disease. These will give good results for four or five years; then buy new plants and grow them on a fresh site.

ALPINE STRAWBERRIES

Either buy the plants in spring or sow the seeds under glass in autumn, overwintering the pricked-out seedlings in an unheated greenhouse or frame. Plant out in a rich soil in a semishaded position in spring, spacing them about one foot apart in each direction.

Fruiting is from midsummer until late fall. Pick the berries regularly and keep the soil moist, to encourage continued cropping throughout the season.

MAKING A START

Plant single-crop varieties as early in the spring as possible, when trees are just starting to leaf. Being slightly less hardy, perpetual varieties need to be planted slightly later, so that spring frosts do not damage their vulnerable blossoms. In the case of single croppers, which usually bear in June, you should nip off the flowers rather than try to harvest a crop during the first season, to insure strong plants. Perpetual varieties planted in spring will crop the following fall; remove the first flowers.

Dig the new strawberry bed well before planting so that it has time to settle. Mix in some rotted manure or compost, and scatter and rake in general fertilizer at two ounces per square yard just before planting.

You can buy plants either in pots or bare-rooted. Both are satisfactory, but both require you to keep the soil damp while new roots form. Set the plants fifteen inches apart in rows two and a half feet apart. For bare-rooted runners, use a trowel to form a hole a little deeper than the roots, with a mound in the center.

For pot-grown strawberries, scoop out a hole large enough to take the soil ball without breaking it or disturbing the roots. Water the plants in.

CARE OF THE CROP

For an early crop, cover established strawberries with cloches from later winter on, spacing or partially opening the covers once pollinating insects are flying.

Keep the soil moistened around recently planted strawberries. During dry weather watering may also be needed from about the time the fruit starts to swell. Well-developed fruit is also a signal to tuck straw under the plants to lift the berries clear of the soil. Many gardeners use black plastic mulch, which also warms the soil.

You will have to decide whether to maintain the plants as individuals, removing all runners except any needed for propagation, or to develop a "matted row" by allowing runners to root between plants. The latter yields a heavier crop, but the berries will be smaller.

PROTECTING AND HARVESTING

Unless you are growing them in a permanent fruit cage, protect strawberries from birds soon after strawing the plants. Netting laid directly over the plants is better than nothing, but the birds will peck through it and you will lose some fruit. Netting is more effective, and is easier to lift for picking, if it is supported above the plants.

As an alternative to using a metal or wooden frame, lay the netting over inverted jam jars supported by short stakes. Pin one side of the netting to the ground with metal or wooden pegs, pull the other side taut, and hold it down with stones or bricks.

Given warm weather, strawberries ripen rapidly once the fruit has grown to full size. Watch carefully for the first signs of color, subsequently checking the plants at least daily. Remove the fruit by pinching the stalk between forefinger and thumbnail. Avoid handling the berries as much as possible, since they bruise easily.

As soon as you have picked the last berries, use a pair of shears to cut off all the mature foliage close to the crown of single-crop plants. Remove the old leaves from perpetual strawberries, leaving the new ones. Add the foliage and the straw to the compost heap. Hoe between the plants and rows, first digging out any perennial weeds, and cut off any surplus runners.

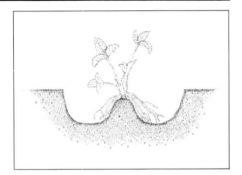

For bare-rooted strawberry plants, dig a hole wide enough for the roots to be spread out, with a mound in the center to raise the crown level with the surrounding soil. Place the crown of the plant on the mound, level with the surface, with the roots spread outward and downward. Replace the soil and firm carefully.

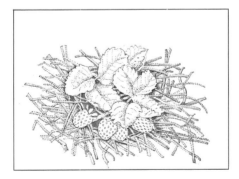

Lay straw, black plastic, or ready-made strawberry mats under the plants when the fruits are quite well developed to prevent them from coming into contact with the soil.

PROPAGATION

Use only vigorous, healthy-looking plants, since any virus infection present will be passed on. The runners used for the purpose are the wiry shoots (stolons), each bearing plantlets, that grow from the parent plant.

During early summer, select up to four strong runners on each plant. Bury a three-inch compost-filled pot in the soil beneath each tuft of young growth and secure the runner to the compost with a wire pin.

Nip off the far side of each runner but leave it attached to the parent for one to two months; keep the compost moist. Plant the young strawberry a week after severing.

It is a good idea to propagate some strawberry plants annually, replacing your oldest stock each time. The maximum age of strawberry plants is about four years.

PROPAGATING

1 Sink pots of compost into the soil close to mature plants. Use bent wires to secure the first embryo plant on each runner to the compost. Cut off the continuation of the runner, but leave intact the piece joining the new plant to the parent plant. Keep the compost moist while roots form.

2 Between four and eight weeks later, when roots have formed, sever the runner joining new and mature plants. Plant out the new strawberry in its permanent position after a few more days.

PESTS AND DISEASES

The pests most likely to occur are aphids, red spider mites, strawberry root weevils, and slugs, snails, and birds.

Common disorders include gray mold, red stele, and verticillium wilt.

RECOMMENDED VARIETIES

Perpetual varieties
'Ozark Beauty' Popular. Heavy crops of medium-sized fruit. Good freezer. Zones 4–8.
'Ogallala' Cold hardy, drought resistant. Best in Great Plains and Mountain states.
'Shortcake' Exceptionally large, elongated fruits, red clear through. Zones 4–8.

Single-crop varieties
'Royalty' Very large, wedge-shaped fruit. Productive and adaptable. Zones 4–8.
'Surecrop' A favorite with commercial growers; disease resistant. Zones 4–8.
'Tioga' A standard in the warm Southwest because of its huge, firm berries.
'Cardinal' Recently introduced, 'Cardinal' yields many sweet berries. Zones 5–8.
'Gurney's Giant' A "bragging berry": produces fruit up to two and a half inches across. Zones 5–8.
'Sequoia' Very large, dark red berries. Only for mild-winter western areas. Early bearer.

Alpine varieties
'Alexandria' Early and comparatively large-fruited.
'Fraises des Bois, Mixed' Golden, red, and crimson fruits are the delicacies served by fine French restaurants. Cold hardy.
'Ruegen Improved' Long, slender fruit, soft when mature. Very fragrant.

STRAWBERRIES IN CONTAINERS

Practical as well as decorative reasons give strawberries a distinct advantage as container plants. Supported off the ground, the fruit keeps clean and is at little risk from slugs. Picking is simple, as is protecting the berries from birds by draping netting over the top.

Barrels and earthenware strawberry pots, both with planting holes in their sides, are widely used for growing strawberries on patios or where space is restricted. If converting your own barrel, make the holes about two inches in diameter and allow about nine inches between holes.

Other suitable containers include hanging baskets, large pots and troughs, and the towerlike plastic containers that provide a succession of planting pockets. Apart from more frequent hand watering and the absence of a need for straw, aftercare is much the same as for strawberries grown in the ground.

After strawberries, raspberries (*Rubus idaeus*) give the highest yield for the space they occupy as well as showing the quickest returns. They are delicious eaten fresh or made into jam and they freeze more successfully than strawberries, with their flavor and texture intact.

Both black and red varieties are available; yellow or golden raspberries are now becoming popular too. Some raspberries do not ripen until around the time of the first frost; for this reason they are best suited to mild zones.

Raspberries grow best in full sun but will tolerate partial shade, and they thrive on light or medium soils. The fruit-bearing shoots are vulnerable to wind damage, so it is an advantage to have a sheltered site. Slightly acid soil, with a pH of 6 to 6.5, is ideal for raspberries.

Early-fruiting raspberries must be trained onto supporting wires. Though not essential for later-fruiting kinds, which have shorter stems, some support will help to keep them upright and make for easier picking.

Protection from birds is a necessity—certainly if you grow only a few canes—and there is much to be said for planting raspberries in a permanent fruit cage. Failing this, you might simply drape the canes with muslin or fine-mesh netting at fruiting time, or try the fake-snake deterrent.

The other major hazard is virus infection, to which raspberries are particularly susceptible. By purchasing certified stock, though, you should be guaranteed good yields for eight or nine years. However, if canes do become infected, they should be dug up and burned.

MAKING A START

It is best to plant raspberries during the early spring, once the soil has begun to warm up. If you live in the South, you may be able to plant raspberries in late winter. Early-fruiting raspberries will crop fifteen months after planting, if planted in early spring, whereas later varieties will bear fruit during their first year.

Dig plenty of organic matter into the site, taking care to remove every perennial weed as you do so. Space the plants about fifteen to eighteen inches apart and about three inches deep, with their roots spread out. Allow five feet between rows. Firm the soil around each cane after planting, and water them in. Either before or after planting, cut back the stems of both early- and late-fruiting raspberries to one foot; this will prevent the plant fruiting too soon and encourage it to develop a strong root system and healthy canes the following year.

CARE OF THE CROP

Each spring rake a handful of general fertilizer into the soil around each plant. Remove any perennial weeds by hand as soon as they appear, but use a sharp Dutch hoe to control annual weeds and to cut off the raspberry suckers that will emerge between the rows. Avoid deep hoeing, which can cut through the roots since they are fairly shallow.

Do not allow the ground to dry out, especially during the fruiting period. Being shallow-rooted, raspberries are quick to suffer from dehydration, so water liberally before any harm can be done. A mulch of rotted manure or compost, or of black plastic, applied in spring will help to conserve moisture as well as suppress weeds.

Use soft string to tie the developing shoots to the wires, spacing them as evenly as possible, about three to four inches apart. This will keep them straight and help to protect them from wind damage.

HARVESTING

Pick the fruit when the raspberries are fully colored but still firm. It pays to go through the canes daily, especially since you are likely to have missed some ripe fruit the previous day. Try not to pick when the fruit is wet—it will quickly go moldy unless eaten at once.

Pull the raspberries gently from the plant, leaving the core of the fruit and the stalk behind. Eat or freeze them as soon as possible after picking.

PRUNING

Early raspberries Fresh canes will grow from the base during the first year after planting. Tie them temporarily as they grow, but remove any weak ones close to the ground. Nip off the flowers from any canes that show signs of fruiting during this first year.

In subsequent years, cut out the old fruit-bearing stems at soil level immediately after gathering the last fruit. Replace them with the current year's shoots which you find growing from the base, and keep these tied to the wires. Retain the five or six best canes from each rootstock, retying where necessary, and cut out the smaller, weaker ones at the base.

By autumn the tallest canes may have grown well above the top wire. Wait until late winter before trimming these back to a bud just above the highest support. This removes any winter damage and encourages the canes to fruit along their full length the following year.

Late raspberries These fruit on shoots formed during the current season. Toward the end of winter, cut out all the previous year's growth to make space for the new shoots that will develop during the coming spring and summer.

SUPPORTING THE CANES

It is sensible to erect the support structure for raspberries at the time of planting. For early-fruiting varieties, this takes the form of three wires stretched tightly between well-braced posts at either end of the row. As they will have to stay in place for a number of years, use stout, treated wood for the posts and firmly sink the ends two feet into the soil. Brace them with an angled support.

Between the posts strain three 13-gauge galvanized wires at thirty, forty-five, and sixty-five inches from the ground. Attach them with eyebolts, which enable you to strain each wire tightly. A couple of horizontal wires will help to keep the canes of late varieties more upright. Space them thirty and fifty inches above the ground.

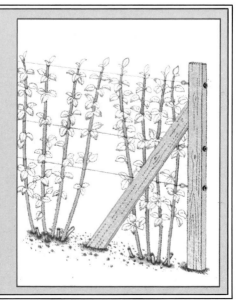

 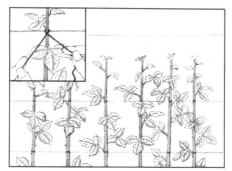 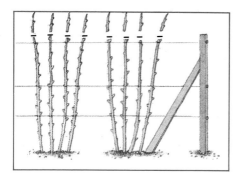

PRUNING

Cutting out the old stems once the plant has fruited provides space for the new ones. Leave up to eight on each plant and keep them tied up as they grow during the summer. By fall they will extend beyond the top wire, but do not prune them back at this stage.

Canes may be tied individually where they cross each of the three wires. Alternatively, use a continuous length of string, passing it round each cane and round the wire alongside. This prevents the canes sliding but is less convenient for securing those that are late to develop.

In late winter cut back each of the canes to a bud just above the top wire. If this was done the previous year when they reached this height, some of the canes will have sprouted new growth from the top. This is also the time to cut back late-fruiting varieties.

PROPAGATION

Restrict propagation to plants in apparently good health, and preferably to those sold as certified virus-free stock within the previous year or two.

During late winter or early spring, dig out some of the suckers that invariably grow near the parent plants, together with some attached fibrous roots and soil. Lift them carefully with their roots intact and sever them from the parent plant with clippers or a sharp knife. Replant where they are to grow, cutting the stems back to one foot. Those that you do not want for propagation should be dug up and thrown away.

Some of the suckers may be dug out for planting elsewhere, provided the plants show no signs of disease. If you can do this in early spring, while the raspberries are still dormant, they will get off to a better start.

PESTS AND DISEASES

Among the most likely pests are aphids, cane borers, and raspberry beetles.

The more troublesome diseases include cane blight, anthracnose, gray mold, honey fungus, spur blight, and virus diseases.

RECOMMENDED VARIETIES
Red raspberries
'Heritage' An everbearing red with firm, conical berries. Produces a smaller fall crop after the main summer crop. Zones 4–8
'Dorman Red' Heat resistant but only moderately productive. Zones 7–10
'Latham' Highly popular winter-hardy variety. Bears for 3–4 weeks. Zones 3–8
'September' Bright red, giant-sized fruits. Zones 4–7
'Canby' A thornless variety that produces well where summers are cool.

Black raspberries
'Bristol' An old favorite for flavor. Large, firm berries. Zones 5–8
'John Robertson' Large, plump berries. Best in northern states and Canada.
'Blackhawk' Large, solid berries that stay intact when stemmed. A drought-resistant

midwestern favorite. Zones 5–8
'Cumberland' A very old variety. Best suited to midwestern and northern states.

Yellow raspberries
'Fallgold' High in sugar but better for cooking than eating fresh. Winter hardy. Zones 4–8

Purple raspberries
'Royalty' Purple when fully ripe but still tasty, if tart, in the red stage. Large fruits. Pest and disease resistant. Zones 4–8
'Brandywine' Very large fruits are tangy at the red stage, quite sweet and purple when fully ripe.

BERRIES, pages 50–51
GROWING BERRIES, pages 66–67
PESTS AND DISEASES, pages 108–111
FREEZING FRUITS, pages 234–235

Cultivated blackberries (*Rubus fruticosus*) bear larger, plumper, sweeter fruits than those gathered in the wild. When successfully grown, each plant will yield between ten and twenty pounds and may even exceed this amount.

Blackberries can be grown almost everywhere, though in exposed areas subject to early frost in autumn it makes sense to avoid the later-fruiting varieties. There are several types that ripen not long after midsummer. One or two varieties are certified as virus-free stock, and these are the best choice if they are suitable in other respects. Chief among these are 'Darrow' and 'Black Satin.'

Strong, tightly strung wires are needed for training blackberries, since they are vigorous plants that grow on long, trailing canes. Many have vicious thorns, although there are also some thornless varieties. Blackberries can be trained against a wall or fence as well as in the open; thornless varieties lend themselves to training over an arch. Summer protection from birds will insure that you harvest a heavier crop, although birds are less attracted to blackberries and loganberries than to raspberries. You may not have to net if you are prepared to lose a few blackberries.

Blackberry plants are sold bare-rooted and in plastic containers from midwinter onward. There is little to choose between these two types, except that container-grown plants generally cost more.

MAKING A START

Plant bare-rooted plants in early spring, if possible, but put plants in in late fall or even winter if you live in a mild southern region.

Container-grown plants may go in at any time, subject to appropriate soil and weather conditions.

Really taut wires are required to restrain and secure the sturdy stems of blackberries. If you are planting in the open, this means rigid end posts, so place a brick at the foot of each bracing strut to prevent the post from being drawn into the ground. For the posts, use three-inch-square lumber sunk two feet into the ground. If you are growing more than one plant, hammer in two-inch stakes every ten feet.

Strain four 10-gauge supporting wires between the braced posts, setting them three, four, five, and six feet above the ground. If you are attaching the wires to vine eyes on a wall or fence, keep to the same spacings.

Dig in plenty of organic matter around

TRAINING

There are several ways of arranging the stems of blackberries, including fanning, roping, and weaving, with the fan method giving the heaviest yields.

In conventional fan training the fruiting canes are trained left and right along the wires, leaving the center open for the new canes, which should be loosely bunched together and tied to the wires as they grow. Once the old canes are cut down (see Pruning, next page), the new canes are securely tied fanwise to the wires, again leaving the center empty.

A variation on this method, which makes for easier pruning and fruit picking, is to secure the new growth to the wires on one side of the plant only, keeping these canes separate from the year-old shoots that are bearing fruit. The plant thus alternately fruits on each side of the rootstock. Apart from making for easier handling, this method of training reduces the risk that infection will spread from the older shoots to the young ones.

To obtain the heaviest yields, train the shoots to the wires in the pattern of half a fan, securing them with soft string at each crossing point. Retain enough canes to allow a space of about four inches between them at the point where they are fastened to the top wire.

The alternative method, called roping, is to train three or four canes up and then horizontally along each wire. This also allows for easy pruning and harvesting, but the yields will be lighter.

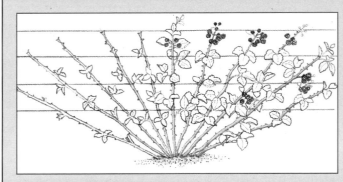

Fan training of blackberries, loganberries, and other hybrid berries requires a lot of tying but gives a heavy crop of fruit. For easier pruning and management, it is best to train the canes that grow in consecutive years to alternate sides. Here, the new canes have been tied on the left; the year-old, fruited canes are on the right. The canes are tied with soft string to the tightly strung wires at each point where they cross.

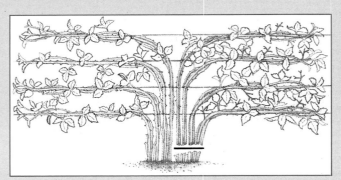

In roping, an alternative method of training, three or four canes are tied horizontally to each wire. This is simple and fairly quick to do, but yields are somewhat lower. As with fan training, the easiest means of separating year-old canes from new ones is to train them to alternate sides. Once the fruited canes have been cut out, that side will remain empty until the following spring.

each planting position; take care that no perennial weeds are left, especially those with creeping roots. Space the plants of trailing varieties, such as 'Olallie,' about six or eight feet apart, with eight feet between rows. Upright varieties, such as 'Darrow' and 'Black Satin,' require only three to five feet between plants.

Cut back bare-rooted plants to a bud nine to twelve inches from the base. Dig a hole large enough to take the spread-out roots, and add some peat or a planting mixture to the soil when replacing it. The soil should just cover the roots of the plant. Leave the stems of container-grown plants untrimmed, but add similar material around the root ball, digging a hole large enough to allow for this.

CARE OF THE CROP
During the first spring rake in a handful of general fertilizer around each plant; increase the area in subsequent years and distribute about two ounces per square yard.

As the weather warms up, water generously if the soil starts to dry out, especially as the fruits start to develop but before they have ripened.

PRUNING
Cut out the old canes immediately after fruiting, leaving the wires on that side of the plant bare. You will need to wear heavy gloves for the thorned varieties of blackberry. Burn the old canes; do not try to compost them.

Keep as many healthy new canes as possible, in case the frost damages some unripe new canes. You can always remove any surplus canes once the winter is over, if they are all unscathed. You can cut back any dead cane tips to the first live bud at the end of winter.

HARVESTING
Pick when the berries are black in color and ripe; pick carefully to avoid squashing the ripest ones, and if possible only when the weather is dry. The core usually comes away with the fruit.

Blackberries can generally be picked over a period of several weeks.

PROPAGATION
Soon after midsummer, peg the tips of healthy shoots to the ground and bury their roots. The following spring, when they have rooted, cut them free just above a bud and replant into their permanent positions.

PESTS AND DISEASES
Raspberry beetles are the chief pest. Crown gall, gray mold, and viral diseases are possible troubles.

PROPAGATING
1 Before attempting tip layering, satisfy yourself that the plant is healthy. The first step, shown here, is to bury the tip of a shoot about six inches deep, replace the soil, and firm it with your foot. If the shoot is springy, secure it to the ground with a length of wire bent to the shape of a hairpin.

2 By the following spring the tip will have rooted. Sever the original stem about one foot from the ground and either move the new plant to its permanent site or grow it on in a nursery bed before planting out a year later. If you prefer, you can layer tips into pots of compost sunk into the ground.

RECOMMENDED VARIETIES
'Rosborough' Heavy crops of firm, sweet berries. Zones 7–9
'Darrow' A popular winter-hardy variety with large, long, slightly tart berries. Good in Zones 4–6.
'Black Satin' Thornless. Heavy-bearing for midsummer harvest. Hardy to −25°.
'Hull' Another winter-hardy thornless variety. Good for eating fresh, frozen, or preserved.

It is said that fruit growers have to thank Judge J. H. Logan of Santa Cruz, California, for spotting this chance blackberry-raspberry cross in his garden more than a century ago. Truth or myth, loganberries are a distinctive fruit in their own right, being less rampant than blackberries and having larger fruit than either parent.

The flavor of loganberries is on the acid side and perhaps not to everyone's taste when eaten fresh. The berries freeze and cook well, however.

There are both thorny and thornless strains, but even the former lack the blackberry's lethal spikes. The fruits ripen during the second half of summer on stems that developed during the previous season.

Loganberries need wire supports, either in the open or attached with vine eyes to a wall. A thornless loganberry can be trained over an archway.

Loganberries also need a slightly acid (pH 6), moisture-retentive soil; medium to heavy loams are ideal. On sandy ground it is essential to add plenty of organic matter.

Virus-free stocks are generally available, but you may have to hunt for them. In general, the thornless varieties bear lighter crops than those with thorns, but much depends on growing conditions.

MAKING A START
Planting, together with the system of supporting wires, is the same as for blackberries (opposite), except for the spacing. Being somewhat less vigorous, loganberries do not need as much growing room as trailing blackberries. The plants should be spaced about five or six feet apart.

CARE OF THE CROP
Feeding and watering are the same as for blackberries, opposite.

TRAINING AND PRUNING
The method is the same as for blackberries. That is, train young shoots of the current year to one side only, keeping them separate from the year-old canes that are bearing loganberries.

PROPAGATION
See blackberries, opposite.

PESTS AND DISEASES
Aphids and raspberry beetles may prove troublesome.

Possible ailments include cane spot, crown gall, gray mold, and spur blight.

BERRIES, pages 50–51
PESTS AND DISEASES, pages 108–111

FREEZING FRUITS, pages 234–235

A number of hybrid berries have been brought into cultivation as a result of crossing various *Rubus* species, notably the raspberry (*Rubus idaeus*) and blackberry (*Rubus fruticosus*). Loganberries (see p.73) are the best known and the most widely grown of these, chiefly because they have been around longer. But home foodgrowers are in a unique position to try the comparatively new hybrid fruits, such as the tayberry and the marionberry. These berries are seldom found in supermarkets, since market growers prefer to concentrate on more familiar fruits for which there is a known demand.

It would be unwise to grow hybrid berries in abundance, at the expense of their parent blackberries and raspberries, until you have tried them. But out of personal interest and for the chance to enjoy an intriguing change of flavor, it is well worth growing one or two, if space permits.

Certain hybrid berries, such as the tayberry, are now reasonably well known and established. But others have failed to catch on, despite the enthusiastic claims of nurserymen. So you might have trouble obtaining one or two of those described from a local nursery.

Though most hybrid berries owe part of their parentage to the raspberry, their cultivation and training are generally the same as for blackberries (see p.72). Nearly all are less vigorous than trailing blackberries, however, and can tolerate closer planting, but this makes them more suitable for the small garden.

Other, rarer berries, such as the Japanese wineberry and the dewberry, are in fact cultivated forms of true species of *Rubus*. They are included here because there is an increasing curiosity about and interest in their domestic cultivation.

TAYBERRY
The tayberry is probably the best hybrid resulting from a blackberry-raspberry cross. The fruits are larger than loganberries and a deeper purple color. They are firm and juicy, with a delicious sweet flavor. They are produced in abundance and freeze quite well.

Tayberries are moderately prickly and of medium vigor. Leave a space of eight feet between plants; otherwise treat them just like blackberries or loganberries. Certified virus-free stock is available.

BOYSENBERRY
There are both thorny and thornless forms of this hybrid (*Rubus ursinus* 'Boysen'), which carries distinctively flavored fruits shaped like raspberries but longer. The berries are dark red ripening to purplish-black and may have a dusty bloom. A yield of up to ten pounds can be expected from each boysenberry plant.

A particular feature of the boysenberry is its resistance to drought, so it could be a good choice for light soils. It is moderately vigorous, and needs a planting distance of eight feet.

MARIONBERRY
Though they look like blackberries, the large, juicy fruits of this relatively new hybrid resemble succulent loganberries in flavor. They are produced over an exceptionally long period—two months or more—from midsummer onward. The plants are vigorous and thorny and need about twelve feet between them.

SUNBERRY
With its vigorous habit and spiny shoots, this hybrid has some drawbacks. But its great asset is the excellent flavor of the dark red loganberrylike fruits. It crops during the second half of summer, and requires a generous planting distance of fifteen feet.

TUMMELBERRY
In many ways similar to the tayberry, which is one of its parents, this hybrid is somewhat hardier and therefore better suited to cold areas. The canes are long and covered in hairs, and it is a reasonably heavy cropper; the fruits are sharp in flavor. Allow eight feet between plants.

JAPANESE WINEBERRY
The Japanese wineberry (*Rubus phoenicolasius*) is one of the most decorative and unusual plants for the food garden. Its fruits are an attractive golden yellow ripening to light red, and the long, arching stems are covered with soft, striking red bristles, making quite a display in winter. It can be grown as an ornamental climber on a fence or trellis with little trouble.

The berries are small and seedy, but they are sweet, juicy, and refreshing, with a mild flavor resembling that of grapes. The aromatic fruits all ripen at once; they make successful, delicately flavored jams, jellies, and preserves.

Since it is not especially vigorous, a six-foot planting distance is sufficient.

DEWBERRY
Rather like a slender-growing blackberry, the dewberry (*Rubus caesius*) has flavorful fruits. The small berries are not shiny but have a white bloom over them.

Though the dewberry produces only a modest crop, the fruits ripen ahead of blackberries. The stems trail over the ground, providing a form of ground cover if the plant is not trained on wires.

WORCESTERBERRIES
The Worcesterberry (*Ribes divaricatum*) resembles a vigorous, gooseberry, with smaller, purple fruits. It might appear to be a cross between a gooseberry and a black currant, but it is in fact a species of currant. The shoots are thorny; the purple berries are tasty and used mainly for cooking and jam making. Planting and care are the same as for gooseberries (see pp.75–76), though with a more generous spacing of eight feet between the berry bushes.

The Worcesterberry's great virtue is its immunity to American gooseberry mildew. It is also a hardy and prolific cropper. However, it is also a host for the deadly white pine blister rust.

BERRIES, pages 50–51
BLACKBERRIES, pages 72–73
PESTS AND DISEASES, pages 108–111
FREEZING FRUITS, pages 234–235

Gooseberries (*Ribes grossularia uva-crispa*), which are rarely available in supermarkets, deserve to be more popular than they are, for they are among the easiest of fruits to grow. They are wonderful in jams and pies, and some varieties, such as 'Poorman,' make excellent fresh dessert fruit.

Like black, red, and white currants, gooseberries are an alternate host of white pine blister rust, so many states prohibit or restrict their sale and growth. Be sure to check with your agricultural extension agent or the forestry commission before proceeding to buy plants.

Gooseberries are long-lived plants, lasting for twenty years or more. The immature berries of all gooseberry varieties are green, but they ripen to an assortment of shades. Some remain green while others turn red, yellow, or greenish-white; color is an indication of ripeness. The fruits ripen, depending on the variety, between late spring and the second half of summer. A mature bush may give a harvest of up to ten pounds.

Any well-drained, fertile soil is suitable for growing gooseberries. If your soil is sandy, be sure to dig in plenty of moisture-holding organic material. The site can be in full sun or partial shade, but it should not be under an overhanging tree. The chief precaution is to avoid a frost pocket, where the early spring flowers could be damaged.

GOOSEBERRY FORMS
Gooseberry plants may be grown as bushes, with a number of branches emerging above a short stem, or as upright cordons (see p.88) with one, two, or three stems. The chief advantages of cordons are the extra-large size of the berries they produce and the limited amount of space they take up.

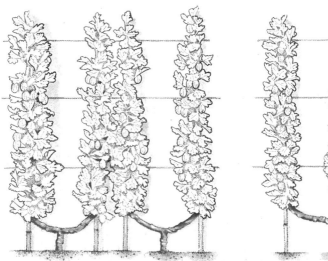

Gooseberry cordons with two stems.

A three-stem (triple) gooseberry cordon.

MAKING A START
Plant bare-rooted gooseberries during early spring, and container-grown specimens at any season, when soil and weather conditions allow.

Prepare the soil well in advance by digging in organic material. In addition, rake in a dressing of organic fertilizer at two ounces per square yard around each position at planting time.

Space bushes five feet apart; for cordons, see the advice given below.

Most gooseberries are sold when two years old. Dig the planting hole with a spade, mixing peat, rotted compost, or a planting mixture with the soil, then replace it and firm it with your feet. Plant bushes so that the soil comes to the same level it

did in the nursery, or just above this level.

After planting a bush, cut back the new growth on each shoot to a bud about halfway along its length. Your eventual aim is to create a goblet-shaped bush with an open center, so choose buds (from which fresh shoots will develop) that are well placed to make this possible. This means that they will be on the upper surface of drooping branches or on the outside of upright growths. A total of about eight branches will form the mature bush; cut out other shoots just above the lowest bud.

SUPPORTING AND TRAINING CORDONS
Cordons may be grown in the open, with the wires tightly strung between posts (see p.70) or fastened with vine eyes to a wall or fence (see p.84). Allow one and a half feet between singles, two feet between doubles, three feet between triples.

After planting, select the number of shoots needed to form the stems (one, two, or three), then cut away any others that are lower than four or five inches.

Once they begin to grow, support each stem of a cordon with a bamboo cane, securing these to wires two feet and four feet above the ground. Fasten the canes for a double cordon six inches on either side of the main stem. For a triple cordon, secure one cane in line with the main stem, the others one foot on either side.

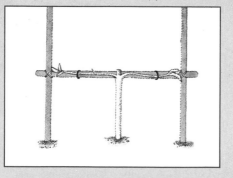

1 To form a double cordon (two stems), prune the stem at planting time to eight inches above the ground. Allow a bud to develop near the top on each side of the stem, rub off those beneath, and train the resultant shoots to the horizontal cane on each side.

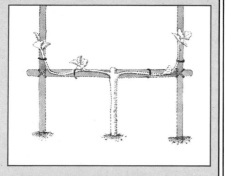

2 When the shoots reach the upright canes, fastened six inches on each side of the main stem, train them vertically. A triple cordon is formed by retaining three buds on the main stem, then training the shoot that grows from the top bud to a cane fastened centrally.

CARE OF THE CROP

Because gooseberries are shallow-rooted, they may be harmed by careless hoeing. A better means of controlling weeds is to keep the soil mulched throughout the year, especially from spring onward.

Before mulching in the spring, scatter a balanced general fertilizer over the surface at two ounces per square yard, with an added half ounce of sulfate of potash. Water liberally if a dry spell coincides with development of the berries.

Pull off any suckers that emerge from the soil near the bushes. In spring, firm in with your foot any plants loosened by frost.

Protection from birds is needed, but less so at harvest time than during the winter, when sparrows may strip off the fruit buds. Use nets if you are not growing your gooseberries in a fruit cage.

HARVESTING

Start picking the berries before they are fully developed, taking them at intervals from along the branches. These smaller berries are suitable for cooking or freezing, and the extended picking period, which amounts to thinning, allows those that are left to develop more fully.

Continue to pick for cooking or for jam making until relatively few, well-spaced berries remain. These are the ones to leave until they become soft and colored, ready for eating fresh.

PRUNING

Continue to prune bushes both winter and summer, with an eye to the eventual shape. Early spring is the best time for winter pruning. Cut back by about half the new growth of branch leaders—that is, the ends

of main branches—just above an undamaged bud. Then reduce the new growths of laterals (side growths) to about three inches. Toward the middle of summer, cut back all laterals—but not main shoots—to the fifth leaf from the base.

In later years, you can cut the current season's laterals back to a bud within one inch of the main branch, and strong new growths from the base can replace congested, aging branches from the center.

Cordons are pruned each summer and winter to keep their shape. Remove about a third of the new growth from the leading shoot and cut back laterals to three buds in early spring. Toward midsummer, cut back all new laterals to five leaves. Do not summer-prune the leaders until they are the right height: singles are usually five feet high, doubles and triples three or four feet.

An established gooseberry bush after it has been pruned in winter. Your major aim should be to avoid overcrowding in the center.

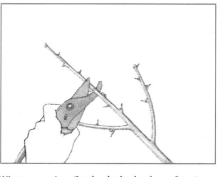

Winter pruning Cut back the leaders of main branches by about half the growth that was made during the previous year. At the same time, shorten laterals by up to three inches.

Summer pruning Between early summer and midsummer, cut back laterals to about the fifth leaf from the base. This reduces the risk of mildew and other fungus diseases.

PROPAGATION

New plants are easily raised from hardwood cuttings, taken in the fall. These will root in open ground, without protection, and be ready for planting out a year later.

Choose shoots that have grown during the current year. They should be reasonably straight, about one foot long, and with the wood firm and well ripened. Cut off the tip and trim the base to just beneath a bud.

Use a spade to form a broad slit about eight inches deep, placing some sterile sand in the base. Position the cuttings six inches apart, with three buds above the soil. Press the soil back, then firm.

PESTS AND DISEASES

The most troublesome pests are aphids and gooseberry sawflies.

White pine blister rust and American gooseberry mildew are possible diseases.

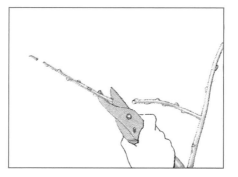

1 Remove straight, well-ripened shoots, each about one foot long, during the autumn. Trim the tip and the base.

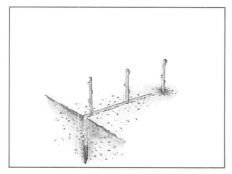

2 Form a slit and place some sand in the base. Position the cuttings six inches apart, each with three buds above the ground.

WATERING AND MULCHING, pages 42–43
BLUEBERRIES AND OTHER BERRIES, pages 52–53

PESTS AND DISEASES, pages 108–111
CANNING, pages 228–229

FREEZING FRUITS, pages 234–235

RECOMMENDED VARIETIES
'Pixwell' A practically thornless variety suitable for Zones 4–6. Berries are large, smooth, and oval, and turn pink when fully ripe. Good for cooking and eating.
'Welcome' Another pink variety, but the fruit is good for pies when still green.
'Poorman' The best variety for eating fresh. Large bushes with short thorns; ripe berries are red.
'Fredonia' Bears heavy crops of very large fruit, which turns a dark red at maturity.

CAPE GOOSEBERRIES
This tender plant (*Physalis peruviana edulis*) is a decorative addition to the fruit garden. Its cherrylike fruits are enclosed in a straw-yellow, lanternlike calyx or husk. The fruits are ready to harvest when the calyxes have turned papery and golden brown; the berries inside have a distinctive sweet taste, and may be eaten raw or used for making preserves. Each plant will produce up to two pounds of fruit.

It is fairly easy to grow Cape gooseberries outdoors if you can give them a warm and sheltered position, or you can grow them in pots or in a greenhouse. In any case, the plants must be started in gentle heat during early spring. Though the Cape gooseberry is a half-hardy perennial, it is usually grown as an annual.

The plants respond to much the same care routines as tomatoes, to which they are related. Plant them two and a half feet apart outdoors or individually in growing bags or pots.

Cape gooseberries will reach about two feet but will spread as much as four feet. A dwarf species, *Physalis pruinosa*, grows to about two thirds this size and is widely available; it makes a good choice for container growing. Both species need protection from wind, and staking is a good idea too.

Keep the plants moist while they are growing, but regulate their watering carefully later on; otherwise they will produce growth at the expense of fruit. Apply liquid fertilizer sparingly after the first flowers have appeared.

Red currants (*Ribes sativum*) are used principally for cooking or for making jelly. They are sometimes eaten as dessert fruits, but white currants are the favorites for this purpose. Both these fruits, which are closely related, need the same general care, propagation, and pruning as gooseberries (see pp.75–76), which is *not* the same as for black currants.

Red and white currants produce their fruit buds in clusters at the base of the one-year-old shoots and on short spurs on the older wood. This means that they may be grown as open, goblet-shaped bushes on a short stem, or as cordons.

Well-drained soil is essential. The bushes are hardy and can be planted in sun or partial shade, but always avoid any frost pockets. Cordons can successfully be grown in the open or against a fence or wall anywhere. Protection from birds is needed for the fruit buds in winter, and for the berries in summer, so use nets unless you are growing the plants in a fruit cage.

Like black currants, red and white currants are hosts for white pine blister rust. Some states prohibit them altogether, and several others restrict planting, so check with the appropriate authorities before planting.

MAKING A START
A supply of compost will help, though red and white currants are less "hungry" than black currants. They need potash, however, so in spring add sulfate of potash at one ounce per square yard, together with twice this amount of balanced fertilizer.

Plant bare-rooted bushes in early spring and container-grown plants at any time when soil conditions and weather allow. Leave five feet between bushes. If the plants are to be grown as single-stemmed cordons, space them about fifteen inches apart; leave two feet between double cordons and three feet between triples.

CARE OF THE CROP
In late winter or spring, check to see whether frost has loosened the soil and/or lifted plants. If it has, firm the earth back gently with your feet.

Each winter apply potash in the same quantities as at planting time. In spring, sprinkle sulfate of ammonia over the root area at one ounce per square yard and spread a mulch of compost or peat.

Pull off any suckers that appear, but avoid regular hoeing.

HARVESTING
Pick the fruits as soon as they are ripe, removing the stalks as well. Eat or preserve them as soon as possible.

PESTS AND DISEASES
Aphids, sawflies, and currant fruit flies are the most likely problems.

Diseases include anthracnose and cane blight.

RECOMMENDED VARIETIES
'Red Lake' Large scarlet berries in long clusters ripen in midsummer. Bushes are 3–4 feet tall and vigorous.
'Wilder' Very large, dark red fruits are easy to pick. Winter hardy.
'White Imperial' Selected from red currants. Yellowish-white berries are large, but yields can be disappointing.

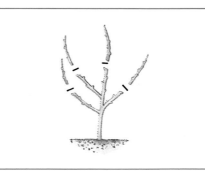

Prune red and white currant bushes immediately after planting. This one-year-old plant has each of its shoots cut back to four buds. New shoots will break at this point.

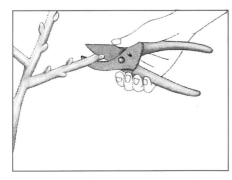

Prune exactly as for gooseberries: trim the shoots back to outward-facing buds that are well placed to promote a sturdy, open, goblet-shaped bush.

For cordons and two-year-old bushes, follow the pruning methods advised for gooseberries, opposite.

Black currants (*Ribes nigrum*) are valued for their high vitamin C content and are used extensively in Europe for cooking and flavoring. Unfortunately, they are favored alternate hosts for white pine blister rust, which can be deadly to pine forests. Many states in which these trees grow consequently prohibit the planting of black currants, so you should check with your agricultural extension agent or the forestry commission before ordering or buying black currant bushes.

Black currants are a very easy crop to grow; their chief need is well-manured soil. Subject to this, a yield of up to ten pounds or more can be expected from each mature bush. The life expectancy of a black currant bush is fifteen years or more, especially for certified virus-free stock.

Choose either an open or a lightly shaded position for planting, but be careful to avoid a site subject to late spring frosts.

MAKING A START

Dig plenty of manure or garden compost into the site before planting, and spread on some general fertilizer, at two ounces per square yard, at planting time. Distribute this around each planting position, setting the bushes five feet apart.

Plant bushes in late fall or early spring (the earlier the better). Dig generous planting holes that will allow the bushes to sit a little deeper in the soil than they were in the nursery, so that the new shoots will grow directly from the soil. Immediately after planting, cut back each stem to the second bud above soil level, to encourage the production of several strong new shoots from the base. This should insure heavy

cropping in future years, although it means sacrificing a crop the first summer.

Spread a deep mulch around the plants in early spring and renew it each year once the soil has warmed up.

CARE OF THE CROP

Sprinkle sulfate of potash over the root area in midwinter, at one ounce per square yard. At the end of winter, before mulching, provide sulfate of ammonia in similar quantities to the roots.

Soak the ground if there is a dry spell from late spring onward. Avoid hoeing, if possible, in case you damage the shallow roots. Hand weeding is safer, but in any case the mulch should keep the weeds down.

HARVESTING AND PROTECTION

Make sure the fruits are fully ripe before you pick them: they turn black a week or two before they are quite ready. There are two methods of picking black currants: one is to strip the berries from the stalks, so that they come off singly; the other is to remove them with the stalks intact. The latter is better if you have to keep the fruit for a while, and does not involve much extra work.

The spring flowers are vulnerable to frost, and the ripening fruits to damage by birds. Drape the bushes with burlap or several layers of net if a night frost is likely, then remove it during the day. Net the bushes against birds when the first fruits begin to turn darker in color.

PRUNING

Black currants fruit on the previous season's new wood, so the aim of pruning is to encourage new growth to develop. During

the first autumn, cut out any weak shoots to a bud a little above the ground. Do the same a year later, purposely removing a few of the weaker growths to stimulate new ones from ground level.

Once the bushes are mature, remove about a quarter of the older, darker growth each autumn, even though this means losing the younger shoots that some of the older ones bear. Cut out badly placed or damaged wood first. Then remove old branches that have no new shoots on them, and finally cut back fruited branches to a strong shoot. This will prevent overcrowding in the center of the black currant bush and encourage new, fruit-bearing growth from the base.

PROPAGATION

As for gooseberries (see p.76).

PESTS AND DISEASES

Two particular pests are black currant gall mites and aphids.

In addition to white pine blister rust, American gooseberry mildew, leaf spot, and reversion are possible ailments.

RECOMMENDED VARIETIES

Only one variety, 'Boskoop Giant,' is easy to find in American nurseries. This is an early currant, vulnerable to frost, but is vigorous and has large, sweet fruit.

European varieties can be ordered through the mail, if your state does not forbid planting. Some good choices might be 'Ben Lomond,' a heavy midseason bearer that is resistant to American gooseberry mildew, and 'Jet,' a late variety that is very vigorous.

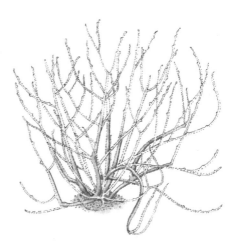

Before pruning

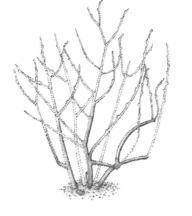

After pruning

The object in pruning black currants is to promote a continuing supply of young, fruit-bearing growths. This is done by cutting out up to a third of the older wood each year (above), though retaining some of the branches bearing year-old shoots. The older wood is darker and thicker.

BLUEBERRIES AND OTHER BERRIES, pages 52–53
WATERING AND MULCHING, pages 42–43

PESTS AND DISEASES, pages 108–111
FREEZING FRUITS, pages 234–235

The highbush blueberry (*Vaccinium corymbosum*) is the ideal fruit for a garden with really acid soil. Whereas soil with a pH level just on the acid side of neutral suits the great majority of fruits and vegetables, blueberries need a pH of about 4.5, to match the peaty environment from which they derive.

In most gardens this means creating special planting places in which acid peat is the main soil component. You might also need an acidifying chemical. The alternative is to grow the plants in containers, using an acid potting soil for azaleas.

The highbush blueberry has a height and spread of around five feet, and makes a striking spectacle in autumn, when the leaves turn a glowing red. The rabbiteye blueberry, grown in the South, often reaches fifteen feet but is similar in other respects. Because they are so decorative, blueberries can be grown in a shrub border with other acid-soil plants, such as rhododendrons.

The dark blue berries, which ripen in midsummer, are covered with an attractive grayish bloom. They have a distinctive flavor, at its best in the pies and muffins for which blueberries are famed.

MAKING A START

Blueberries are unlikely to succeed in soil with a pH of 5.5 or higher. If your soil is less acid than this, dig individual planting stations two feet square and one foot deep. Break up the subsoil a little, but do not remove any of it. Allow five feet between the planting stations.

Mix dampened sphagnum moss or a lime-free compost in equal quantities with the soil removed, and add some sterile sand. The heavier the soil is, the more sand you will need, up to a maximum of 25 percent.

Return the mixture to the planting hole; the job should be completed a few weeks before you buy the plants. This may be in autumn or spring, if the plants are bare-rooted, or at any time of the year if they are container-grown.

Soils on the borderline of being too alkaline can be further acidified by simply adding sulfur at four to eight ounces per square yard every two or three years; the heavier the soil, the more you will need.

Water the roots or soil ball before planting if there is any hint of dryness. Plant the bushes in their individual stations at the same level as previously grown, and firm the soil-moss mixture thoroughly around their roots. Spread a mulch of peat or an acid leafmold (such as oak leaves), or sawdust, over the surface afterward.

GROWING IN CONTAINERS
Growing blueberries in tubs or pots is a good idea if your soil is alkaline. The containers need to be substantial, however, since blueberries have extensive root systems: the minimum suitable size is approximately fifteen inches square and deep. Each tub or pot must have a drainage hole. Fill it with a lime-free compost, or a peat-based potting soil with no added lime.

Pay close attention to the watering needs of container-grown bushes, and use rainwater if your groundwater supply is hard. A drip watering system is especially convenient.

Unless the soil is naturally acid (ideally pH 4.5), you should prepare special planting stations for blueberries. Mix sphagnum peat moss or a lime-free compost with the soil in equal parts, and add sterile sand unless the soil is naturally light. Allow a few weeks for the mixture to settle before planting.

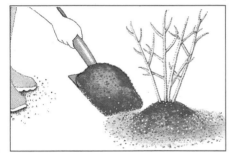

A mulch of peat or lime-free compost added after planting will help to maintain the acid conditions and prevent the soil and roots from drying out. Renew this mulch each spring after the plants have been fed and when the soil has had a chance to warm up. If applied too early, it prevents heat reaching the soil.

CARE OF THE CROP
Do not prune the stems after planting, but prevent fruiting during the first year by rubbing off the plump fruit buds with your thumb, leaving only the smaller buds that will form leaves.

It is vital not to let the roots dry out at any stage; even in spring there is an occasional risk of this. Water plants thoroughly at the first hint of dryness. Continue watering throughout the summer as necessary. A drip system of watering could save you some time, and is particularly useful for plants grown in containers (see p.42).

Every year, provide a balanced general fertilizer at two ounces per square yard in early spring, followed about a month later with a dressing of sulfate of ammonia at half this rate. Fork or rake this gently into the existing mulch, then add a fresh layer of peat. Manure is unsuitable for a blueberry bed. Apply a high-potash liquid food (as sold for tomatoes) while the berries are forming and ripening.

Hoeing is inadvisable, since the bushes have a network of roots near the surface. Any weeds that appear, despite the mulch, are best removed by hand.

BLUEBERRIES AND OTHER BERRIES, pages 52–53
WATERING AND MULCHING, pages 42–43

PESTS AND DISEASES, pages 108–111
FREEZING FRUITS, pages 234–235

HARVESTING AND PROTECTION

Wait until the berries are fully ripe before you pick them. Berries picked prematurely lack flavor. When ripe they are soft, blue-black with a waxy bloom, and part easily from their stalks. Eat the blueberries fresh, or use them for cooking, within a couple of days; otherwise freeze them.

Protection from birds is essential. If you are not growing the bushes in a fruit cage, drape netting over them.

Blueberries are irresistible to birds. If you do not have a fruit cage, drape nets over the bushes for reasonable protection.

PRUNING

After the first three years, some pruning is needed annually in early spring. Cut back a few (one to four) of the oldest stems; either remove them altogether, if there are plenty of young basal shoots, or trim them back to strong young shoots. The aim is to stimulate growth that will bear fruit a couple of years later; blueberries fruit on the tips of the previous season's growth. It is also necessary to thin out established bushes that are becoming too dense.

Remove dead or weak branches and those spreading close to the ground at the same time.

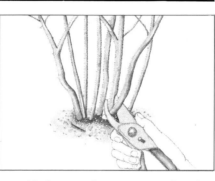

Prune blueberries in late winter or early spring by cutting back up to four of the oldest stems. This will encourage the plants to produce new fruit-bearing shoots.

PROPAGATION

Blueberries can be propagated either by layering in the autumn or by taking semi-hard cuttings in midsummer. In the autumn, select one or two long shoots and cut a nick in each so that it can be bent to touch the ground. Peg each shoot down with a pin of bent wire. After one or two years, sever the new plant from the parent.

Alternatively, take a semiripe shoot in midsummer by cutting cleanly just above a bud. Dip the heel in hormone powder and plant it in equal parts of peat and sand in a cold frame or unheated greenhouse. Mist the cutting with water until it has rooted.

PESTS AND DISEASES

Aphids may be troublesome occasionally. The plants are rarely affected by disease, but too much lime may cause chlorosis.

RECOMMENDED VARIETIES

Though the plants are self-fertile, they will fruit better if you grow at least two plants, each of a different variety.

Highbush blueberries
'**Earliblue**' An early, disease-resistant variety with large berries.
'**Berkeley**' Delicious midseason berries.
'**Jersey**' A vigorous, late-bearing blueberry, winter hardy in Zones 5–8.

Rabbiteye blueberries
'**Woodard**' Very early. Fragrant, slightly tart berries. Zones 7–9.
'**Southland**' Heavy crops of medium-sized fruit in mid- to late summer.

The cranberry (*Vaccinium macrocarpon*) is a close relative of the blueberry and needs much the same growing conditions—acid, free-draining soil—but even more moisture. It has a prostrate, creeping habit, however, so is unsuitable for containers. The foliage is evergreen and the plant takes a long time to grow.

The oval red berries, which are good for making muffins and bread as well as for cranberry sauce, ripen during late summer and early autumn.

GROWING AND HARVESTING

It is not practical to form individual stations, as is done for blueberries, since cranberries are planted only one foot apart in each direction. Instead, prepare a bed by mixing equal parts of soil and acid peat, with added sand, to a depth of about eight inches. Lower the pH level, if necessary, by adding some sulfur.

Plant cranberries during the spring, preferably in a sunny position, and from then on make sure that the bed is constantly moist. A covering of sterile sand will reduce evaporation and suppress weeds.

Leave the picking until all the berries are ripe. Pruning, in early spring, consists of trimming to prevent any overcrowding and to remove untidy, wispy stems.

PESTS AND DISEASES

You are unlikely to have any troubles, except perhaps for aphids.

RECOMMENDED VARIETIES

You will probably have to obtain commercial varieties. Good choices might be '**Early Black**,' '**Searle's Jumbo**,' and '**Stevens**.'

The large, velvety-skinned kiwi fruits (*Actinidia chinensis*) are also called Chinese gooseberries. They are indeed of oriental origin, but commercial production is concentrated in New Zealand—hence the more commonly used name. The fruits are refreshing, with a mild but delicious flavor. They are eaten raw, in both sweet dishes and salads.

Kiwi fruits are produced on a vine. The plant is a vigorous climber, entwining around any support. It has large, heart-shaped leaves and the female flowers are creamy white, so it can look attractive grown over a porch or a trellis. The vines do not usually produce a harvest for three years or more if they are grown outdoors, and the fruits they bear are generally smaller than the imported varieties that are usually sold in supermarkets.

The kiwi vine is a tender plant, winter hardy only in mild areas, although hardy varieties are beginning to be available. Still, it is best grown in a sheltered spot, preferably against a south-facing wall. Avoid known frost pockets at all costs, and protect the vine if necessary.

Low winter temperatures and spring frosts, which are the two potential dangers for kiwi fruits, can both be countered by planting the vine in a large, unheated greenhouse. If it is grown against an outside wall, a temporary shelter, in the form of a sheet of polyethylene, will reduce the risk of damage from severe winter winds and consistently low temperatures.

Any average, well-drained soil will do, provided some organic matter is dug in to help retain moisture. The fruits will mature in late summer or early fall.

MAKING A START

As well as a female, fruit-producing plant, a male is needed for pollination. Actinidias are rampant vines, so unless you have unlimited space, the best plan is to plant the two together, training the male one way and the female the other. Their potential spread is at least fifteen feet, so you might have to restrict the growth of plants raised in a greenhouse.

The best method of support is much the same as for blackberries (see p.73), though the wires should be fixed a little farther apart. Stretch the wires between posts if plants are grown in the open, or attach them to vine eyes set in a wall or to screw eyes in a greenhouse.

Plant the kiwi vines in spring. Before you do so, prepare the planting position by mixing peat or well-rotted compost in with the soil, together with a half ounce of a general fertilizer. Alternatively, use a prepared planting mixture. Set the two plants side by side and firm the mixture around the root balls.

If you have the space and want to grow more than one female kiwi fruit, space the plants ten to fifteen feet apart. One male plant will pollinate up to six females.

CARE OF THE CROP

Feed annually, in spring, with a general fertilizer at two ounces per square yard, scattering this over a broad area around the stems. Spread a deep mulch, preferably organic, over the same area.

Water generously during dry weather, at least until about midsummer, and especially if the plants are growing against a wall or in a greenhouse.

PRUNING AND TRAINING

Grow the male and female plants as espaliers—that is, each with one upright main stem, and with the shoots growing from this trained along the wires in one direction only.

To start the training process, cut each stem level with the bottom wire immediately after planting. Allow two shoots to develop; leave one to grow upright and train the other horizontally along the first wire by tying it loosely with string.

Tie a string to the wires as an additional support for the main, upright shoot. Repeat the cutting-back procedure at each wire, to encourage the development of more shoots that can be trained horizontally. Rub off any buds that appear on the stem between the supporting wires.

During the summer, remove the tip of each horizontal branch, and eventually those of the side shoots that will then form behind the pinched-back shoots. The purpose of this is to encourage the formation of fruiting spurs.

In later years, thin out any congested growth during winter. Cut the three-year-old fruited laterals back to a dormant bud near the main cane to renew the fruit-bearing lateral shoots.

PESTS AND DISEASES

Aphids may prove a minor problem. Diseases seldom occur.

RECOMMENDED VARIETIES

'Hayward' Late-flowering, and with large, well-flavored fruits.
'Miller's Northern' A new winter-hardy variety that bears in midsummer.

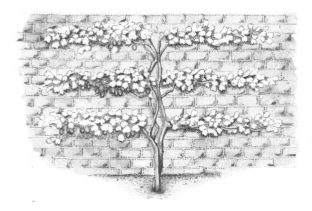

A male and a female kiwi fruit are planted together. The shoots from each have been trained in a single direction to form a conventional espalier shape.

In extremely mild and sheltered districts it is possible to grow kiwi fruits as freestanding plants on a pergola. Elsewhere, some form of protection is necessary.

The sweet, luscious flavor of melons (*Cucumis melo* and *Citrullus vulgaris*) is particularly rewarding when these warmth-loving fruits are grown in a mild climate. Yet melons are by no means a difficult crop: their cultivation demands close attention rather than great skill.

Melons are tender plants, and seed cannot successfully be sown outdoors except in the warmest of climates. For reliable results, sow the seeds in warmth—in a greenhouse, in a soil-warmed frame, or on a sunny windowsill inside the house.

Although most American gardeners grow melons outdoors, those in northern zones might consider the European method of growing melons in greenhouses, which lengthens the growing season and provides the constant warm temperatures these fruits covet.

Melons generally divide into three groups. Muskmelons include the familiar cantaloupe types and ripen in about three months. Winter melons, which include Crenshaws and casabas, usually require at least four months, and they are generally larger than muskmelons. Watermelons, the third group, range from small to very large.

MAKING A START

Sowing time depends on where the melons are to grow. A midspring sowing will provide plants that you can move outdoors in late spring, after the last frost. But you can sow seeds in early spring if the young plants are to remain in a warm greenhouse. Slightly staggered sowing times will insure that the melons do not ripen all at once.

A temperature of about 65°F is needed for germination, and it should be kept within a degree or two of this as the seedlings develop. A propagator (see p.38) is ideal for maintaining the fairly high germination temperature, especially if you are using a windowsill indoors.

Sow each seed alone in a three-inch pot of planting medium or in a peat pot. Press it into the middle of the pot, then water the mix and cover the pots, first with glass and then with paper. Remove the paper and glass as soon as the seeds germinate. Stand the pots in a light, warm place and keep the planting medium moist.

Prepare the soil for planting, indoors or out, by forking in some well-rotted garden compost. You can use peat instead, in which case add a handful of general fertilizer to each square yard. Do not use manure, which would produce too much foliage at the expense of fruit. Melons can also be planted in growing bags, provided that some additional feeding is given from a fairly early stage.

To warm the soil in northern areas, lay black plastic mulch two weeks before planting. Use row covers to protect the melons.

CARE OF THE CROP OUTDOORS

Wait until the risk of frost is completely over before planting out. By this stage, the plants should have at least two or three true leaves. Water the melons in their pots first so that the root balls are not disturbed. Set the plants three feet apart and cover them if necessary, or place two plants in a cold frame. Draw the soil into a slight mound first, then make a hole wide and deep enough to take the root ball. The mound will help to keep the stem dry, since melons are susceptible to root rot.

If you live in the South, plant seeds directly in the garden as soon as there is no danger of frost. Thin seedlings to two-foot intervals, or plant two or three together on hills four feet apart. The melons will need about six feet of space around them however they are planted.

Arrange plants in cold frames in well-spaced pairs, trained in opposite directions. Once the flowers appear, remove the covers or leave frames open, weather permitting, to allow insects in to pollinate.

Leave frames open, and pull row covers aside (or space them a little apart), whenever the weather is warm. Remove covers altogether during prolonged sunny spells and warm weather.

An alternative is to mulch the melons with black plastic or with an organic mulch such as straw. Plastic is particularly effective for keeping weeds down and retaining moisture in the soil, but be sure to check regularly in hot weather so that the roots do not dry out.

Keep the soil moist, especially as the fruit develops. At this stage feed plants every week or two with a high-potash liquid fertilizer. When the melons are the size of apples, support them off the ground on an upturned plant pot or something similar, to prevent any possibility of rotting.

CARE OF THE CROP IN A GREENHOUSE

Europeans have had great success with melons in greenhouses. Although this method is usually used for the hard-shelled true cantaloupe, which is rarely available in this country, it might be worth experimenting with if you live in a harsh climate.

Transplant the young melons in the prepared border or in growing bags when they have five rough-edged leaves. Set them two and a half feet apart, first forming a slight mound as advised for outdoor plants.

The object is to grow the plants as twin-stemmed cordons, first up to the eaves and then along the underside of the roof. For support, push two canes into the soil six inches to each side of the plant. Tie the tops of the canes to a horizontal wire at eave level, then fasten wires at one-foot intervals up the wall, behind the plants, and on the underside of the roof. Use vine eyes to secure the wires to the bars of the greenhouse. An overall width of three feet is about right for a single melon plant.

Pinch out the tip of the plant when it is six inches high. Remove all but two of the shoots that will develop, and secure each of these to a cane, using soft string. Continue to tie them at intervals until they are about six inches long, then pinch out their growing points.

The effect of stopping the main shoots will

Sow the seeds on edge, pressing them into the planting mix. If you sow them singly, prepare one or two spare pots in case of failures. Otherwise, sow two per pot and remove one seedling if they both germinate.

Swelling of greenhouse fruit is a signal to pinch out the ends of shoots two leaves beyond each one. Do this when the fruit is marble-sized, leaving one fruit per shoot.

POLLINATION

You cannot rely on insects for pollination when you are growing melons inside, so this will have to be done by hand. Pollinate the female flowers, each of which will have an embryo fruit beneath the petals, by brushing the pollen from a male flower onto the center. Do this when four female flowers are open at the same time on different shoots of the same plant, and repeat the procedure on the following day. Try to pollinate in the middle of the day, if possible, when the temperature in the greenhouse is at its warmest. Remove any flowers that grow on the main stem.

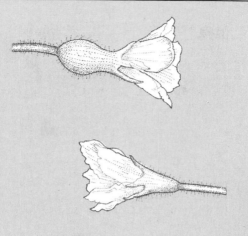

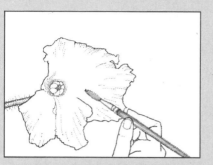

Female flowers (upper left) are easily distinguished by the embryo fruit behind the petals. To pollinate greenhouse melons, use cotton or a brush to transfer pollen from the male to the female flowers.

be to encourage the production of side shoots, or laterals. Tie these to the wires, and remove the tip of each lateral once it has developed five leaves. Flower-bearing shoots will start to grow from the laterals.

Provide temporary shade in the greenhouse on hot, sunny days by means of blinds or liquid shading. Ventilate the house freely during the day but close it up completely at night.

When the fruit starts to develop, pinch out the tips of the shoots two leaves beyond them. Remove the largest and the smallest fruit, and any others, to leave two equal-sized melons on each stem. Any large melon left on would continue to grow at the expense of the others. Allow only one melon to remain on a side shoot.

Feed with a high-potash liquid fertilizer every week or so, from the time that the fruit starts to swell. Support the weight of the fruit by placing the melons in nets or pantyhose secured to the wires. If any are lying on the ground, place them on an upturned flowerpot or some other support.

Melons need ample watering throughout the growing period; water daily as a rule, but do not saturate the soil. In particular, be careful not to wet the soil immediately around the stem.

HARVESTING

A softening of the outer end of the melon, opposite the stalk, is a sure sign of ripening. By then the characteristic scent will be obvious. Pull the fruit carefully from the stalk. Eat without too much delay.

PESTS AND DISEASES

Mites can be troublesome in a greenhouse, and cucumber beetles are common. Root rot and bacterial wilt are possible.

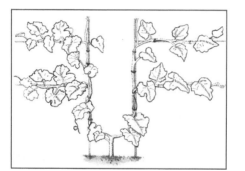

Above Fruit-bearing laterals will develop on a twin-stemmed cordon when the tip of each stem is pinched out.

Right Use nets to take the weight of greenhouse melons.

RECOMMENDED VARIETIES

True cantaloupes (for greenhouses)
'**Charentais**' The small, greenish fruits average two or three pounds. Very sweet and unusual European variety.
'**Ogen**' Long vines produce fragrant melons with greenish-white flesh.

Muskmelons
'**Earligold**' An extra-early, semihardy melon with dense netting and orange flesh.
'**Easy Rider**' A good variety for the West and Southwest. Round, sweet, netted melons.
'**Burpee's Ambrosia Hybrid**' A very popular, flavorful melon. Fruits average four pounds and have thick flesh.
'**Tam-Dew**' A large honeydew melon with thick, juicy flesh. Disease resistant.

Winter melons
'**Crenshaw**' A late-bearing yellow-green melon. Fruit averages nine pounds and is pale pink.
'**Casaba**' Wrinkled skin and sweet white flesh characterize this large melon.

Watermelons
'**Garden Baby**' Compact vines produce round, dark green melons with faint striping. A small, flavorful watermelon.
'**Sugar Jade**' A midseason bearer. Fruit is elliptical, about fifteen to twenty pounds, and very sweet.
'**Dixielee**' A late watermelon, good in hot, humid climates. Twenty- to thirty-pound fruit with dark red flesh.

Grape growing, or viticulture, has a long and illustrious history; the grapes are grown for making into wine and for drying as raisins as well as for eating as a dessert fruit. Table grapes are easiest to cultivate domestically, although many varieties are suitable for wine making and preserving in addition to eating.

The grapevine is a perennial deciduous climber that clings to its supports by means of tendrils. Though you cannot expect to harvest any fruit for at least three years, the vine, once established, is a long-lived plant and will last between twenty and forty years, so its cultivation could be a lifelong commitment. You can expect an established wall-trained grapevine to yield up to twenty pounds of fruit in a good year.

Grapes, usually produced in bunches, are generally described as being black, red, or white, but in fact the white grapes may be any shade between green and amber-yellow, and the black varieties range from purple to deep blue-black in color.

Grapes need a sheltered place in the sun if they are to ripen properly in the North. Success is more likely in a mild area, especially if you grow the vine against a sunny, south-facing wall or fence. Such protection is easily provided in many gardens. A wall is preferable since it serves as an overnight "heat bank." However, grapes are subject to mildew if they are grown in still air next to a wall in hot climates, so southern gardeners may want to consider the popular grape arbor as an alternative.

Grapevines may also be grown in open ground, as they usually are commercially. This method of growing requires a more complicated system of training and pruning than the one covered here. The important thing is to provide good air circulation, protection from cold winds, and plenty of sun throughout the season.

The type of soil is not critical, except for its drainage, which must be perfect. European varieties evolved in fairly arid conditions and the roots will not stand any hint of waterlogging. A gritty, sandy soil is ideal since it insures free drainage. Heavy, soggy ground is unsuitable unless it can be improved by artificial drainage.

MAKING A START

Depending on which method of training you are using (see p.85), sink in posts, secure wires or monofilament, or set up a trellis or arbor in the spot you have chosen for your grapevines. Take steps to improve the soil's drainage if necessary (see p.26).

Toward the end of winter, dig plenty of manure or compost into the topsoil around each planting position. Space these five feet apart if you are growing more than one vine. Leave the soil to settle for a month or two, then rake a handful of general fertilizer into the surface a few days before planting.

Spring is the best time to plant both bare-rooted and container-grown vines. Firm the soil around the plants at the same level as they were in the nursery, with bare roots spread out evenly, but make sure not to disturb the root balls.

After planting, shorten the leading shoot (which will form the main stem, or rod) to about two feet and cut the others to a single healthy-looking bud.

PRUNING AND TRAINING

Pruning and training are vital to the establishment of healthy, heavy-bearing grapevines. Any of the systems described on page 85 might be appropriate, depending on what kind of grapes you are growing.

Training will keep the fast-growing vine under control, will insure that all parts of the vine are exposed to the sun, and will make care and harvesting easier.

The purpose of pruning is to maintain the vine's vigorous growth, encourage the development of new shoots for the next year, and limit the number of fruit-producing buds so that the vine does not produce too many small or inferior bunches of grapes. If you follow the pruning procedures outlined, you should have a small harvest of grapes when the vine is three years old.

TYPES OF GRAPES

Most grapes grown by American gardeners are descended from wild native varieties, which are notable for their slip-skins. Such familiar bunch grapes as 'Concord' and 'Niagara' are among the native type.

Southerners often cultivate the less hardy muscadine grapes, which grow in loose clusters and do well on arbors, as the vines are rampant growers.

European wine grapes (*Vitis vinifera*) also prefer a mild climate, but some varieties and hybrids can be grown successfully as far north as Zone 6.

When choosing a variety to grow, be careful to find out whether the grape is self-fruitful. If it is not, plant such a variety nearby to improve flavor.

Vines against a wall. The wires are one foot apart and leading shoots have been shortened to two feet.

On a trellis, the rods are secured to canes and the laterals trained to alternate wires on each side.

THE KNIFFEN SYSTEM

A good method for cultivating most American bunch grapes, this system relies on four new fruiting spurs each year to produce the crop. Like the European system, it requires careful training and drastic pruning for the first few years, until the vine is well established. As with all grapes, grapes pruned under the Kniffen system should be cut back in the spring, when the vine is dormant but after all danger of heavy frost is over.

FIRST- AND SECOND-YEAR PRUNING

In the first year, allow the strongest stem to develop and pinch back all other shoots to a single leaf.

In the second year, tie the rod to the top wire, if it is long enough; if not, secure it to the lower wire. Cut off any of the rod that extends above the top wire, and remove all the other shoots.

SUBSEQUENT PRUNING

In the third year, decide which four shoots are the strongest and train them along the wires, two to each side of the stem, to form arms. Cut them back so that each arm has about ten buds. Choose four more shoots to form renewal arms in the fourth year, and prune them so that two or three buds remain on each. Remove all other shoots.

Beginning in the fourth year, cut off the fruit-bearing arms from the previous year and tie the renewal shoots, which should be pruned to ten buds each, to the wires as replacements. As in the third year, choose four shoots to become the next year's fruiting spurs and remove all others.

SYSTEMS FOR TENDER GRAPES

To train muscadines on an arbor, prune the vine to form a strong trunk six or seven feet long before you allow branch shoots to develop. Cut back any shoots that are weak, trying to keep two feet between each branch on a side.

The Munson system involves a two-branch pruning method, but requires you to tie the arms to a wire four and a half feet above the ground and drape the fruit-bearing shoots over another wire six or eight inches higher. This is a particularly good system in humid climates, where poor air circulation can be a problem.

In extremely cold zones, the modified Chautauqua system might be appropriate. In this case you allow a low-growing shoot to develop into a rod, which is tied to a wire about a foot above ground. Each spring, tie new growth to higher wires, but prune this growth back in the fall to short spurs. Remove the vine from the trellis each year and bury it in about eight inches of soil for winter protection.

THE EUROPEAN SYSTEM

The object of this method is to secure a single rod from which horizontal stems are trained left and right on alternate wires.

To begin, form a trellis by sinking strong posts three feet into the ground at ten- or twelve-foot intervals, depending on the variety and how many vines you are growing. Alternatively, secure a series of horizontal wires five inches away from a wall at one-foot intervals. In either case, the bottom wire should be about one and a half feet above the ground and the top wire should stand at about five feet. If necessary, add one or more intermediate wires. Nine- or eleven-gauge galvanized steel wire or heavy monofilament is best. Tie a cane vertically to the wires; you can use this subsequently as a support for the main stem.

When a new shoot grows from the top of the rod, keep this tied to the cane. Train the side shoots to the wires on alternate sides, and pinch out any that are not needed.

Pruning during the first and second years is particularly critical, since this will affect the quality of the fruits the vine is allowed to produce from the third year onward. Pruning should be done in late spring or early summer, once all danger of frost is over.

FIRST-YEAR PRUNING

During the early summer, cut off the tips of the side shoots beyond the fifth leaf. Pick off any flower trusses, too, since growth will suffer if the vines are allowed to bear fruit during their first two years.

In the autumn, cut back the leading shoot—that is, the new growth at the top of the rod—by about half, cutting just above a bud. The purpose is to remove soft, unripened wood. At the same time, cut back each of the horizontal growths to leave stubs with just two buds each.

This pruning may seem drastic, but remember that the fruiting growths will be taken from these spurs each year, throughout the life of the vine.

SECOND- AND THIRD-YEAR PRUNING

During the autumn of the second year, repeat the same pattern of pruning and flower removal. Also pinch back to a single leaf any smaller growths that develop on the main horizontal shoots.

Keep the main stem tied to the cane, and fix a second cane to the wires when necessary. When the stem reaches the top wire, stop it at an adjacent bud.

Allow one shoot to grow from each stub, or spur, during the third year. Pinch out the weaker shoots once you can see which is the strongest. Leave the flowers on three of the shoots to form fruits, then prune the ends of these shoots three leaves beyond each cluster. Tip the other shoots at five leaves, as previously. Tie the laterals onto the supporting wires where necessary.

Allow another bunch or two to develop each subsequent year, continuing until two or three bunches are left on each lateral. The fewer bunches you allow to develop, the better the quality, and size, of the fruit will be.

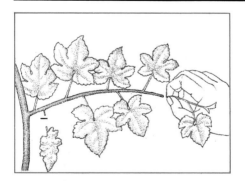

During the first summer, cut off the ends of laterals just beyond the fifth leaf. Remove flowers before fruits can develop.

In the autumn, reduce the leading shoot by half. Cut back laterals to form stubs that have only two buds.

GREENHOUSE EQUIPMENT, pages 14–15
IMPROVING DRAINAGE, page 26

GRAPES AND KIWI FRUITS, pages 56–57
PESTS AND DISEASES, pages 108–111

CARE OF THE CROP

Water an outdoor grapevine regularly, especially during dry spells and if it is planted against a wall. A spring mulch of manure or compost is beneficial if your soil is particularly poor; otherwise, do not provide any fertilizers unless the plant shows signs of nutrient deficiencies. Weeds can be controlled by mulching or by shallow hoeing or cultivating, but be careful not to damage the young plant's roots.

Birds are likely to be a considerable problem as the fruit ripens, so drape the vine with netting if you are not growing it in a fruit cage.

GROWING GRAPES INDOORS

In extremely harsh climates you have the option of growing grapes in a heated greenhouse, provided you have the necessary space. Although two vines can take up a lot of room—and you will probably want two vines so that the fruit sets properly—there are some advantages to greenhouse cultivation: the grapes tend to retain a waxy bloom on their skin, and they are sometimes sweeter than those grown outdoors. The European grapes in particular thrive in the controlled environment of a greenhouse.

Grapes grown indoors should be planted, trained, and pruned like outdoor grapes, but they require a bit of additional care. First, be sure that your greenhouse is well ventilated and free of drafts. Supply a mulch of manure or compost each year at the end of winter, and add some general fertilizer at two ounces per square yard.

For an early harvest, increase the heat to a minimum of 50°F toward the end of winter and begin to water the vines generously each day, spraying the leaves and damping the paths if necessary to maintain a moist atmosphere. When the vines begin to flower, cut back on spraying, but be sure to maintain a daytime temperature of about 70°F. For a good set of fruit, assist pollination by tapping the flowering stems each day or by brushing the flowers with a ball of cotton or a soft-bristled brush.

Once the flowers have set, increase the humidity once again by regular spraying, and be sure to keep the air vents shut at night to retain warmth. Water regularly; do not let the soil dry out.

After your greenhouse vines are established, keep them free of disease with annual winter care. Each year, untie the rods from the wires, lower them to the ground, and scrub them gently with a clean, dry brush to remove loose bark that might shelter pests. While the vines are down, clean the glass in the greenhouse thoroughly with a mixture of water and disinfectant. Then carefully retie the vines to the wires.

Pruning during the second summer is much the same as during the first. As well as trimming shoots and removing flowers, reduce sublaterals to a single leaf.

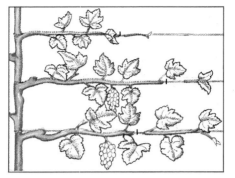

In the third year, allow up to three bunches of fruit to form on each vine. Prune the shoots concerned just beyond the second leaf after the bunch.

HARVESTING

The first signs of color in the grapes are a signal to gradually reduce the amount of watering. If wasps are a nuisance when the fruit is ripening, leave a jar containing some honey or a sugar solution by the vine in order to attract and drown them.

Ripening is a fairly lengthy business, and takes several weeks from the first change of color. When the grapes are ready (taste them if necessary), cut through the stem with clippers. Handle the grapes as little as possible; eat them immediately or keep them in a cool, dark place for several days.

PESTS AND DISEASES

Chief among the several pests that may affect vines are red spider mites, Japanese beetles, grape berry moths, aphids, and scale insects. Phylloxera can be a problem on wine grapes in California and the East. Wasps and birds will probably attack the fruit as it is ripening.

Diseases include black rot, anthracnose, powdery mildew, and downy mildew.

RECOMMENDED VARIETIES

Black grapes

'Black Monukka' A large, late-ripening, seedless table grape. Not hardy.

'Concord' A hardy, blue-black, medium-sized grape used for juice, jelly, and wine as well as eating. Zones 5–7.

'Fredonia' A Concord type that is larger and more vigorous.

White grapes

'Niagara' Sweet light-green fruit suitable for table use and wine making. Zones 5–7.

'Edelweiss' An extremely hardy, very sweet white grape.

'Remaily' A very large, late-ripening, seedless variety for general use. Zones 5–8.

THINNING
Thinning insures that the individual grapes are a good size. When the grapes are starting to swell, start to remove the smaller fruits from the center of overcrowded bunches, using scissors with long, pointed blades.

'California Thompson Seedless' The most widely grown variety of seedless grapes. The light green fruits are sweet and refreshing.

Red grapes

'Zinfandel' A medium-sized European wine grape, suitable for eating.

'Red Caco' The oblong, seeded fruit is late-ripening, and the vine is resistant to temperature extremes.

'Tokay' A popular large grape for wine making and eating. Not hardy.

Muscadine grapes

'Jumbo' A large, round black grape with thick skin, good for cooking and jelly and wine making.

'Summit' A very sweet, bronze grape for table use and preserves.

'Scuppernong' An old favorite. The bronze-skinned fruit has a distinctive sweet flavor.

Many gardeners who will happily grow a row or two of cane or bush fruits will hesitate at the thought of apples or apricots. But tree fruits need not be any harder to grow than berries, and even space need not be a problem, if you choose one of the restricted forms. However, growing tree fruits is a long-term project. Most fruit trees reach their full fruiting capacity only after several years, but with care, they will continue to produce fruit for a lifetime. And the rewards can be considerable. A pair of apples are capable of yielding two hundred pounds of fruit, or a single, fan-trained apricot twenty pounds.

FRUIT TREE FORMS
Fruit trees can be grown in two basic ways, restricted and unrestricted. Restricted forms, grown on wire supports, include cordons, espaliers, and fans, any of which are a suitable choice for a small garden. A fan-trained tree is generally grown against a sunny wall or fence; it is the best form for apricots, peaches, and nectarines. Cordons, which have a main stem with short fruiting spurs, are usually grown at an oblique angle against a wall or trained on wires in the open; the yield per tree is relatively small, but a row of cordons can be very productive for the ground space occupied. Espaliers have a main stem and carry their fruit on a number of horizontal branches. They can be grown against a wall or fence,

but like cordons, they make good screens and dividers within the garden when grown in the open.

Restricted forms are created by pruning and training. Only certain kinds of fruits lend themselves to this treatment; these are detailed in the individual descriptions.

Unrestricted forms are freestanding, and they naturally occupy more space; bush trees and dwarf pyramids are the main forms as far as gardens are concerned. Depending on their rootstock (see below), a pair of apple trees need at least ten feet between them, and dwarf pyramids need four to six feet between them.

ROOTSTOCKS
Many fruit trees, notably apples and pears, are not grown on their own roots. This is because they would not come true to type from their own seeds or stones. Instead, the breeder grafts a shoot (called the scion) from the desired variety onto the roots of a different species, called the rootstock.

The significance of rootstocks is that the strength of their growth—their vigor—is known with some precision. This is important, for it plays a major part in determining the eventual size of the tree. Apple rootstocks are particularly well classified, and each is identified by a numbered prefix.

When you buy a fruit tree, make sure that its rootstock is suitable for the available space and the type of soil. In practical terms,

this means that trees on a dwarfing rootstock are the best choice for a small garden. The more dwarfing the effect, however, the better the soil needs to be to insure satisfactory growth. The influence of a dwarfing rootstock will help to counteract that of a vigorous variety of fruit tree (the scion) and vice versa.

This is really less complicated than it sounds. You need to choose a rootstock principally with apples, and even then there are only about four that need concern the home gardener. Remember that the same variety of apple may be available on two or three different rootstocks. As a result, a tree might grow from as little as four feet in height to as tall as eighteen feet.

BUYING FRUIT TREES
It makes sense to grow the more unusual, and often more flavorful, dessert varieties of fruit, which are not often produced commercially. Plant two or three different varieties, if possible, and choose them carefully so that you can enjoy the fruit over an extended period. This is more practical with restricted forms such as cordons and espaliers than with larger fruit trees, unless you have a large garden.

Two- or three-year-old trees are the best buy, since they will bear fruit sooner than maidens (one-year-olds), and in the case of restricted forms, you will not have to do the initial training.

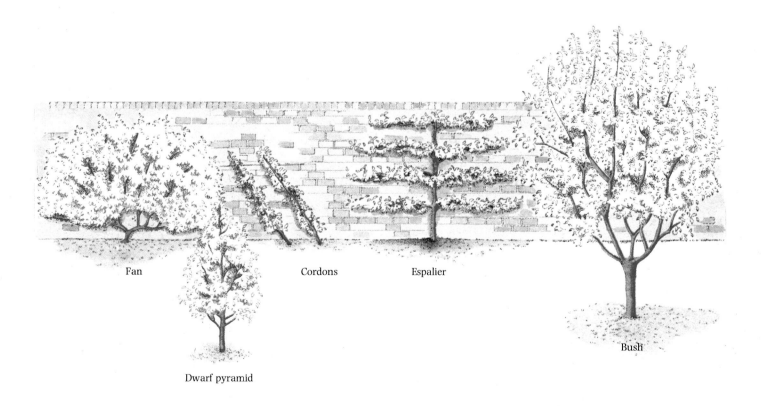

Fan

Cordons

Espalier

Bush

Dwarf pyramid

SITE AND SOIL

Spring frosts, rather than cold winters, are the chief hazard to fruit trees, since it is the blossoms that are most vulnerable. Avoid planting fruit trees in hollows or other places where cold air is liable to be trapped.

Some fruits—notably peaches, figs, and apricots—need a warm, sheltered position if they are to succeed. They are therefore unsuitable for cold northern gardens. A wall facing between southeast and southwest is ideal. A Bing cherry is one fruit tree that likes a north-facing wall.

As long as they have good drainage, most fruits will grow in a wide range of soils. Any exceptions are explained in the individual descriptions. It is important to prepare the planting positions well, however, and to dig in plenty of organic matter.

SUPPORTS

All fruit trees need staking during their early years. The restricted forms require a permanent system of support wires. Erect the stakes or wires before you plant.

Bush trees and dwarf pyramids Drive a stake that is two or three inches in diameter about one and a half feet into the ground. Secure the stem with a plastic tree-tie.

Cordons and espaliers Ideally, buy pressure-treated end posts, or fix the posts into metal sockets. For cordons, run wires or monofilament between the posts at two and a half, four and a half, and six and half feet above the ground. For espaliers, fasten them at the same levels as the horizontal branches.

Fans Fasten supporting wires every six inches, with the first one and a half feet above the ground.

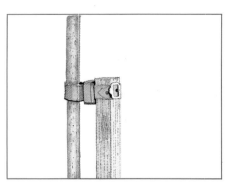

Support a bush tree or a dwarf pyramid with a stake. Trees on vigorous rootstocks can dispense with such support after a few years, but those on dwarfing stock need lifelong support. This tree-tie has an antifriction buffer.

To tighten the wires used to support espaliers and cordons, fasten one end to an eyebolt passed through a hole in the post. Fit a washer under the nut and tighten with a wrench.

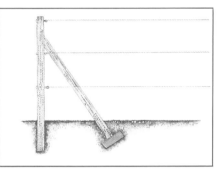

Provided the post has been pressure-treated against rot, it can be set straight in the soil, about two feet deep. Ram the soil back around it, then brace it with an angled strut mounted on a brick or slab.

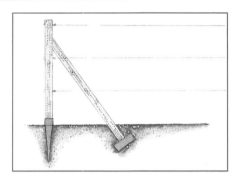

Instead of digging a hole, you can set the post into a metal post socket. This is hammered in and, by keeping the post out of the earth, avoids the need for pressure treatment.

PLANTING

You can choose between bare-rooted trees, for planting in fall or spring, and container-grown trees, for planting at any time. Avoid planting in frozen or very wet soil.

Prepare each planting position by digging out a spade-deep hole that is half as broad again as the area of the spread-out roots, or the same as the width of the root ball in the case of container-grown trees.

Fork some well-rotted manure, compost, or a prepared planting mixture into the bottom of the hole and mix some compost with the soil that you have just removed.

If a supporting stake is needed—for a bush or dwarf pyramid—hammer this in a little off-center. Shorten the long, thick roots and cut off any that are damaged or appear dead. Plant cordons with the stems leaning toward the north, if possible, so that they receive maximum light.

Check that the soil mark is level with the surrounding ground. Add or remove a little soil as necessary. Regardless of the soil mark, make sure that the bulge on the stem, where the upper and lower parts of the tree were grafted, is well above the surface.

Place some soil-compost mixture over the roots, and shake the stem up and down so that it settles in between the roots. Repeat the process until the hole is filled, then firm the soil with your foot. With a container-grown tree, simply firm the prepared soil mixture around the root ball.

Finally, secure the tree to the stake or the supporting wires.

POLLINATION

Some trees will bear fruit when fertilized by their own pollen. Peaches, apricots, and some plums come into this category and so can be grown singly. Others are wholly or partly self-sterile and must be cross-pollinated by another variety, which means that you have to grow at least two varieties to get a good crop. If they are planted in the same garden, they will be close enough for insects to pass between them.

An obvious condition for cross-pollination is that the flowers of the two varieties should be open at the same time.

PROTECTION

Damage by birds is a problem for all fruit tree growers. Winter and spring are the critical times, for it is the blossoms and the fruit buds that are most at risk.

You can grow restricted forms in a fruit cage, but this is hardly practical for a row of cordons planted as a screen. Spray-on bird repellent, applied frequently, is an alternative, or moving reflectors can be effective for a while. You may be able to net small trees.

TREE FRUITS, pages 58–64
THE FRUIT GARDEN, page 65
APPLES, pages 90–95

PRUNING

The initial training and subsequent pruning of fruit trees are essential to keep them in good shape and insure that they are productive all their lives. Particular pruning needs are explained in the descriptions of individual fruit. It helps, however, to be aware of the basic aims and principles.

The initial purpose of pruning, during the first few years, is to train the tree to a particular shape, to create the framework on which crops will later be borne. Winter pruning, which stimulates growth, is the usual method for bush trees. Summer pruning, which retards growth, forms part of the plan for restricted trees.

Once the framework is established, after about four years—and as the tree matures—the emphasis changes to maintaining a balance between creating new, non-fruit-bearing replacement shoots and encouraging the older growths to bear fruit. Overcrowding has to be remedied too, and it is essential to remove dead or badly placed branches.

Pruning cuts are made just above a growth bud (not the larger fruit bud) that faces in the appropriate direction. The bud will develop into a shoot. The more severely a branch is pruned, the stronger the resultant new growth will be. Strong growth is the aim during the early years of shaping the tree, since it creates nonfruit-bearing stems that form part of the tree's framework. Subsequently, lighter pruning will foster the production of fruit buds.

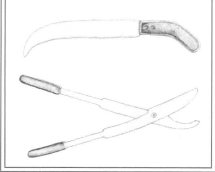

PRUNING TOOLS
A pruning saw is useful for cutting thick branches of fruit trees. Long-handled pruners (bottom) will cut medium-sized branches one inch or more thick.

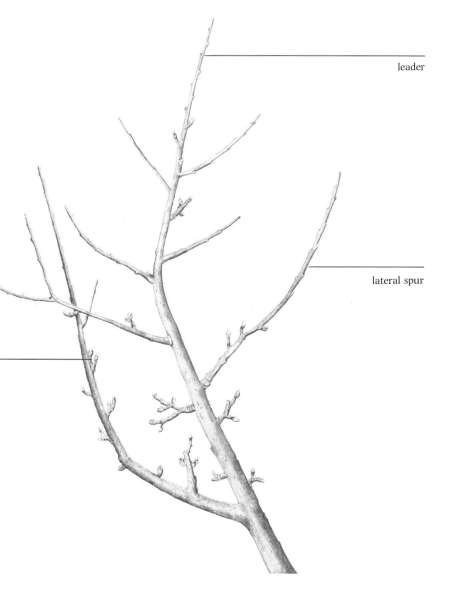

leader

lateral spur

Make a pruning cut, slanted as here, just above a bud pointing in the direction in which you wish a shoot to grow.

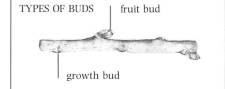

Spurs are growths with multiple fruit buds. Some trees, in contrast, carry their fruits on the tips of shoots.

TYPES OF BUDS | fruit bud

growth bud

When pruning, you must distinguish between fruit buds and growth buds. Fruit buds are plump and rounded; growth buds, which develop into shoots, are small and flat by comparison.

Apples (*Malus* sp.) are one of the most worthwhile of tree fruits to grow. They are consistent croppers, provided the variety and form chosen are right for the site, and provided the trees are carefully grown. They are also versatile trees, since they comprise an extensive range of eating and cooking varieties and lend themselves to a number of trained forms. There are hundreds of apple varieties available, and many will keep well if correctly stored.

ROOTSTOCKS

Rootstocks have a considerable influence on the vigor and size of apple trees, as explained on p.87. In addition to their varying dwarfing properties, they have different susceptibilities to pests and diseases, different soil and moisture requirements, and different degrees of hardiness. Therefore, it is important to choose a rootstock that is suitable to your particular area. Among the possibilities are:

M27 One of the most dwarfing rootstocks, this produces apple trees that are only four to six feet tall, so that they can even be grown in containers. The rootstock requires soil with good drainage and needs to be staked throughout its life; it is rather tender, but encourages early fruit-bearing.

M26 This has a less dwarfing effect than the M27 rootstock, growing to ten or twelve feet, but it is hardy and a good all-round choice for the average garden.

M9 This is a very dwarfing rootstock that will do well in a clay soil, although it too needs permanent staking. The average tree is about six or eight feet tall and slightly larger across. M9 is often interstemmed —placed between the rootstock and the scion—with MM106 to produce hardy, disease-resistant trees.

MM106 This semidwarfing tree is vigorous and reasonably hardy, and is resistant to woolly aphids, which are a serious pest of other varieties. Trees with this rootstock generally reach about fifteen feet.

Antonovka This is a standard-size rootstock that produces an extremely vigorous, hardy, and adaptable tree up to twenty-eight feet tall. It resists most pests and diseases, and can be interstemmed with more dwarfing rootstocks to produce excellent trees for smaller gardens.

APPLE FORMS

Most American gardeners grow apples as freestanding trees, usually on dwarf or semidwarf rootstocks. If you have a small garden, however, you might want to train your trees as cordons, espaliers, or dwarf pyramids.

Dwarf trees can appear rather deceptively named, since they have a spread (and planting distance) of from eight to twelve feet, depending on the rootstock. Even so, on M27 and M9 rootstocks they are a practical proposition for very small gardens. Obviously, the more dwarf they are, the easier they are to prune and to harvest, and they bear fruit relatively quickly; they crop less heavily than larger trees, but they are easier to protect against birds.

Semidwarfs, with a height and spread of fifteen feet, are large for the average-sized garden, but they make a striking spectacle in the spring. Remember that all apple trees need a companion for pollination (this could be a crabapple tree).

Cordons are thoroughly practical, offering the best means of planting several varieties in a restricted area. Allow three feet between rows. Plant with the stem at a forty-five-degree angle, and secure it to a stake tied to the horizontal wires.

Espaliers are elegant and surprisingly easy to prune. They make ideal trees flattened against a sunny wall or fence. Leave ten to fifteen feet between trees planted in a line against the same support.

Dwarf pyramids have a Christmas-tree shape, which explains their name. They are usually about seven feet high and are suitable for growing where space is somewhat restricted. Plant them four to six feet apart in the open.

FAMILY TREES

Grafting three or more varieties onto a single rootstock enables one tree to produce several different kinds of apple. The varieties are selected for their simultaneous flowering, so there is no need for a second tree for pollination. Such a tree is generally pruned to a freestanding form.

A number of nurseries offer family trees. They are an ingenious means of saving space, but careful pruning is needed to achieve a balance and even fruiting.

The extreme dwarfing effect of M27 makes it suitable only for the most vigorous varieties. Apples grown on this rootstock usually bear fruit at an early age.

Trees on M9 rootstock, though still very dwarf, are somewhat larger than on M27. Being less robust, dwarf trees need really good soil and plenty of attention.

M26, which has a less dwarfing effect, is a good all-round rootstock for apples grown in average soils. Growth is still sufficiently restricted for the majority of gardens.

Dwarf pyramids are a good compromise: they take less space than a bush form but need no supporting wires, as required by the trained forms of tree, such as cordons.

MAKING A START

Choose varieties of apple that are able to cross-pollinate one another (see p.95), and since the blossoms are vulnerable to frost, give preference to late-flowering kinds if you live in a cold climate.

Choose an open, sunny, but sheltered site if possible. The ideal soil is moist and slightly acid, but most soils are suitable, provided they drain well and do not contain too much lime. Shelter is important, since strong winds can damage the blossoms and also because pollinating insects fly in still conditions. If you live on the coast, or in an exposed situation, you may need to consider planting a windbreak (see p.96).

Prepare the site with the addition of well-rotted organic matter, then plant the trees as described on p.89. Plant in early spring or, if you live in the South, in the late fall. Make sure the union between rootstock and scion is at least two inches above the soil.

After planting—or during the following spring if planted in fall—rake in a dressing of fertilizer (preferably organic) over the root area, at a rate of three ounces per square yard. Spread a mulch of rotted manure or garden compost around the trees to discourage weeds and conserve moisture, but do not let the mulch touch their stems, since this could encourage them to put out roots at the union between scion and rootstock.

CARE OF THE CROP

Make certain that the soil does not dry out during the first season or two, while the root systems develop. Give each tree a thorough soaking in spring and repeat this a week or two later if necessary.

In subsequent years, apply sulfate of potash at one ounce per square yard during the winter, followed by a similar application of sulfate of ammonia during the spring. Every two or three years, apply super-phosphate in the spring at two ounces per square yard. Treat an area just a little bigger than the spread of the branches, which corresponds roughly to the root area of the apple tree.

Renew the mulch annually, after the spring fertilizer application, at least during the first few years of a tree's life.

Trees on dwarfing rootstocks may flower and fruit precociously, whereas those on vigorous rootstocks may take several years. Discourage fruiting during the first year by removing any flowers. Thereafter, allow an increasing amount of fruit to set as the tree becomes established.

THINNING THE FRUIT

Mature trees benefit from having their fruit thinned if the crop is heavy. As well as reducing the strain on the tree itself, this will increase the average size of the fruit.

Wait until after the so-called June drop, when a number of small apples are likely to fall. Then remove one or two apples from each overcrowded cluster, including the central "king fruit," which is generally deformed. Leave only the two best fruits.

If, despite thinning, there is a risk that branches will break, secure a stout pole to the tree's stem, with its top well above the upper branches. Tie nylon twine to any branches that are overloaded, and fasten the twine to the pole to take the weight.

PICKING AND STORING

An apple that is ready for picking will part easily from the tree, with its stalk still attached, when it is gently lifted and simultaneously twisted. This test applies also to late varieties that mature in storage for eating at a later date.

An earlier sign of ripening may be a change of color—the skin of dessert apples becomes brighter—or the sight of windfalls. Not all apples on a tree ripen together, so do not strip them all as soon as the first fruit is ready to be harvested.

Handle the apples with great care, for the slightest bruising impairs their keeping qualities. Store sound fruits of the keeping varieties in a dark, cool, but frost-free place where there is some humidity, such as a garage or porch.

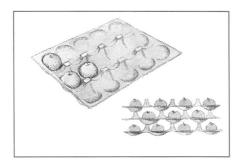

Depending on the variety, apples will keep for several months in a cool room. Ready-made papier-mâché trays are inexpensive, reusable, and allow easy sorting during storage. Wrapping is an advantage if humidity is low.

Thinning a heavy crop of apples reduces the strain on the tree and helps to insure larger, better-quality fruit. It is less likely to be needed on trained trees. On freestanding trees, leave about five inches between eating apples and half as much again between cooking fruit.

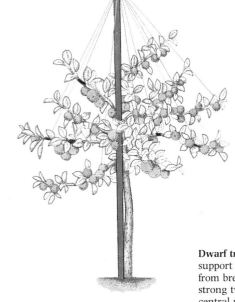

Dwarf trees, especially, may need support to prevent a heavy crop from breaking some branches. Tie strong twine to the top of a central pole during the weeks before picking.

The principles of pruning fruit trees are described on pages 88–89. The purpose of pruning is to create the framework and desired shape of the tree in the first few years, after which you must try to keep a balance between new growth and the production of fruit.

Depending on the form of apple tree you are growing, these aims are realized in different ways and at various times of the year. It is therefore important to follow carefully the pruning program for a particular form of apple tree.

You can use either clippers or loppers—long-handled pruners—for this formative pruning. A pruning saw is usually required only for a mature freestanding tree or for pruning a long-neglected apple tree that you have inherited.

PRUNING FREESTANDING TREES

Apple trees pruned to a central leader or trunk are commonplace (see Pruning Dwarf Pyramids, p.93, for method), but the open-center system advised here is often preferable, particularly if you want heavy crops in a limited space.

Two-year-old trees These will have several branches. The object during the first few years is to get these main branches, and the laterals that will grow from them, to form an open-centered, goblet-shaped tree, called a bush tree. Three or four branches are needed, so remove any others.

Since pruning stimulates growth, in the winter after planting a two-year-old tree, cut back each of the branches to just above an outward-facing bud. Shorten strong, vigorous branches by about half. Reduce weaker growths by two thirds to encourage stronger shoots to develop.

Do not prune container-grown trees planted during the growing season until the following winter.

Three-year-old trees Lateral shoots will now have grown from the main branches. Retain about four of these in all, to help fill in the branch structure, and choose those best placed to fill gaps between the original shoots.

Cut back each selected lateral and the leading shoots of the original branches. Reduce them by a third if they are vigorous and two thirds if they are weak. Prune the other laterals to about four buds from their base, to form future fruiting spurs.

Fourth year onward Some further formative pruning will be needed, but from now on the purpose and pattern of the operation change. While developing and maintaining the tree's shape and preventing overcrowding, you now want to encourage the formation of fruit buds.

The pruning of a mature tree takes one of

Prune a two-year-old bush tree with the aim of establishing a sturdy, open framework of branches. Reduce the stronger branches by half, the weaker ones by two thirds. Hard pruning is a means of encouraging stronger growth.

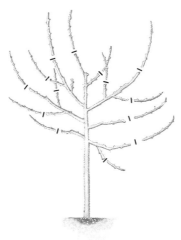

A three-year-old bush tree will have laterals growing from the branches that were pruned a year ago. Cut back both the main branches and laterals to buds that are well placed to extend the framework.

two different forms, depending on the variety of the apple. Some bear their fruit on two-year-old shoots and on spurs (short growths) growing from older wood, and others carry it mainly on the tips of shoots formed during the previous year. Some varieties combine both habits.

Spur-bearing bush trees Until the tree is fully grown, continue to cut back the leading tips of branches by about a quarter, or a little more if growth is weak. Trim or cut out any laterals (year-old shoots) growing too close to the branch leaders.

On older trees, remove or shorten any branches that are too crowded or that cross or rub against each other. Keep the center of the tree reasonably open.

To induce spur formation, prune to about six buds each of the laterals that will have formed at a lower level—that is, away from the branch leaders. The following year, spur-prune the sublaterals that will grow from these (in addition to fruit buds), or else remove them altogether. Space is the deciding factor.

Tip-bearing bush trees Apart from keeping the center open and removing crowded branches, as for spur-forming trees, you will need to do comparatively little pruning.

Cut back branch leaders by about a third, to a growth bud, even on mature trees, but leave all except the most vigorous laterals unpruned. Cut back by half any that are more than ten inches long.

Trees that bear some of their fruit on the tips of shoots and the rest on spurs are best treated as spur-bearers.

Protect the cut with a wound-sealing paint.

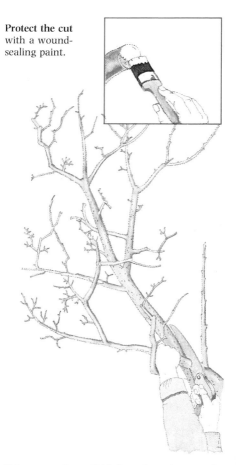

When removing a thick branch, make a small cut on the underside, then complete the job by sawing through from above. Protect the cut with a wound-sealing paint.

PRUNING AND TRAINING CORDONS

Only tip-bearing varieties need pruning after planting, by shortening the leader by about a quarter.

Mid- to late summer is pruning time, when laterals that have grown during the previous months are maturing. A typical mature shoot is at least nine inches long, with a woody and firm base. Cut back these laterals to just above the third leaf from the base, excluding the little group of leaves where lateral and main shoot meet. Reduce to a single leaf any mature side shoots that are growing from existing spurs, but again exclude the basal cluster. If secondary growth occurs after early pruning, cut this back to a basal bud in the fall.

When the main stem has grown to the top wire, you can lower the cordon to a more acute angle, if you want to extend its length. In winter, untie the stem from its stake, lower it by a few degrees each year, taking care not to damage it, then retie it to the stake. Lowering the angle checks the growth of an overvigorous cordon by slowing the movement of sap but at the same time encourages fruit production. Do not lower the stem to less than a thirty-five-degree angle from the horizontal.

Allow the tip to grow a little beyond the top wire each year, then cut it back in late spring to leave a thumbnail's length of year-old wood, terminating in a bud.

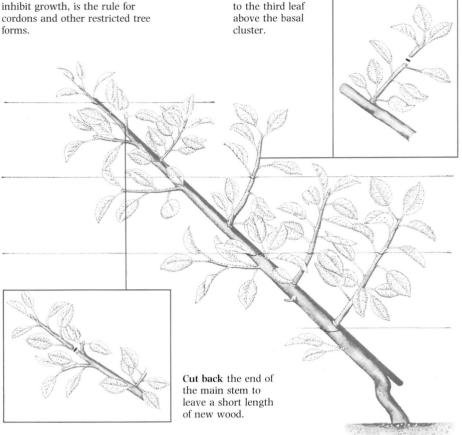

Summer pruning, which tends to inhibit growth, is the rule for cordons and other restricted tree forms.

Laterals are pruned to the third leaf above the basal cluster.

Cut back the end of the main stem to leave a short length of new wood.

PRUNING DWARF PYRAMIDS

Two-year-old trees After planting, cut back the previous year's growth of the central stem to about nine inches. To keep the leader straight, cut to a bud on the opposite side to where a similar cut was made a year before, as shown by the kink in the stem. Prune the branch leaders slightly shorter than this; cut to buds on their undersides.

Three-year-old trees During the winter, reduce the central stem in the same way as you did a year ago; again, cut to a bud on the opposite side. This alternate cutting prevents the stem from becoming lopsided. If you are starting with a three-year-old tree, the nursery will have followed the same pruning procedure.

Do not prune branch leaders at this stage. From now on, until the tree is fully grown, prune them during the second half of summer; wait until the darkness and firmness of the wood show that it is mature.

Summer pruning consists of cutting these branch leaders back to about five leaves, excluding the small cluster at the base, then reducing the length of the laterals. As with cordons, cut these back to three leaves above the basal cluster, or to a single leaf in the case of growths arising from existing side shoots. Wait until autumn before cutting back to a single bud any secondary growths induced by the earlier pruning.

Continue with this winter–summer pruning routine, shortening the central stem in winter and other growths in summer, until the tree has attained full height. This will be between six and twelve feet, depending on the rootstock.

At this stage, prune the central leader by half its length in late spring and at the same time reduce the length of any growths that are tending to crowd the central stem. In subsequent years, cut the leader's new growth back to a half-inch stub, also in late spring, to restrict the tree's size.

To prevent the main stem of a dwarf pyramid from becoming lopsided, winter-prune to a bud on the opposite side to the one chosen a year previously. Continue in this way until the tree is fully grown.

If you are a beginner at fruit growing, it is best to buy a container-grown tree. You then have only to master the simple technique of creating additional tiers. The added advantage of buying a tree that already has two or more tiers of branches, trained by the nurseryman, is earlier fruiting. Alternatively, you can buy a maiden (one-year-old) tree, without any tiers, which will be less expensive but slightly more difficult to train.

Container-grown espaliers Erect the wires against the wall after planting (see p.88), so that they correspond to the spacing between the existing tiers. At the same time, add a further wire or wires, the same distance apart, if you wish to extend the tree. Tie the horizontal branches to the wires with soft string.

If you are content with a low tree and satisfied with the existing number of tiers, wait until late spring before cutting the previous year's growth of the main stem—the part above the upper tier—to a half inch. Do the same in subsequent years.

However, since a taller tree takes no more ground space, most gardeners want to extend an espalier to at least four tiers. In this case, immediately after planting (or during the following winter in the case of a summer-planted tree), cut the main stem to a bud two inches above the next wire—that is, the third wire from the ground if you bought a two-tier espalier.

Fasten a vertical cane to the upper wires in line with the main stem; secure two others at 45°, forming a V with its base on the third wire, behind the top of the main stem.

Allow only three shoots to grow near the top of the stem during the following spring. The uppermost will form a continuation of the main stem; two others, on opposite sides of the stem and in line with the wires, will form the next tier of horizontal growths. Rub off any other buds with your thumb to leave a clean stem.

As the shoots grow, keep the top one tied to the vertical cane, and tie the others to the angled canes. If the shoots at the sides develop unevenly, raise the weaker one to a less acute angle for a while. In the autumn, lower both side canes closer to the horizontal wire. A year later, remove the canes altogether and tie the branches to the wires with soft string.

Repeat this procedure each year until the desired number of tiers is established. When you have formed the top tier, cut back the main stem to two side buds, leaving no third, upper bud.

If growth is sufficiently vigorous, leave the ends of the horizontal branches unpruned until they are long enough. If it is not, provide a boost by cutting back the previous year's growth by about a quarter.

This formative pruning and training is carried out in winter, but late spring is the time to cut the new growth on the main stem and branches back to a half inch, once they are long enough. In addition, summer pruning is needed to encourage fruiting growth on the branches. The method is exactly the same as the method described for cordons on p.93.

Maiden espaliers The method of creating the first tier on a one-year-old tree is the same as for forming additional tiers on a partly trained tree. Set up the wires, with the lowest about fifteen inches above the ground, then prune the newly planted tree to a bud about two inches above this lowest supporting wire.

Fasten a vertical cane and two angled canes as described; secure the shoots to them as they develop, from spring onward.

PESTS AND DISEASES

Among several troublesome pests are apple maggots, plum curculios, green fruit-worms, codling moths, tarnished plant bugs, aphids, red spider mites, tent caterpillars, and woolly aphids.

Potential diseases and disorders include fireblight, apple scab, apple-cedar rust, canker, and powdery mildew.

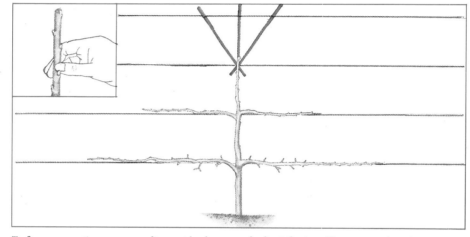

To form a new tier on an espalier, cut back the main stem to a bud two inches above the next wire. Rub off all but three well-placed buds at the top. Tie canes to the wires as supports for the shoots that will develop.

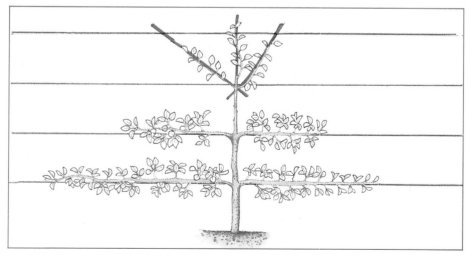

Shoots have grown from the three buds that were left, but one (on the right) is a little less robust than the other. To give it a boost, the cane and shoot have been raised nearer the vertical. Lowering has the opposite effect.

RECOMMENDED VARIETIES

Red varieties

'Red Delicious' The most popular eating apple: crisp, fine-grained, and sweet. The fruit is slightly elongated, with indistinct knobs on the blossom end.

'Starkrimson' An improved 'Red Delicious' type that is a good keeper. Trees are semi-dwarf and winter hardy.

'Stayman Winesap' A small, bright red apple with a pungent aroma and a fine-grained flesh. Good for both eating fresh and cooking.

'Cortland' This tart midseason fruit is another favorite for both eating fresh and for cooking.

'McIntosh' Yet another popular all-purpose apple, this variety produces fruit heavily in midseason.

'Wealthy' This variety's yellow skin ripens to scarlet with red stripes. A heavy-bearing, winter-hardy apple, 'Wealthy' is favored in the Midwest.

'Carefree Liberty' A good keeper that is resistant to scab, fireblight, and apple-cedar rust. Juicy.

'Stark's Jumbo' These red apples weigh as much as two and a half pounds each, but are produced by a dwarf tree. In flavor they resemble 'Winesap.'

'Red Rome' A well-known cooking apple that ripens late in the season.

'Arkansas Black' The dark-red skin and tart flavor of this late-ripening variety make it popular in the South.

'Red June' An early-ripening apple suitable for cooking and making cider. Fruit is very tart in flavor.

'Red Duchess' Another early apple with a tangy flavor. Trees are winter hardy, but fruit should be used right away.

'Beacon' An early to midseason apple that is resistant to scab and fireblight. A good variety for the North.

'Freedom' A very heavy-bearing variety with juicy flesh, good for cooking as well as eating. Trees are highly resistant to most apple pests and diseases.

'Sweet Sixteen' This is another resistant variety. The apples are quite sweet and keep very well.

'Regent' A good all-purpose apple for gardeners in Zones 3–5, as it is cold hardy.

'Northern Spy' A late-blooming and late-bearing variety that has a crisp, juicy texture and keeps well.

'Baldwin' This large, round red apple is a classic. It keeps well, cooks well, and tastes delicious fresh. Midseason.

'Snow Apple' An "antique" variety that ripens early. The fruit is medium to large and has pure white flesh.

'Cox's Orange Pippin' A classic English apple with superb flavor.

Green varieties

'Granny Smith' The most popular and best known of the green apples. The fruit is crisp and tart and keeps well.

'Summer Granny' is an early, winter-hardy version of this crisp, tangy fruit.

'Newton Pippin' A large green apple that turns yellowish when mature. The cream-colored flesh is firm and juicy.

'Northwest Greening' This variety bears very large apples with a yellow cast to their pale skin. Crisp and mild, the fruit keeps exceptionally well.

'Anna' is a heat- and humidity-resistant variety somewhat like 'Golden Delicious' in taste and texture. The early-ripening fruit has green skin with a red blush.

'Gordon' A sweet-smelling apple with a bright red blush. Trees bear heavily and do well in mild winters.

'Bramley's Seedling' produces large, green-yellow apples that hold shape well in cooking. Very vigorous, so a dwarfing rootstock is needed. Keeps about four months.

Yellow and variegated varieties

'Golden Delicious' A popular, slightly tart apple that is ideal for eating fresh. Fruit is borne late but in quantity.

'Ein Sheimer' An early 'Golden Delicious' type that is heat resistant.

'Honeygold' This 'Golden Delicious' type bears late, keeps well, and is winter hardy.

'Yellow Transparent' This variety is a favorite in the West. Medium-sized apples have clear yellow-white skin and firm flesh.

'Dorsett Golden' is a good choice in the South, as it tolerates hot summers.

'Beverly Hills' Another variety suitable for mild climates. Crisp and juicy.

'Golden Russet' A very fine old variety that ripens late. The apples have golden skin with a bronze blush and are good both fresh and dried.

'Jonagold' Large fruits have red-streaked, bright yellow skin. The tree is vigorous and productive but susceptible to mildew. Not a very satisfactory pollinator.

'Lodi' is a popular apple in the West. Its fruit is large and round; trees are heavy-bearing, hardy, and vigorous.

'Winter Banana' A heavy-cropping old variety good in Zones 5–10. Fruit is aromatic and tangy.

'Roxbury Russet' This old-fashioned apple makes wonderful cider and keeps exceptionally well. A good all-purpose variety.

'Lady' Also known as the Christmas apple. Small fruit smells sweet and has firm, juicy flesh; skin is red and green.

Crabapples

Crabapples can be planted near other apple trees for cross-pollination. The trees are beautiful in the spring, and the fruit makes wonderful jellies and preserves.

'Chestnut' An eating crabapple. The fruit is relatively large, bronze-red, and juicy.

'Dolgo' A hardy variety that is especially good for jelly making.

'Whitney' This early-ripening variety has yellow fruit with red stripes, used for pickling and spicing.

'Hyslop' A good crabapple for mild climates. Medium-sized yellow apples have tart flesh.

Pears (*Pyrus communis*) are a rewarding crop to grow. Unlike some commercially grown pears, which are tough-skinned to withstand bruising during travel, the best of garden-grown fruits virtually melt in the mouth. Provided they are planted in a suitable site, pears are not especially difficult to grow.

Pears come into flower earlier than apples, so spring frosts are a hazard. Besides avoiding a frost pocket, you should thus choose a sheltered spot in the garden if possible. There are fewer pollinating insects around when the flowers of pear trees are open, and you want to insure that they will fly, even in windy weather. You may have to plant a hedge as a windbreak.

Pears also benefit from warmth. Although they are not an obvious choice for exposed or northern gardens, you can choose a hardy rootstock or grow them in cordons against a wall. Pears give the best results on well-manured, moisture-holding soil. Shallow soils are unsuitable.

Pears can be grown in any of the forms described for apples. Supports, training, and pruning are essentially the same. Yields from pear trees are lower than from apples grown in the same way, as a rule.

ROOTSTOCKS

Pears are very vigorous trees, often reaching forty feet in height, so a dwarfing rootstock is essential for most home-grown pears. The usual rootstock is quince, which generally produces a tree that will grow to twelve or fifteen feet and that will begin to bear fruit in its fourth or fifth year.

Unfortunately, there are several drawbacks to the quince rootstock: it is rather weak, susceptible to fireblight, and not reliably hardy north of Zone 5. To counteract these problems, nurserymen sometimes interstem a quince rootstock with a hardier pear variety, such as 'Old Home.' This will produce a semidwarf tree capable of withstanding cold and blight.

For northern growers, the only option is to buy standard pears grafted onto a smaller pear rootstock; the most common choice is 'Bartlett,' although the Siberian pear is also sometimes used. These trees will not bear until their sixth year or so.

POLLINATION

As with apples, most pears need another variety nearby to insure cross-pollination. The varieties must flower at the same time. If your neighbor has a pear, you might get away with planting only one, but you must first identify the variety and flowering group of both trees.

MAKING A START

Pears thrive in moist, organically rich soil, so dig in plenty of manure or compost a few weeks before planting. Immediately before planting, rake in some general fertilizer at two ounces per square yard.

Plant bare-rooted trees in early spring, and container-grown trees at any time soil and weather conditions allow. Follow the method of planting and supporting outlined on pp.88–89. Make sure the union between rootstock and scion is above soil level; if your trees are interstemmed, plant the lower graft three or four inches deep.

Planting distances are as follows:
Standard trees 20–25 feet
Semidwarfs 15–20 feet
Dwarfs 12–15 feet
Cordons 2½–3 feet
Dwarf pyramids 4–5 feet
Espaliers 10–15 feet

Wire the plastic windbreak to strong wooden posts; wrap it around the end supports before doing so.

A plastic windbreak three feet high is adequate for sheltering a living windbreak until it becomes established. Plant the hedge two to three feet from it on the leeward side. Fast-growing plants, such as the *X Cupressocyparis leylandii*, should be set four feet apart; they will reach six feet in two years.

A six-foot hedge will give shelter for a hundred feet on the leeward side; its effectiveness diminishes as the distance increases. Plant fruit trees at least eight feet away from the windbreak; otherwise the hedge will compete for nourishment and moisture.

Shelter pear trees from strong winds if the garden is very exposed. A living screen, protected by a plastic windbreak while it becomes established, is better than a wall or fence. A solid barrier would result in air turbulence.

CARE OF THE CROP

Feed the trees annually, in winter and spring, as for apples (see p.91). A moisture-retaining mulch is particularly valuable for pears, since they do not perform well in dry soil. Renew this each spring after applying the fertilizer.

Water the root area thoroughly during a dry spring or summer; pears are less able than apples to withstand drought. Repeat the watering after a week if there is still no rain. It is essential to soak the soil, not merely to wet the surface; allow about four gallons per square yard.

Support any overladen branches with props as the fruit develops, or remove developing fruit from weak branches.

HARVESTING

Gather early varieties while they are still firm, before they ripen. Their texture will suffer if they are left longer. Cut through the stalks if they do not part easily from the tree. Leave midseason and late varieties until the pears are easy to remove by lifting and gently twisting.

Store pears in slatted trays. An unused room in the house is suitable, although pears keep longer if they are refrigerated. Handle the fruit carefully, since it bruises easily. Any of the eating varieties of pear can be cooked, provided they are still firm and not fully ripe.

PRUNING

Follow the same pruning procedures as for apples (see pp.92–94), although established bush pears will put up with somewhat heavier pruning when necessary.

Pears usually fruit on spurs growing from wood that is at least two years old. Shorten the new growth of leaders by about a third and cut back laterals to three or four buds. Shorten or remove spur systems that become crowded or overgrown. Also, cut back any main branches that cross each other or crowd the center of the tree.

Summer pruning of trained forms of pear tree is the same as for apples, except that it can be done a week or so earlier, when the summer growth matures.

Because fireblight is a serious problem with pears in most parts of the United States, it is important to prune out diseased branches as soon as you find them. Cut them off six inches beyond the infection.

PESTS AND DISEASES

Among potentially troublesome pests are aphids, codling moths, pear psylla, apple maggots, cherry fruit flies, plum curculios, and mites.

Ailments that affect pears include fireblight, fungus diseases, and pear decline.

RECOMMENDED VARIETIES

'Bartlett' The most familiar commercial pear, also suitable for home growing. Can be eaten fresh, cooked, or canned.

'Moonglow' Often called 'Red Bartlett,' this soft-fleshed fruit has yellow skin with a deep red blush. Resistant to fireblight.

'Lincoln' A winter-hardy variety with medium to large golden fruit.

'Seckel' A very sweet pear that ripens late. Fruit is small; trees are winter hardy and blight resistant.

'Tyson' Known as 'Summer Seckel,' this sweet pear matures early.

'Stark Honeysweet' A firm-fleshed, smallish variety that is good for canning or eating fresh. Blight resistant.

'Comice' The pear found in winter gift boxes. Fruit is very large, golden, and juicy, with a wonderful flavor. Does best in the Pacific Northwest.

'Duchess' A large, late-maturing variety that keeps well when refrigerated.

'Pineapple' A very large pear with a unique pineapple flavor. Well adapted to conditions in the Deep South.

'Baldwin' Another good choice for the South. Pears are medium to large and semi-hard; trees are disease resistant.

'Kieffer' This variety is very resistant to fireblight and is best used for canning or making pear syrup.

'Maxine' is a fairly hardy pear with very large golden fruit that ripens early.

'California' A pleasant-smelling variety with white, juicy flesh.

'Bosc' The best known of the long-necked pears; good for eating or canning.

'Beurre d'Anjou' A good keeper. Large fruit has green skin with a yellow blush.

'Fan Stil' has bell-shaped fruit that is crisp and juicy. Blight resistant.

'Shinseiki' This oriental variety is apple-shaped, sweet, and crisp, and keeps well.

'Twentieth Century' Another oriental type. Trees are highly ornamental.

'Monterrey' A Mexican pear with smooth, sweet, grainless fruit.

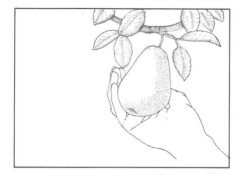

Pears must be picked before they are fully ripe; otherwise their texture will suffer. A lightening of skin color is a good indication of readiness. The stalks of early varieties may have to be cut, but later kinds should part easily when gently twisted.

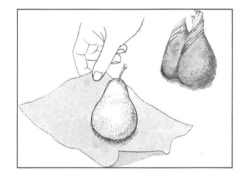

Though wrapping pears in paper may help to check the spread of rot, it makes it more difficult to tell when fruit is ripening. Frequent inspection is vital, as the fruit stays in top condition only briefly. Many growers prefer not to wrap.

Lay the pears in slatted trays, either singly or in tiers, and leave spaces between them. For the final stages of ripening, place the fruit in a warm room for a day or two. Handle it with the greatest care to avoid bruising.

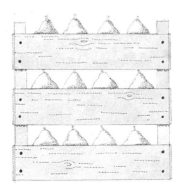

Quince (*Cydonia oblonga*) is a long-lived tree of ancient origins, and merits a place in the garden for its decorative qualities as well as for its fruit. It bears white or light pink blooms in spring, has bright autumn tints, and presents a winter spectacle of bent and twisted branches. The golden yellow, apple- or pear-shaped fruit ripens in the fall. It is too astringent to be eaten raw but can be made into flavorful jams or jellies, or added to apple pies to give them a special zest.

Quinces grow steadily, and once established they require little attention. They are slow to fruit, however, taking a minimum of four years, and possibly as long as eight. They eventually reach a height of twelve to fifteen feet, with a similar spread, depending on whether they are grown as semidwarfs or dwarfs.

Although the quince is not an ideal tree for cold northern states, it might be worth trying in a particularly favorable spot in the garden, such as a sunny corner sheltered by two walls. The danger in cold zones is that the fruit may not be fully ripened by the time of the first autumn frost.

Quinces will grow in most soils but do best in those that hold moisture during dry spells. Avoid poorly drained ground, however. Quinces are self-fertile, so a single tree will fruit satisfactorily on its own.

MAKING A START

Plant quince in the early spring if the tree is bare-rooted, or at any time if it was raised in a container (see p.88 for instructions on planting). Support is needed during the formative years, so drive in a firm stake before planting, with its top level with the lowest branches, and tie the plant's strongest branches to it.

Make sure that the soil does not dry out during the first years, while the tree becomes established; a deep mulch of well-rotted manure or compost is worthwhile. Apply a general fertilizer each spring at three ounces per square yard.

HARVESTING

Quinces should be left on the tree as long as possible to develop their characteristic flavor. But even if the fruits are still unripe, you

must gather them before the first autumn frost. They will ripen indoors over a period of several weeks; they can sometimes last until Christmas, if stored in a cool place unaffected by frost. Keep them away from other fruit, the flavor of which can be adversely affected by the distinctive aroma of quinces.

PRUNING

Initially, you can help the formation of a branch framework by pruning branch leaders during the winter. For the first year or two, cut back new growth by a half, pruning to an outward-facing bud, to create a goblet-shaped tree with an open center. Reduce the amount of pruning during the next two years, and then stop pruning the quince altogether.

Prune mature quince trees only when branches appear to be diseased or dead, or if they are badly placed.

PESTS AND DISEASES

A number of pests may attack the leaves and fruits of quinces. The principal ones are aphids, codling moths, oriental fruit moths, and mites.

Brown rot and mildew are among the possible diseases.

RECOMMENDED VARIETIES

'Cooke's Jumbo' Very large, pear-shaped fruit has yellow-green skin and white flesh.
'Pineapple' Another large variety. The fruit is smooth and golden, with a flavor reminiscent of pineapple.
'Smyrna' Large, oblong, lemon-yellow fruit. Very fragrant.
'Champion' A winter-hardy variety with medium-sized yellow fruit.

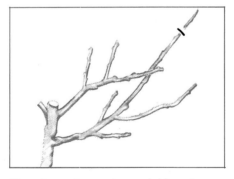

The only regular pruning needed by quince trees is leader tipping during the early years. This will assist the growth of strong branches. Thereafter, occasionally remove dead, diseased, or badly placed branches in winter.

The mulberry (*Morus* sp.) is a large tree originally grown for its leaves, which were used to feed silkworms. The white, pink, or purple berries, similar in appearance to loganberries, ripen in late summer. They have a distinctive flavor and can be made into jams and wines as well as eaten fresh. Birds are fond of them, and will eat them instead of cherries if they ripen first.

The mulberry is slow to fruit (eight years at the earliest), and is therefore suitable only for those who have space to spare in their gardens and who plan to stay in their homes for some time. Its eventual height may be thirty feet or more, with an almost equally large spread.

Mulberries are unsuitable for very cold areas and will not grow north of Zone 4, but they do well in sunny, fairly sheltered gardens. The white mulberry, *Morus alba*, is most commonly available; varieties include the Russian mulberry, which is fairly hardy, and the weeping mulberry.

Mulberries are self-fertile, so a companion is unnecessary. Start with a young tree with the beginnings of a branch framework.

PLANTING AND PRUNING

Choose a well-drained spot and dig in plenty of organic matter some weeks before planting. Keep the tree staked for a few years until it is well established. Make sure that the soil does not dry out for a year or two while the root system develops. The roots are brittle, so take care not to damage them when planting, and do not dig around them. Mulch with well-rotted manure.

During winter in the first few years, cut back to four or five buds any strong laterals longer than twelve inches that are not required as framework branches. Pruning thereafter consists of removing dead wood or misplaced branches. The fewer cuts made, the better, since mulberries tend to "bleed" when cut. Protect the cuts with a wound sealant.

Gather the fruit when ripe by shaking the branches over a large sheet of plastic laid on the ground.

PESTS AND DISEASES

Mulberry whiteflies may prove a problem. Bacterial blight is a possible disease.

Its gnarled trunk and heart-shaped leaves make the mulberry an interesting feature for a large lawn.

Cultivated elderberries are more widely grown in North America, where *Sambucus canadensis*, or American elder, is the favored species, than in Europe. The European elder, *Sambucus nigra*, grows wild throughout Europe, the U.S.A., and Canada. *S. canadensis* is less vigorous than other species: it can be pruned to form a large bush that grows about eight feet high.

In late summer and fall, both species bear numerous clusters of small black berries, which are used for cooking and wine making; elderflowers also make good wine.

Elderberries are ornamental, extremely hardy, and will grow in most soils and positions. A fair amount of sunshine does assist fruit production and ripening, however.

MAKING A START

Where named varieties are available, it is best to grow two different kinds to assist pollination and improve flavor.

Plant container-grown bushes at any time when the soil and weather are suitable. Plant a bare-rooted bush in early spring, to the same depth as it was in the nursery. Prepare the site by mixing well-rotted compost or manure, or a prepared planting mixture, with the soil removed from the hole (see p.88). Allow eight feet between elderberry bushes.

PRUNING AND FEEDING

After planting, prune each healthy shoot back to an outward-facing bud. Remove poor shoots altogether, and cut back any unwanted suckers to ground level.

From the next winter onward, prune to maintain a sturdy, open framework of branches. Cut about a quarter of the old wood back to ground level on a regular basis to promote new shoots, and cut out any dead branches at the same time.

Feed each spring with a general fertilizer at two ounces per square yard. Mulch the area with well-rotted manure or compost in spring if the weather is dry.

HARVESTING

Pick the fruit when it is dark in color and has a slight bloom. Use or preserve the berries as soon as possible; they should, however, keep in a cool place for up to two weeks.

PESTS AND DISEASES

The elder borer is the only likely problem.

PEARS AND OTHER TREE FRUITS, pages 60–61
GROWING TREE FRUITS, pages 87–89

PESTS AND DISEASES, pages 108–111
STORING FRUITS, pages 226–227

FREEZING FRUITS, pages 234–235

The fig (*Ficus carica*) is a handsome tree and well worth including in the food garden, provided you can give it a sunny position, protect it in winter, and induce it to crop well. It will develop fruit without fertilization, so a single tree can be grown. The fruit is sweet and aromatic and can be eaten fresh or dried. The skin color varies from green to deep purple, depending on the variety, and the skin is edible. The fleshy inside contains masses of tiny edible pips.

Figs are semitropical plants, and fruit best in warm climates; they need warmth to ripen the fruit and protection from heavy freezes. However, they can be grown as far north as Zone 6, if they are placed in the sunniest position the garden can offer and are protected in winter. Further north they can be grown in containers or in a heated greenhouse, although they can be rampant growers and need a lot of space.

The best way to grow a fig is by training it as a fan against a sunny south- or southwest-facing wall. An alternative, particularly in more northern zones, is to grow it as a freestanding bush in the protection of a corner of your house or garage. If you want to plant your fig in a container, such as a large pot or tub, you can place it on a patio or deck for the summer and move it indoors when frost threatens. Take special care to see that a pot-grown fig never dries out.

Wherever you decide to plant, keep in mind that any frost at all can damage both the young shoots and the fruit buds of figs. If the tree is sufficiently protected, it will crop prolifically and grow vigorously; in fact, some old trees in the South and Southwest have reached twenty feet in height and about thirty feet in girth.

In tropical climates, figs will yield up to three crops a season, but one or two are more usual in most of the United States. One crop, the result of fruit buds formed during the previous season, ripens in mid- to late summer. The second crop grows on the current year's wood and often does not have time to ripen before winter.

MAKING A START

Buy a two-year-old tree—if possible, one that has been partly trained. Prepare the site by digging a hole or trench about two feet deep and adding lime, compost, or bonemeal to the soil. If you use a container, be sure to provide good drainage.

Plant the fig in spring, about six inches from the wall and approximately four inches deeper than it was in the nursery. Spread the roots out over the planting hole, then cover with soil and firm the ground with your foot. Be sure that the soil or compost does not dry out.

Fasten the horizontal wires for a fan-trained tree at six-inch intervals, with the lowest eighteen inches above the ground. Allow for a twelve-foot span.

To restrict the roots, which can help a fig to crop well, make a concrete- or brick-lined planting hole. Leave the base uncovered.

Place a deep layer of rubble or stones in the bottom of the hole, up to a depth of about one foot. Fill the remainder with soil, with some mortar rubble added to it.

CARE OF THE CROP

Spread a mulch over and beyond the root area of the fig, and renew this each year in early winter. Water frequently during dry spells. Beware of nematodes and mites.

Apart from the mulch, do not feed the tree for the first two or three years. After this interval, rake in a handful of bonemeal each spring, followed by an application of a high-potash liquid fertilizer as the fruit swells. Add lime if necessary every two or three years. Do not fertilize a mature fig, or water it heavily, in late summer, since this will force it to produce new growth which will be vulnerable to frost damage.

Replace the top layer of the soil for pot-grown figs a year after planting. A year later, repot the tree in fresh potting soil; tease away a proportion of the old soil before repotting it. Repeat this replacing-repotting pattern in later years.

HARVESTING

During the second half of summer, hang netting over the tree to protect the ripening fruit from birds. The fruit is ripe and ready to pick when it becomes soft to the touch and hangs downward from its stalk. The skin may start to split. Eat or preserve the fruit immediately.

WINTER PROTECTION

How much winter protection you provide for your fig depends largely on where you live. In Zones 8 to 10, where figs are grown commercially, a thick mulch may be enough to protect the roots; the delicate shoots and fruit buds should withstand occasional temperatures in the 15° to 20°F range. In Zones 6 and 7, however, you will need to do more.

To protect freestanding bushes or trees, it is a good idea to tie the branches loosely and cover them with straw or leaves and burlap. If they are securely wrapped in this way in late fall, they should produce well the next year, provided you do not remove the covering too early in the spring. A hard spring frost will quickly kill the vulnerable fruit buds that will bear the late-summer crop of figs.

You can protect fan-trained figs by lowering the branches to the ground and covering them with a thick mulch of straw and/or soil. Alternatively, dig around the plant's root ball and then turn the entire bush to the ground; cover it with straw or soil and burlap and leave the mulch in place until there is no danger of a hard frost.

Bring container-grown figs indoors as soon as frost threatens. They will do well in a garage or shed as well as in a greenhouse, as long as the winter weather is not too severe and they receive enough light.

PRUNING AND TRAINING

In order to establish a framework of branches, prune bush and container-grown figs in the same way as bush apples (see p.92) during their first three years. By then they will be approaching the fruiting stage of development.

For a fan-trained tree, fasten canes to the wires at a 45° angle. Train the first branches, which may already have been started in the nursery, onto these canes. Further canes will be needed in due course for the secondary branches that develop.

If the tree you have planted is two years old, cut back both branches in spring to a bud about a foot and a half from their base. During the summer allow four shoots to develop on each branch—two on the upper side, one on the underside, and one at the end. Tie these to the wires or to additional canes with soft string. Remove all other growths by rubbing them off.

The following year, in early spring, prune each shoot to a bud that will continue the direction of growth; leave two feet of the previous year's wood. Summer-prune again to provide more shoots for adding to the fan structure. Continue, if necessary, during the following year until the whole space is occupied. Expect a fan-trained fig to take about three to four years to cover the wall.

Once bush trees and fans have made their framework, trim all young growths back to five leaves in early summer—no later—to promote fruiting growth for the following year. Keep shoots tied to the wires during the summer. Do not overcrowd the framework, since both the new growth and the figs themselves need plenty of sunlight.

In late spring, remove any diseased branches or any damaged by frost. Also cut off outward-pointing shoots and those growing toward the wall.

During late fall, remove any partly grown fruits that are too small to develop and ripen before the first frost. This is the second crop; if the growing season has not been long or hot enough, the figs will still be small and green by autumn.

Take care not to disturb the embryo fruits near the tips of the shoots. The fruits for the first harvest develop at the apex of these shoots, and remain throughout the winter as pea-sized buds.

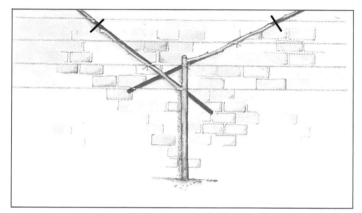

Secure two canes to the wires at fairly flat angles as supports for the two young shoots. Cut each of these back to a bud about a foot and a half from the main stem, then tie the remainder of each stem to a cane.

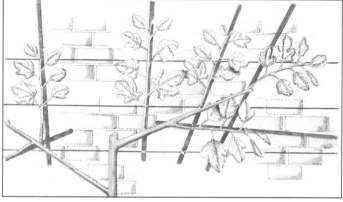

Allow just four shoots to develop on each of the two branches during the summer—one at the end, to form an extension, two on top, and one on the underside. Fix canes to the wires for support and tie the shoots to these. Rub off other buds.

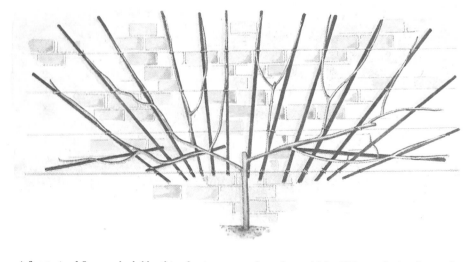

A fan-trained fig may look like this after two or three years. Note the even spacing of the branches, which still have plenty of scope for growth along the canes.

PESTS AND DISEASES

Nematodes can be a real problem in the Gulf states and other places where the soil is light. Scale and mites are other possible pests, and rust, mildew, and dieback can affect figs.

RECOMMENDED VARIETIES

'**Black Mission**' Medium to large pear-shaped figs with strawberry-colored flesh.
'**Celeste**' A very sweet variety that has purplish-brown skin and white flesh.
'**Brown Turkey**' Fruit is medium to large and bell shaped; flesh is pale red.
'**Texas Everbearing**' A good variety for those with short seasons. Medium-sized fruit.
'**Conadria**' A large, light-green fig with white flesh. Heat resistant.
'**White Kadota**' A good variety for drying.

MULCHING, page 43
PEARS AND OTHER TREE FRUITS, pages 60–61

GROWING TREE FRUITS, pages 87–89

Plums grow in a wide range of colors, shapes, and sizes and are popular around the world. In North America, they generally fall into three categories: European plums (*Prunus domestica*), Japanese plums, and native or bush plums. Hybrids and wild beach plums are also available.

European plums, including such familiar varieties as damsons and greengages, are usually self-fruitful and prolific. They will grow wherever temperatures are not too extreme, although some varieties need the protection of a south-facing wall to do well. The fruit, which is often purple, stays on the tree longer than that of Japanese plums, and it keeps better after harvesting.

Most red or reddish plums are Japanese types, which often require cross-pollination (though not with European varieties). Japanese plums do not tolerate cold well but will thrive where summers are hot, so they are a good choice in Zones 5–9.

American plums, in contrast, are extremely winter hardy, and some hybrid varieties are grown successfully in the northern Great Plains. These disease-resistant plums are usually red or yellow.

All three kinds of plums can be grown as a bush or a dwarf pyramid, and European plums can be fan-trained against a wall. Wall-trained trees are easier to protect from birds and spring frosts. Plums are not suited to the other restricted forms, however.

Most plums ripen between midsummer and early fall, but some ripen later. A fan-trained plum should yield up to twenty-five pounds of fruit in a good year; a dwarf pyramid will produce perhaps twice this amount. All plums can be canned, made into jam, or used for cooking, but some varieties are too tart for eating fresh.

ROOTSTOCKS
Standard plum trees are often grafted onto peach rootstocks, which increase yield; the trees are vigorous but highly susceptible to root-knot nematodes.

Plum rootstocks, such as 'Myrobalan' cherry plum, have a slight dwarfing effect and are far hardier. One popular rootstock is 'St. Julien,' a damson plum that produces cold-hardy, disease-resistant trees with a fifteen-foot spread.

Fully dwarfed trees are usually propagated on a sand or Nanking cherry rootstock. The resulting bush can be as small as four feet tall and is ideal for fan training.

MAKING A START
Plums require a deep, moisture-retentive soil and a sheltered, frost-free site if possible, since they flower early. Clear the ground of perennial weeds before planting.

Plant bare-rooted trees in early spring, the earlier the better. Container-grown trees may be planted at any time of year, if soil and weather conditions are favorable (see pp.88–89).

Space bush trees and dwarf pyramids to suit the rootstock, from ten to twenty-five feet apart. Allow about ten or twelve feet between fans if you are setting more than one against a wall.

Plant a fan-trained tree nine inches away from the wall. Fasten wires to the wall at six-inch intervals, with the lowest a foot and a half above the ground. Support bush trees and pyramids by inserting a stake before planting (see pp.88–89).

CARE OF THE CROP
Mulch the tree after planting and insure that the soil does not dry out during the first season or two. Take care not to disturb the roots when weeding, or the tree will throw up suckers. If suckers do appear, pull them up rather than cut them off.

Except on the poorest soil, feeding is unnecessary until the tree has started to bear fruit. Thereafter, apply a late-winter dressing of sulfate of potash at a half ounce per square yard, followed by a similar amount of sulfate of ammonia in the spring. Supply a spring dressing of superphosphate at two ounces per square yard every two or three years.

If you prefer, apply a general fertilizer at two ounces per square yard. This should keep the tree growing well and cropping satisfactorily.

Cover wall-trained trees overnight if frost is expected while they are flowering. Fine-mesh plastic sheeting, sold for greenhouse shading, can be used as a roller blind if you support it just clear of the tree's branches on wire runners.

PRUNING AND TRAINING
Prune young plums during the spring and mature plums during the summer. Late winter, which is the normal season for pruning many other fruits, brings a greater risk of disease. Japanese plums grow especially vigorously, so they will need more attention than European or native varieties.
Bush trees Leave newly planted two- and three-year-old trees unpruned for a year—that is, until the second spring after they are planted. Then, if you bought the tree as a two-year-old, choose three or four of the best-placed shoots to form the main branches, and cut each back by half to an outward-facing bud. Remove any others.

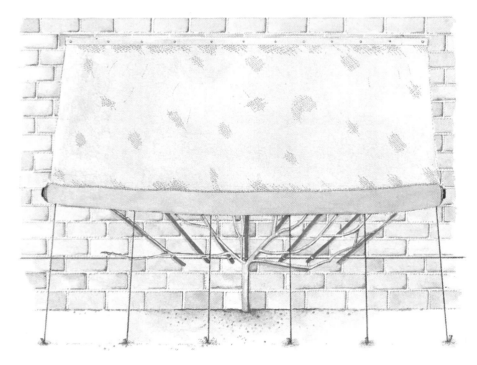

Protect a wall-trained tree from frost by means of a roll-down blind made from fine-mesh greenhouse shading. Support it on canes or wire runners. A similar device made of netting will keep birds off ripening fruit.

The following year—or, if you buy a three-year-old, in the first spring after planting—cut back branch leaders by a third of the previous year's growth. This will include those that have grown as laterals from the original shoots. From then on, prune only to remove or shorten misplaced or diseased branches.

Dwarf pyramids During the spring after planting, prune the previous year's growth on the main stem by two thirds. Cut to a bud on the side opposite to the one chosen last year, in order to keep the stem in balance.

Each summer, shorten the current year's growth on branch leaders to eight inches and side shoots to six inches. Once the tree has reached the required height, cut the main leader back almost to its base. Do this in spring and repeat each year.

Fans Build up the framework of branches as described for figs (see p.101). Once the tree is established, summer-prune it; shorten to about six leaves any shoots that are not needed to extend the fan structure. After harvesting, reduce these same shoots by half their length.

THINNING AND HARVESTING
Plum trees—especially Japanese plums—can carry remarkably heavy crops in good years. Since their branches tend to be brittle, thinning the fruit is recommended to prevent branches from breaking. Thin when the fruits are the size of marbles and once the stones have formed; thin again when fruits are about twice this size. Leave two inches between European plums and three or four between Japanese plums.

Later, if there still seems a risk of damage, support the trees with a central pole, as described for apples on p.91.

Pick Japanese plums just before they are ripe, but leave European varieties to ripen fully on the tree. Pick plums with their stalks intact. Since plums do not ripen simultaneously, you should have a good succession of fruit from your trees.

PESTS AND DISEASES
The chief pest is the plum curculio. Nematodes and peach borers can also be troublesome in some areas.

Among possible diseases are brown rot and black knot.

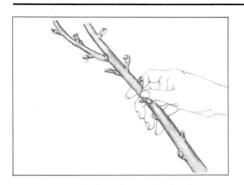

On a fan-trained plum, keep only the shoots that grow parallel with the wall. Rub off buds pointing outward or inward.

Summer-prune fan-trained trees by shortening to about six leaves those shoots not intended to extend the framework.

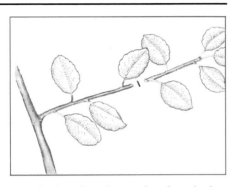

After the fruits have been gathered, cut back by half the shoots that were shortened earlier in the summer.

RECOMMENDED VARIETIES
European varieties
These plums are self-fruitful, but most will bear better if a compatible variety is planted nearby.

'**Stark Blue Ribbon**' Very large, elongated freestone plums with purplish-red skin.

'**Stanley**' Freestone plums with large, oval, purplish-blue skin and yellow flesh.

'**Earliblue**' This variety bears early but flowers late, so is good for northern zones.

'**French Improved**' The leading variety for commercial production of prunes. Tender, finely textured flesh, dark blue skin.

'**European Green Gage**' A flavorful plum that is yellow-green when mature. Trees are productive and winter hardy.

'**Blue Damson**' The classic plum for jams and jellies. Fruit is small and tart. Hardy.

Japanese varieties
Cross-pollination is essential. Remember that European and Japanese varieties will not pollinate each other.

'**Shiro**' A very early golden plum good for cooking, canning, and eating fresh.

'**Waneta**' This plum is a natural dwarf that produces large round fruit with sweet yellow flesh.

'**Elephant Heart**' Very large plums with red skin and flesh.

'**Tecumseh**' Medium-sized fruit with dark red skin and yellow flesh. Extremely hardy.

'**Santa Rosa**' The most popular plum. Large purplish-red fruit with a blue bloom has a nice texture and a slightly tart flavor.

'**Superior**' Very large, early, hardy variety.

'**Ozark Premier**' A tart, yellow-fleshed plum with bright red skin.

'**Wickson**' This large yellow variety has strongly marked red skin and firm flesh.

'**Redheart**' A medium-sized plum with dark red skin and blood-red flesh.

'**Ember**' Bears heavy crops of large golden-yellow fruits with sweet, firm flesh. Good for canning, cooking or eating fresh.

PLUMS AND OTHER STONE FRUIT, pages 62–63
GROWING TREE FRUITS, pages 87–89
CANNING, page 230
FREEZING FRUITS, pages 234–235

Peaches and nectarines (*Prunus persica*) are closely related and their cultivation is broadly similar. Nectarines are smooth-skinned sports or mutations of the peach, which has a naturally downy or fuzzy skin. They have juicy yellow flesh like most peaches (some have white flesh), and both fruits have an excellent flavor. They can be frozen, canned, or used in cooking but are at their best eaten fresh.

Of more practical importance, nectarines are more susceptible to disease, particularly brown rot, than peaches, and sometimes produce smaller fruit as well. Peaches are the safer choice for most food gardens, unless you prefer to grow nectarines for their singularly rich flavor.

Peaches are relatively hardy and will tolerate moderately cold winters, provided the summers are sufficiently warm and sunny to ripen the fruit. The chief hazard to peaches is spring frosts while they are in flower, since they are an early-flowering tree. Peaches are also adversely affected by strong, cold winds, so shelter is needed if you live in an exposed area. In general, if your winter is cold enough to provide the necessary dormant period but temperatures do not drop below 0°F, you should be able to grow peaches successfully.

Well-drained soil is essential, though it needs to contain plenty of moisture-holding organic matter. A pH fairly close to neutral is ideal, so you may need to add lime from time to time if the soil is markedly acid.

Provided there is shelter, peaches may be grown as freestanding (bush) trees in the open or fan-trained against a wall. Either way, they need plenty of sunshine. An average annual yield from a bush peach is around forty pounds, and a fan peach will produce half this amount. The crop from a nectarine is comparable.

Peaches and nectarines are self-fertile, so you can grow only a single tree. Nevertheless, hand pollination helps to insure a maximum set of fruit.

Birds can be a hazard to the fruit buds in winter and the ripening fruit in summer. It is difficult to protect bush trees, which are too tall for a standard fruit cage, but it is fairly easy to devise a plastic netting cover for wall-trained trees (see p.102).

Most peaches come on a standard rootstock such as 'Lovell' or 'Halford,' which results in a tree with a spread of about fifteen feet. Dwarfing rootstocks are generally unsuccessful, but true dwarf varieties are available, as are rootstocks for very cold regions.

MAKING A START

For a fan-trained peach, fasten horizontal wires to the wall with vine eyes; space them six inches apart with the lowest about a foot and a half above the ground. Prepare the planting positions for all trees by digging in some well-rotted manure or garden compost. Improve the drainage first if necessary; peaches will not tolerate too much water around their roots.

Buy one-year-old or two-year-old trees from a nursery. Plant bare-rooted trees during the spring; hammer in a supporting stake for bush trees first (see p.88). Dig a large hole so that the roots can be well spread out, and plant the tree to the same depth as it was in the nursery.

Allow fifteen feet between freestanding trees if you are planting more than one. Plant fan trees at least six inches from the wall, and twelve to fifteen feet apart if you are growing more than one. Incline the stem slightly toward the wall. For both kinds of tree spread a mulch of well-rotted manure or compost over and beyond the root area.

CARE OF THE CROP

Make sure that the site does not dry out during a dry spring or summer, especially for the first two years.

From the third year onward, fertilize the tree each year. Apply a late-winter dressing of sulfate of potash at a half ounce per square yard, followed by a similar amount of sulfate of ammonia in spring. Add super-phosphate in the spring at two ounces per square yard every two or three years. If you prefer, apply a general fertilizer every spring at two ounces per square yard, instead of the various straight fertilizers. An adequate supply of nitrogen is essential during the first few years of growth.

Since the flowers often open before many insects are flying, it is worth trying to assist fertilization throughout the flowering period. It is important to try to protect the flowers if frost threatens.

Hand pollination helps to insure a maximum crop. Make this a daily task while the flowers are open. Transfer the pollen by touching the flowers lightly with a tuft of cotton wool or a fine-haired brush. The best time for this is around midday and when the sun is shining.

THINNING AND HARVESTING

Thin the fruit from early summer onward if you are fortunate enough to get a heavy crop. Thin over a period, starting when the fruits are the size of large peas. Aim to leave six to nine inches between them.

Ripe peaches and nectarines part easily from the tree when lifted and gently twisted. Handle them very carefully and store them unwrapped in a cool place for a week or two if you cannot eat them at once.

PEACHES, PLUMS, AND OTHER STONE FRUITS, pages 62–63
GROWING TREE FRUITS, pages 87–89
FIGS, pages 100–101
PLUMS, pages 102–103

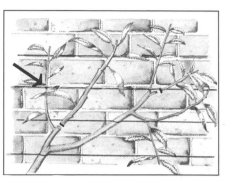

This year-old shoot will carry the coming season's fruit. In spring, leave a replacement shoot to develop at its base but reduce other growths to a single leaf.

The branch has been trained and tied up as an extension of the main framework. Shoots growing from it are thinned out in spring to a spacing of about six inches.

At the end of summer, after you have picked the fruit, prune the laterals that carried the peaches back to the replacement shoots that were left at their base.

PRUNING AND TRAINING

Fans Build up the framework in the same way as described for figs (see pp.100–101); train the shoots to canes attached to the horizontal wires.

Once the tree is mature, fruit will be borne on shoots that developed during the previous season. The aim of pruning is therefore to stimulate the constant annual renewal of young shoots. To start the process, allow upward- or downward-pointing shoots to develop at about six-inch intervals along the branches. Rub off surplus shoots, including any growing outward or toward the wall. Tie the chosen shoots to the wires and cut the tips off if they are more than eighteen inches long.

During each successive spring, pinch out inward- or outward-pointing buds as soon as they break. Allow a growth bud near the base of each year-old lateral to develop into a replacement growth, and reduce the others to a single leaf. Tie the replacement up as it grows, but tip it if it becomes longer than the year-old lateral that it will replace.

During the early summer, repeat the thinning and tying of shoots that develop along the branches. Shorten the fruit-bearing laterals to six leaves and their replacements to ten leaves. In early fall, after picking, prune back the fruited laterals.

Bush trees Establish the branch framework by pruning in late spring in the same way as for bush plums (see p.103). Cut back to four inches shoots that are not required to form secondary branches. Remove all blossoms during the first spring after planting, and most of them during the second year.

Once the tree is mature, prune in early spring to remove badly placed branches and to encourage new growth. Cut off a proportion of older, unproductive wood. Apply a wound-sealing paint, since peaches are susceptible to bacterial canker.

PESTS AND DISEASES

Peach tree borers and plum curculios are the most likely pests, and nematodes can be a problem in the South and West.

Brown rot, canker, peach leaf curl, and powdery mildew are common ailments.

RECOMMENDED VARIETIES
Peaches

'Elberta' A classic variety. Large yellow fruit has yellow flesh; freestone. Zones 5–8

'Red Haven' A firm, sweet freestone peach with red-blushed yellow skin. Zones 5–8

'Reliance' An extremely hardy variety. Zones 5–8

'Sun Haven' This very early freestone peach has firm yellow flesh. Zones 5–8

'Starking Delicious' An early-ripening type, good for canning, freezing, and eating. Zones 5–8

'La Feliciana' A heavy producer. Zones 8–9

'Belle of Georgia' A white-fleshed freestone peach with yellow skin. Zones 5–8

'Strawberry Cling' Large, creamy white fruit is juicy. Clingstone. Zones 5–8

'Indian Blood' An old, winter-hardy clingstone peach with dark crimson skin and flesh.

Nectarines

'Mericrest' A hardy, disease-resistant type.

'Stark Sunglo' Very large fruit has a smooth, waxy skin. Winter hardy.

'Desert Dawn' An aromatic variety suitable for very warm climates.

PESTS AND DISEASES, pages 108–111
CANNING, pages 228–229

FREEZING FRUITS, pages 234–235

Home-grown apricots (*Prunus armeniaca*) usually have a much better flavor than the fruit sold in stores, provided they have been exposed to sufficient sunshine. Besides being eaten fresh and dried, they are suitable for canning, freezing, and jam making.

Apart from their need for summer warmth, apricots need a protected site in all but the warmest, most temperate areas. Apricots flower very early in the year—even earlier than peaches—so their blossoms can easily be destroyed by frost. This means that you must delay their blossoming in cold regions by planting near a north-facing wall, and even in milder areas it is a good idea to grow apricots fan-trained against a wall that will radiate heat overnight. The wall will also help to protect the blossoms if flowering coincides with frost.

Since apricots are generally self-fertile, you can grow a single tree, but fruit set is often better if another variety is planted nearby. Full-size trees can reach thirty feet, but genetic dwarfs are available.

A well-drained medium loam is the ideal soil, with a pH close to neutral. But other soils give reasonable results, provided they contain sufficient organic matter.

MAKING A START

Buy a one-year-old tree if possible. It may be bare-rooted and dormant, or container-grown. Plant bare-rooted trees as early in the spring as possible (see p.89).

Prepare the soil by digging in well-rotted manure or compost some weeks ahead of planting. Once the tree is planted, rake some lime into the surface if the soil is acid.

Fasten horizontal wires to vine eyes in the wall every six inches, with the lowest about a foot and a half above ground level. Set the tree at least six inches away from the wall. After planting, spread a mulch of manure or compost over and beyond the root area.

CARE OF THE CROP

Protect the blossoms with a plastic screen, as suggested for plums on p.102. Hand-pollinate the flowers with a fine brush or cotton wool as for peaches (see p.104).

Feeding is unnecessary until the tree has started to bear fruit. Then apply a late-winter dressing of sulfate of potash at a half ounce per square yard, followed by a similar amount of sulfate of ammonia in spring. Supply superphosphate in the spring at two ounces per square yard every two or three years. If you prefer, you can add a general fertilizer every spring instead of the individual straight fertilizers, at two ounces per square yard. Renew the mulch each year.

Do not allow the soil around apricots to dry out, especially while the tree is young or bearing a crop.

Wall-trained trees are particularly at risk from drying out. Water regularly during dry spells, especially while the tree is still young or when it is bearing fruit. A good soaking is essential and is most easily applied with a heavy sprayer on the end of a hose. This helps to prevent the water from running off the surface of the ground.

Thinning is advisable if there is a heavy set of fruit. Start when the apricots are the size of small grapes, and leave a space twice their width between each fruit. Later, thin again to leave spaces twice as big; aim for a final spacing of about three inches.

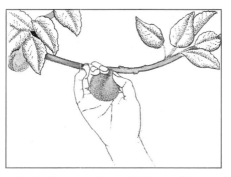

Pick the fruits complete with their stalks to maximize their keeping qualities. Leave the fruits to ripen fully before picking them, which may be some time after they first soften. When fully ripe they should come away easily, especially if you hold the stalk between finger and thumb.

PRUNING AND TRAINING

Build up the fan structure of an apricot in the same way as for a fig (see p.101). Carry out the initial work in late winter.

By about the fourth summer, promote fruiting growths by pinching out the ends of laterals once they reach three inches; remove later side shoots altogether.

Heavy pruning is unnecessary on a fruiting tree, since apricots produce their best fruit on two- or three-year-old short spurs. Every five years or so, cut out some of the older fruited shoots, including the main laterals of a fan, to make way for new young shoots. Retain and tie up the same number of replacement shoots as you cut out.

Freestanding trees should be pruned as for bush plums (see p.103). Prune them in early spring, while they are dormant and before the new growth begins.

HARVESTING

Protect the trees from birds with netting before the first signs of ripening. Leave the fruit to ripen fully before picking.

PESTS AND DISEASES

Codling moths, peach tree borers, and plum curculios may prove troublesome, as can gophers. Brown rot is a common disease.

RECOMMENDED VARIETIES

'Harcot' A cold-hardy variety bred in Canada. Disease resistant; early ripening.
'Moorpark' Exceptional flavor and aroma. An old favorite that ripens unevenly.
'Gold Kist' A good variety for warm climates; bears early and has superb flavor.
'Sungold' Medium-sized, gold-orange fruit.
'Stark Sweetheart' The kernels of this variety are edible; fruit is good fresh or dried.

PEACHES, PLUMS, AND OTHER STONE FRUITS, pages 62–63
PLUMS, pages 102–103   PEACHES AND NECTARINES, pages 104–105

There are two main types of cherry, and their cultivation is slightly different. Sweet cherries, which are varieties of *Prunus avium* or crosses between *P. avium* and *P. cerasus*, produce heavy crops of fruit, ranging in color from pink to deep purple-black. Sour cherries (*Prunus cerasus*) are usually red and are used mainly for making desserts and preserves.

SWEET CHERRIES

Sweet cherries are not the easiest fruit to grow, but if you live in a suitable region, choose your varieties carefully, and pay attention to care, you can reap up to fifty quarts of cherries from a single tree. Sweet cherries are not self-fertile, so you need to plant compatible varieties nearby.

In general, sweet cherries do best in Zones 5–7 and on the West Coast, although some varieties do well elsewhere. Fan train-ing on a high wall is recommended for sites with good air circulation.

Cherries need a good, well-drained, and deep soil, with a pH between 6.7 and 7.5.

PLANTING AND AFTERCARE

Plant sweet cherries in a sunny sheltered position where spring frosts will not trouble the early blossoms.

Dig a hole wide and deep enough to take the roots when they are fully extended. Plant a fan-trained cherry at least six inches from the wall, after you have fastened support wires at six-inch intervals, the lowest a foot and a half from the ground. Drive a supporting stake into the ground before planting a tree in the open (see p.89) and tie the young tree to it. Young bush trees are susceptible to wind damage.

Insure that the soil never dries out, especially while the roots become estab-lished. An annual spring mulch will help in this respect. Afterward, apply a balanced fertilizer at three ounces per square yard.

Protect the blossoms from frost with a netting screen (see p.102). From early summer onward, cover dwarf trees with netting to keep birds off the fruit. Sweet cherries are harvested in midsummer. Pick them complete with their stalks, and eat or preserve them as soon as possible.

PRUNING AND TRAINING

Fans Build up the branch framework for a fan as for a fig (see p.101). Subsequently, prune the mature tree by restricting the ends of laterals to six leaves during early summer; reduce the same shoots to four buds in late summer. Each spring, remove new shoots that grow outward or inward.
Bush trees Prune in the same way as for a plum (see p.103).

Pinch back lateral shoots on mature trees in early summer, once they have produced five or six leaves.

In late summer or early autumn, reduce the shoots that were pinched back earlier in the summer to four healthy fruit buds.

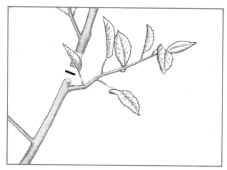

After harvesting sour cherries, prune back fruited laterals to their replacement growths. These will fruit the following year.

SOUR CHERRIES

Sour cherries have some advantages over sweet cherries. They are less vigorous; both semidwarf and dwarf varieties are common, and are easier to protect against damage from birds than standard cherries. Sour cherries are self-fertile, which means you can experiment with a single tree. They are also hardier than sweet varieties, and they resist disease better.

PLANTING AND AFTERCARE

Fix wall supports or a stake and plant the tree as for a sweet cherry, spacing dwarfs about eight feet apart. Make sure the soil does not dry out. Supply general fertilizer and renew the mulch every spring.

When harvesting, cut the stalks of sour cherries. This avoids damage to the fruiting spurs, and helps prevent disease.

PRUNING AND TRAINING

Fans Build up the branch framework of a fan in the same way as for a sweet cherry.

The annual pruning of mature trees is different, however. Because sour cherries fruit on year-old shoots, the aim is to encourage continual fresh growth. During early summer, thin out new shoots to a spacing of about three inches, and secure these to the wires. Keep as many as possible of the shoots at the base of year-old laterals, which are fruiting during the current year.

After harvesting, cut back these laterals to replacement growths. In spring, remove outward- or inward-growing new shoots.
Bush trees Prune as for a plum (see p.103).

PESTS AND DISEASES

Plum curculios, cherry sawflies, and apple maggots can attack both sweet and sour cherries. Potential diseases include brown rot, cherry leaf spot, and powdery mildew.

RECOMMENDED VARIETIES
Sweet cherries
'Starkrimson' Extremely sweet, very large fruit is borne early. Zones 5–8
'Stella' Available in standard or dwarf form. Cherries are wine-red and sweet.
'Van' A productive, crack-resistant variety.
'Early Ruby' Popular in California.
'Kristin' The most winter hardy of the "black" sweet cherries.
'Stark Gold' A tangy golden cherry; hardy.
Sour cherries
'Montmorency' The best-known sour cher-ry. Fruit is firm; trees produce heavily.
'North Star' A winter-hardy dwarf.
'Meteor' This semidwarf crops heavily and has dense foliage that limits bird damage.

CHERRIES, page 64
GROWING TREE FRUITS, pages 87–89

FIGS, pages 100–101
PESTS AND DISEASES, pages 108–111

CANNING, pages 228–229
FREEZING FRUITS, pages 234–235

The following pages help you to identify and control the various pests and diseases that may affect fruits. Those most likely to blight particular fruits are listed in the individual descriptions, but if you are careful, your fruit may not be attacked by any of them.

The best way to prevent pests and diseases is to make sure that your soil is nourished and improved regularly and kept free of weeds, so the plants you grow are strong and healthy. Following the correct cultivation and pruning procedures also helps to make the plants less vulnerable.

It is a matter of individual choice whether you make use of commercial pesticides or rely on homemade remedies and organic sprays. Both courses of action are suggested here, where alternatives exist for the pest or disease in question.

The commercial chemicals mentioned are a selection from the many options often available; they are described by their chemical names, not by brand names. You will have to check labels carefully to be sure of what you are buying. Government regulations regarding pesticides and their use vary from state to state, so you might want to check with your local agricultural extension service agent for expert advice.

When using chemicals, always carry out the manufacturer's instructions to the letter, and follow the guidelines given on p.21, Care with Chemicals. Do not spray fruit trees when they are in flower, because bees and other pollinating insects may be killed.

Organic remedies are recommended whenever possible, but they too should be used with caution and care. Many organic pesticides are available at garden centers and through the mail; others are simple to make yourself. For details of some remedies and how to make them, see pp.20–21.

APHIDS
These small insects live in clusters on buds, leaves, and the tips of shoots of fruit trees and bushes. They feed on the sap, causing distortion and stunted growth, and often spread disease.
□ During spring and summer, spray active colonies with malathion, pyrethrum, or rotenone.
△ Spray with rhubarb and elderleaf mixture, or spray hard with water.

WOOLLY APHIDS
These aphids form tufts of waxy wool. Apples are particularly susceptible.
□ Spray trees in winter with an anti-insect oil. During the active season, spray with dimethoate or brush with a spray-strength solution of pyrethrum, malathion, or rotenone.
△ Use natural parasites and predators such as lacewings and ladybugs.

GALL MITES
These damaging pests, which resemble microscopic worms, cause buds to swell, then cease to develop—hence the disorder's common name, "big bud." Includes pear leaf blister mites, which attack apples as well as pears.
□ Pick off affected buds in late winter. Spray with dormant oil in winter and malathion in summer.
△ Spray with diluted permanganate of potash (one ounce in two gallons of water).

CAPSID BUGS
Apples, gooseberries, and currants are vulnerable to these pests. They cause ragged holes in the leaves, and deformed and scabbed fruits.
□ As prevention, spray after petal fall with malathion or dimethoate, or dust or spray with rotenone. Follow manufacturer's instructions for repeat sprays.

CATERPILLARS
Caterpillars attack buds and young leaves of fruit trees. In addition to evident damage, leaves may be spun together with silken threads. Tent caterpillars and gypsy moth caterpillars, in particular, can be a problem on apple trees.
□ Spray with *Bacillus thuringiensis*, malathion, or dimethoate. Spray with dormant oil in winter.
△ Place grease bands around the tree trunks in autumn. Use pheromone (sex-lure) traps in early spring.

PLUM CURCULIOS
A serious pest of most stone fruits as well as apples and pears. The larvae feed on the fruit, causing it to rot, drop, or develop unevenly. Adult beetles also feed on the fruit.
□ Malathion and diazinon are effective sprays, used at two-week intervals during the growing season. Rotenone is also effective.
△ Keep ground free of windfalls and leaves, and remove mulch in winter; the beetles hibernate in the soil.

PEAR PSYLLA
Immature and adult insects feed on leaves and stems and spread fireblight. They also coat the leaves with a sticky substance that encourages a black mold.
□ Malathion and carbaryl are effective chemical controls.
△ Spray with dormant oil in the fall and again in late winter. Use an insecticidal soap during the growing season.

CODLING MOTHS
Codling moth larvae are usually the maggots found in apples and pears.
□ Diazinon and methoxychior are effective sprays.
△ Spray with ryania when most blossoms have fallen. Trichogramma wasps and *Bacillus thuringiensis* can be effective, or you can trap larvae with burlap strips or corrugated cardboard tied around the trunk.

CHERRY SAWFLY
These dark, mucous-covered caterpillars consume the foliage of cherry trees in spring and summer, sometimes reducing it to a skeleton.
□ Malathion is an effective spray. Alternatively, spray or dust with rotenone and/or pyrethrum.

EUROPEAN RED MITES

These tiny sap-sucking insects cause discolored leaves and early leaf fall on apples, plums, and apricots.
□ Malathion and dormant oils are effective sprays; also the systemic insecticide dimethoate.

MEALYBUGS

The leaves of grapevines and apples become stunted, with patches of waxy threads covering grubs or eggs. Damage can be serious if unchecked.
□ Spray with malathion every two weeks. A winter spray of dormant oil breaks the life cycle.

STRAWBERRY ROOT WEEVILS

The larvae attack roots, whereas the large black or brown beetles feed on leaves.
□ Diazinon or malathion sprays may be effective, and carbaryl will certainly work.
△ You might trap beetles in jars buried in the soil.

RED SPIDER MITES

A number of fruits, including peaches, strawberries, grapes, and melons, may be affected. Mottling and yellowing of the leaves are followed by leaf fall. Fine, silky webbing may be seen.
□ Spray at 10-day intervals with dimethoate or malathion.
△ Spray hard with water or insecticidal soap. Apply dormant oil in early spring to smother eggs before they hatch.

PEACH TREE BORERS

The white caterpillars of these moths hatch in the summer and burrow into the trunks of peaches, plums, cherries, and apricots. A heavy infestation can kill young trees in a single season.
□ The usual treatment is to spread a repellant such as moth crystals (paradichlorobenzene) beneath the tree in the fall, cover them with soil, and leave them for a month or two, depending on the age of the tree. Endosulfan is an effective spray.

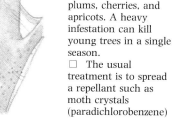

SAWFLIES

Different species attack apples, gooseberries, and plums. The caterpillars of apple and plum sawflies burrow into the fruitlets, causing them to drop. Gooseberry sawflies strip foliage.
□ If there has been trouble previously, spray with carbaryl or dimethoate after petal fall. Spray affected gooseberry plants with the same chemicals.
△ Spray with rotenone, pyrethrum, nicotine, or *Bacillus thuringiensis*.

LEAFHOPPERS

These aptly named insects cause the upper surface of many kinds of leaves to become mottled. Damage is slight but disease may be spread.
□ Malathion, carbaryl, and dimethoate are effective sprays.

NEMATODES

These tiny worms, also known as eelworms, live in the soil and feed on and injure the roots of strawberries and various trees, notably peaches.
□ Fumigate the soil before planting with Vapam, a commonly available and fairly toxic weedkiller.
△ A grass cover crop will virtually eliminate soil nematodes in two or three years in some parts of the country, since organic matter fosters beneficial fungi. Some varieties of marigolds will attract the pests if planted and pulled up before the tree is planted.

SCALE INSECTS

The clusters of tiny scales sometimes found on the stems and leaves of peaches, apricots, and vines are in fact the females of this sap-sucking species of insect. Sometimes the scales are coated with a thick, waxy substance.
□ Winter spraying with a dormant oil emulsion gives good control. Malathion and dimethoate are suitable sprays for the growing season.

APPLE MAGGOTS

Known as the railroad worm because of their tunneling habits, the larvae attack the fruit of European plums, pears, and cherries as well as apples.
□ Dormant oil sprays in winter and general-purpose insecticidal sprays applied when the flies are active are the usual treatment.
△ Trap adult flies in sticky ready-made traps. Use one trap for each 100 apples; hang them in early summer.

RASPBERRY BEETLES

The grubs feed on the ripening fruits of raspberries, blackberries, and loganberries.
□ Spray with malathion every two weeks between flowering and harvesting.
△ Spray with pyrethrum.

SLUGS AND SNAILS

Strawberries are most at risk; the fruit may suffer considerable damage during damp weather if no counter-action is taken.
□ Scatter metaldehyde pellets or meal before the mulch is laid around the plants. Keep the surrounding area free of weeds.
△ Collect the pests by hand at night, or trap them by sinking a shallow bowl containing sweetened beer level with the soil.

AMERICAN GOOSEBERRY MILDEW

Leaves, shoot tips, and fruit are covered with a white, powdery growth, which results in distortion. Black currants are also affected.

□ Spray with dinocap or benomyl. Manufacturer's instructions give most effective spraying time.

△ Spray with micronized sulfur before the bushes have begun to blossom.

BROWN ROT

A fungus that attacks ripe fruit, especially plums, including those in storage. Spreads rapidly to other fruit by entering where the skin is damaged.

□ Spray with benomyl or captan. The main safeguard is to remove and burn infected fruit as soon as you see it. Wash your hands before touching other fruit.

CANE BLIGHT

A fungus disease that attacks the base of raspberry canes; it results in discoloration and brittleness. The leaves wither and die back. Black raspberries are generally more susceptible than red or purple varieties.

□ Spray with captan or ferbam.

△ Cut back damaged canes to beneath soil level and burn the wood removed. Spray new growth with Bordeaux mixture.

ANTHRACNOSE

This fungus disease principally affects raspberries, blackberries, and various hybrid berries. Purple-edged brown spots develop on the leaves and canes. Leaves and fruit may be distorted.

□ Spray with Bordeaux mixture, benomyl, captan, or folpet after cutting out and burning the worst-affected canes.

CANKER

The fungal canker that afflicts apples and pears causes the bark on branches to shrink and expose the inner wood. The gummy canker that develops on peaches, plums, and cherries causes the leaves to wither; it is bacterial in origin.

□ To treat apple canker, cut off badly affected spurs and small branches. Trim away damaged wood from larger branches and apply a fungicidal paint. Spray in winter with dormant oil.

□ Remove branches damaged or killed by bacterial canker; treat cuts with a fungicidal paint. Spray with Bordeaux mixture.

△ Prune damaged wood in summer; spray with streptomycin during the blooming period.

CORAL SPOT

A fungus infection that may attack figs and currants. Its name describes the color of the spore masses that appear on old or dead shoots and branches.

□ Cut off affected wood a few inches beyond the spores. Treat cuts with a fungicidal sealing paint.

△ Feed red and white currant bushes only with low-nitrogen organic material.

CROWN GALL

A number of berries, including blackberries and loganberries, may be affected by this bacterial disease. Rounded growths, or galls, develop on the roots, sometimes stunting growth.

□ Prevent by avoiding root damage and by buying certified stock. Plant bushes on newly cleared land.

CUCUMBER MOSAIC VIRUS

The leaves of infected melons become mottled and the plants stunted. Highly infectious, it is often spread by aphids.

△ As a precaution, prevent aphid colonies from becoming established. Burn infected plants as soon as you see them. Avoid carrying the disease on hands or tools.

BLACK ROT

This fungus disease attacks grapes, causing the fruit to develop brown spots, then shrivel and turn black. The vines and leaves may also be infected.

□ Spray the grapevines with benomyl, folpet, or maneb just before and after the blooms appear. Continue spraying every two weeks if warm, wet weather prevails in spring and early summer.

DOWNY MILDEW

A disease of melons, downy mildew is apt to strike when the weather is very wet or humid. Brown or yellow spots on leaves have a fuzzy white mold on the underside. The melons are small and bitter.

□ Spray every week or 10 days with maneb or folpet.

△ Keep upper leaf surfaces free of water.

FIREBLIGHT

Both apples and pears may be attacked by this bacterial disease. It causes foliage to wither and shoots to curl over, with cankers forming at their base. Affected branches and fruits turn black and die.

□ Cut off infected branches six or eight inches below the wilted area, and disinfect the pruners after each cut. Spray with Bordeaux mix or streptomycin during blossoming.

BOTRYTIS (GRAY MOLD)

A widespread fungus disease particularly troublesome on strawberries. Fruits with the soft gray covering invariably rot.

□ Because the infection starts at flowering time, spray preventively from the time flowers open with captan. Repeat every 14 days. It is worth spraying as soon as you see any symptoms.

△ Use a mulch to keep fruit off the ground, and thin if necessary.

HONEY FUNGUS
Named for the color of the toadstools that emerge from the base of the infected trees and bushes, this is a particularly persistent and widespread organism that weakens and eventually kills infected plants.
☐ Remove and burn infected trees and bushes, together with as many of their roots as possible. Treat the infected soil with a sulfur compound.

LEAF SPOT
Various bacterial and fungal infections cause spotting and browning of the leaves and early leaf fall. Weak trees and berry bushes are most likely to succumb.
☐ Most fungicides, including those based on copper, benomyl, and dodine, give good control.
△ Burn fallen leaves in autumn. Spray affected plants with Burgundy mixture.

PEACH LEAF CURL
A fungus specific to peaches, nectarines, and other *Prunus* species. It causes leaves to blister, followed by premature fall.
☐ Spray in winter with Bordeaux mixture or a copper fungicide, or spray at two-week intervals with ferbam after leaves emerge.

POWDERY MILDEW
The leaves, flowers, and shoots of many trees and bushes may develop a powdery coating, which causes them to shrivel.
☐ Spray every two weeks, from the time the buds burst, with benomyl, dinocap, Bayleton, or sulfur-based fungicide.
△ Spray with Burgundy mixture in midwinter.

BLACK KNOT
The branches of plums, and occasionally of cherries and apricots, develop large black galls that stunt and eventually kill the wood beyond them. Caused by a fungus, the galls sometimes take a year or more to become noticeable.
☐ Prune out any infected branches in early spring, cutting four inches into the healthy wood. Spray with lime sulfur or ferbam when buds are about to open.

RUST
A fungus infection that attacks a wide range of plants, including apples, blackberries, and black raspberries. Symptoms are brown or orange masses of spores on the leaves.
☐ Remove and burn badly affected foliage. Improve growing conditions. In severe or persistent outbreaks, spray apples with ferbam, thiram, or micronized sulfur.

SCAB
The scabs form on the fruit of apples, pears, or peaches and often result in cracks. The leaves of affected trees are blotched.
☐ Spray with benomyl, captan, or dodine (specifically for apple scab).
△ Observe trees closely at pruning time and remove any shoots with blisters or cracked areas. Rake leaves and burn them. Spray with Burgundy mixture.

SUNSCALD
A condition caused by excessive heat, which shows as pale, wrinkled patches on fruit, or by too much light, which can burn tree bark in winter by reflecting off snow.
△ Cut off damaged fruit. Provide shade and ventilation if possible. Paint tree trunks white.

BACTERIAL WILT
Melons affected by bacterial wilt gradually wilt until the leaves and stems of the plant are dead. Although leaves may wilt naturally in hot weather, infected plants often have a sticky white sap in the stems.
☐ Control the cucumber beetle, which spreads the bacteria as it feeds. Use a rotenone dust or spray preventively once a week, and keep leaves covered with cloches or floating row covers, especially when plants are young.

RED STELE
This soil-borne fungus infects the roots of strawberries and causes stunting, wilting, and failure to bear fruit. The leaves turn yellow and red, and the core of the roots is red rather than yellow.
△ No chemicals are known to remedy this disease, which thrives in heavy, poorly drained soil. Use raised beds to improve drainage, enrich the soil with compost, and rotate the strawberry crop to fresh soil every year.

SPUR BLIGHT
A fungus disease causing purple patches to appear on raspberry and loganberry canes and brown spots on their leaves. Spurs and axillary buds shrivel and die.
☐ Cut out and burn affected canes after they have borne fruit. In spring spray the emerging canes with Bordeaux mixture or benomyl. Repeat the procedure every two weeks if necessary.

VIRUS DISEASES
Although many fruits are affected, strawberries and raspberries are particularly vulnerable to virus infections, which cause distortion, wilting, and oddly colored foliage and stems. The diseases are spread principally by insects.
△ There is no cure. Dig up and burn infected plants, and replace them with certified virus-free stock in fresh ground. Keep insects, especially aphids, in check; for methods, see p.108.

The
VEGETABLE COLOR
CATALOGUE I

Much of the appeal of home-grown vegetables lies in their variety as well as in their flavor and freshness. Although the following color plates are not totally comprehensive, they suggest the scope available to food growers within certain categories of vegetable: legumes (peas and beans), stalks and shoots, tubers and root vegetables, and fruiting vegetables such as tomatoes and peppers. (The color plates for brassicas, salad greens, and herbs can be found on pages 176–192.)

The separate vegetable entries, on pages 134–171, give specific details about sowing and individual cultivation requirements as well as recommendations for varieties other than those illustrated in the color plates.

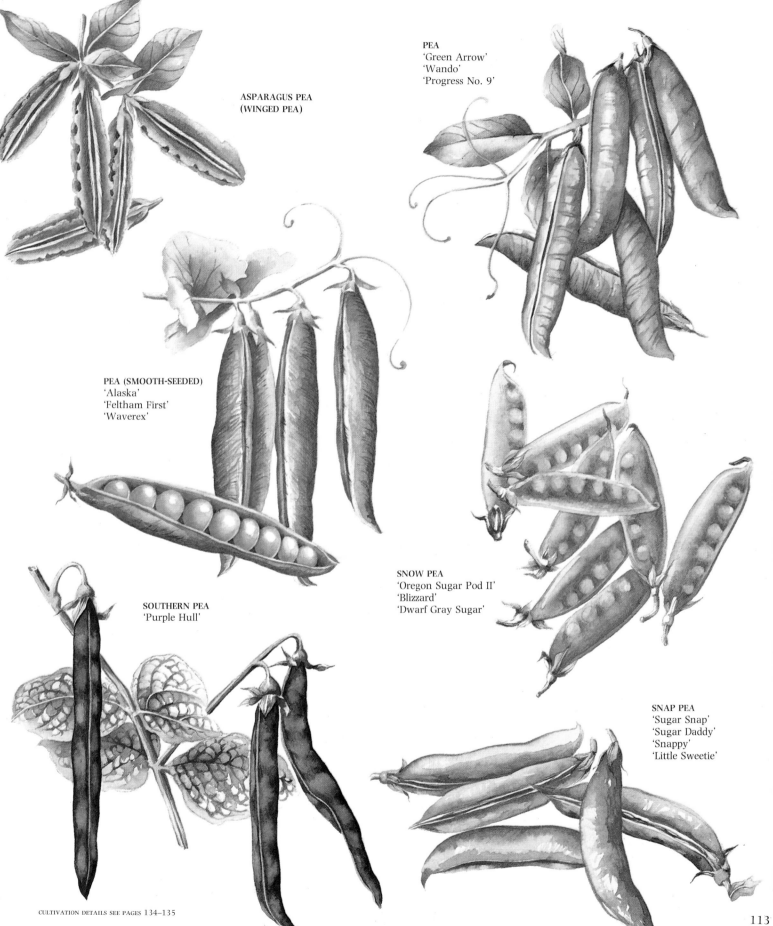

ASPARAGUS PEA
(WINGED PEA)

PEA
'Green Arrow'
'Wando'
'Progress No. 9'

PEA (SMOOTH-SEEDED)
'Alaska'
'Feltham First'
'Waverex'

SNOW PEA
'Oregon Sugar Pod II'
'Blizzard'
'Dwarf Gray Sugar'

SOUTHERN PEA
'Purple Hull'

SNAP PEA
'Sugar Snap'
'Sugar Daddy'
'Snappy'
'Little Sweetie'

BEANS, SWEET CORN, AND ARTICHOKES Selected varieties

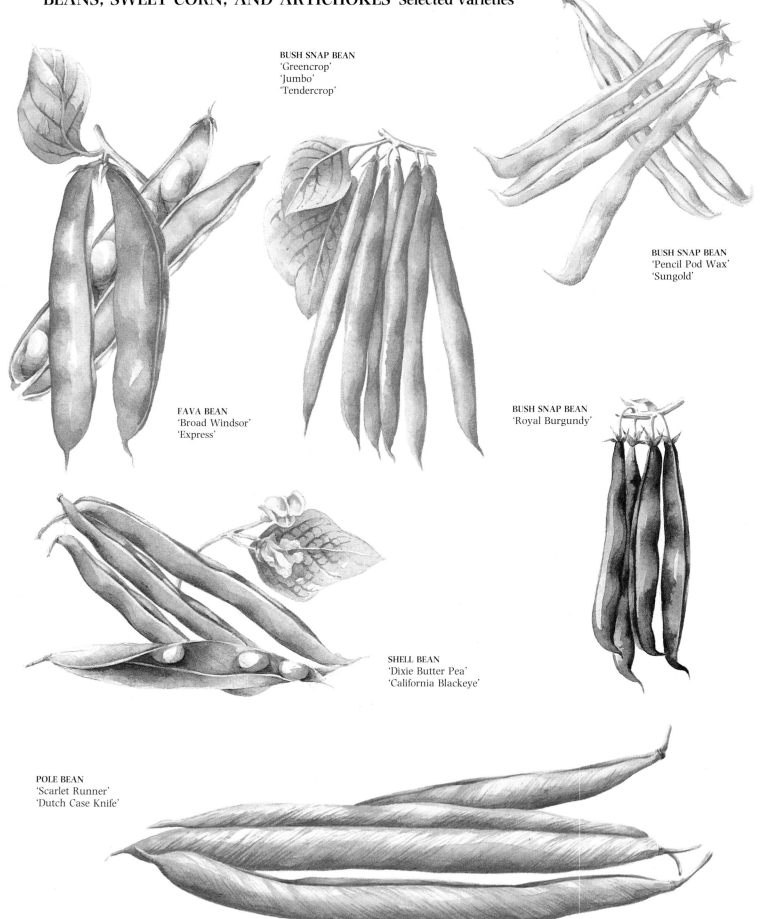

BUSH SNAP BEAN
'Greencrop'
'Jumbo'
'Tendercrop'

BUSH SNAP BEAN
'Pencil Pod Wax'
'Sungold'

FAVA BEAN
'Broad Windsor'
'Express'

BUSH SNAP BEAN
'Royal Burgundy'

SHELL BEAN
'Dixie Butter Pea'
'California Blackeye'

POLE BEAN
'Scarlet Runner'
'Dutch Case Knife'

CULTIVATION DETAILS SEE PAGES 136–142

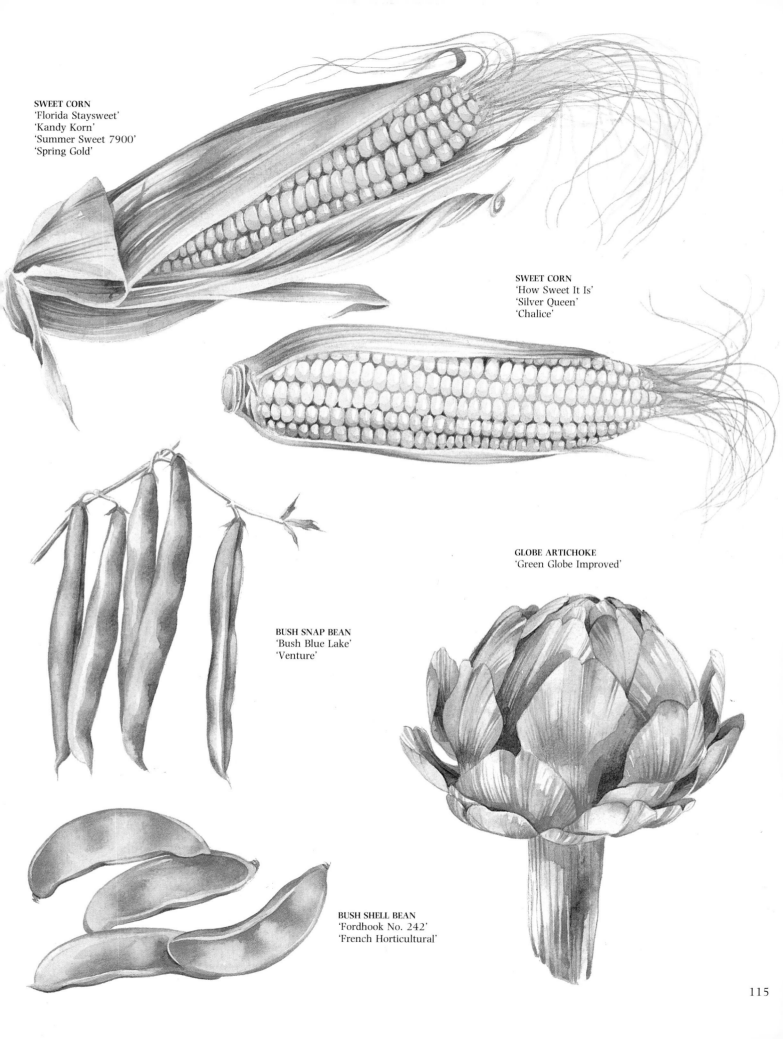

SWEET CORN
'Florida Staysweet'
'Kandy Korn'
'Summer Sweet 7900'
'Spring Gold'

SWEET CORN
'How Sweet It Is'
'Silver Queen'
'Chalice'

GLOBE ARTICHOKE
'Green Globe Improved'

BUSH SNAP BEAN
'Bush Blue Lake'
'Venture'

BUSH SHELL BEAN
'Fordhook No. 242'
'French Horticultural'

115

STALKS AND SHOOTS Selected varieties

CELERY
'Golden Self-Blanching'
'Golden Plume'

CELERY
'Tendercrisp'
'Deacon'
'Utah'
'Ventura'

CELERY
'Giant Red'

CARDOON

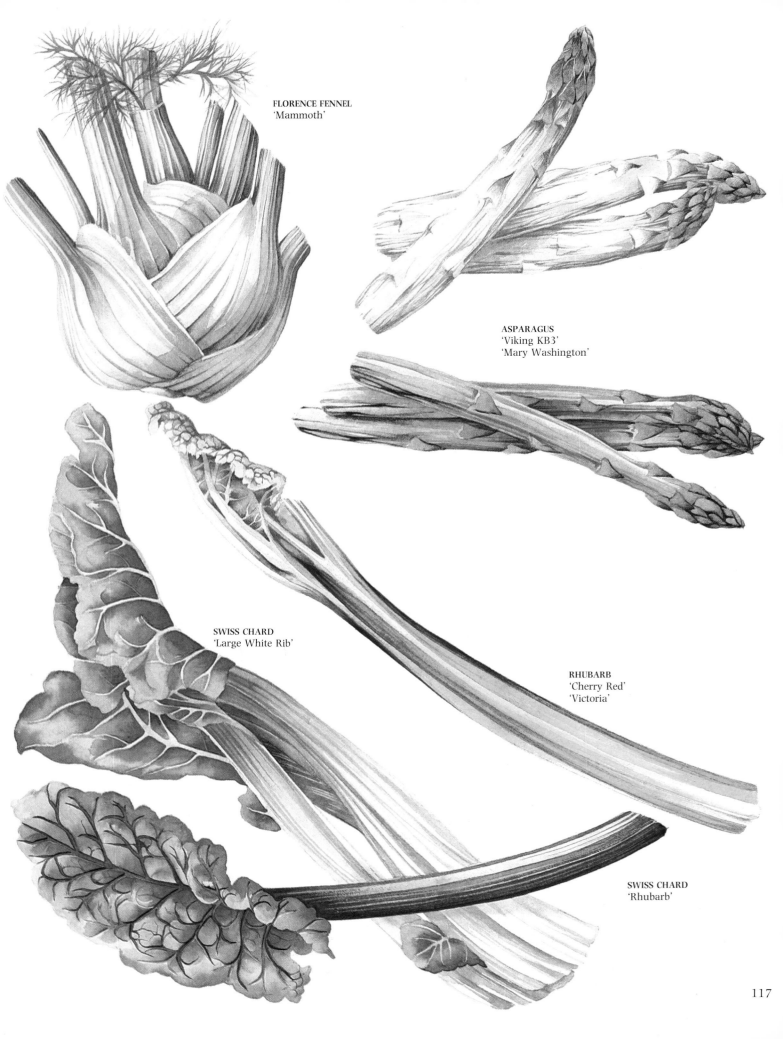

FLORENCE FENNEL
'Mammoth'

ASPARAGUS
'Viking KB3'
'Mary Washington'

SWISS CHARD
'Large White Rib'

RHUBARB
'Cherry Red'
'Victoria'

SWISS CHARD
'Rhubarb'

POTATOES AND OTHER TUBERS
Selected varieties

IDAHO BAKING POTATO
'Russet Centennial'
'Butte'

JERUSALEM ARTICHOKE

WHITE POTATO
'Katahdin'

RED POTATO
Young or "new" potato

RED POTATO
'Red Pontiac'
'Norland Red'

RED POTATO
'Red LaSoda'
'Sangre'

WHITE POTATO
Young or ''new'' potato

WHITE POTATO
'Kennebec'

WHITE POTATO
'White Cobbler'

NOVELTY POTATO
'Blue'

CULTIVATION DETAILS SEE PAGES 150–151

CARROTS AND OTHER ROOT CROPS Selected varieties

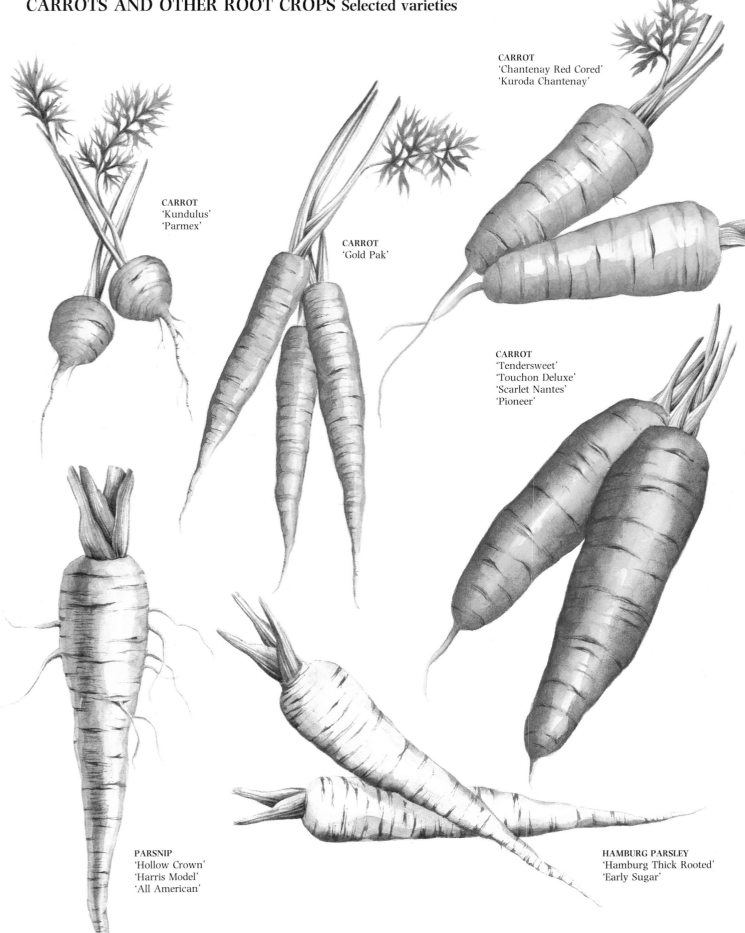

CARROT
'Chantenay Red Cored'
'Kuroda Chantenay'

CARROT
'Kundulus'
'Parmex'

CARROT
'Gold Pak'

CARROT
'Tendersweet'
'Touchon Deluxe'
'Scarlet Nantes'
'Pioneer'

PARSNIP
'Hollow Crown'
'Harris Model'
'All American'

HAMBURG PARSLEY
'Hamburg Thick Rooted'
'Early Sugar'

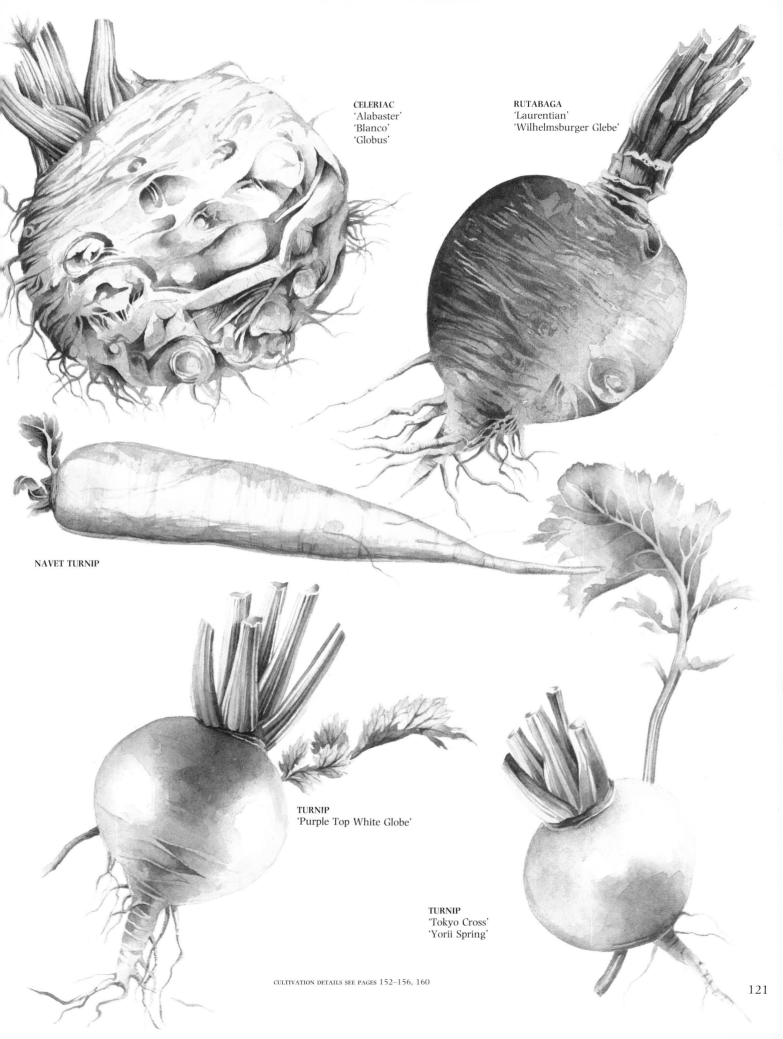

CELERIAC
'Alabaster'
'Blanco'
'Globus'

RUTABAGA
'Laurentian'
'Wilhelmsburger Glebe'

NAVET TURNIP

TURNIP
'Purple Top White Globe'

TURNIP
'Tokyo Cross'
'Yorii Spring'

CULTIVATION DETAILS SEE PAGES 152–156, 160

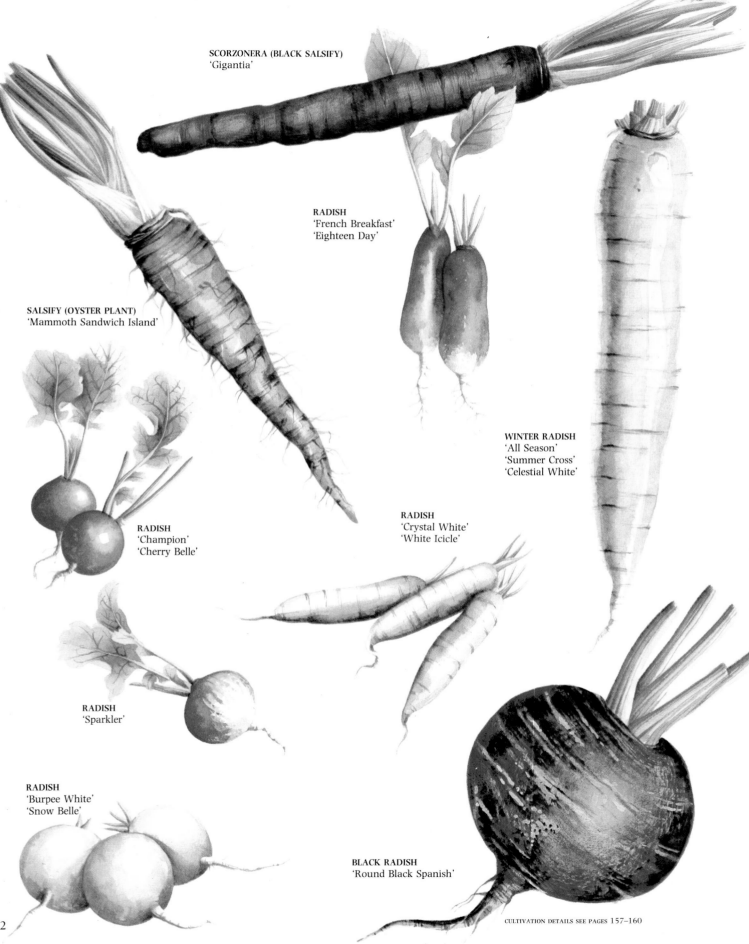

SCORZONERA (BLACK SALSIFY)
'Gigantia'

RADISH
'French Breakfast'
'Eighteen Day'

SALSIFY (OYSTER PLANT)
'Mammoth Sandwich Island'

WINTER RADISH
'All Season'
'Summer Cross'
'Celestial White'

RADISH
'Champion'
'Cherry Belle'

RADISH
'Crystal White'
'White Icicle'

RADISH
'Sparkler'

RADISH
'Burpee White'
'Snow Belle'

BLACK RADISH
'Round Black Spanish'

122

KOHLRABI (STEM TURNIP)
'Purple Danube'

KOHLRABI (STEM TURNIP)
'Kolpack'

BEET
'Mobile'
'Sweetheart'
'Early Wonder'
'Pacemaker III'

BEET
'Formanova'
'Forono'

BEET
'Burpee's Golden'

123

SQUASH AND PUMPKINS Selected varieties

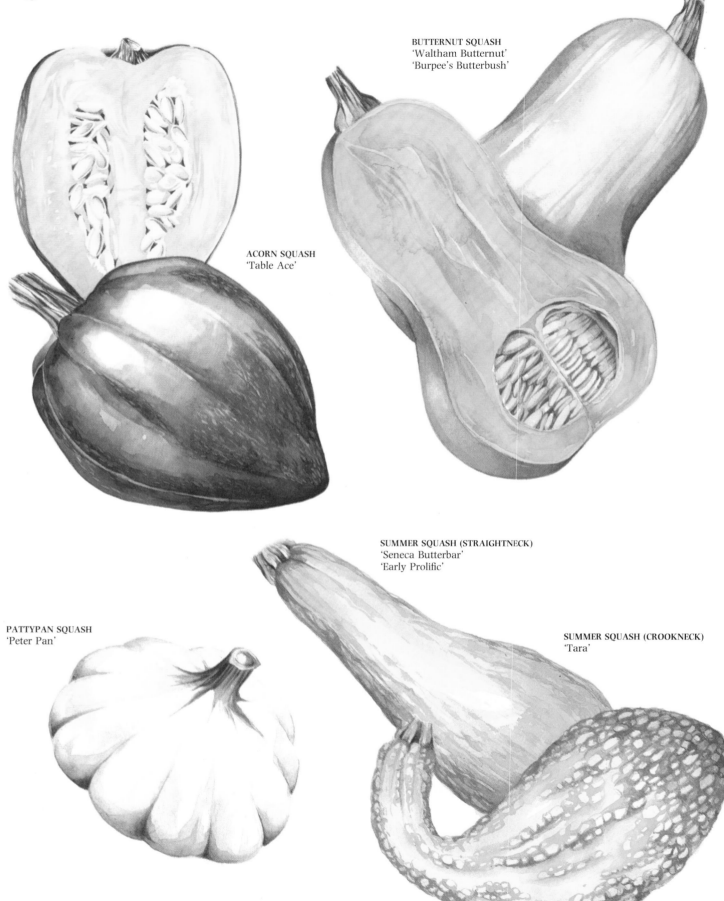

BUTTERNUT SQUASH
'Waltham Butternut'
'Burpee's Butterbush'

ACORN SQUASH
'Table Ace'

SUMMER SQUASH (STRAIGHTNECK)
'Seneca Butterbar'
'Early Prolific'

PATTYPAN SQUASH
'Peter Pan'

SUMMER SQUASH (CROOKNECK)
'Tara'

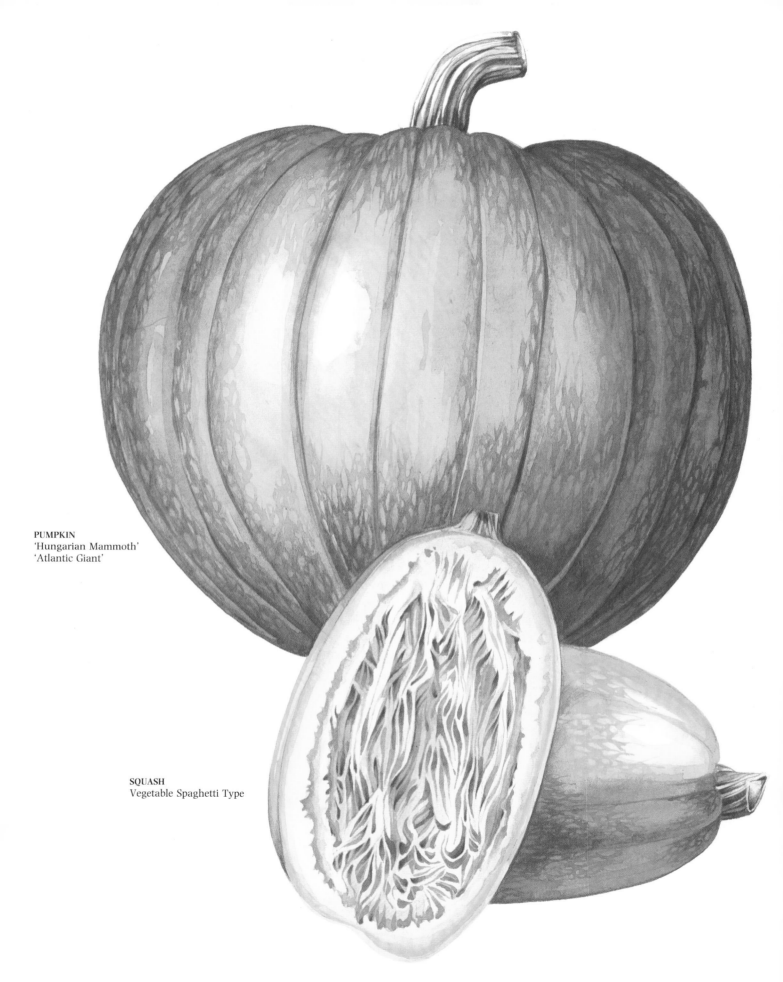

PUMPKIN
'Hungarian Mammoth'
'Atlantic Giant'

SQUASH
Vegetable Spaghetti Type

CULTIVATION DETAILS SEE PAGES 161–163

125

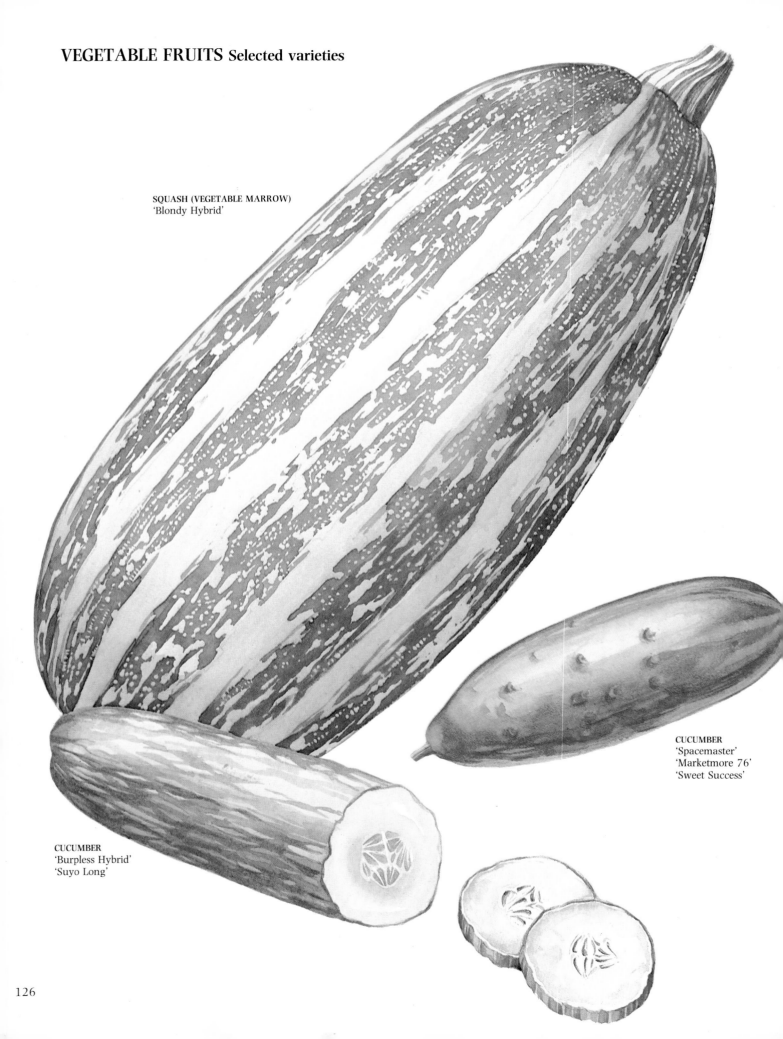

VEGETABLE FRUITS Selected varieties

SQUASH (VEGETABLE MARROW)
'Blondy Hybrid'

CUCUMBER
'Spacemaster'
'Marketmore 76'
'Sweet Success'

CUCUMBER
'Burpless Hybrid'
'Suyo Long'

126

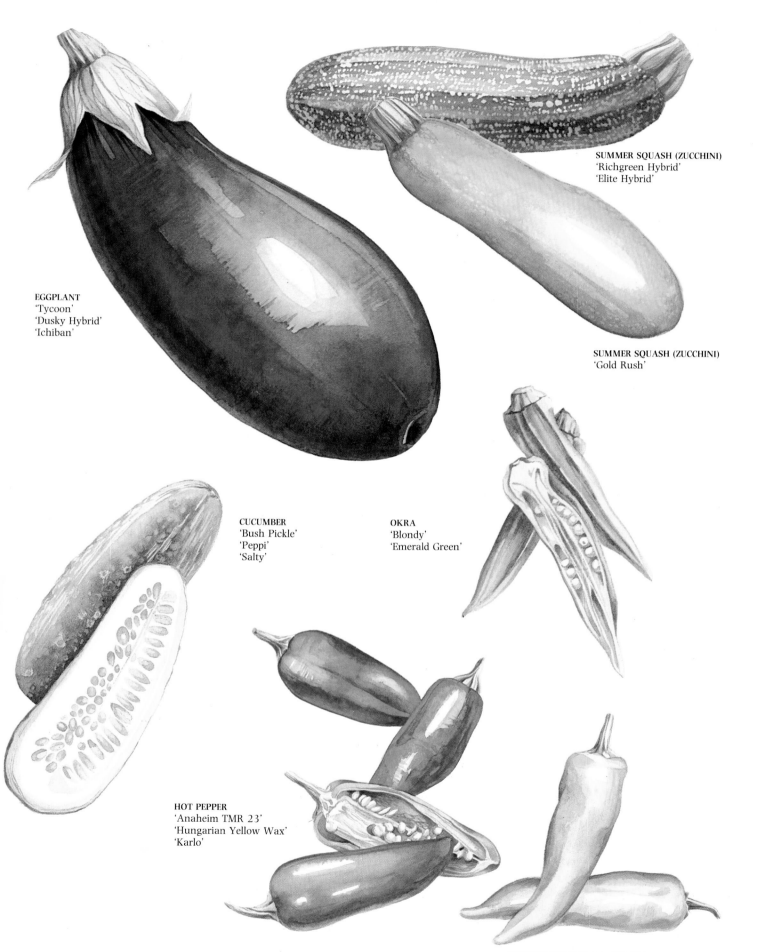

EGGPLANT
'Tycoon'
'Dusky Hybrid'
'Ichiban'

SUMMER SQUASH (ZUCCHINI)
'Richgreen Hybrid'
'Elite Hybrid'

SUMMER SQUASH (ZUCCHINI)
'Gold Rush'

CUCUMBER
'Bush Pickle'
'Peppi'
'Salty'

OKRA
'Blondy'
'Emerald Green'

HOT PEPPER
'Anaheim TMR 23'
'Hungarian Yellow Wax'
'Karlo'

CULTIVATION DETAILS SEE PAGES 161–167

TOMATOES, PEPPERS, AND MUSHROOMS Selected varieties

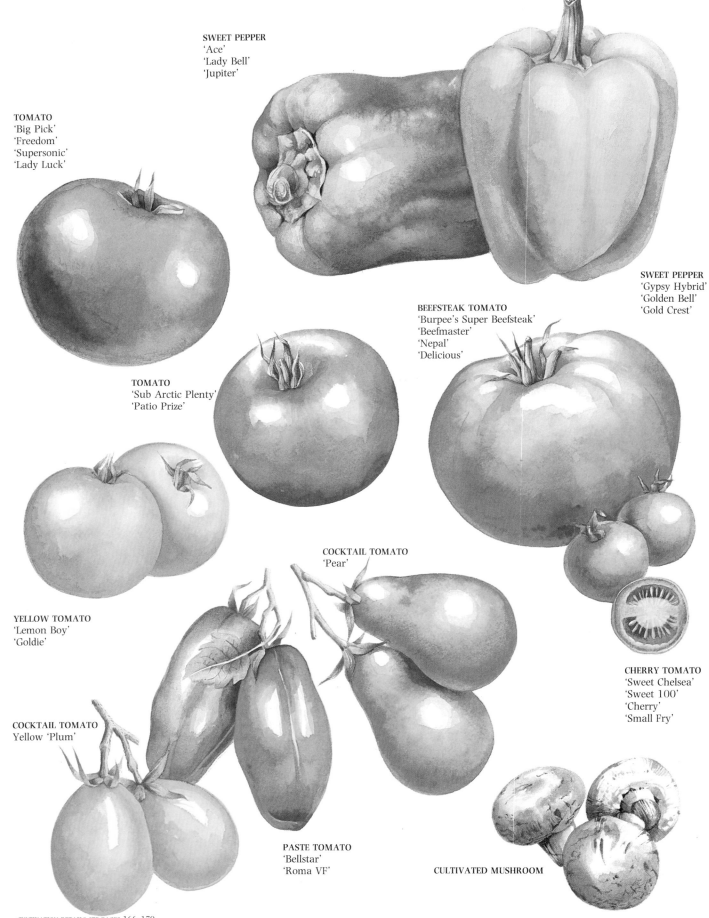

SWEET PEPPER
'Ace'
'Lady Bell'
'Jupiter'

TOMATO
'Big Pick'
'Freedom'
'Supersonic'
'Lady Luck'

SWEET PEPPER
'Gypsy Hybrid'
'Golden Bell'
'Gold Crest'

BEEFSTEAK TOMATO
'Burpee's Super Beefsteak'
'Beefmaster'
'Nepal'
'Delicious'

TOMATO
'Sub Arctic Plenty'
'Patio Prize'

COCKTAIL TOMATO
'Pear'

YELLOW TOMATO
'Lemon Boy'
'Goldie'

CHERRY TOMATO
'Sweet Chelsea'
'Sweet 100'
'Cherry'
'Small Fry'

COCKTAIL TOMATO
Yellow 'Plum'

PASTE TOMATO
'Bellstar'
'Roma VF'

CULTIVATED MUSHROOM

CULTIVATION DETAILS SEE PAGES 166–170

VEGETABLE GARDEN I

Vegetable gardening is an intensely personal matter, not least because it offers you the opportunity of choosing to cultivate those vegetables you and your family most like to eat. By growing your own crops, you can enjoy the food in the knowledge that it is not only full of flavor and goodness but free of harmful chemicals and pesticides.

The selection of vegetable crops available to today's food gardener is huge—and increases every year as seed suppliers introduce new varieties. Yellow beets and tomatoes, white radishes, pink celery, purple beans and onions, snap peas, and miniature, globe-shaped carrots are just a few of the many new vegetables you can choose from.

The techniques of vegetable cultivation depend more on the group of plants to which each belongs than on individual variety. Because plants with common characteristics share the same basic needs, the vegetables in the following section are grouped together according to those needs. The major groupings are pods and seeds, stalks and shoots, root vegetables, vegetable fruits, brassicas and other leafy vegetables, the onion family, and herbs.

As well as heeding and following the best cultivation techniques, as detailed throughout the book, you also need to plan carefully to get the best out of your vegetable garden. Forethought is needed, for example, if you want to have fresh vegetables on your table every week—or even every day—of the year, if you want to harvest your favorite crops for the longest possible period, or if your aim is to grow as wide a range of vegetables as possible.

When planning your vegetable garden, you must take into account the climate (and any ways you can protect plants from the weather with cloches or a greenhouse), the space you have available, and the need to practice crop rotation. The last of these is vital to the health and welfare of the vegetable garden, since growing the same sorts of crops in the same place each year can lead to a damaging buildup of disease organisms in the soil.

Unless your garden is very large, space is likely to be one of your greatest constraints. Again, planning can help you make the most of the area you have available for vegetables, particularly if you aim for some interplanting or catch cropping (see pp.132–133). If space is at a premium, you should aim to set plants as close together as possible, without restricting their growth or depriving them of the light they need in order to thrive. Often, grouping vegetables in wide beds rather than in single rows is a good way of maximizing your use of space, as is growing plants on trellises or fences.

Whatever vegetables you choose to grow, never forget that the key to success lies in the soil. Well-nourished soil is the vital ingredient for growing your own vegetables, and tending the soil is an ongoing task, since you must always return to the ground what has been taken out of it in the form of food crops.

Planning the vegetable plot means considering what kinds of crops to grow each year and where to grow them, as well as deciding on when to make a start. It does not mean drawing up a precise, row-by-row annual cropping plan; this would inevitably be disrupted by tricks of weather and variations in temperatures.

PLANNING THE VEGETABLE PLOT

Crop rotation and its manuring routine (see p.25) are significant factors in how you allocate the space each year. If you practice crop rotation, your vegetable plot will probably be divided into three, whatever its shape, with possibly some extra space allowed for permanent vegetables. The size of each section will depend on your favorites among vegetables.

Before planning the plot in detail, make a note of how much space you need to allow rows of particular crops. Plan a bed at a time, and remember to allow space for a seedbed. To make the best use of the space, aim to follow one crop with another immediately: this practice is known as *succession planting*.

WHERE TO GROW VEGETABLES

Most vegetables need all the light and warmth they can get, which means a site open to the sun for at least six hours a day. They simply will not grow in more or less permanent shade. An exception, which does reasonably well in partial shade (although not under trees), is Jerusalem artichokes. A quick-maturing crop of lettuce will grow in partial shade during the warmest months of the year.

Good drainage is another essential. Though celery, celeriac, and leeks do best in moist soil, no vegetable will put up with waterlogging. Dry soil checks growth also, but you can remedy this by irrigating and by digging in plenty of organic material. Dry, light soils warm up quickly in spring and give the earliest crops.

Shelter is not essential, but growth is faster when crops are protected from strong winds—particularly those that blow cold. If your whole garden is exposed, consider planting a hedge or erecting a fence or screen as protection.

Don't think that you can't grow food crops if you don't have much space. An area of only about four square yards should keep a family in summer salads. A double row of pole beans ten feet long will yield up to forty pounds of beans, whereas nearly thirty pounds is considered a good yield for a single container-grown tomato. Forget the dream of total self-sufficiency and concentrate instead on a relatively small number of carefully chosen crops.

If you simply don't have space, or conditions are unsuitable, consider growing at least a few vegetables in the flowerbed or in containers (see p.132). Suitably decorative crops include globe artichokes, asparagus, beets, ornamental cabbages, sweet corn, and tomatoes. For containers, which include pots, tubs, and growing bags, choose any of the salad crops (lettuces, radishes, spring onions), or carrots, Swiss chard, and such semiornamental summer crops as peppers, eggplants, zucchini, and tomatoes.

CHOOSING YOUR CROPS

The most obvious choice is to grow what you most enjoy eating, but this needs qualifying. Among your favorite crops, it makes sense to concentrate on kinds not always readily available in the supermarket—some Chinese vegetables, for instance—or those that taste best when they are freshly gathered, such as early peas and sweet corn.

Choose vegetables suited to the conditions that you can provide. This means, for example, avoiding watermelons and eggplants if you live in a particularly cold area, and celeriac if your soil is sandy and dry. Do not plant vegetables that will mature when you will be away on your annual vacation.

Likewise, choose crops to match the available space. There is little point in planting cabbages or midseason potatoes in a garden where every bit of ground is precious. Crops should not be crammed together at less than the recommended spacings, though very close planting is acceptable in beds (see p.133).

Finally, choose crops that are known to do well in your part of the world. Soil and weather conditions, pests and diseases, and first and last frost dates can differ dramatically within a single state, so it is wise to seek the advice of a local nurseryman or agricultural extension service agent before deciding what to buy.

CROP CATEGORIES

Some vegetables are sown in rows in the place where they are to grow; this applies, for example, to most root crops. After the seedlings have emerged, they are thinned to allow them adequate space to develop. Peas are grown in this way, too, but the seeds are spaced at sowing time and no further thinning is needed.

Late fall Only a few vegetables remain in the ground; most of the plot is left vacant for digging. Most gardeners try to complete this task by Thanksgiving, especially if the soil is heavy. Leave the ground rough for the frost to crumble.

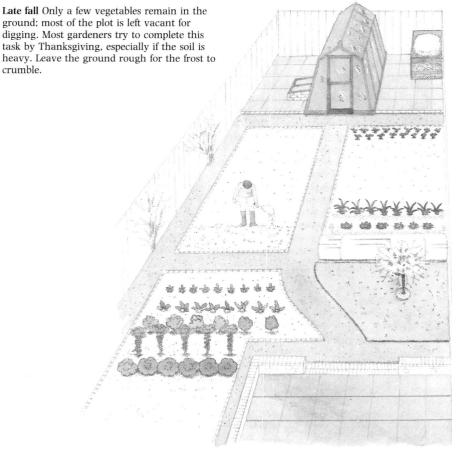

Many other crops are sown in a separate seedbed, and the seedlings are transferred to their final quarters when they are partly grown. Many brassicas are planted in this way. They need a lot of growing space, and the two-stage operation means that the ground is occupied for less time.

Tender plants, such as tomatoes and peppers, are also grown in two stages. They are started indoors in spring, then moved outdoors when the soil has warmed up and the risk of night frosts is over. Between the two environments they must have a period of acclimatization, termed *hardening off*, in a cold frame or possibly under cloches.

By sowing many vegetable seeds in a warm environment, then setting young plants outdoors under protection, you can get earlier crops of hardy vegetables, such as lettuces and cauliflowers.

A few crops are planted as bulbs (shallots and onions) or tubers (potatoes and Jerusalem artichokes). These are placed in their final growing position.

A few perennial vegetables remain in the same position for a number of years. The chief crops of this type are asparagus, globe artichokes, and rhubarb. Despite occupying their site all year round, each provides only a single harvest. Such crops therefore offer poor value for space in a small or average-sized garden, although you may still choose to grow them as a luxury vegetable—asparagus and globe artichokes are rarely inexpensive to buy.

HERBS
There is room for herbs in even the smallest garden (see p.41). If you are restricted to two or three pots on a patio or a windowbox outside the kitchen, this still allows you to grow basic herbs, such as mint, basil, chives, parsley, and thyme. If a small patch of garden can be set aside for growing more, so much the better. Position perennials where they will not interfere with the annual rotation of crops.

Further suggestions on what herbs to grow and how to set about it are given on pp.219–223.

WHEN TO START
Aim to have the plot cleared of perennial weeds, then manured and dug ready for the first spring sowing and planting. On most soils this means completing the work by early winter, since it is likely to be too cold and wet after that. This will also give time for frost to crumble the clods. Heavy soil dug in spring breaks down for seed-sowing less readily than fall-dug soil.

To make a spring start on undug, heavy soil, wait until the surface is reasonably dry and then turn over a few random patches with a fork. Once you can break the lumps into a reasonably crumbly tilth—with neither sticky nor rock-hard clods—it is worth digging or tilling the whole area.

Such problems do not arise on light, quick-draining soil. When dug at any time of year, the soil crumbles readily, so spring manuring and digging can be followed almost at once by sowing or planting. Let the soil settle for a week or two, however.

If you make a start in summer for some reason, on soil of any type, it will be too late to sow slow-growing crops such as parsnips, Brussels sprouts, leeks, or onions. Concentrate for this first season on such rapid growers as lettuce, radishes, spring onions, beets, carrots, and turnips. In the North, sow quick-maturing cabbage seeds between mid- and late summer for a harvest in the late fall.

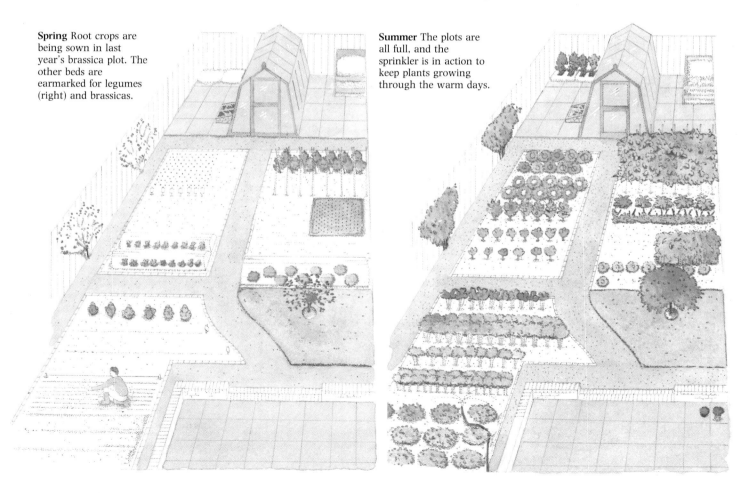

Spring Root crops are being sown in last year's brassica plot. The other beds are earmarked for legumes (right) and brassicas.

Summer The plots are all full, and the sprinkler is in action to keep plants growing through the warm days.

TOWARD BETTER SOIL, page 25
PLANTING VEGETABLES AND HERBS, pages 40–41

SPACE-SAVING METHODS, pages 132–133

If your food garden is smaller than you would like, there are several ways in which to make better use of the available space. If you follow any, or all, of these suggestions, you will have a significantly greater output from a given area. All the intensive methods depend for success on a high level of soil fertility; if necessary, take steps to improve this (see p.25).

CATCH CROPPING

The idea of catch cropping is to make use of patches of ground left empty between harvesting one crop and planting another. For instance, if squash or melons are to be planted out in late spring or early summer on a part of the plot where parsnips or rutabagas were grown during the winter months, there should be time to grow a crop of lettuce or spring onions after the last root

vegetables have been harvested and before the soil is warm enough for the squash or melons to go in. There will be even more time to spare before late-maturing cabbages and broccoli are planted out.

The fast-growing vegetables most suitable for catch cropping include—as well as lettuces and spring onions—short-rooted carrots, beets, dwarf peas, turnips, radishes, kohlrabi, and spinach. In all cases choose quick-maturing, early varieties.

Catch cropping can also be practiced at the other end of the season, using a fast-growing vegetable to follow a midsummer harvest of new potatoes, bush beans, or early-maturing cabbages. Unoccupied soil should be a rare sight between late spring and autumn in regions where the growing season is moderately long, if the food garden is producing as much as it can.

INTERPLANTING

This is a space-saving method that exploits the differences in growth rates between crops. Fast-growing crops of the types mentioned above are sown between those that mature more slowly. By the time the slow-growing vegetables are big enough to fill the space around them, the fast growers have been harvested. The spaces between rows and between slow-growing plants within a row can be used in this way. Late-maturing brassicas, in particular, lend themselves to this treatment. Fast-maturing crops can be grown between them before they become too large.

The success of this intensive planting depends to a large extent on well-fed soil and plenty of moisture. Always remove the secondary crop before the row or bed becomes overcrowded with plants.

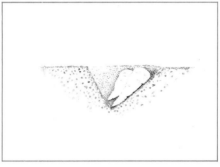

Late-maturing crops, such as parsnips and leeks, may still be occupying valuable space at sowing time. A simple solution is to dig a shallow trench elsewhere, then dig up the remainder of the crop and place it in the trench with a covering of soil. This space-saving process is termed *heeling in.*

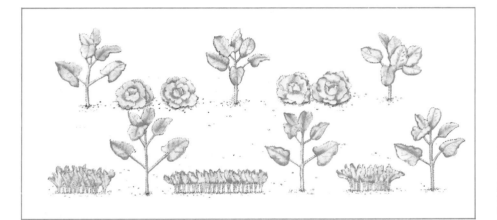

Interplanting makes use of the spaces between slow-growing plants, such as parsnips and some brassicas. Here, fast-maturing lettuces and radishes have been sown between Brussels sprouts. They will be harvested before the main crop needs the space.

GROWING IN CONTAINERS

Many vegetables can be grown in large containers on the patio, which saves precious room in the vegetable plot. They may even benefit by being given a sunnier position. Tomatoes, eggplants, peppers, and cucumbers are all suitable for this method of growing. Pots, tubs, and boxes need to be at least nine inches deep and wide, and it helps if they are somewhat larger, since smaller containers can dry out in a matter of hours.

Garden soil is seldom suitable as a growing medium for container-grown crops, and the cost of ready-made potting soil can be high. Use garden soil in containers only if you have a crumbly, fertile loam; even then you will probably have to add sand and peat to achieve good moisture retention and drainage.

When buying potting soil, choose a soilless mix or a peat-based product. The soilless mix will tend to retain moisture longer, particularly if it contains plenty of vermiculite, but in both cases the crop will need supplementary liquid feeding as it develops. Tomatoes in particular need generous feeding. If you are using homemade planting mix, add some thoroughly rotted manure or garden compost during the preparation stage, together with a balanced fertilizer.

Be sure that there is a drainage outlet in the bottom of the container. If you wish, cover the hole with curved crocks, then place a layer of small stones over the base. Stand containers on slats or bricks so that the drainage outlet is clear. All containers will need watering daily, even twice daily during hot weather.

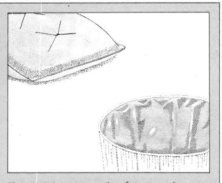

To minimize evaporation from growing bags (top), cut only small holes, or slits, for the plants. You can simply lift a corner for watering. Never let the compost dry out: apart from harming the plants, it may prove difficult to saturate again.

Reduce evaporation from wooden containers by lining them with plastic.

GROWING VEGETABLES IN BEDS

The wide-bed system of growing crops, rather than growing them in long rows, is another means of saving space. The beds need to be narrow enough to allow you to plant, weed, and perform other cultivation tasks from the sides, without stepping on top of them. This allows closer spacings and therefore a higher production rate.

Extra output is not the only advantage. On heavy ground, especially, walking between the plants on an ordinary plot compresses the soil and spoils its texture. The looser soil in beds drains better, warms up earlier in spring, and is much easier to work into a tilth for seed-sowing. There is a marginal advantage, too, in that closely spaced plants tend to suppress weeds. To some extent this is countered, however, by the greater difficulty of hoeing.

Though the paths may be left as bare earth—on light soil, anyway—it is a considerable advantage to provide a firmer surface that will suppress weeds and not be reduced to mud. Bricks or small paving stones are ideal, but grass or wood chips also work well.

For most gardeners a convenient bed width is four feet, making the maximum reach two feet from either side. If you use cloches, make at least some of the beds sufficiently wide to take a double row; a single row of cloches would waste space.

There is no limit to the length of a bed, though it might be convenient to divide a long plot by means of a central path. There is then no need to walk the length of the bed in order to reach the other side. Make the paths about a foot and a half wide.

MAKING THE BEDS

In making the beds, double digging (see pp. 34–35) really does pay, at least for the initial preparation. Once you have formed the beds, it should be necessary to double dig only every few years. Double digging will also help to raise the level of the bed, thereby assisting drainage.

Mark out the bed shapes before you start to dig, and once you have given some thought to layout and spacing. Some gardeners like to leave a slightly broader path between each pair of beds to allow room for the wheelbarrow. This is certainly an advantage if space is not too restricted.

Remove the topsoil and loosen the subsoil; take care not to mix any of the latter with the topsoil. Subject to the requirements of your crop rotation (see p. 25), fork plenty of compost or manure into the upper layer, or add some lime to the dug surface. Try to complete the digging and preparation well in advance of sowing or planting so that the beds have time to settle.

PLANTING THE CROPS

When sowing and planting, remember to maintain the same spacing between plants in every direction. That is, the distance between plants across the bed should be the same as the distance between plants along the bed. This will be greater than that between plants in a row, but less than the space between rows.

For instance, if you normally leave one foot between rows of beets and thin the plants to a spacing of four inches, allow about five inches in each direction when growing them in a bed. As a general rule, the more space you allow, the larger the plants will grow, though size is also influenced by soil fertility. You will have achieved the ideal spacing if the leaves of fully mature plants just reach those of their neighbors on each side.

MANAGING THE BEDS

Keep the beds weeded and hoed while the plants are small. As plants grow, they will tend to suppress further weed growth. A short-handled onion hoe is useful for working between closely planted crops.

Carry out all cultivation from the paths, and never walk on the beds. Once a bed is established, it should be possible to turn the soil with a fork, mixing in manure or compost as you do so, instead of digging with a spade.

Staggered planting, with the vegetables in one row set opposite the spaces in adjoining rows, makes maximum use of bed space. By the time plants reach maturity, most of the ground should be covered with foliage. Because cultivation is carried out from the side, there is no need to walk between the plants.

It is easier to organize rotation of crops when vegetables are grown in beds. During a given year, set one bed aside for brassicas, another for root crops, and a third for legumes and/or solanaceous plants. Earth paths are fine on light soil; on heavier ground, especially where drainage is poor, it is an advantage to lay bricks, gravel, or paving stones.

FEEDING THE SOIL AND PLANTS, page 28
DIGGING THE PLOT, pages 34–35

DECIDING WHAT TO GROW, pages 130–131

Peas (*Pisum sativum*) are a cool-weather crop, so they must be planted as early in the spring as possible, or in late summer for a fall crop. Many varieties require a trellis for support, and most are susceptible to fungus and virus infections. In spite of these potential difficulties, though, it is worth growing peas for their wonderful fresh-picked flavor.

In general, peas can be divided into dwarf and climbing or pole varieties, each of which has its virtues. Dwarf types, which typically grow to about eighteen inches, rarely need supporting and are suitable for small gardens and for producing early crops. Climbing peas, which can reach as much as six feet in height, bear later in the season but produce more heavily and for a longer period. Obviously, these varieties must be grown on a trellis or some other kind of support.

TYPES OF PEA

Peas are also classified according to the characteristics of their pods, which affect their uses as well as size and date of harvest. The three major categories are garden peas, edible-podded peas, and snap peas.

Garden peas include the traditional varieties that have tough, fibrous pods and tender, sweet peas. They come in both dwarf and climbing forms and have either wrinkled or smooth seeds, the latter being more resistant to rot. Garden peas planted in March or early April are ready for harvesting by mid-June, and continue to bear if the weather is cool.

Edible-podded peas, also known as sugar or snow peas, are harvested when their pods are tender and fleshy but before the peas have developed. They are good raw or cooked, and freeze well. Edible-podded peas, like garden peas, come in both dwarf and climbing varieties, and are often disease resistant. As the name "snow pea" implies, they will withstand light frost.

Snap peas are the most recent development of plant breeders. Like snow peas, they have edible pods, but these are best when the peas themselves are mature and crisp. Snap peas are suitable for eating raw, for cooking whole, for shelling, and for freezing.

All types of pea grow best in soil that holds moisture well but is free-draining. As this implies, it must contain plenty of organic matter, either dug in well ahead of sowing or mixed into the bottom of a trench (see pp. 138–139). Early or over-wintered crops do best in light soil.

MAKING A START: PROTECTED SOWINGS

For an overwintered crop, which is possible in most parts of Zones 9 and 10 and in greenhouses elsewhere, sow a dwarf, smooth-seeded variety in late fall and cover with cloches.

Use a hoe to form flat furrows eight inches wide and two inches deep; allow two feet between furrows. Sow the seeds in three rows, spacing them two inches apart in each direction. Cover the seeds with the soil removed to form the furrow. Set mouse traps under the cloches.

Follow exactly the same sequence for a sowing in late winter or early spring, as soon as the soil is workable. Cover with cloches until the soil begins to warm up.

Place the cloches in position a week or two ahead of sowing to help warm and dry the soil. It is pointless to sow in cold, wet soil, since germination will be slow and the risk of disease great; the seeds may even rot.

You can also sow peas indoors in late winter for subsequent planting outdoors. This enables you to make a start while the soil outside is still too wet and cold. A good method is to sow the seeds individually in two-inch peat pots, then cover them with glass and paper until they germinate. Gentle warmth—about 45°F—will help to get them started.

Aim to plant out the seedlings in early to midspring, complete with the pots, before they get too leggy. Harden them off in a cold frame for a week or two before you do so.

Leave just a little space between the pots when planting.

As an alternative to peat pots, sow the seeds in lengths of plastic guttering filled with planting mix. Sow in two rows, two inches apart, and germinate in gentle warmth. When planting out in midspring, after hardening off, form a rounded furrow to match the guttering and simply slide the row of plants into it.

UNPROTECTED SOWINGS

Peas are usually one of the first crops to be sown in the spring; they can be planted as soon as the soil can be worked, although it is a good idea to encourage quick germination by sowing them in raised beds or under cloches.

Because they often go into cold, wet ground, peas are susceptible to fungus diseases that will cause them to rot. To avoid this problem, treat them with a powdered fungicide. An alternative is to inoculate them with a bacterial preparation that helps them to use the nitrogen in the air. Add some high-phosphate and -potash fertilizer before planting.

Peas need support as soon as they are five or six inches tall; otherwise they will trail along the ground and be at risk from attack by slugs and snails. Insert dead sticks and branches along the row, or fix some form of netting, as shown in the illustrations. You can also make or buy a trellis like those suitable for pole beans (see pp.138–139).

In general, climbing varieties of peas will bear heavily throughout their growing season, so they can use a side dressing of sulfate of ammonia when they are tall enough to need support. Mulch them well, adding some well-rotted manure if you have it.

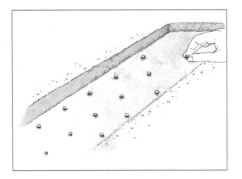

In light, sandy soil, sow peas in wide, shallow trenches; space the seeds two inches apart in each direction. A covering of cloches will protect early crops from birds and squirrels as well as from the weather.

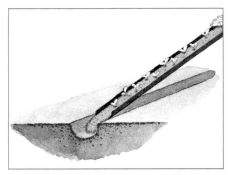

Germinating the seedlings in a length of fairly broad guttering allows you to transfer them from greenhouse to outdoor bed without root disturbance. Simply slide them out into a furrow of matching shape.

CARE OF THE CROP

During dry weather, keep the rows well watered from the time the peas start to flower. A mulch of finely crumbled manure or compost will help to keep the soil moist.

If aphids are a problem, spray the plants with cold water early in the day, or dust with rotenone in the evening. Slugs can be controlled by trapping or hand picking.

HARVESTING

Pick garden varieties when the peas are well developed but before they quite fill the pods. Pick edible-podded varieties when they are about two inches long and before the seeds swell. Harvest snap peas daily: do not let them exceed one and a half inches in length. Picking every day or two insures continuous cropping.

If you want to dry peas for use in soups and stews, leave them to ripen on the plants. To finish the process, lift the complete plants and hang them upside down in an airy shed or shelter. When fully dry, shell the peas and store them in airtight jars.

When all fresh peas have been harvested, sever the main stem of each plant at ground level and put the plants on the compost heap. Leave the roots in the soil so that the beneficial nitrogen stored in their nodules can be released to aid soil fertility.

PESTS AND DISEASES

Among several pests that affect peas, the most troublesome are aphids, slugs, seed corn maggots, and rodents.

The most likely ailments are powdery mildew, root rot, and fusarium wilt.

Dead branches of shrubs and trees provide one of the best supports for peas. Insert them along the row, and make sure that there is plenty of support fairly close to the ground to which the tendrils can cling.

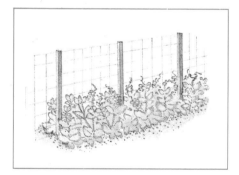

A length of netting provides a good alternative form of support. Secure it to firm stakes and, if necessary, loop twine around the main stem of the plant to insure that it clings securely, even in wet or windy weather.

RECOMMENDED VARIETIES

Garden peas

'Green Arrow' A midseason, medium-sized variety that bears pods on the top of the plant. A heavy-bearing, disease-resistant variety of pea.

'Wando' Acknowledged as the best garden pea for heat resistance. Heavy yields; bears in midseason.

'Progress No. 9' The earliest long-podded pea; bears well.

'Little Marvel' An early dwarf pea that freezes well.

'Frosty' Another early variety good for freezing. Dwarf plants are resistant to wilt.

'Lincoln' An old favorite because of its sweetness. Midseason; medium-sized.

'Alaska' A very early pea; good for freezing, canning, and drying.

'Feltham First' Another very early variety.

'Waverex' Very short vines bear small pods with tiny *petits pois*.

'Alderman' A late-season, vigorous variety that is easy to shell.

'Thomas Laxton' This early, adaptable pea bears well; peas are good for freezing.

'Lacy Lady' A dwarf variety that has little foliage and can be planted close together in small gardens. Early.

Edible-podded peas

'Oregon Sugar Pod II' A midseason snow pea that bears well and retains its flavor and tenderness for a few days. Very vigorous.

'Blizzard' An early, dwarf variety.

'Dwarf Gray Sugar' A medium-sized pea that is tolerant of both heat and cold. Vigorous.

Snap peas

'Sugar Snap' The first snap pea, a 1979 All-America winner. Tall, productive, and frost and wilt resistant.

'Sugar Daddy' A late variety with stringless pods. Medium-sized; good for cooking.

'Snappy' Very early; mildew resistant.

'Little Sweetie' This dwarf variety produces short, stringless pods early in the season.

SOWING UNDER GLASS, pages 38–39
PLANTING VEGETABLES, page 40

CROP PROTECTION, page 44
PEAS, page 113

PESTS AND DISEASES, pages 172–175
FREEZING VEGETABLES, pages 232–233

Most people are familiar with shell beans, or at least with the ever-popular lima (*Phaseolus limensis*), but more and more gardeners are now growing beans for drying, such as favas (*Vicia faba*) and soybeans (*Glycine max*), as well. Although the distinction is usually made, both types are often suitable for both eating fresh and drying, and they offer special advantages to those in the more extreme climate zones.

Beside limas, the shell bean family includes French horticultural beans and Southern or cow peas. These beans require a long, hot growing season and are popular throughout the South, although they can be grown elsewhere if they are germinated in warm soil. They are often available in both bush and pole varieties.

Among dried beans, kidneys, pintos, and Great Northern beans are well known, but many others are now available, including garbanzos, cranberry beans, and soldier beans. Many of these are suitable for northern climates; the fava bean is especially hardy, and can be planted a few weeks before the last frost or (on the West Coast) in the fall or early winter for a spring crop. These beans, which are very popular in Europe because of their sweet flavor, are a good alternative for northerners who lack the conditions to grow lima beans.

Most soils will suit shell and dried beans, but avoid using the same part of the plot in successive years (see Crop Rotation, p.25). Neutral or slightly acid soil is ideal. Choose a fairly sunny position, and provide support for the growing beans. Like snap beans, shell and dried beans do not require much fertilizer, although pole limas will benefit from light side dressings of nitrogen.

MAKING A START
Shell beans To germinate properly, lima beans need soil temperatures of 65° to 75°F, so sow the seeds a few weeks after the last frost date or in individual pots indoors two to three weeks before. Other shell beans can be planted somewhat earlier, but be sure the soil is warm.

Treat seeds with a bacterial inoculant to help them fix nitrogen—that is, utilize the nitrogen in the air for growth—then make holes one inch deep and two to four inches apart in rows two and a half feet apart, and put one seed in each hole. Water, then cover the rows with cloches. Alternatively, plant the seeds slightly closer in a bed.

If you are setting out seedlings started indoors, warm the soil with cloches and be careful to harden the plants off completely. Set plants about four inches apart in rows, water them well, and cover them with cloches if the weather is cold or windy.
Fava beans Sow seeds two or three weeks before the last frost date, or in the fall if you live on the West Coast. Add a little general fertilizer to the soil first, and cover the beds with cloches to speed germination.
Dried beans Plant as for shell beans, but leave slightly more space between plants and between rows if possible.

CARE OF THE CROP
Support bush types by inserting stakes or canes around the outside of paired rows; tie string between them and across the rows. Pole varieties can be supported in the same way as other pole beans (see pp.138–139).

Mulching is a good idea for dried beans, which need a moist, cool soil to grow in. Use straw, hay, or leaves, and apply it thickly.

HARVESTING
Shell beans Harvest limas when the pods are plump and green; if you leave them too long, the beans will become starchy and dry. Southern peas and soybeans are best when the pods first change color.
Dried beans Leave the pods on the plants until they are brown and dry, then pick them and store them in a dry place for a few weeks. Remove the beans and let them dry again before you store them permanently.

PESTS AND DISEASES
Mexican bean beetles, Japanese beetles, and leafhoppers are the principal pests; bean weevils can infest dried beans.

Diseases include anthracnose, blight, powdery mildew, and virus infections.

RECOMMENDED VARIETIES
Shell beans
'Dixie Butter Pea' A bush lima with small, plump beans. Heat resistant.
'Fordhook No. 242' An All-America Winner. Large, plump lima beans; heavy yields.
'Florida Butter' A speckled pole lima. Rampant grower; very heat resistant.
'King of the Garden' A popular pole lima.
'California Blackeye' Bush beans with large cream-colored seeds. Disease resistant.
'Mississippi Silver' A tasty Southern pea.
'French Horticultural' Very hardy, disease-resistant pole bean.
Dried beans
'Fiskeby' Dependable northern soybean.
'Broad Windsor' Standard fava variety.
'Express' The earliest fava bean.
'Midnight Black Turtle' Small black beans.
'Jacob's Cattle' Pure white beans have dark red speckles.

Sow fava beans and other large-podded beans in double rows. Place the seeds in each row opposite the spaces in the other. Leave nine inches between pairs of rows and between the seeds in a row.

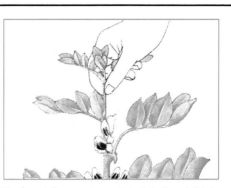

Pinch out the growing point of shell and dried bean plants to deter aphids. Do this when the first pods start to develop – or sooner if these pests appear. Pinching the tip also speeds the development of the crop.

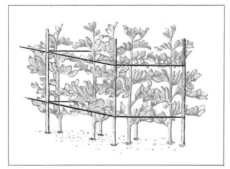

Support all but the shortest varieties with stakes and string. The best method is to insert pairs of stakes on each side of the row, secure string between them around the outside, and then pass it across between plants.

Bush snap beans (*Phaseolus vulgaris*) are probably the most common garden vegetable in America, and summer meals are scarcely complete without them. They are ready at least two weeks earlier than pole beans. If you have enough space to grow both bush and pole beans, you will have a supply of fresh beans throughout most of the summer months.

Snap beans come in several forms and may be yellow or purple as well as green. There are both flat-podded and round-podded types; the flat-podded beans sometimes tend to become stringy if allowed to grow large. Most varieties of either type can be cooked snapped or whole, and the ripe seeds of some varieties can also be shelled and stored for use as dried beans. Most snap beans form dwarf, bushy plants, but there are also climbing varieties.

All snap beans need a sunny site and a light, well-drained soil. To provide enough nitrogen, either mix some compost into the soil or coat the seeds with a bacterial inoculant. Choose a sheltered spot to protect the plants from the wind.

You can advance crops by sowing the seeds in a greenhouse and planting the seedlings out under cloches. Alternatively, sow directly in the ground.

MAKING A START

Dig the site during the fall, and add plenty of manure or compost.

For direct sowing outdoors, wait until the soil is dry and has started to warm up, which usually means fairly late in the spring. Snap beans cannot withstand frost, and sowings in cold, wet soil invariably fail. Set cloches in place two weeks beforehand.

Make a furrow an inch and a half deep, and sow the seeds of bush snap beans three inches apart. Allow one and a half feet between rows.

If you are growing the beans in a bed, leave five inches between plants in each direction. It is easier to make separate holes with a trowel than to sow in furrows.

To start plants in an unheated greenhouse, sow the seeds in midspring. Set them two inches apart in trays or plant them in individual pots; cover them with glass and paper until they germinate.

If necessary, add general fertilizer to the row or bed at three ounces per square yard. Harden the plants off in late spring, but wait until after the last frost before planting them out if they are to be unprotected. If you are planting them under cloches, set them out two or three weeks earlier. Allow one and a half feet between rows and three to four inches between plants.

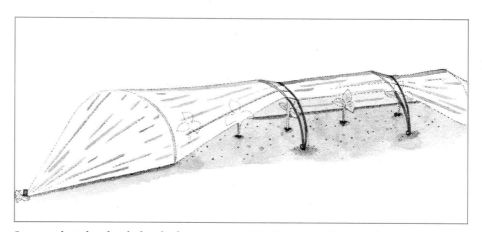

Sown or planted under cloches, bush snap beans get off to a better start and produce an earlier crop. Cloches can be left in place until the plants are well grown, but some ventilation may be needed during warm weather.

CARE OF THE CROP

A mulch around established plants will help to keep the weeds down and the soil's moisture in. Water generously during dry spells. If the plants blossom but fail to develop pods, provide partial shade to keep temperatures down. If the plot is exposed, insert stakes at intervals for support.

HARVESTING

Bush snap beans will start to crop within eight weeks of sowing, and may produce pods for up to eight weeks after that. Start picking when the pods will snap in half and before the seeds have developed. Pick all the pods that are ready so the plant will continue to produce.

To guarantee a good supply of snap beans throughout the summer, plant several rows in succession. If you plant every ten days or two weeks, you should be able to harvest bush snap beans from June until late September in most parts of the country.

PESTS AND DISEASES

Bush snap beans may be attacked by Mexican bean beetles, aphids, leafhoppers, or Japanese beetles.

Potential diseases include anthracnose, bacterial blight, mosaic viruses, powdery mildew, and gray mold.

RECOMMENDED VARIETIES

Green varieties

'**Greencrop**' An All-America Winner that has long, flat, stringless pods. Resistant to common bean mosaic virus.
'**Bush Romano**' The short, very broad pods are meaty and have a distinctive flavor.
'**Jumbo**' An extremely productive bean with very long pods.
'**Cheverbel**' A flageolet bean that is good fresh or shelled.

The plants have relatively insecure roots and benefit from the support of stakes and string. When picking, avoid loosening the roots by holding the plants with one hand while removing the beans with the other. Frequent picking insures heavy yields.

'**Bush Blue Lake**' Round bean pods are medium long and straight.
'**Venture**' An early 'Blue Lake' type, adaptable to climate extremes.
'**Provider**' An early, vigorous variety.
'**Tendercrop**' The classic bush snap bean. Disease resistant, productive, and flavorful.
'**Tenderpod**' This early, very tender bean is an All-America Winner.

Other varieties

'**Royal Burgundy**' The pods are short, round, and dark purple. Bushes do well in cold soil.
'**Sungold**' Stringless and meaty yellow pods have white seeds. Disease resistant.
'**Pencil Pod Wax**' A productive, reliable yellow wax bean with very round pods.

SOWING SEEDS OUTDOORS, pages 36–37
SOWING UNDER GLASS, pages 38–39

BEANS, SWEET CORN, AND ARTICHOKES, pages 114–115
PESTS AND DISEASES, pages 172–175

FREEZING VEGETABLES, pages 232–233

137

This vigorous, tall-growing crop might seem an odd choice for a small garden, yet in fact it is ideal. Limited ground area puts a premium on vertical space, which pole beans exploit to the full. On good soil they will grow to eight feet or more, and bear a prolific crop from close to ground level upward, though most gardeners are content with a more manageable six feet.

Pole beans include varieties of snap and lima beans as well as kidney and runner beans (*Phaseolus* sp.). Runner beans are larger and coarser than bush beans, with a more pronounced flavor. In general, pole beans require more warmth than bush beans, and respond best to a warm, sheltered spot in the garden. They grow readily almost everywhere, but they need a well-manured raised bed for maximum root development. In cold areas it is a great help to sow the seeds in a greenhouse and to plant the seedlings out under cloches. It also helps to choose a quick-maturing variety.

Because they are vining plants, pole beans need some form of support. This can be provided in a number of ways, as shown in the illustrations. Whatever system you use, it needs to be strong.

Arbors and teepee structures are the most familiar supports for pole beans; they are easy to make with bamboo, branches from trees, or wooden stakes, and they will last for several years if they are constructed well in the first place.

An alternative is to use a trellis or netting, which you can place either within the vegetable plot or against a fence or wall. Many varieties of pole bean, especially the red-flowered runner beans, present a brilliant spectacle when in full bloom, and make a welcome addition to a flowerbed or against the side of a garage. Trellises, too, can be used for many seasons if you clean them carefully in the fall.

The pole bean harvest extends from summer into autumn, provided the pods are picked every two or three days and before the seeds begin to bulge in the pods. Never leave old pods on the plants because they are past their best; they will inhibit the development of new flowers and pods.

The sowing times suggested are the earliest that are safe for spring crops. You can extend the season, though, by succession planting until midsummer.

Overall, the yields from pole beans reflect the amount of care you put into the soil preparation. Though you can expect some sort of harvest even on poor soil, your yields will increase dramatically if you dig in a generous amount of organic matter during the previous fall. You will also want to provide dressings of a general fertilizer during the growing season.

MAKING A START

First decide how you are going to support the beans and where you will position the plants. Then mark out the planting site and dig a spade-depth trench, about fifteen inches wide. Place a thick layer of manure or compost on the bottom and fork this into the soil. Mark the position of the trench with sticks when you replace the topsoil.

Rake a general fertilizer into this planting site, at three ounces per square yard, during the spring before sowing or planting. Erect supports at the same time to avoid disturbing the young plants later on, even if you propose to use cloches.

For the earliest crop, or if you live in a cold area, sow the seeds in a greenhouse during midspring. Either place them two inches apart in a box of planting mix or, even better, use peat pots and sow two seeds in each pot. Cover them with glass and paper until they germinate. Remove the weaker seedling in each pot if both seeds germinate; be careful not to disturb the roots of the stronger one.

Start to harden off the seedlings in late spring and plant them out ten to fourteen days later. If you are planting them against angled poles, set them on the underside, one to each support. In the case of peat pots, plant the whole container. Either protect the seedlings with individual cloches or, if

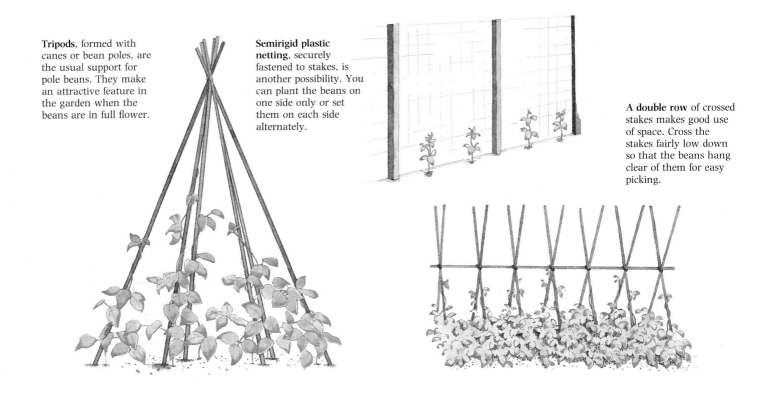

Tripods, formed with canes or bean poles, are the usual support for pole beans. They make an attractive feature in the garden when the beans are in full flower.

Semirigid plastic netting, securely fastened to stakes, is another possibility. You can plant the beans on one side only or set them on each side alternately.

A double row of crossed stakes makes good use of space. Cross the stakes fairly low down so that the beans hang clear of them for easy picking.

When planting pole beans that you have started indoors, keep the root ball or peat pot intact. Set a plant beneath each supporting pole, and water them if the soil is dry.

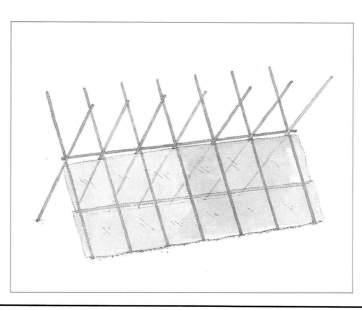

Polyethylene sheeting can be stapled or tacked to the lower part of the poles to form a giant cloche, which will protect the plants until they are growing strongly. Draw soil around the base of the plastic.

the supports are already in position, secure polyethylene sheeting to the poles with staples or thumbtacks to form a kind of giant cloche.

If you are planting against netting or a trellis, allow six inches between plants. When planting peat pots, make sure that the ground does not dry out afterward, particularly in beds close to walls, and tear off any rim that projects above the soil to help the plants retain moisture.

It is not safe to sow pole beans without protection until late spring, after the last frost. The alternative is to sow under cloches. Again, you can fasten plastic sheeting to the poles if these are already in position. Sow two seeds in each station, two inches deep, and remove the weaker seedling if both germinate.

Most pole beans require the same planting conditions as bush snap beans, but pole limas are particularly susceptible to cold, so be sure to plant out seedlings when the soil is warm and the plants are well established. If you live in a warm region and sow your pole lima beans directly, wait until the soil temperature is at least 65°F.

Like other legumes, pole beans are able to utilize atmospheric nitrogen for growth because of the bacteria that live on their roots. If you have not enriched your soil with compost or manure, help the beans to fix nitrogen by coating the seeds in a bacterial inoculant before you sow them. Do not use fungicides on seeds that have been inoculated, however.

CARE OF THE CROP

Remove cloches or plastic protection as soon as the plants are growing strongly. At this stage, with the soil well warmed, spread a mulch of manure around the plants. If necessary, tie the shoots to the support or give the plants an initial twist or two around the support. Their inclination is to climb counterclockwise, but sometimes they seem reluctant to start.

Take care that the soil does not dry out, especially when the plants extend up the supports and start to flower. Pinch the tip from each main shoot when it reaches the top of its support.

HARVESTING

Start picking when the beans are about six inches long, or when the pods are plump. The secret of prolonged cropping is to pick every day or two, and always remove the pods of pole snap beans before the seeds have time to swell. They are easily seen from the outside. The more frequently you pick, the heavier the harvest will be. Most pole beans are at their best if cooked or frozen while still young and tender; for information on harvesting pole varieties of shell and dried beans, see p.136.

After you have harvested the crop, cut down the stems but leave the roots in the ground, since they add nitrogen to the soil.

PESTS AND DISEASES

Like other beans, pole beans are susceptible to attacks from the Mexican bean beetle and the Japanese beetle. Nematodes can also be a problem in some regions.

Anthracnose, mosaic viruses, and bacterial blight are possible diseases.

RECOMMENDED VARIETIES

'Dutch Case Knife' An old variety of runner bean with long, flat, twisted pods. White seeds; prolific.

'Kentucky Wonder' A standard pole bean with stringless, flavorful pods and brown beans.

'Kentucky Wonder White Seeded' The beans have the same flavor as 'Kentucky Wonder,' but are better for freezing. Pods are straight and dark green.

'Romano' An Italian pole bean. Short, broad pods are good fresh or frozen; vines are prolific but relatively short.

'Selma Zebra' A very early stringless variety. Flat pods are streaked with purple.

'Scarlet Runner' A very ornamental bean that grows to 10 feet. Pods are very large; beans are black and scarlet.

'Burpee Golden' The butter-yellow pods are flat and stringless; beans are tender.

'Purple Pod' A vigorous, flavorful bean with green pods tinged with purple.

'King of the Garden' A very large pole lima, with extremely tasty beans. Late bearing.

'Florida Butter' This sweet butterbean is well adapted to hot, humid climates and has small, speckled beans.

'Christmas' Another speckled variety; bears earlier and more prolifically than 'Florida Butter.' Seeds are flecked with red.

'Burpee's Best' Thick, fat green beans are borne in large, broad pods. Tall vines.

SOWING SEEDS OUTDOORS, pages 36–37
SOWING UNDER GLASS, pages 38–39

BEANS, SWEET CORN, AND ARTICHOKES, pages 114–115
PESTS AND DISEASES, pages 172–175

FREEZING VEGETABLES, pages 232–233

139

The globe artichoke (*Cynara scolymus*) is a herbaceous perennial that is prized for the distinctive flavor of parts of its flower buds. This thistlelike plant is equally at home in the flowerbed, the container, and the vegetable plot: not only does it bear large flower heads, but its silvery-gray, deeply cut leaves also form a splendid backdrop for more colorful plants. This large vegetable demands a fair amount of space right through the year, which is another reason why you might want to grow it as a landscape plant.

The globe artichoke is a native of North Africa and is not especially difficult to grow, but it needs a long growing season. Except in the mildest coastal districts, such as northern California, where it is grown commercially, the root base must be protected during the colder months. With a good covering of leaves or straw, it should survive in mild inland gardens; elsewhere it is best grown in containers that can be moved indoors.

The usual (and best) way to start is with rooted suckers, which are obtainable from many nurseries and garden centers. The alternative is to raise the plants from seed. This saves money but gives rather variable results. If your seed-raised plants do not crop well, take your own suckers from the best plants when they are old enough, and start again. You should expect about six flower heads on each mature plant.

Fertile, well-manured soil with good drainage is needed if globe artichokes are to produce plenty of large flower heads. Sticky clay is unsuitable until it has been improved with generous additions of organic matter. A sunny, sheltered spot is the best position for globe artichokes.

MAKING A START

Spring is planting time, but well before then decide where the plants are to grow, so that you can dig and manure the site. The artichokes, which will grow up to five feet tall, have a spread of up to three feet, so allow for this amount of space around each plant. They require an open position, well away from the shade of trees.

Work in plenty of rotted manure or compost, at least a bucketful to the square yard, together with a good dressing of bonemeal. Up to one pound per square yard is not excessive, bearing in mind that the plants will remain in the same site for three or four years. Their production invariably declines after this time.

Growing from suckers During spring, place the suckers two and a half to three feet apart in each direction, and at the same depth as they were previously. The soil mark is easy to see. Use a trowel to plant them, and afterward firm the soil with your foot. Water the plants in and make sure that the soil remains damp while the suckers grow fresh roots.

In dry weather, the plants may wilt and become dormant. Reduce this risk by trimming off the outer quarter of each leaf immediately after planting to reduce moisture loss. Temporary shading with newspaper is a help, or you can place an open-ended cloche over each plant and paint it with greenhouse-shading liquid.

In late spring, spread a mulch of rotted manure or compost around the plants to help conserve moisture.

Growing from seed Start the plants in a seedbed by sowing the seeds one inch deep, with one foot between rows. Thin the seedlings to six inches apart. Grow these on for a year and then plant them in their permanent positions the following spring.

CARE OF THE CROP

Keep the plot hoed to prevent competition from weeds. Water during dry spells before the soil becomes parched and the plants suffer. From the second spring onward, rake in general fertilizer around the plants at two ounces per square yard.

It is better to resist harvesting a crop the first summer. It would, in any case, be very small. Nipping off the flower buds as they appear will help to insure more and better flower heads during later years.

Harvesting starts during the second year. For the largest artichokes, restrict the number of stems to five or six, and cut off the others near ground level. Also pinch out some of the smaller flowers that form on the side shoots.

In autumn, cut down the main stems close to the ground. If you live in a cold area, draw some soil over the crowns and then cover them with leaves or straw. Put wire netting on top to prevent the material from being blown away. In warmer areas, the soil may not be essential, but it is nevertheless a good precaution.

Another precautionary measure appropriate for colder gardens is to remove some suckers at this time and grow them on in six-inch pots in a cold frame for the winter. They will serve as replacements if the older plants are lost.

In cold zones, a covering of straw or leaves will protect the crowns during a hard winter. Encircle this with netting to prevent the material from being blown away or scattered by birds.

HARVESTING

Starting with the largest buds, which will be on the ends of the main stems, cut the flower buds, together with four to six inches of the stems, while they are still green and before they start to open. The edible parts are the fleshy, curving segments at the base of the petals, together with the bottom of the flower, called the heart; this is revealed by removing the hairy choke from inside the flower bud.

After removing the bud, cut back each stem to half its original length. Encourage a further crop of flowers by applying a liquid fertilizer every two weeks for a couple of months after you cut the first flower buds.

Use clippers to remove the flower buds, starting with the largest one at the top of each main stem. Harvest when these buds are fully developed but before they change color and start to open.

THE CROPPING PLAN
Year 1 Restrict flower buds as they appear in order to produce larger buds in the next two years.

Year 2 Restrict each plant to four to six stems and let flower buds develop on these. Nip off any smaller buds from side shoots. Harvest the flower buds.

Year 3 Harvest four to six flower buds per plant. Remove other buds.

Year 4 Globe artichokes are past their prime by this stage. Take suckers from plants in spring or fall. Aim to replace a third of your artichoke stock in this way each year.

PROPAGATION

Take root suckers in spring or fall. First scrape some soil away from the base of the plant, then cut downward, close to strong shoots, to remove them from the rootstock; make sure each shoot has a section of root attached. A large, sharp knife is the best tool. Once you have taken the suckers, discard the rest of the plant.

If you take suckers in spring, plant them out immediately. If you take them in the fall, overwinter them in pots in a cold frame before planting them out the following spring. Since the plants of globe artichokes are past their prime after three or four years, it is a good idea to replace up to a third of them every year.

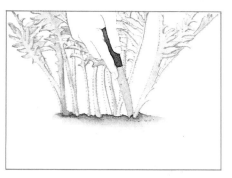

To propagate globe artichokes, use a long, sharp knife to remove offsets from the main plant, each with a good section of root. Trim the leaves back to reduce moisture loss after they have been transplanted.

Offsets taken during the spring should be replanted at once. Those taken during late autumn will stand a better chance if planted in potting soil and overwintered in a cold frame.

PESTS AND DISEASES
Aphids, together with slugs and snails, are the most likely pests.

The flower buds may be affected by petal blight disease.

RECOMMENDED VARIETY
'Green Globe Improved' is the variety generally available from seed catalogues, but will produce variable results. Either take root suckers from the best plants in the first year, or try to find commercial varieties in containers.

CHARDS
Chards are blanched leaf shoots, obtained from three- or four-year-old plants that have borne their final crop of flower buds and that are not needed to supply suckers.

To produce chards, cut down the main stems after harvesting to within one foot of the ground, and allow new shoots to grow. Mulch and water the plants frequently. When the shoots are about two feet high, tie them together, then tie black plastic around them to exclude the light. Treat them like celery or cardoons to blanch them. The stems and leaf tips are cooked and eaten like cardoons, to which they are related (see p.143).

SOWING SEEDS OUTDOORS, pages 36–37
BEANS, SWEET CORN, AND ARTICHOKES, pages 114–115
CARDOONS, page 143
PESTS AND DISEASES, pages 172–175

141

Sweet corn (*Zea mays*) is exceptionally tender and delicious if it is cooked just after it has been picked, so you will probably want to find space for this easily grown vegetable in your garden. Many kinds are available, including white, yellow, and bicolor varieties as well as the new supersweet hybrids, which have a more compact growth and keep better than standard sweet corn.

Sweet corn requires warm soil for germination, but it grows quickly on a fertile site with good drainage. If you can supply plenty of nutrients, enough moisture, and an early start, you can grow corn in any part of the United States. Obviously, northern gardeners are advised to start corn seedlings indoors and plant out when all danger of frost is past, whereas those in milder regions can sow directly into warm soil. Cloches and row covers are useful for corn in any region.

It is a good idea to plant sweet corn in blocks rather than rows, as pollination of the female silk by the male tassels is accomplished by the wind. Be careful to plant different varieties far enough apart to avoid cross-pollination, and succession-plant to insure a continuous crop.

Corn is a heavy feeder, so prepare the site, which should be sunny, the previous autumn by digging plenty of manure or compost into the soil. Clear away any perennial weeds, and be sure you will be able to provide an adequate supply of water.

Among the pests that might affect your crop, squirrels, deer, and raccoons are especially difficult to control. An electric fence is often effective; otherwise, try protecting the ears with bags or netting.

To aid pollination, plant sweet corn in blocks of four or five rows.

MAKING A START
Just before sowing or planting outdoors, rake a generous amount of general fertilizer into the soil (at least four ounces per square yard). Repeat this when the plants are growing well.

Sweet corn does not like being disturbed by transplanting. If you start seeds indoors, sow them in peat pots or other small pots—two per pot—in midspring. Germinate them at about 60°F, and keep them covered with glass and paper until the seedlings appear. Remove the weaker one if two germinate. Harden the seedlings off in late spring and plant them out, complete with their peat pot or soil ball, after the last frost, either in the open or under cloches. Space them as for outdoor-sown plants.

For a protected sowing outdoors, first warm the site by using cloches. Then sow the seeds under cloches or floating row covers from midspring onward. Place each seed a half-inch deep and space them eight inches apart in rows two feet apart. You can also plant two seeds at each station, then leave only one seedling after germination.

If you are not protecting the crop, wait until late spring to sow. The soil must be warm and the danger of frost past.

CARE OF THE CROP
Sweet corn grows rapidly, so remove cloches as soon as the tallest plants reach the glass or plastic, and do not let floating row covers hamper growth.

Avoid deep hoeing, since the plants are shallow-rooted. Mulching, once the soil is really warm, is a better way to check weeds. Make sure that the soil does not dry out, and supply high-nitrogen fertilizer whenever leaves turn yellow. Protect seedlings from birds with fake snakes or net cloches.

HARVESTING
Start harvesting when the silk of the sweet corn becomes brown and withered. The kernels, exposed by pulling away the husk, exude a watery fluid if unripe and a milky liquid if ripe when pricked. Pick them by twisting or "snapping" the ears off the plants. Cook or freeze as soon as possible.

PESTS AND DISEASES
Corn earworms, European corn borers, and earwigs are among the many pests.

Common diseases include corn smut, leaf blight, bacterial wilt, and mosaic virus.

RECOMMENDED VARIETIES
White varieties
'How Sweet It Is' A recent supersweet All-America Winner that keeps very well.
'Silver Queen' Late-season standard hybrid.
'Chalice' An early 'Silver Queen' type.
Yellow varieties
'Florida Staysweet' Widely adapted, disease-resistant supersweet corn.
'Kandy Korn' An enhanced-sugar variety.
'Summer Sweet 7900' Ultrasweet late-season hybrid. Large ears, many kernels.
'Seneca Chief' A very popular hybrid.
'Spring Gold' Early, standard corn.
Bicolor varieties
'Bi-Queen' Late, disease-resistant.
'Burgundy Delight' A flavorful midseason corn. Stalks sometimes produce two ears.
'Sprite' An early standard variety.

Draw soil around the base of developing plants to increase their stability and to insure that the roots are adequately covered. Additional support with fencing may be needed on a site that is particularly exposed.

Browning of the silks, or female flowers, is a sign that the corn may be ready to eat. Before picking, test by peeling back part of the husk and piercing a kernel with your thumbnail. The liquid exuded should be milky. If it is watery, the corn is not yet ready.

CLOCHES AND ROW COVERS, pages 16–17
SOWING SEEDS OUTDOORS, pages 36–37

SOWING UNDER GLASS, pages 38–39
PLANTING VEGETABLES, page 40

BEANS, SWEET CORN, AND ARTICHOKES, pages 114–115
PESTS AND DISEASES, pages 172–175

Cardoons (*Cynara cardunculus*) are tall, handsome plants, similar to globe artichokes in appearance and cultivation requirements. Cardoons need similar soil and growing conditions to celery (see pp.146–147). Their blanched stems and leaf midribs are usually served as a cooked dish.

MAKING A START
Prepare the site during the late fall by forking in a generous amount of manure or compost. In late spring, after the last frost, rake in a dressing of general fertilizer at two ounces per square yard just before sowing.

Sow the seeds directly in the ground in groups of three or four, and set the groups one and a half to two feet apart in each direction. Subsequently, remove all but the strongest seedling from each group. Alternatively, sow the seeds singly in pots indoors in early spring and harden them off ready for planting out in late spring. You can put cloches over the seedlings for the first four weeks or so. Keep the plants well watered throughout the summer and supply a weak liquid food every week or two.

BLANCHING AND HARVESTING
In late summer, tie each plant's leaves together with string, then tie black plastic around it, leaving only a little of the top uncovered. Blanching takes four or five weeks. From that stage onward, the plants may be dug up. Remove the plastic and discard the tough outer leaves. Use the crisp inner stems for cooking: first cut them into pieces, then boil or steam them until tender.

RECOMMENDED VARIETY
The variety most commonly available in the United States is '**Large Smooth**,' and you may have to hunt for it.

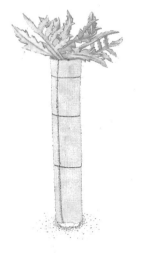

Secure black plastic around the stems to blanch the stalks of cardoons before eating.

Florence fennel (*Foeniculum vulgare*), also known as finocchio, belongs to the same species as the herb called sweet fennel and has a similar aniseed flavor. But it is the bulbous base that is harvested for eating as a cooked vegetable; its crisp texture, much like that of celery, also makes it suitable for eating raw in salads. Florence fennel needs a richer soil than the herb. Its feathery foliage, which grows to about two feet and can be used in cooking, makes Florence fennel a plant attractive enough to plant in the flower border.

Florence fennel grows best in light, well-drained soil that has been well supplied with manure or compost. It needs a sunny, sheltered position.

MAKING A START
One of the difficulties of growing Florence fennel is that it easily flowers too early, or bolts. It may do this if the seeds are sown too early or if the plants suffer a setback, perhaps because of dryness, during the growing season.

First add general fertilizer to the bed at two ounces per square yard just before sowing. Sow the seeds in early spring and late summer; avoid sowing when the plants could bolt early in the season, when the weather first begins to be hot. Plants sown in late summer will mature in autumn, whereas early sowings provide a summer harvest.

Sow the seeds sparingly in shallow furrows about a half-inch deep; leave a foot and a half between rows. Thin the seedlings to spacings of about eight to twelve inches. Water the bed at the first hint that a dry spell is on the way; this helps to produce bulbous stems and reduces the risk of bolting.

Use a hoe to draw soil around the base of Florence fennel when the stem starts to swell. Repeat, if necessary, so that the bulb remains covered and becomes blanched.

BLANCHING AND HARVESTING
Swelling of the stem base is a signal to draw earth around and over this part of the plant. Continue to keep the swollen base covered until it is about the size of a tennis ball, which will be about two or three weeks later. Then sever it from the roots with a sharp knife. Cut off the tops, too, which may be used in the same way as the herb fennel (see p.221).

PESTS AND DISEASES
Florence fennel is not subject to any particular troubles.

RECOMMENDED VARIETIES
Florence fennel is usually sold under its generic name in this country, although varieties such as '**Mammoth**' are also available. If possible, try to find a variety that matures early and that is sold for its bulb, not for its properties as an herb. Several seed catalogues make the distinction, but some do not.

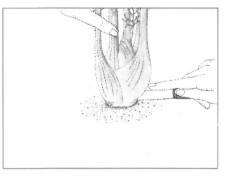

Florence fennel can be harvested once the bulbs are fully formed. Use a sharp knife to cut close to the ground. If the stumps are left, secondary shoots will grow.

Asparagus (*Asparagus officinalis*) is generally regarded as an aristocratic or luxury vegetable, mainly because of the delicate flavor of its young shoots, or spears. Asparagus is always expensive in grocery stores and supermarkets, not only on account of its limited season, but because growing it is labor-intensive. It has to be picked by hand.

Whether you choose to grow this perennial vegetable yourself depends on how highly you value its flavor and whether you have enough room. Asparagus needs a considerable area of ground, which it occupies right through the year. Growing it also requires a lot of patience, since it takes two seasons to produce its first crop. However, once established, it will go on providing its annual six-week harvest for twenty years, and possibly longer.

Asparagus needs good soil. The ideal soil is fertile, well drained, and neutral or just slightly acid. If your soil is on the damp side, it will help to grow asparagus in a raised bed (see p.133). Choose a sunny, fairly sheltered position, and avoid a frost pocket.

Asparagus can be raised from seed, but it then takes an extra year to produce spears for cutting. It is best to buy asparagus as one-year-old crowns, which you can purchase directly from a nursery or by mail order. If you buy them from a nursery, the asparagus crowns will have been growing in soil, so take care not to allow the roots to dry out before they are planted. Crowns sent through the mail are purposely dispatched dry, and not in moist wrappings, to survive the journey. It is important to allow air to circulate around these roots before they are

planted, to prevent the development of molds or fungi. If you cannot plant the crowns as soon as they arrive, put them in the refrigerator or in a cool dry room until you are able to plant them.

MAKING A START

It is worth preparing an asparagus bed with some care, bearing in mind the length of time the crop will be growing in the same site and the plant's extensive root system. The first step is to dig the site during the autumn; remove every trace of perennial weeds as you do so. Work in plenty of rotted compost or manure; allow a bucketful to the square yard.

You will need a planting trench one foot wide, with three feet between trenches if you plan to grow more than one row. Set the plants eighteen inches apart. If you are growing twelve plants, which will give a good yield, dig two nine-foot trenches.

In early spring, dig out the trench to a depth of eight inches. Mix some sterile sand

with the soil you have removed, then replace enough to form a ridge along the base of the trench about three inches high. Leave the rest of the soil beside the trench.

Set the plants or one-year-old crowns on the ridge in the trench and spread out the roots. Cover them immediately with a further three inches of soil.

GROWING ASPARAGUS FROM SEED

Soak the seeds in tepid water for several hours, then sow them two or three to a pot in small peat pots filled with mixed manure and potting soil. Thin to one plant per pot when the seedlings are two inches high, and transplant to larger pots if necessary.

Plant the seedlings in the same way as crowns, in the spring.

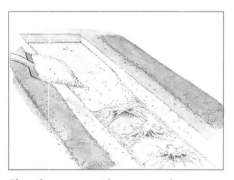

Place the crowns, with roots spread out, on a shallow ridge of free-draining soil laid in the trench. Cover them at once with soil. Leave surplus soil on the surface alongside the trench for the time being.

CARE OF THE CROP

Replace the remainder of the soil little by little during the first summer, by gently drawing soil from the sides of the trench while hoeing. By the autumn, you will have filled in the trench.

Do not cut any shoots during the first spring after planting. A year later, cut just a few of the thicker ones, taking one or two from each plant.

Hand-weed between the plants, or hoe very carefully once shoots have ceased to emerge. You must use a hoe with great care between asparagus plants, since there is a risk of causing root damage. A better plan is to use a thick mulch—eight inches is not too much—of leaves, straw, bark, or some other bulky organic material.

Make sure the bed never dries out. Early each spring, remove the mulch and apply a general fertilizer at two ounces per square

yard: mix this gently into the surface. Then spread a two-inch mulch of well-rotted manure or garden compost over the soil surface, or replace the leaves or straw. This should control weeds, but if weeds still prove troublesome, you will have to remove them carefully by hand.

Asparagus can be hilled up, like potatoes; this process will produce longer, blanched spears. To make ridges, draw up a little soil from the surrounding area to a depth of about five inches. Do this just before the asparagus is ready to be cut, and spread the soil out again in the autumn. If you prefer, you need not hill up asparagus, in which case the spears will be shorter, but ready for cutting earlier. The annual process of mulching gradually builds up ridges along the rows to a certain extent.

Pick berries from the ferns before they can fall; otherwise your trench will be

invaded by unwanted seedlings. Support the ferns with string and stakes if they are exposed to wind. If you allow the plants to blow and sway, their roots may be loosened and rot can develop.

Cut the stems down to within one inch of the soil once the growth turns yellow in autumn, then spread a mulch of well-rotted manure or compost over the asparagus bed.

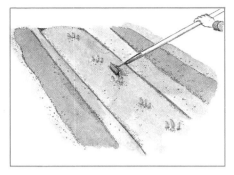

Draw more soil around the plants when the shoots emerge, pulling in the remainder from the sides during the summer to fill the trench flush with the surrounding soil. Weed the bed often, and take special care not to allow any perennial weeds to become established.

Cut the stems down almost to ground level during the autumn once the foliage has changed color. Collect and burn the stems, and remove the supporting stakes if you used any. Spread a mulch of compost or well-rotted manure over the bed afterward.

ASPARAGUS: THE FIVE-YEAR PLAN
Year 1 Plant out young roots grown from seed the year before or purchased as one-year-old crowns.
Year 2 Do not cut any shoots.
Year 3 Cut only one or two of the thicker stems from each plant.
Year 4 Cut all spears when four inches high. Cut for five weeks only.
Year 5 Cut all spears, for up to seven weeks.
Continue harvesting all spears annually for 15 to 20 years.

HARVESTING

Two years after planting, cut the emerging spears when they are four inches high; sever them three inches below the surface. Do this with a sharp knife, since the base of the stalk is tough. Stop cutting after five weeks, and allow any shoots that emerge later to grow into ferns. This will build up the crowns for the next season's crop. Cut the spears during a period of six or seven weeks in subsequent years.

Rather than let the spears grow longer than six inches, cut a few each day as they reach this size, until you have enough for a meal. Stand them in iced water for a while, then cover and refrigerate them until you have enough.

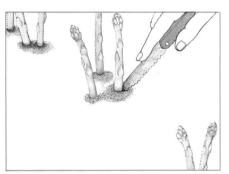

A sharp, serrated knife, preferably a purpose-made asparagus knife, is best for cutting asparagus. Wait until each shoot, or spear, is about four inches above the ground and make the cut well below the surface. Cut for five weeks during the first year of cropping.

PESTS AND DISEASES

Asparagus and Japanese beetles are the chief pests of this crop.

Damage may also be caused by rust and fusarium wilt, but well-kept asparagus beds are seldom troubled by disease.

RECOMMENDED VARIETIES

'Viking KB3' A good variety to grow from seed; bears heavy crops of thick dark-green spears. Plants tolerate heat and cold and are resistant to rust and fusarium wilt.
'Mary Washington' The most common garden asparagus. Very straight spears have tight buds tinged with purple. Rust resistant.
'Martha Washington' Another popular variety. Spears are straight and thick; plants resist asparagus rust and fusarium wilt.
'Brock' A hybrid asparagus that grows well from seed. Vigorous, rust resistant.

Celery (*Apium graveolens*) is a valuable crop, both for eating raw or cooked and as flavoring for soups and many cooked dishes. Its crisp texture and distinctive flavor also make it ideal for salads and hors d'oeuvres. The leaves of celery are also strongly flavored and are used for seasoning and garnishing. There are several types of celery: the most familiar has green stems, but there are pink- and red-stemmed varieties, as well as self-blanching types, which are golden.

When grown in the traditional European way, by using a trench, celery can be a demanding vegetable. The stems must be blanched for at least a couple of months, a process necessary to improve their flavor and texture and increase the length of the stems. Blanching is accomplished by grow-ing the plants in trenches and drawing soil around them. Trench-grown celery has an excellent flavor and, being relatively hardy, is a useful winter vegetable in milder regions; it can remain in the ground well into the new year in some southern and coastal zones.

If you want to save yourself some effort, however, you will probably choose to grow celery in beds or rows, as most American gardeners do. You can either plant a self-blanching variety, leave your celery green, or blanch a green-stemmed type with boards or tin cans during the last few weeks before harvesting.

In either case, the requirements of celery are the same: a long growing season and plenty of moisture. It does best in areas that have moderate temperatures both day and night, but can be grown nearly everywhere in the United States.

All types of celery need rich, moisture-retentive soil in an open situation; a heavy soil is suitable. The key to holding moisture lies in ample supplies of organic matter, such as rotted manure or garden compost. The best results are obtained in ground that is neutral or only slightly acid.

TRENCH CELERY: MAKING A START

Prepare the ground during the fall by removing the soil from a trench fifteen inches wide and one foot deep. This is the width for a single row. If you prefer to plant a double row, make the trench two feet wide. Single rows are better for small quantities; although a double row saves space, it makes hilling up more difficult.

Spread a thick layer of manure or compost over the bottom of the trench—it should be at least two inches deep—and work this into the soil with a fork. Then replace most of the soil that you have dug out, to leave the trench just four inches deep. Leave the rest of the soil beside the trench for future hilling up.

Sow the seeds in early to midspring if you have a greenhouse for growing the seed-lings. They require a temperature of about 50° to 60°F, so an electric propagator is useful if the greenhouse is not heated to this temperature. Indoors, choose a warm but light place for germination and avoid too early a start.

Sow the tiny seeds in small pots or flats and cover them with glass. Celery seed germinates better in light, but it takes at least two weeks for seedlings to emerge. Transfer the seedlings to individual peat pots when they are large enough to handle. Grow them in gentle warmth; do not allow the temperature to fall too low at night. Throughout their entire growing period it is important to avoid a sudden change in the growing conditions.

If you are raising the seedlings indoors, place them close to a well-lit window to reduce the risk that they will become spindly and pale.

Harden the plants off in late spring by moving them to a cold frame for ten to fourteen days. If possible, wait for some mild weather to do this; cool weather will cause them to bolt. Prepare the trench and rake in some general fertilizer at three ounces per square yard. Add a further two ounces per square yard when you are hilling up.

When the plants are fully hardened, set them nine inches apart in the trench. If you are planting a double row, leave fifteen inches between the rows and ten inches between the plants. Set them in pairs and water them thoroughly after planting.

Make sure that the soil does not dry out during the summer by watering generously as soon as a dry spell begins.

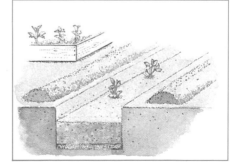

To allow for subsequent hilling up, plant celery in a prepared trench some four inches deeper than the surrounding ground. Leave the surplus soil in a low ridge along each side.

Before hilling up, tie the stems loosely together below the leaves. Take care that no soil falls between the stalks of the celery when you are hilling up, if you have not tied paper around the plants.

Pull earth around the plants a little at a time, on at least three occasions, until only the leaves remain visible. Blanching will be complete from about two weeks after the final hilling up.

TRENCH CELERY: HILLING UP

Hilling up is done in three stages, the first when the plants have grown at least one foot tall, which is during the second half of summer. Water the trench and remove any side shoots from the base of the plants, then tie the stalks together loosely just beneath the leaves, allowing room for the hearts to develop. If you wrap thick brown paper or corrugated cardboard around the stalks before tying them, this will help to prevent soil from falling between them. Draw a little soil from the sides of the trench to cover the lower part of the stalks.

Repeat the hilling up three weeks later, and bring the soil nearer to the leaves. Give the celery a final coating of soil after another three weeks, this time encasing the stalks right up to the base of the leaves.

Slope the sides sharply, to insure that the rain runs away from the plants and into the ground, rather than into the celery heart, which would foster rot. You may need some additional soil.

TRENCH CELERY: HARVESTING

Start harvesting the celery with a fork during the fall, about two weeks after the final hilling up. Open the ridge from one end and cut the plants close to the roots with a sharp knife. Then hill up the ridge again as a protection against frost.

A touch of frost improves the crispness and flavor of celery, but late crops may rot if they are frozen in the ground. In severe weather, it is worth protecting the plants by putting down a mulch of straw or leaves on top of the ridge.

Dig up the celery with a fork; take care to insert it beneath the plant and not through the stalks. Use red varieties first, followed by those with green stalks.

BED OR ROW CELERY: MAKING A START

Planting celery in beds makes sense, as it saves space, helps conserve moisture, and is easier to mulch than rows. Whichever method you choose, though, plan how much room you will need for plants spaced nine inches apart. Dig the ground during the fall, and work in a generous amount of rotted manure or compost—allow at least a bucketful to the square yard.

Sow the seeds in early to midspring, as for trench celery. Transplant the seedlings as soon as they can be handled. Harden the seedlings in a cold frame during late spring and scatter a general fertilizer over the planting site at three ounces per square yard. Give another dressing at two ounces per square yard every two or three weeks. Plant out about a week before the last frost date, when the seedlings have five or six leaves. The plants have a tendency to bolt if they are subjected to cold nights, so do not plant them out too early.

Set the plants nine inches apart in each direction, with their crowns flush with the soil, to form a square block; or plant them in rows thirty inches apart. Water them well, and keep the plants watered as necessary throughout the growing season to prevent the soil from drying out. Apply a thick mulch of straw.

In midsummer, when the plants are well developed, blanch their stalks by pulling straw around them or by covering them with large tin cans or heavy paper. Alternatively, use planks placed on edge to form a light-excluding box around the plants. However, you will still need straw to cover plants that are exposed when harvesting starts. Many gardeners do not bother to blanch their celery at all, though.

BED OR ROW CELERY: HARVESTING

Start harvesting during the second half of summer, using a fork. Aim to finish before the first autumn frosts. Tuck straw against the plants that are exposed when others are removed. If there is a surplus, you can freeze the stalks for subsequent cooking, though not for eating raw since the texture of celery is adversely affected during freezing.

PESTS AND DISEASES

Aphids, earwigs, carrot rust flies, and tarnished plant bugs can sometimes be troublesome.

Various kinds of blight are the principal diseases, and leaf spot can be a problem. Black heart, a disorder caused by nutrient deficiencies, can be avoided.

Pack straw around a bed of celery to cover the outer plants. The plants' own dense foliage will exclude light from those that are on the inside.

RECOMMENDED VARIETIES
French celery
This type is especially suitable for trench cultivation.

'Dinant' A fairly early variety with slender round stems. Strongly flavored; good for cooking and salads.

Green varieties
'Tendercrisp' An early, productive hybrid with smooth, ribless stalks that are excellent eaten raw.

'Deacon' This variety has short, thick stalks and large heads that are green all the way to the heart.

'Utah 52-70R' Improved from a standard commercial celery. Very productive and tall; resistant to black heart disorder and bacterial disease.

'Ventura' An early-maturing green celery with tight, crisp hearts. Widely adapted to various growing conditions.

'Fordhook' A crisp celery with short stalks that turn silvery-white when blanched. Keeps well in fall and winter.

Red and golden varieties
'Giant Red' This very cold-hardy type has light green stalks tinged with reddish purple. If grown in trenches or otherwise blanched, it turns light pink.

'Golden Self-Blanching' A standard variety that is slow to bolt. Plants are compact and early; stalks are tender, stringless, and yellow when mature.

'Golden Plume' This early celery produces large golden heads.

SOWING UNDER GLASS, pages 38–39
PLANTING VEGETABLES, page 40

STALKS AND SHOOTS, pages 116–117
PESTS AND DISEASES, pages 172–175

FREEZING VEGETABLES, pages 232–233

Although it grows like a vegetable, rhubarb (*Rheum rhaponticum*) is invariably eaten as a form of dessert fruit. There are few more accommodating food plants, for it tolerates most well-drained soils and goes on producing its spring harvest for five years or much more if you dig it up and divide it regularly. Furthermore, its large leaves smother weeds and reduce the need for hoeing. Rhubarb can also be forced to provide an earlier crop of slender, delicately flavored stalks; leftovers are easily frozen.

Like most vegetables, rhubarb needs a sunny spot. It can be grown almost anywhere in the country, though it prefers a cool climate. And, although it will produce some sort of crop even on poor soil, the reward for generous feeding and summer watering is a much greater yield of thick, succulent stalks.

Rhubarb may be grown from root divisions (crowns), which are widely available at nurseries and garden centers, or from seed. Though they save a little money, seed-grown plants produce variable results and must be left for an extra year before you can take the first harvest.

MAKING A START
From crowns Plant crowns at any time in the early spring when soil and weather conditions allow. Each crown will need up to a square yard of growing space. Prepare the planting stations a few weeks in advance by digging holes a foot and a half square and a foot deep.

Place a thick layer of rotted manure or compost in the hole and fork this into the soil. Mix some more manure with the topsoil before replacing it. Mark each position with a stick and make sure that no perennial weeds are left in the area. A week before planting, work in some general fertilizer at five ounces per square yard.

Plant with the buds just on the surface, and firm the soil around each crown.
From seeds Sow in a seedbed in spring: sow the seeds about one inch deep, and thin the seedlings to nine inches. Set the plants out in prepared stations, as for crowns, the following autumn.

CARE OF THE CROP
Keep the plants watered during dry summer weather. Give crowns and older plants a spring dressing of general fertilizer at five ounces per square yard, and repeat this after a few weeks. Hoe the fertilizer in carefully so that the crowns are not damaged. Spread a mulch of rotted manure or compost around them and top this up in autumn, before the ground freezes.

Cut off any seed stalks as they appear, since they weaken the plants.

HARVESTING AND FORCING
Unforced stems are ready for gathering from spring until late summer. Take a few stalks from each crown a year after planting, but wait another year for rhubarb grown from seedlings. Even on mature plants, always leave a few stalks behind at any one picking. To gather them, grasp the stalk near the base and pull from the roots with a slight twisting action. Cut off the leaves, which are poisonous, and put them on the compost heap.

Wait until the plants are at least three years old before you attempt to force them. For a really early crop, dig up one or two plants in autumn, when the leaves die back, and leave them on the surface to freeze. This gives the plants the impression that it is winter, and they become dormant. Place them the right way up in boxes early in winter, with moist peat or soil packed around them, and stand the boxes in a shed, basement, spare room, or greenhouse where the temperature is about 45° or 50°F.

If necessary, cover the crowns with black plastic to exclude the light. The stalks will be ready in five to six weeks. After harvesting, replant the crowns, but do not force them again for several years.

To advance the main harvest by two or three weeks, cover some of the outdoor crowns after the ground has thawed with boxes or an upturned bucket, and pack straw or compost around them. Do not force these roots again for a couple of years.

PROPAGATION
When new plants are needed—and, in any case, every five years or so—dig up the roots in late fall or early spring and divide them into several segments. Make sure that each has a growth bud.

PESTS AND DISEASES
Rhubarb rarely attracts pests, although Japanese beetles may investigate it.

The plants may be susceptible to crown rot and honey fungus.

RECOMMENDED VARIETIES
'Cherry Red' One of the richest red varieties. Stalks are long, large, and tender.
'Victoria' is a good variety to grow from seed. Broad stalks are green tinged with red; plant is upright and hardy.
'Valentine' produces few seed stalks but quantities of dark red leaf stalks with excellent flavor.

Divide mature rhubarb crowns with a spade; they can be split into four or five segments. Those round the outside of the clump are best. Each must have a bud and part of the root.

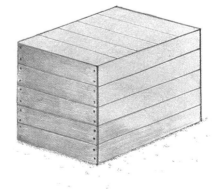

An upturned box, a bucket, and a large pot are equally suitable for forcing an early crop of rhubarb outdoors. Do this in early spring, after the ground has thawed. Forcing weakens the plant, so do not repeat it the following year.

Jerusalem artichokes (*Helianthus tuberosus*), also known as sun chokes, are unrelated to globe artichokes. Their tubers have a distinctive yet delicate sweet flavor and are a good winter standby. The plants are hardy members of the sunflower family, and will grow as tall as ten feet, although by removing the upper, flowering part of the stem in midsummer you can keep them to about half this height. This helps reduce the risk of wind damage and assists the production of artichoke tubers.

Jerusalem artichokes are not unlike knobbly potatoes in appearance, though some smoother-skinned varieties are now available. They are recommended for baking and roasting and for eating raw, and are a popular ingredient in several cuisines, notably Italian and Middle Eastern. They can be boiled in their skins, then peeled afterward if you prefer.

Treat Jerusalem artichokes as an annual crop, even though any tubers left in the ground will survive the winter and send up fresh shoots the following spring. Remember that unless you clear the site each year, it will soon turn into a jungle of stems and undersized tubers.

The plants are not fussy about soil, provided it is reasonably well drained, and they will also tolerate partial shade. This makes them ideal for planting in odd corners and patches within the garden—perhaps beside the compost bin, or in some other place where few other crops can be successfully grown. Be careful, however, not to let them take over by leaving tubers in the ground from year to year.

They are also a good first crop to plant when you are breaking new ground, including heavy soil. Their fibrous roots help to improve the soil structure, and there is plenty of space to hoe between plants. Alternatively, a row of Jerusalem artichokes can make a screen or an effective windbreak in the summer when plants are fully clad with foliage.

MAKING A START

Dig the site in late autumn or early winter, and remove any perennial weeds, together with their roots, as you do so. Add some manure or compost to improve the yield of tubers on poor soil, but remember that this can result in an excessive amount of foliage on more fertile ground.

Plant the tubers at the end of winter or during spring. The plants are quite hardy, and a reasonably early start provides an extended growing season.

You can buy tubers at many health-food stores or order them from a seed catalogue if none are available at your local garden center. Although named varieties exist, they can be hard to find. Tubers should be firm and about the size of an egg. Any that are much larger may be cut in half, but make sure that there is a bud on each piece.

Plant the tubers four or five inches deep and about fifteen inches apart, using a trowel. Leave three feet between rows.

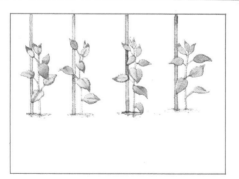

Use a trowel to plant the tubers at fifteen-inch intervals in averagely fertile soil. If the site is exposed, draw soil around the stems and support the plants with stakes.

CARE OF THE CROP

Pull some soil around the stems when they are a foot high to help keep plants more stable. If the garden is exposed or subject to wind eddies, insert a stout bamboo cane alongside each plant so that you can tie the developing stem to it. Even if unsupported plants are not flattened by the wind, constant rocking disturbs their roots and checks their development.

Another way to reduce wind disturbance is to plant the artichokes on "hills" or raised beds, so the soil's drainage is improved. During the autumn, after the leaves have withered, cut the stems down to within six inches of the ground. The tubers will continue to develop slowly until they are harvested.

In exposed areas, support artichoke plants by tying them to bamboo stakes with soft string. Choose stakes at least six feet tall. Such support will prevent root movement, which hinders tuber development.

HARVESTING

Tubers may be dug up as needed from autumn onward, once the leaves have withered. Dig each root with a fork and take great care not to leave behind any tubers, however small.

You can store Jerusalem artichokes in the same way as potatoes, but they retain more flavor if left in the soil throughout the winter and used as needed. Remember to keep some of the smaller, healthy-looking tubers for planting out the following spring.

PESTS AND DISEASES

Cutworms and root aphids can sometimes prove troublesome. Disease is seldom a problem with these hardy plants.

PLANTING VEGETABLES, page 40
POTATOES AND OTHER TUBERS, pages 118–119
POTATOES, pages 150–151
PESTS AND DISEASES, pages 172–175

Potatoes (*Solanum tuberosum*) are the most widely grown and most commonly eaten vegetable in the western world. Though they are always available in stores and supermarkets, the main advantage of growing your own is that you can choose from among dozens of interesting varieties, most of them far superior in flavor and texture to the heavy-cropping commercial types.

Despite this, potatoes are not necessarily a crop for every garden. If you have limited space, you might want to use it for crops that are rarely seen or very expensive in supermarkets. Although average potato yields are quite impressive—up to eighty pounds for storage potatoes, for instance, from a plot ten feet square—whether you grow them or not depends on how much ground you can spare.

If your garden is small, you might consider growing a few early potatoes. If harvested in early summer, when their skins are still not set, they have a wonderful flavor. After the potatoes are harvested, you can use the ground for later crops such as brassicas or leeks. If you cannot spare any space in the vegetable plot, you can even grow a few earlies in pots.

Potatoes are an excellent first crop for ground that has just been cleared of weeds.

All potatoes are half-hardy and need a sunny unshaded position. Most soils are suitable, though somewhat acid conditions are best: a pH of 6–6.5 is ideal. For early potatoes, choose a sheltered position and avoid known frost pockets. Heavy yields depend on plenty of well-rotted manure or compost dug into the soil before planting.

> **TYPES OF POTATO**
> **Early or new potatoes** are quick-maturing varieties that are planted in early spring and harvested about ten weeks later.
> **Midseason potatoes** are planted a few weeks after earlies and harvested from July on in most of the country.
> **Storage potatoes** are planted at the same time as midseason varieties, but they are harvested after the vines have died in the fall. Southern and coastal gardeners plant in August or September for a fall or spring harvest.
>
> Within each of these groups, individual varieties differ in texture, shape, color, size, yield, and cooking qualities. It is worth experimenting with different varieties to see which you prefer.

MAKING A START

The tubers supplied for planting are called seed potatoes. Try to buy certified seed, which means that it is free from virus disease, and look for tubers that are, on average, about the size of an egg. If many are significantly larger than this, cut them into egg-sized pieces, each with at least one "eye," and dust them with sulfur to protect them from rot.

You can give early potatoes a prompt start, well before the last of the spring frosts, by encouraging them to form shoots before they are planted. This is termed sprouting, or chitting. Midseason and storage potatoes can be treated in the same way, although the advantage is less marked.

Stand potatoes that are to be sprouted in a shallow box or tray: place them so that

their eyes (embryo shoots) are uppermost. Put the box in a cool but frost-free room or shed where there is a reasonable amount of light, but never in direct sunlight.

Shoots will develop over a period of four to six weeks. They should be short and stubby (about an inch long) rather than long, thin, and straggling.

Early potatoes Plant the sprouted tubers as soon as the ground is dry enough to be easily worked: from March onward in the North, and from January on (or in late August for a fall crop) in the South.

Just before planting, rake in a dressing of general fertilizer at five ounces per square yard. Either use the trench method, described below, or plant the potatoes in a row, using a trowel to make individual holes. Place the bottom of each tuber about

four inches deep, with the sprouts uppermost. Allow one foot between potatoes and eighteen inches between rows. As each row is planted, pull a little soil over it from each side to form a shallow ridge.

Midseason and storage potatoes Plant these about a month after earlies if you live in the North, or two weeks later if your garden is in a mild coastal region.

The conventional method is to dig a trench about six inches wide and four or five inches deep, sprinkle some fertilizer in the bottom, cover it with soil, and place the potatoes or pieces of potatoes about a foot apart on the bottom. Cover the potatoes with soil. Trenches should be about three feet apart. Tamp down the soil carefully so the potatoes are tightly covered; this encourages them to develop strong roots.

CARE OF THE CROP

Look for the emerging shoots, which will first show as a slight disturbance of the soil. For earlies, especially, it is important to draw or hill up some extra soil over this first growth as protection against frost. Use a hoe to do this, and take care not to cut through shoots just beneath the soil. If frost threatens when growth is well advanced, cover the shoots overnight with straw, newspaper, or soil.

Hilling up must continue throughout the growing period for all potatoes. Hill up the plants when they are about ten inches high, and then every two weeks or so until the foliage meets between rows. If they are not covered with soil, some of the tubers will develop close to the surface, where the light will cause their skins to turn green and become poisonous.

Another reason to hill up is to bury the

Early potatoes can be started even sooner if you sprout them before planting. If they are placed in the light and protected from frost, strong, stubby shoots will develop. Lack of light or too much warmth will result in long, thin, pale shoots.

Planting with a trowel is the easiest method for potatoes; make the holes four inches deep. The alternative is to dig a trench about five inches deep. Plant the tubers with sprouts uppermost. The spacing is the same whether they are early, midseason, or storage potatoes.

roots more deeply; the extra moisture farther down will aid root and tuber development. Hilling up also suppresses weeds, though these will tend to decrease as the foliage meets over the rows.

All potatoes, but especially earlies, need generous watering throughout the season to maintain high yields. With storage potatoes, the long growing period may help to balance the effect of wet and dry spells.

To safeguard against late blight, which cannot be cured once it becomes established, spray or dust in early summer with an approved fungicide or Bordeaux mixture. Continue to spray every two weeks throughout the summer months. The disease is especially troublesome during warm, wet summers.

Hilling up, using a hoe, insures that the new tubers forming on the roots will be covered with soil. Left uncovered and therefore exposed to the light, they will turn green and become poisonous to eat.

Preventive dusting or spraying, starting early in summer, is the only practical way to combat late blight. Direct the fungicide onto both the upper and lower surfaces of the plants' foliage.

HARVESTING AND STORING

Early varieties should be ready as soon as the plants are in full flower. For the first harvest, scrape a little soil from the ridge and remove any egg-sized tubers that you find; replace the soil afterward. These new potatoes are at their best when the skin can be rubbed off easily with your thumb.

Subsequently, to harvest the main crop, push in a broad-tined fork well to the side of the plant; otherwise some of the tubers may be speared. Dig up only as many as you can eat for one or two meals.

Dig up midseason potatoes as needed, to follow the earlies.

Storage potatoes can be dug up once the foliage has withered, but you can dig a few earlier than this for eating. Before digging

them, make sure that the skins are fully set—that is, they cannot be rubbed off.

Harvest storage potatoes on a sunny day, and leave them on the soil surface for an hour or two to dry. Dig up all the tubers, however small; otherwise they will foster any disease in the soil. Use any damaged potatoes immediately, and burn any that appear to be diseased.

To store potatoes, first dry them for a week or two in a dark place with temperatures around 60°F. Then move them to a dry, frost-free room or shed where there is plenty of ventilation and the temperature remains around 40°F. Store them in bins, boxes, or burlap bags, and be sure that no light reaches them. Check them regularly and throw out any that are rotting.

When digging up whole plants, push the fork well to the side; otherwise you might spear some of the tubers. Use a broad-tined potato fork to lift the crop, if you have one. Dig up only as many early potatoes as you can eat for one or two meals; the longer they are out of the ground, the harder they are to peel.

PESTS AND DISEASES
The Colorado potato beetle is the most serious pest; others are flea beetles, wireworms, aphids, and leafhoppers.

Diseases include early and late blight, scab, verticillium wilt, and mosaic virus.

RECOMMENDED VARIETIES
Red varieties
'**Red Pontiac**' A good early potato for boiling, with a thin skin. Yields are high; plants are heat tolerant and thrive in heavy soil. Potatoes keep well.
'**Red LaSoda**' A widely adapted variety that is popular in the South. Matures in midseason or later.
'**Norland Red**' Plants are resistant to potato scab; tubers are oblong, and are ready early. A prolific cropper.
'**Sangre**' Rounded, medium-sized potatoes are good keepers.

White varieties
'**White Cobbler**' A very popular early potato that is ideal for baking since it has a mealy texture. Not good for long storage.
'**Kennebec**' Firm, rounded tubers are good all-purpose potatoes. Plants bear in midseason and are resistant to late blight.
'**Explorer**' A seed-grown variety that can be harvested in midseason for boiling or later for baking.
'**Katahdin**' This storage potato can be used in various ways and is widely adaptable to climate and soil conditions.
'**Russet Centennial**' The long, brown-skinned tubers have white flesh and can be baked or boiled.
'**Butte**' A new variety of baking potato. Plants yield well.
'**Superior**' A popular variety on the East Coast, 'Superior' has white skin and yields well; does not tolerate drought.

Novelties
'**Blue**' An old-fashioned potato that has blue skin and flesh. The tubers are high in protein and good baked or boiled.
'**Lady Finger**' The tiny, finger-shaped potatoes have brown skin, yellow flesh, and a wonderful flavor.

Sweet potatoes
Sweet potatoes are grown from slips, or sprouts, and require a long warm season and sandy soil to produce well. They are a different species from common potatoes, but are harvested in the same way.
'**Centennial**' A popular variety that produces well in the north. Yields are high and the tubers store well.
'**Jewel**' Disease-resistant plants bear moist orange sweet potatoes.
'**Vardaman**' A bush variety; yields well.
'**White Yams**' White all the way through.

POTATOES AND TUBERS, pages 118–119
PESTS AND DISEASES, pages 172–175

STORING VEGETABLES, page 227

The carrot (*Daucus carota*) is a surprisingly varied vegetable—in flavor, shape, and rate of growth. The earliest kinds, given good conditions, can be on the dinner table a mere ten or twelve weeks after sowing. Others, with larger roots, will take twice as long to mature.

The delicate taste and texture of the fastest-growing carrots is typical of early summer vegetables. Those of intermediate size, which mature a little later, are almost as delicious when pulled young, and they taste wonderful when grated for salads. Larger varieties are an invaluable ingredient in soups, casseroles, and many other winter dishes, as well as for eating fresh or cooked on their own.

To enjoy home-grown carrots for most of the year, it is a great help to have cloches or a cold frame. Either will enable you to grow a really early crop for harvesting from early summer onward, as well as a crop of tender young roots in early winter, when usually only large roots are available. The carrots most suitable for these first and last sowings are the short-rooted kinds—either finger-shaped, such as 'Mini Express,' or round, such as 'Parmex.'

At other times and depending on your soil conditions, you might do better with one of the intermediate types—intermediate, that is, between the small-rooted early carrots and some of the very long varieties, which need deep soil to grow well. Among these are stump-rooted, cylindrical, and tapering varieties.

All carrots thrive in light, free-draining soil in a sunny position, though some varieties will tolerate partial shade. The ideal pH is 6–6.5; apply a high-potash fertilizer for extra sweetness.

If you do not have a light soil, do not despair: there are many varieties of carrots available that will thrive in heavy ground. Choose a stump-rooted or round type, and be sure to clear the site of any stones and to work the soil into a smooth tilth. Never sow carrots in ground that has been recently manured or that has not been made friable, or the roots will fork in all directions. Choose a sheltered spot for early crops, if this is possible.

MAKING A START

Dig the site during autumn or early winter and leave the surface rough. In the spring, break down any remaining lumps with a pronged cultivator and scatter a dressing of general fertilizer at about one ounce per square yard. Rake the surface to a fine tilth.

Sowing under cloches

Prepare the soil in late winter or early spring, as soon as it is dry enough to crumble. Place cloches in position two weeks before sowing, since the seeds will not germinate in cold soil. Sandy soil is an advantage for these early sowings.

Either scatter the seeds very thinly, then rake them lightly into the surface, or make shallow furrows two to three inches apart and sow the seeds thinly in these. You should have room for several rows, about four inches apart, under an average-sized cloche. After the seeds have germinated, thin the seedlings to about two inches apart.

Sowing in the open

From early spring onward, once the soil has begun to warm up, sow seeds every two or three weeks for harvesting in summer and fall. Leave four inches between rows and thin to about two inches apart. In beds, space the carrots about three inches apart in each direction.

Sow the last of your large varieties, which may be stored for the winter, by early summer. A late-summer sowing of short-rooted carrots, cloched from early autumn onward, will provide tender young roots for early winter.

THINNING

The characteristic aroma given off when carrot seedlings are thinned attracts carrot rust flies; these are damaging pests that lay their eggs against the roots of those remaining. Minimize the need for thinning by sowing sparsely. This is easier if you mix the seeds first with dry sand or fine soil, or if you use pelleted seeds.

The new spun-bonded fiber row covers are becoming very popular for deterring carrot rust flies. Other recommended precautions include planting garlic and onion in alternate rows with carrots, spreading fresh grass clippings between the rows, or hanging rags soaked in kerosene nearby. The idea is to disguise the distinctive smell of the carrots.

The best time for thinning is on dull or damp evenings; water around the plants both before and after thinning them out. Thin them first when they are about three quarters of an inch tall, and remove enough so the remaining carrots are an inch apart. Thin again after a month or so, for a final spacing of three inches between plants. You may be able to eat the thinned carrots from the second thinning, but the first batch will be too small and should be put on the compost heap.

Thinning is a time-consuming task, but it must be done if carrots are to have the space they need to grow. Overcrowding will deprive roots of essential moisture and nutrients, so although the carrot tops seem to thrive, you will not harvest much of a crop. If you plant the seeds carefully and thin the seedlings late, you may be able to thin only once. Alternatively, if you plant your carrots in wide rows or beds, you can draw a rake through when the seedlings are tiny and thus avoid the more tedious work.

Sow carrot seeds thinly to reduce the need for further thinning, with its attendant risk of carrot rust flies. To make this easier, mix the seeds as evenly as possible with some dry sand before sowing them.

When thinning, preferably during damp weather and in the evening, place the carrots that you remove into a tray or pot. If they are left on the ground, their smell is liable to attract carrot rust flies to the crop.

CARE OF THE CROP

Remove cloches after midspring, or as soon as the seedlings are up and the weather is sunny. Do this in stages to prevent a sudden shock to the young plants.

The need for hoeing will be kept to a minimum if the plants are closely spaced. The best means of keeping weeds in check initially, before the foliage spreads, is by hand weeding or by using a short-handled hoe to cultivate around the plants. Later on, spread a mulch of straw to protect the tops of the roots, and fertilize lightly.

Water frequently during dry weather and keep the soil moist at all times. Once the soil has been allowed to dry out, rain or sudden watering may cause the roots to split.

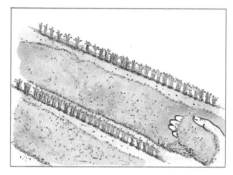

A scattering of grass clippings between rows of young carrots, especially after thinning, is helpful in preventing the attention of carrot rust flies. Attacks are most likely to occur if the soil is dry.

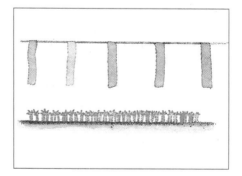

Another way to confuse carrot rust flies, which are attracted by the smell of the crop, is to hang rags of absorbent material soaked in kerosene over the rows of seedlings.

HARVESTING

Harvest early carrots from late spring onward: they are very sweet and tender. Treat this as a final thinning: the space left between the remaining carrots will speed their growth. Water the rows before pulling up any carrots.

Continue harvesting carrots throughout the summer, as needed. In the autumn, pick the remaining carrots: ease them out of the ground with a fork before the first frost occurs. Either use or discard any that are damaged, and store the rest. Trim the leaves to within a half inch of the crown and place the carrots in layers of dry peat in a box. Examine them for rotting regularly throughout the winter.

It is also possible to leave carrots, like parsnips, in the ground during the winter, provided the soil is free-draining and the roots are healthy and undamaged. A mulch of leaves or straw prevents frost damage.

PESTS AND DISEASES

Carrot rust flies, carrot weevils, carrot beetles, wireworms, and leafhoppers are the only common pests.

Aster yellows is a possible disease.

RECOMMENDED VARIETIES

'**Kundulus**' is a quick-maturing round carrot that does well in cold frames.

'**Parmex**' A round variety that has good flavor and color when young.

'**Mini Express**' A very early, smooth carrot that averages three and a half inches and freezes well.

'**Chantenay Red Cored**' This broad-shouldered carrot is good for heavy soils, as the tops don't break when pulled. The carrots are crisp and tender.

'**Kuroda Chantenay**' A late-maturing variety, this large carrot is resistant to alternaria blight.

'**Tendersweet**' Carrots are coreless and deep orange, with a fine sweet flavor.

'**Touchon Deluxe**' Vivid orange carrots are smooth and color early.

'**Scarlet Nantes**' This very popular blunt variety is known for the uniform shape and color of the smooth roots, which average six inches in length.

'**Pioneer**' A medium-length, cylindrical hybrid with smooth, flavorful roots.

'**Gold Pak**' Carrots are very long and pencil-thin; ideal for deep, free-draining soil. Good for freezing and canning as well as for eating fresh from the garden, either raw or cooked.

'**Danvers**' A popular tapering carrot that crops heavily and reliably.

'**Kinko**' A stubby carrot that averages four or five inches and does well in heavy soil.

Hamburg parsley (*Petroselinum crispum*), sometimes known as turnip- or parsnip-rooted parsley, is a dual-purpose vegetable with edible roots and leaves that deserves to be more widely grown. The plant is a member of the same species as the parsley grown as an herb and has the same distinctively flavored leaves, but because it is a good deal hardier, the leaves stay green and edible throughout the winter. Despite a relatively coarse texture, they are valuable for flavoring and garnishing winter soups and casseroles. The roots of Hamburg parsley resemble small parsnips and are cooked in a similar way; they taste something like a cross between celeriac and turnip.

The roots of Hamburg parsley mature during the autumn and can be harvested as needed during the winter; in this, as in their growth cycle, the plants have more in common with parsnips and salsify than with parsley. Hamburg parsley will also thrive in the same conditions as parsnips, though it will tolerate a little shade. A fertile, moisture-retaining soil, preferably one that has been manured for a previous crop, is best. Dig it during the autumn or early winter before sowing.

MAKING A START

Sow seeds in midspring; apply general fertilizer to the soil at two ounces per square yard two weeks before planting. Leave ten inches between the rows of parsley, and thin the seedlings twice, until they are six inches apart.

CARE OF THE CROP

Hoe regularly, or use a thick mulch, to prevent competition from weeds. Water during dry spells to insure that these rather slow-growing plants continue to make steady progress throughout the season.

HARVESTING

Start digging up the roots from fall onward, when they are about six to seven inches long. Unlike most vegetables, the largest roots of Hamburg parsley taste best. Either leave the crop in the ground to use as needed during the winter, or dig up and store the roots in damp peat or sand before the turn of the year. This is generally the best idea in very cold areas or on heavy soil.

PESTS AND DISEASES

Pests are seldom a problem, although parsley worms, a type of butterfly larvae, may appear.

Diseases rarely affect Hamburg parsley.

PARSNIPS

Parsnips (*Pastinaca sativa*) are one of the slowest-growing root vegetables: they can occupy their section of the garden for nearly twelve months on end. However, they are an undemanding vegetable and extremely hardy. Unlike most other root vegetables, they are hardy enough to be left in the ground until they are needed. Their sweet flavor makes a welcome change during the winter, which is their main season of use. Parsnips can be boiled, steamed, sautéed, fried, or puréed, and they can also be made into wine.

Their extended growing period may seem to make parsnips inappropriate for small gardens, but remember that it is possible to grow a quick crop of lettuce or radishes on the same strip of ground. These should be sown in the same furrows as the parsnips and harvested before the principal crop needs its full quota of space.

Some varieties of parsnip have much longer roots than others. These need deep, well-worked soil with few stones; otherwise they will become stunted or distorted, with forked roots. Choose a shorter-rooted variety if you have shallow soil, or else prepare individual planting holes with a mixture of sifted soil and peat.

Because parsnip seeds take as long as three weeks to germinate and the plants require a growing season of six months or more, it is a good idea to start the crop off in soil that is completely free of weeds. Choose a site that did not have many annual weeds in the previous year, and cultivate the ground immediately before sowing the parsnip seeds.

Like most vegetables, parsnips grow best in a sunny position. They like a fertile, well-drained soil, but the ground must not have a fresh application of manure, or the roots will fork. Instead, plant your parsnips on a part of the plot that has received a heavy organic mulch or addition for an earlier crop. Dig it during the autumn or early winter, before sowing, and add lime if the soil is on the acid side (with a pH reading of 6 or lower).

MAKING A START
Be sure to use fresh seed. Seeds left over from the previous year may not germinate.

Because parsnips develop slowly and need a long growing period, sowing in early spring is often advised, but unless you have a light soil, which warms up rapidly in spring, it is usually better to wait for a few weeks. Later sowings usually catch up, with fewer losses. In the South and in mild coastal regions, parsnips can be sown in the fall for a spring harvest.

Around midspring, apply general fertilizer at three ounces per square yard and rake the soil to a fine tilth. Make the furrows ten or twelve inches apart, depending on the size of the variety, and about half an inch deep.

Sow the seeds in groups of three or four; leave from four to eight inches between adjacent groups, depending partly on the size of the variety but also on how large you wish the roots to grow. On very shallow or stony soil, dig individual holes for each plant with a crowbar.

If you wish to interplant radishes or small lettuce, choose the larger spacings and sow the catch-crop seeds thinly between the groups of parsnips. They will mature before the parsnips grow significantly large. Since parsnip seeds take a long time to germinate, sowing radishes or lettuce will also mark the rows before the seedlings appear, enabling you to hoe around them carefully.

Use a crowbar to form individual planting holes for parsnips on stony ground. Drive it in as deep as possible, and rotate it at a slight angle. Fill the hole with peat or sifted soil, then sow the seeds on top.

CARE OF THE CROP
Apart from removing the surplus seedlings to leave the strongest one in each group, and thinning any other crop growing between them, the chief summer task is hoeing. A mulch of rotted compost is beneficial, if you have plenty available. Otherwise, side-dress the plants once a month with a general fertilizer.

Keep the soil moist by watering occasionally during prolonged dry weather. If you do not, there is a danger that a sudden downpour will cause the roots to split.

HARVESTING
Roots can be eaten from autumn onward, as soon as the leaves die back. However, their flavor improves if they are left until after the first few frosts. Cover the plants with straw or leaves and soil, to mark the rows and protect the roots.

Start harvesting parsnips with a fork after the first frosts. The foliage will soon die away, but a covering of straw or leaves will mark the position of the roots and help to prevent the soil from freezing hard.

PESTS AND DISEASES
Parsnips are affected by the same pests as carrots (see p.153), and can also be attacked by flea beetles and leaf miners.

Leaf blight is a possible disease.

RECOMMENDED VARIETIES
'Hollow Crown' This is the most widely available variety. The roots are about a foot long and three inches in diameter when mature; they are white, smooth, and tender. The plants yield heavily and overwinter well in the North.

'Harris' Model' is a long, slim parsnip that seldom branches. Its flavor is delicate and sweet after a few frosts.

'All America' An old variety with excellent flavor. The roots are ten to twelve inches long and sharply tapered.

Rutabagas (*Brassica napo napobrassica*) are often neglected as a crop in this country, though they are popular in Europe and Canada, where they are known as swedes or Swedish turnips. They are a cool-weather crop and will not thrive during the hot summer months, but rutabagas are quite hardy and will tolerate hard frosts. Their flavor is surprisingly delicate; they are milder and sweeter than ordinary turnips. The flesh is yellow, as a rule, but in some cases it is white. The "purple top" cultivars are considered the best garden varieties.

From a gardener's viewpoint, rutabagas are an undemanding crop, but they do need a fairly long growing season. A sowing in early or midsummer will provide roots for harvesting from autumn onward, and they should last through the winter. Alternatively, sow in early fall for a winter harvest in mild regions.

Any fertile, well-drained soil is suitable, provided it is not acid. The ideal pH is 6–6.5, so be prepared to apply lime if necessary.

The soil must also be moisture-retentive if the plants are to maintain steady growth throughout the season. This means that it must contain plenty of organic matter, but do not sow rutabagas in freshly manured ground. Instead, plant them in soil that was enriched for a previous crop.

Rutabagas are members of the brassica family and as such are prone to some of the same ailments as other brassicas, including club root. For this reason, it is better not to include them in the "root" section of the three-year rotation of vegetables, which normally follows brassicas. Instead, include them in the brassica plot, so that there is a two-year interval before crops in this group are grown in the same spot again.

Dig the ground during the previous autumn or spring, and add some lime if needed. Leave this on the surface for the rain to wash in. It is a good idea to add some general fertilizer to the soil before planting.

MAKING A START
Sow seeds in late June or early July for a fall crop, or in August or September for a winter crop in the South and West. Early spring sowing is possible, but is likely to lead to crops that bolt because of prolonged exposure to cold weather.

Make the furrows fifteen inches apart and about a half-inch deep. Sow the seeds thinly, and later thin the seedlings to leave about ten inches between plants.

Some gardeners also sow rutabagas late in the season to provide a crop of green tops for the following spring. For this purpose, set the rows closer together or broadcast the seeds in a small patch. The plants can be left practically unthinned.

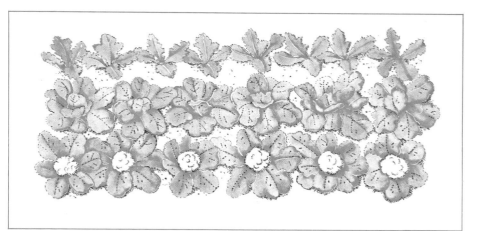

Rutabagas, although a root crop, are also brassicas and therefore subject to such soil-borne ailments as club root. With this in mind, include them with cabbages, cauliflowers, and other brassicas in the crop rotation scheme.

CARE OF THE CROP
Thin the seedlings as soon as they are large enough to handle, and be on the lookout for cabbage root maggots, which thrive in cool, damp conditions. To prevent the adult flies from laying eggs, protect the seedlings with floating row covers or dust the soil with diatomaceous earth or wood ashes. Row covers also help deter flea beetles.

Water the rows as needed to prevent the soil from drying out. As well as discouraging splitting in the event of heavy rain, this will help the plants to grow steadily instead of becoming stunted and woody. Watering whenever necessary will also improve the size and quantity of the roots, though it may make their flavor less pronounced. Hoe often to prevent competition from weeds.

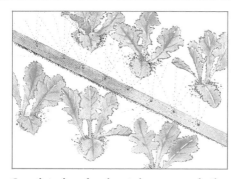

Growth is slowed and roots become woody if the ground in which rutabagas are grown becomes too dry. Start watering before this can happen; an irrigation hose is ideal for row crops.

HARVESTING
Immature rutabagas, which have a mild, sweet flavor, can be harvested in late summer. Otherwise, the roots are ready from autumn onward; dig them up with a fork. You can leave them in the soil, well mulched, during the winter, or dig them up before the ground freezes. Twist their tops off, and store them in peat.

Rutabagas are less likely to become woody if they are stored, and harvesting them all at once avoids the need to dig them out of wet ground later in the winter. Keep them in a cool room, a root cellar, or a refrigerator.

PESTS AND DISEASES
Rutabagas are subject to the same pests as other brassicas, including cabbage root maggots and flea beetles. Club root and mildew are possible diseases.

RECOMMENDED VARIETIES
'Laurentian' This is the leading yellow-fleshed variety. It has purple shoulders.
'Wilhelmsburger Glebe' is an early variety with pink shoulders; it is resistant to frost and good for northern gardens.
'American Purple Top' Another purple-topped rutabaga with yellow flesh, this cultivar has been popular for many years.
'American Yellow' Rutabagas are light amber with reddish-purple tops and yellow skin. This variety stores especially well.

CROP ROTATION, page 25
SOWING SEEDS OUTDOORS, pages 36–37

CARROTS AND OTHER ROOT VEGETABLES, pages 120–121
PESTS AND DISEASES, PAGES 172–175

STORING VEGETABLES AND FRUITS, pages 226–227

Celeriac (*Apium graveolens*) is a turnip-rooted form of celery, grown for its swollen base. From a cultivation point of view, it offers a less troublesome alternative to celery, since there is no blanching involved and the plants seldom run to seed; pests and diseases are also less of a problem. Celeriac makes a good substitute for celery when used as a flavoring in soups, stews, and other cooked dishes; the celery-flavored root can also be cooked as a separate vegetable in its own right, or grated and used raw in salads.

The roots should be allowed to swell to a good size, unlike comparable vegetables such as kohlrabi, and this means a long growing season is needed—usually about 120 days. Although celeriac is a hardy plant, it has to be started indoors in the early spring in order to give it an adequate length of time to grow. After hardening off, the seedlings are planted in their final, outdoor bed during late spring. (In warm climates, the crop does best if it is set out in late summer for a winter harvest.) Choose a position that gets the sun if you can, though celeriac will also tolerate light shade.

Celeriac demands plenty of moisture and can be grown in damper parts of the garden. On dry, light soil lacking organic matter, the roots will swell little if at all. On soils of all types, they need frequent watering throughout the summer if the weather is dry. The surest way to provide favorable conditions is to dig in a healthy amount of rotted manure or compost—at least a bucketful to the square yard—during the autumn before planting. A generous mulch is also beneficial.

MAKING A START

Sow in early spring, sprinkling the tiny seeds thinly over a propagating tray of seed-starting mix and just covering them. After watering lightly, place glass and paper over the tray and germinate in a temperature of not less than 50°F; 70°F is ideal. Uncover as soon as the seedlings emerge.

Seeds can also be germinated in a warm place indoors, and the seedlings raised on a sunny windowsill, but in this case sow a week or two later to reduce the risk that seedlings will become spindly and pale.

Prick the seedlings out two inches apart into a tray of potting soil as soon as they are large enough to handle. Grow them on steadily, with sufficient heat to prevent too much of a temperature drop at night; five to ten degrees is about right.

Toward late spring, move the tray to a cold frame to allow the plants to harden off. Rake general fertilizer into the bed where they will be planted at two ounces per square yard. Ten to fourteen days later, depending on the weather, plant them out one foot apart in each direction, with the bottom of each stem just level with the soil surface. Water the plants in gently.

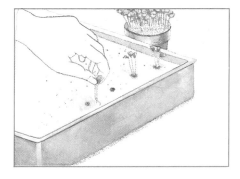

Celeriac plants must be started indoors to give them the long growing season that they need. Prick out the seedlings, which were sown in early spring, into a seed tray at two-inch spacings. Provide some warmth, especially at night, to encourage steady growth.

In common with other plants started indoors, celeriac needs a hardening-off period before being planted outdoors. Place young plants in a cold frame for ten to fourteen days, and gradually increase the amount of ventilation in order to acclimatize them to colder conditions.

CARE OF THE CROP

Keep the soil moist throughout the summer; water the plants immediately if a dry spell begins. Spread a mulch of rotted compost around the plants once they are established. From this stage onward, give the plants some liquid food every two weeks.

Cut off any side shoots that appear, since they will spoil the shape and size of the root. During mid- or late summer, remove the lower, older leaves from each plant, exposing the crown. Draw a little soil around the swollen roots to help keep them white.

HARVESTING

Harvest the roots from autumn onward, once they have attained maximum size. They do not deteriorate if left in the soil, so you can use them as needed.

If you give them a good covering of straw, secured with netting (see p.159), they can remain in the ground throughout the winter. However, in particularly cold areas or on heavy soil, it is better to harvest them and store them in damp peat or sand in a cool, well-ventilated room.

PESTS AND DISEASES

Celeriac is often relatively pest- and disease-free, though it is subject to the same problems as celery (see p.147).

RECOMMENDED VARIETIES

In general, modern varieties have smoother and whiter roots than the older celeriacs. 'Alabaster' is an example; its roots are harvested when they are two to four inches across, have a slightly minty flavor, and keep well. 'Blanco' and 'Globus' are similar varieties, as is 'Marble Ball,' which yields well. 'Jose,' a new cultivar, has a hollow heart and little pithiness.

Remove some of the older, outside leaves at some time after midsummer, to expose more of the crown, or root. It is vital to keep the soil moist throughout the growing period, or the plants will produce only leaves. This can be difficult on sandy soil.

Of all vegetables, radishes (*Raphanus sativus*) are probably the easiest and most accommodating. Their germination is reliable and their speed of growth phenomenal. It is not unusual to start harvesting spring radishes a mere three weeks after sowing.

Radishes are also hardy plants, which means the first sowing under a cloche or frame can be made in late winter. Cloches can also be used at the end of the year to protect sowings made until the end of autumn. If you sow radishes both early and late, it is therefore possible to enjoy spring radishes during most months of the year; these are eaten young, when fresh and crisp, as a raw salad vegetable. The white types of spring radish are longer-rooted than most red ones.

In addition, you can also try the much larger winter radishes, with roots weighing as much as one pound or more. They are suitable for storing during winter, just like carrots or beets. They are somewhat coarser and stronger-tasting than the spring types, so they may need to be cooked, rather than used raw in salads.

Spring radishes are shallow-rooted and need a crumbly, rich, moisture-retaining soil. They do not need a deeply dug soil, since they are not in the ground for more than a few weeks. The essential factor is rapid growth: they need to grow fast in order to be crisp and mild. Slow-grown radishes are soft or woody in texture and quite hot in taste.

Winter radishes do best in light, well-drained ground that was enriched with organic matter for the previous crop. Peat will help if the ground is on the heavy side. Sow the radishes in ground that was dug the previous autumn or winter.

A sunny spot will aid the rapid growth of spring radishes. Long summer days will cause radishes to bolt, so plant winter varieties in partial shade in midsummer.

Spring radishes are ideal for catch cropping and interplanting (see p.132). By growing them on ground temporarily vacant between crops, or between plants that develop more slowly, you will not need to allocate a special space to them. Even so, treat radishes as part of the crop rotation, and avoid growing them on the same ground in successive years.

MAKING A START

For an early crop of spring radishes, put cloches in position or close the cover of a cold frame soon after midwinter. At the same time, apply general fertilizer at one ounce per square yard to the ground where the radishes are to grow.

Allow two or three weeks for the soil to become a little drier and warmer, then sow the seeds in shallow furrows a half-inch deep and six inches apart. If the seeds are spaced about one inch apart, little or no thinning will be needed and the plants should grow rapidly.

Plant unprotected radishes in the same way, from early spring onward. Sow a small amount often so that there is a continuous supply of tender roots. During dry weather, water each furrow before sowing the seeds.

Sow winter radishes around midsummer or in the fall in furrows a half-inch deep and ten inches apart; thin the seedlings to five-inch spacings. Water the furrows first during dry weather. Oriental and Spanish varieties may run to seed if they are sown too early or in full sun.

Frequent sowings are needed for a continuing supply of radishes, but germination may prove slow in warmer weather. One solution is to water the furrows before sowing, using a fine rose on the watering can or a gentle stream from a hose so as not to disturb the soil.

CARE OF THE CROP

If flea beetles prove troublesome, dust the rows with rotenone as soon as the seedlings emerge. Cabbage root maggots can be deterred with cloches or floating row covers, or by spreading wood ashes or diatomaceous earth around the plants.

Water frequently during dry weather to maintain rapid growth, and hoe to prevent competition from weeds.

HARVESTING

Harvest spring radishes as needed while they are still young and tender—that is, before they are fully grown.

Winter radishes should be ready to eat about two to three months after sowing. Pull them up during the autumn, then remove their leafy tops and store them in dry peat or sawdust in a box.

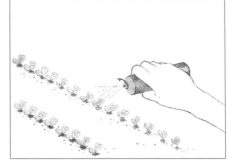

Flea beetle attacks on young seedlings are very common, especially during dry weather. The simple answer is to spray the rows with an organic solution made with hot peppers, or dust with rotenone, using a package that puffs the dust. A single application is often sufficient, but you may need to apply a second dose after a few days.

PESTS AND DISEASES

Flea beetles and cabbage root maggots are the chief pests. Disease is unlikely to prove a problem.

RECOMMENDED VARIETIES

'Cherry Belle' An early, medium-sized, bright scarlet radish for close spacing.

'Pink Beauty' Rosy pink roots are easy to digest and stay crisp longer than others.

'French Breakfast' Olive-shaped roots are pink on top, white on bottom.

'Eighteen Day' Ready in just 18 days.

'White Icicle' A very white, well-flavored early variety that matures slowly.

'All Season' Roots are like large white carrots; flesh is brittle and mild.

'Celestial Rose' has rosy pink roots that grow to eight inches; mild and crisp.

'Round Black Spanish' A strong radish with smooth roots the size of oranges.

SOWING UNDER GLASS, pages 38–39

CARROTS AND OTHER ROOT VEGETABLES, pages 120–121
PESTS AND DISEASES, pages 172–175

STORING VEGETABLES AND FRUITS, pages 226–227

The sweet, richly colored roots of *Beta vulgaris* are delicious served as a hot vegetable or made into soups such as borscht; the young ones are good raw, too, and beets are often canned or pickled for use in salads. The globe-shaped varieties are the ones to grow for salad use and should be chosen for early plantings. Beets can also be stored during the winter, and the more usual choice for this is one of the slower-growing, long-rooted kinds.

As many gardeners have discovered, a bonus in growing beets is the tasty tops, or beet greens, which can be cooked like spinach to make a nutritious and unusual vegetable. Greens can be harvested as soon as the leaves are large enough, so there is no need to thin the crop.

A beet "seed" normally produces a cluster of plants, because each one is actually a seed ball containing several seeds. This makes thinning a difficult and time-consuming task, which can be avoided by sowing a monogerm variety, which produces single seedlings instead of clusters. Another consideration to bear in mind when buying seeds is that the earliest sowings are liable to bolt. Avoid this by choosing a bolt-resistant variety.

Beets are quite easy to grow, especially if you have light but fertile soil that is either neutral or only slightly acid, which may mean that you need to add lime. Never sow beets on freshly manured ground, or the roots will fork. Good crops can also be grown on heavier soils that have been improved with organic matter.

Prepare the soil by digging during late autumn or early winter; spread lime on the surface afterward if it is too acid.

MAKING A START

Spread a general fertilizer over the ground, at three ounces per square yard, a week or two before sowing. Supply a further five ounces while the crop is growing. If you use cloches for an early crop, put these in position two weeks before planting.

Provided the soil is dry enough, sow seeds under cloches or in a cold frame in late winter or early spring; soak the seeds first for an hour in slightly warm water. Sow thinly in furrows a half-inch deep and eight inches apart; thin to three inches apart.

A few weeks later, sow directly outdoors at the same spacings; soak the seeds first. For sowings made in late spring or early summer, leave one foot between the rows and three to four inches between plants.

CARE OF THE CROP

Thin the seedlings as soon as they are large enough to handle. A well-sharpened, short-handled hoe can be a help. Subsequently, keep the ground free of weeds until the beets' foliage meets over the rows and prevents weeds from growing.

Keep the soil moist during dry weather, especially while the seeds are germinating and the roots are forming. Sudden wetting may cause the roots to split; dryness causes stringy, fibrous roots.

Remove cloches as soon as temperatures begin to rise so that the plants can take advantage of cool conditions.

Late thinnings of half-grown roots are excellent to eat, and the extra growing space gives a boost to those that remain.

Soaking beet seeds for an hour or two before sowing helps to soften their outer coat and insure prompt germination. This is less important when sowing in damp ground but still reduces possible delay.

Beets are hungry feeders. In addition to applying fertilizer before sowing the seeds, apply a heavier dressing of general fertilizer once the plants have started to grow strongly.

HARVESTING

Pull up the globe-shaped roots by hand before they become too big and woody. The smaller ones taste sweetest.

Dig up larger roots for storing in early autumn; use a garden fork to loosen the soil around them. Twist off the tops, but leave the bottom two inches of stalk attached. The roots will "bleed" if the tops are cut off too close to them.

Store the roots in boxes of dry peat or sawdust in a frost-free room or shed. High humidity is essential for long storage.

PESTS AND DISEASES

Leaf miners and leafhoppers are significant pests; wireworms, flea beetles, and Mexican bean beetles may also prove troublesome.

Diseases and disorders include boron deficiency and curly top virus.

After removing beets from the ground, whether for eating at once or for storage, twist the leafy tops off rather than cutting them with a knife. This reduces "bleeding" from the root. Leave a two-inch tuft of stalks.

RECOMMENDED VARIETIES

'Mobile' Uniform round roots are dark red throughout. A monogerm hybrid.
'Sweetheart' This variety is a sugarbeet hybrid, so it is exceptionally sweet.
'Dwergina' is a European beet that is intensely red and sweet when small.
'Early Wonder' A dual-purpose variety: greens are vigorous and glossy, roots are small and round or top-shaped.
'Burpee's Golden' Beautiful round golden beets are early and keep very well.
'Albino' is a white beet that doesn't "bleed"; tops are delicious cooked like spinach.
'Formanova' A long, cylindrical red beet that is good for slicing. Cooks and cans well.
'Winter Keeper' This variety bears very large, slightly rough-skinned, top-shaped red roots that are sweeter after they have been kept for a while.

This relatively uncommon vegetable (*Tragopogon porrifolius*) is also known as oyster plant or vegetable oyster. The name derives from its taste—a delicate, elusive flavor reminiscent of oysters.

Salsify is grown principally for its roots, which are long, off-white, and slender, not unlike immature parsnips. There is a second, quite different crop, known as chards, harvested from the same plants in spring.

The best conditions for salsify are a deep, well-worked soil, preferably fairly light and without too many stones. It should have been enriched with plenty of manure or compost within the last year or two, but do not add any more before sowing, since this might cause the roots to fork.

Choose a sunny, well-drained site and double dig the rows or beds.

Double digging provides the deeply worked soil in which salsify thrives. It will assist development of the long roots and insure that there is no hardpan to impede growth. Fork over the lower layer before replacing the topsoil, and sprinkle lime over the surface if the soil is on the acid side (below pH 6).

This plant (*Scorzonera hispanica*) closely resembles salsify and is often known as black salsify. Its long, tapering roots have a similar flavor, and they need exactly the same growing conditions.

The chief difference is in the color of the skin: scorzonera has a dark, purplish-brown skin, quite unlike the creamy color of salsify. The flesh, however, is white and has a more pronounced flavor than that of salsify. Scorzonera is also a perennial, whereas salsify is a biennial.

Choose and prepare the site as described for salsify. Double digging is a valuable aid to root development; avoid fresh manure or compost on the site.

The sowing and aftercare are the same as for salsify, but remember that scorzonera tends to bolt if sown too early.

MAKING A START
Salsify is a slow-growing plant and needs a long season to develop. You therefore need to sow seeds in midspring to provide this. A week or two beforehand, prepare the site by spreading a general fertilizer over the ground at three ounces per square yard. Scuffle this into the surface with a pronged cultivator or a rake, but leave the final raking and firming until just before you sow the salsify seeds.

It is worth noting that salsify seeds do not remain viable for very long—two years at the most. Rather than risk disappointment, buy fresh seeds each spring.

Make the furrows ten to twelve inches apart and about a half-inch deep. The seeds may be sown in clusters of three or four at six-inch spacings, or else distributed evenly and then thinned to this spacing.

CARE OF THE CROP
Thin the seedlings, or reduce clusters to single plants, as soon as they are large enough to handle. At the same time, hand-weed around the plants to reduce the risk of competition.

Subsequently, keep the crop watered during dry weather, and hoe as necessary to keep the ground weed-free. A mulch of peat or rotted compost will help to provide the right conditions for steady growth.

HARVESTING
The roots are ready for eating from midautumn onward. When digging them up, bear their length in mind and try not to break off the lower part. You may find it easier to use a spade than a fork: thrust this in on each side of the plant as deeply as possible in order to loosen the soil before attempting to pull the root free.

The roots are extremely hardy, and may be left in the ground throughout the winter in mild regions. Alternatively, to avoid having to dig them out of muddy or frozen ground, harvest them in late fall and store them in a box of peat. If you do leave them in the ground, mulch them with a covering of straw or leaves, secured with netting.

PESTS AND DISEASES
Pests and diseases are rare for salsify, although aphids can be troublesome.

RECOMMENDED VARIETIES
The variety most commonly available in this country is 'Sandwich Island Mammoth,' which produces smooth, thick roots about eight inches long with creamy white flesh. Salsify can be baked, fried, made into soup, boiled, steamed, and frozen.

HARVESTING SALSIFY CHARDS
For a harvest of blanched shoots, leave some of the roots undug. Cover them with a deep layer of straw or leaves, up to six inches thick, when they first show signs of growth in the spring. A chicken-wire cage, supported by short stakes, will prevent the covering from blowing away.

Gather the blanched shoots when they are about six inches long, and use them raw or cook them like asparagus.

If you prefer to leave the shoots unblanched, you can harvest them green and cook them like spinach.

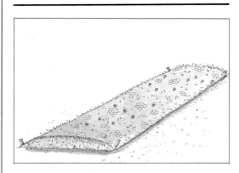

A winter covering of straw or leaves not only helps to protect the crop but also keeps the ground from freezing, and provides a good way to keep scorzonera or salsify in mild regions of the South and West. Secure netting over the top to stop the mulch from blowing away and to keep mice out.

HARVESTING
The roots may be left in the ground or dug up and stored, as for salsify. Any that are unused by spring may be left to continue growing during the new season. The roots will have expanded by the following autumn and winter, but will not have become coarse.

PESTS AND DISEASES
Pest and disease problems are rare.

RECOMMENDED VARIETIES
The most common variety of scorzonera is called 'Gigantia,' and produces very long, slender, brittle black roots with white flesh. The plants resemble thistles.

SOWING SEEDS OUTDOORS, pages 36–37
RADISHES AND OTHER ROOT VEGETABLES, pages 122–123

PESTS AND DISEASES, pages 172–175
STORING VEGETABLES AND FRUITS, pages 226–227

Home-grown turnips (*Brassica rapa*) have little in common with the tired, limp roots that find their way into supermarkets. If they are grown quickly, their flavor is as delicate as their texture. Good growing conditions will insure that their flavor is sweet and their texture is firm but not woody, whether you grow them for eating fresh or for storing.

Early, quick-growing turnips are ideal for catch cropping and interplanting (see p.132). Protect the earliest crops with cloches or a cold frame. A late-summer sowing of turnips will supply an abundant crop of tender turnip greens, which are filled with vitamins and minerals, or you can harvest the sweet young roots before the ground freezes.

Turnips belong to the brassica family and are subject to the usual pests and diseases. For this reason, include them with other brassicas in your rotation plan.

Turnips tolerate all types of soil, but grow best on a light, fertile one. Choose an open, sunny situation where the soil was manured for a previous crop. After digging during the previous fall, apply some lime if the soil is below pH 6.

The aboveground "root" of this strange-looking vegetable is actually its swollen stem. Kohlrabi (*Brassica oleracea*) has a turniplike flavor and, as with turnips, is best eaten while still young and tender. It also needs the same soil and similar growing conditions as turnips and can be grown as a catch crop or interplanted with late-maturing vegetables.

The main difference between the two vegetables is that kohlrabi can be grown where summers are hot and dry, where turnips would probably fail. Kohlrabi can stand conditions of drought and heat without losing its flavor. A member of the brassica family, kohlrabi should be grouped with other brassicas in the rotation scheme.

Sow kohlrabi from late winter onward (under cloches for the earliest sowings),

MAKING A START

Sow seed from late winter onward if you are using cloches or a cold frame, or from early spring without protection. In both cases, the soil must be sufficiently dry and crumbly. Spread general fertilizer at two ounces per square yard two weeks before sowing. At the same time, place cloches in position.

Sow the seeds in furrows nine inches apart and a half-inch deep; firm the seedbed. Thin the seedlings to five inches. Continue with one or two further sowings until midspring, to give a succession of crops.

You can also sow turnips in mid- or late summer. Make the furrows one foot apart and thin the seedlings to nine inches to encourage large roots. For greens, sow in early spring or late fall, and allow three to four inches between rows. Sow thinly and do not thin again.

CARE OF THE CROP

Thin turnips as soon as seedlings are large enough to grasp between finger and thumb. Watch out for cabbage root maggots. Keep the soil moist during dry weather, or the plants will stop growing.

HARVESTING

Pull up spring turnips when they reach the size of golfballs. Harvest midsummer sowings from autumn onward; either leave them in the soil until needed (if you live in a mild area), or store them in peat in a large box. Twist off the leafy tops first.

PESTS AND DISEASES

The principal pests are cabbage root maggots and flea beetles.

Ailments include boron deficiency, club root, and black rot.

Instead of being grown for their roots, turnips can be sown for a harvest of greens. Broadcast a small area of seeds in autumn or early spring, and cut the greens with shears one inch above the ground when they are six inches high.

Harvest kohlrabi by pulling the entire plant from the ground. If pulled up before the "roots" (swollen stems) become tough, the leaves can be cooked in the same way as turnip greens. Though winter storage is possible, the crop is better eaten straight from the ground.

RECOMMENDED VARIETIES

'Purple Top White Globe' is the most commonly available variety. Turnips are round, smooth, and white with reddish-purple shoulders; flesh is mild and crisp.
'Tokyo Cross' An All-America Winner. Plants are disease resistant and produce pure white roots early. The roots are never pithy or coarse.
'Just Right' A dual-purpose variety: greens are prolific, roots are slightly flattened, white, and tender.
'Yorii Spring' An extra-early variety that can be harvested before the summer heat begins. Roots are small, flattened, and white, with a sweet flavor.
'Presto' This early turnip is slow to bolt and has very delicately flavored roots.
'Gilfeather' An heirloom variety bred in Vermont. Flavor is exceptionally sweet.

with the same spacings and care as you give to turnips. Take particular care not to damage the roots when hoeing.

Harvest the plants when the bulbous stems are the size of tennis balls. Late kohlrabi can be left in the ground or else harvested and stored, though the stems shrivel more than root crops in storage.

Pests and diseases are the same as for turnips (see opposite).

RECOMMENDED VARIETIES

Kohlrabi varieties are quite similar except in color and the relative thickness of their leaf stems. **'Grand Duke'** and **'Rapid'** have blue-green skin with a powdery bloom, **'Purple Danube'** has reddish-purple skin, and all three have crisp white flesh. A new variety, **'Kolpack,'** is an extra-early, light-green kohlrabi that stays free of fiber or pithiness.

CROP ROTATION, page 25
SOWING SEEDS OUTDOORS, pages 36–37
CARROTS AND OTHER ROOT VEGETABLES, pages 120–121
RADISHES AND OTHER ROOT VEGETABLES, pages 122–123
SPACE-SAVING METHODS, pages 132–133
PESTS AND DISEASES, pages 172–175

Squash and pumpkins are cucurbits, which means they are members of the cucumber family and grow on annual bushes or vines with large, lobed leaves and yellow flowers. Although their cultivation requirements are broadly similar, there are significant differences between these vegetables, not only in shape, size, and color, but also in flavor and texture.

Squash has always been very popular in America and is becoming increasingly available in Europe too. The fruit comes in many forms but falls into two basic groups—summer and winter types.

Summer squash (*Cucurbita moschata*) has soft skin and pale, soft, fine-grained flesh. It is eaten fresh, as soon as it is gathered, which is usually at an immature stage. This group includes straightneck and crookneck squash, zucchini, and squash with scalloped rims, known as pattypan squash. Though there is some variety in the flavor of the different summer squash, the texture of the cooked flesh varies considerably. Vegetable marrows, which are very popular in Europe, are the mature fruit of some varieties of zucchini, and taste like other summer squash.

Winter squash, on the other hand, has a tough, shell-like skin that enables it to be kept for long periods. Winter squash (*Cucurbita maxima*) is less watery than summer squash; the fibrous flesh has a

more solid texture and contains more nourishment. However, winter squash needs several months of sunshine to mature, so it is best suited to those areas that have reasonably long summers. The winter squash group includes small acorn squash and the larger Hubbard, butternut, and banana squash. In a class of its own is the unusual 'Vegetable Spaghetti' squash: when it is cooked whole, the inside comes away in strands like spaghetti.

Pumpkins (*Cucurbita pepo*) are similar to the largest of the winter squash and take up a lot of room; they are not a good choice for those with limited space in the food garden. They have orange or yellow skin and coarse, strongly flavored flesh. When grown for show, pumpkins may reach weights of over five hundred pounds.

Much smaller pumpkins than this can be grown, however. They have several culinary uses, and some varieties make excellent Halloween jack-o'-lanterns when hollowed out. The miniature kinds weigh only a pound or two. Many pumpkins can be stuffed, steamed, boiled, baked, or, of course, used as the basis for pumpkin pie.

Both summer and winter squash plants are obtainable in bush and vine varieties, although most summer squash for gardens are bush types, and most winter squash are vine types. Bush varieties need less space and crop earlier; they do not form a true

bush, but they have a reasonably compact habit, which is practical for most gardens.

The vining varieties throw out long shoots that extend over the ground for a considerable distance. You can train large plants, such as pumpkins, into a circular form by pinning down the main shoots with wire, plastic, or wooden pegs. Alternatively, you can train vining plants up tripods made of stout poles or over strong trelliswork of some kind. Growing the plants on a trellis also enables the fruit to get more sun and to ripen faster. It makes harvesting the crop easier, too.

Most pumpkins have a vining habit and need a great deal of space. The fruit can grow to an enormous size, which is of interest mainly in exhibitions, but smaller, better-tasting pumpkins can be harvested earlier from suitable varieties.

If space is at a premium, winter squash or pumpkins can be trained over a trellis or similar structure. Heavy fruit may need to be supported individually in nets or pantyhose.

The bush form of squash is compact and usually considered more suitable than vines for most gardens.

Squash and pumpkins, like other members of the cucumber family, need a sunny position in the garden and rich, moist, well-drained soil. It should be neutral or just a little acid—about pH 6 to 6.5.

The best way to provide these conditions is by preparing the planting area some weeks ahead of sowing or planting. If you are growing only a few plants, dig holes one foot deep and about one and a half feet square. Mix a bucketful of rotted manure or compost with the soil you have removed. Loosen the subsoil with a fork before replacing the topsoil. If your ground is sandy and light, leave the surface a little below ground level so that plants receive as much moisture as possible in dry weather. Dress the surface with lime if the soil is too acid.

When deciding where to dig, bear in mind that you will need to allow two to three feet between bush plants and six feet between groups of vining types. If vining varieties are to be trained upward, however, it is sufficient to allow two feet between plants. Zucchini plants need only twenty inches between them, whereas the largest varieties of pumpkins will require as much as eight feet between hills (hills are not mounds, but circular depressions in which three or four vining pumpkins or squash are planted together).

Squash and pumpkins need soil rich in organic matter in order to sustain rapid growth and heavy fruiting. Prepare the soil in advance, and mix plenty of manure or compost with it before replacing it.

MAKING A START
For a slightly earlier start, you can sow the seeds indoors around the middle of spring. Only gentle warmth is needed. Sow each seed individually in a three-inch peat pot (pumpkins and squash do not like having their roots disturbed by transplanting). Sow one or two extra pots in case any fail to germinate. Cover the pots with glass and paper until the seedlings appear.

Toward the end of spring, harden these plants off in a cold frame, ready for planting out ten to fourteen days later. At the same time, rake a handful of general fertilizer into each planting position. You can use cloches or plastic mulch to warm up the soil in preparation for the plants.

Members of the squash family are only half-hardy, and at no time must the plants be exposed to frost. When putting them in their final positions, provide temporary protection with cloches or row covers if the weather is dull and cold.

The alternative means of raising the plants is to sow the seeds directly outdoors in prepared hills, rows, or individual planting holes. With cloche protection, this may be done while there is still just a chance of a late frost. If you do not have cloches, you can place a glass jar or a plastic jug with the bottom cut out over each seedling; remove it when the plant is established.

If plants have no form of protection, wait for a week or two after the last frost. Sow two seeds in each position and remove the weaker seedling in due course. Cucumber beetles are very partial to the young plants, so protect them with row covers if possible.

Cloche protection is valuable whether you sow the seeds directly or transfer plants from a greenhouse. If you don't have cloches, cover seeds with a large glass jar or plastic jug until a week or two after they have germinated.

CARE OF THE CROP
Water frequently during dry weather, and be sure to supply enough to penetrate the soil deeply. Make sure you water around the plants rather than over them, to prevent mildew and rot. Watering is particularly important when the plants are flowering and when the fruit is growing. A mulch of well-rotted compost or black plastic will reduce evaporation. Provide a little liquid fertilizer to winter squash once the fruit has formed. Keep weeds down by hand weeding or mulching.

Winter squash and pumpkins often throw out roots from their stems. Cover these with soil so they root and increase the plant's food and water supply.

If you want to train squash onto a trellis, you will have to tie up the long shoots regularly and support the fruit with slings.

ENCOURAGING FRUIT DEVELOPMENT
Pinch out the shoots of winter squash and pumpkins when they are two to three feet long, or when a few fruits have developed, to stimulate growth. If you are training them on fences or tripods, however, wait until the shoots are five feet long before stopping them. Pinch out the fuzzy tips as often as necessary to restrict the vines.

If the plants flower while the weather is cloudy or windy, transfer pollen from male to female flowers with a brush, or by gently rubbing a female flower with a male bloom. It is easy to recognize the female flower by the swelling behind it.

HARVESTING

Once the fruit is established and is beginning to swell, pinch back the main shoots at two leaves beyond the fruit. Keep larger squash well mulched with straw or plastic to prevent it from rotting or being attacked by pests. Turn the squash regularly to encourage even ripening.

Cut zucchini and other summer squash as soon as it is ready, using a sharp knife. Harvest elongated types when they are four to six inches long if you want to eat them whole; otherwise leave them until they are a little longer, for slicing. Pattypan types are best when they are three to four inches across. Small summer squash freezes well if you have a surplus.

Soft-skinned summer squash is generally picked young and eaten raw or cooked. Test the skin with your thumbnail: it should be soft and pierce easily. If it is hard, the squash is past its best. Larger squash can be hollowed out, stuffed, and baked, but do not let the fruit grow larger than about twelve inches long, or the flavor will deteriorate.

With winter squash and pumpkins it is usual to allow only two or three fruits to develop on each plant, depending on the variety. Remove any surplus fruits toward the end of the summer. Stop watering the plants when they reach their mature size. Pumpkins are ready for harvesting when they turn completely orange and the vines die. You can leave late ones to mature on the plants, but cut them before the first frost.

Use a sharp knife to cut the stems of pumpkins and winter squash, since rot will set in if the stem pulls away from the fruit. Leave a two-inch stub of stem, and handle the fruit carefully, without scratching the skin. Brush off any soil, but do not wash the fruit. The pumpkins or squash can then be stored indoors for winter use.

To keep winter squash and pumpkins for several months, first cure their skins by drying them thoroughly in the sun or near a stove for a week or ten days. Wipe them with a weak solution of bleach, then spread them out in a cool, well-ventilated, dark room. Check them frequently and throw away any that appear to be rotting.

PESTS AND DISEASES

Cucumber beetles, squash vine borers, squash bugs, and stinkbugs are among the pests that prey on squash and pumpkins.

The most likely ailments include fusarium wilt, bacterial wilt, downy mildew, powdery mildew, and blossom end rot.

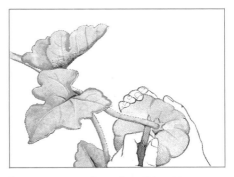

Cut summer squash, such as this pattypan squash, as soon as it is large enough and while the skin is still soft. Winter squash is left on the plants until just before the first frost.

To cut vegetable marrows and other large squash, place a board under the fruit to steady it and cut through the stem with a sharp knife. Leave a two-inch stub, and be careful not to bruise the fruit.

RECOMMENDED VARIETIES

Summer squash
'Richgreen Hybrid' A zucchini type with glossy, dark green fruit.
'Gold Rush' Small, productive plants bear golden zucchini.
'Dixie' An early-producing, compact crookneck squash with light yellow fruit.
'Tara Hybrid' Tadpole-shaped yellow squash is smooth and delicately flavored.
'Seneca Butterbar' Vigorous bushes bear for extended periods. Straight, long, pale yellow fruit.
'Early Prolific' An old standard; slightly bulbed fruit has straight neck.
'Sunburst' A bright yellow pattypan squash with good flavor.
'Scallopini' Fruit is early and thick.
'Peter Pan' Semibush plants bear large, greenish-white pattypan fruit.

'Blondy Hybrid' A vegetable marrow type that is popular for cooking and storing.
'Cousa' Also known as Lebanese zucchini. Fruit is pale greenish-white and short.
'Vegetable Marrow Bush' A compact, productive bush that bears white fruit.

Winter squash
'Table Ace' An almost black acorn squash. Deeply ribbed fruit is borne on semibush vines, has bright orange flesh.
'Jersey Golden Acorn' A golden squash that is good raw or cooked and stores well.
'Early Butternut Hybrid' Numerous small, hard-shelled fruits mature early.
'Waltham Butternut' A popular squash with deep orange flesh. Keeps well.
'Burpee's Butterbush' Compact plants bear large fruit with good flavor.
'Tahitian' A very large variety with long vines, resistant to heat and humidity. Squash are immense, semicircular, and deep red-beige in color.
'Buttercup' Drum-shaped fruit has exceptional flavor and texture, no stringiness.
'Blue Hubbard' A good keeper that weighs 10–15 pounds. Skin is warty, blue-gray.
'True Hubbard' This variety has fine-grained, light orange flesh.

Pumpkins
'Atlantic Giant' An exhibition pumpkin; one fruit weighed over six hundred pounds. Thick flesh makes good pies.
'Spirit Hybrid' Uniform, symmetrical fruit is ideal for jack-o'-lanterns.
'Jack Be Little' Miniature fruit fits into your hand; ideal for decorating.
'Howden' Large pumpkins are good for carving and for pies.

The cucumber (*Cucumis sativus*) is a warmth- and moisture-loving semitropical plant that has long been a favorite with home gardeners. There are essentially two kinds, slicing cucumbers and pickling varieties, though a number of new hybrids and exotic types are now available as well.

In general, slicing cucumbers bear fairly long, smooth-skinned fruit with crisp flesh. They include the European varieties, which are exceptionally sweet and thin-skinned, and the oriental or "burpless" cucumbers, which grow quite long and are practically seedless. Many slicing cucumbers are disease resistant, and they are available in both bush and vining forms.

Picklers, in contrast, tend to be short, chunky, and rather knobbly; the plants are often very productive, and they usually bear earlier than slicing varieties. Gherkins, which are actually a different species, have very short, burrlike fruit, and are one of the few cucumbers that cannot be used for both eating raw and pickling.

Standard cucumbers of all types produce both male and female flowers and thus require pollination by bees to set fruit. However, some varieties are "all-female" or gynoecious; these are pollinated by standard varieties (a few seeds of which are included in the packet) and bear earlier and heavier because their blossoms are mostly fruit-bearing ones. Parthenocarpic, or nonpollinating, cucumbers will crop regardless of the presence of bees.

All cucumbers need warm soil, long, hot days, plenty of moisture, and warm nights to produce at their best.

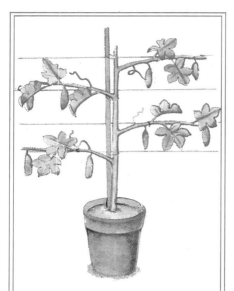

GROWING CUCUMBERS OUTDOORS
Cucumbers can be grown outdoors anywhere in the United States, as long as you choose a variety appropriate for your region and climate. In the South and in coastal areas, plant any cucumber that can tolerate humidity and disease; in colder regions, choose an early-maturing, prolific variety.

Cucumbers will do well in rows or beds, on trellises, and in containers. The crucial factor is rich soil that will retain moisture and supply plenty of nutrients.

MAKING A START
Prepare the planting site in advance, in a sunny, sheltered spot. Dig the soil one foot deep, mix half a bucketful of well-rotted compost or manure with each square foot of soil, and then replace it. Allow for two feet between ordinary varieties and slightly more between supported oriental types. Gherkins, which are best sown where they are to grow, need to be two feet apart.

In midspring, sow seeds in peat pots indoors, as described on the opposite page, and harden off the seedlings for a couple of weeks before planting them out. Two weeks before planting, rake a handful of general fertilizer for each plant into the planting site. Set the young plants out very carefully, preferably under cloches, to cause as little root disturbance as possible.

Alternatively, wait until late spring and then sow the seeds directly, when the soil is quite warm. Sow seeds about six inches apart, or in hills with five or six seeds each.

GROWING GHERKINS
Gherkins are small cucumbers (*Cucumis anguria*) used for pickling. They are usually grown on flat ground, but it is also possible to plant them in a pot of organically rich potting soil standing on a sunny patio. Support the stem with a stake and tie the laterals to wires or similar supports.

True gherkins, which are usually ready for harvesting about two months after they are planted out, have a distinctive sweet flavor and can be made into relishes as well as pickles.

CARE OF THE CROP
It is a good idea to erect a netting or trellis support five feet high for vining varieties. Train the stems to this, tying them as necessary, and pinch out the tips when they reach the tops of the support.

Water frequently and generously, and never let the soil dry out. A mulch of straw or black plastic will reduce evaporation, suppress weeds, and deter pests. Feed every ten to fourteen days with a high-potash liquid fertilizer once the fruit starts to form, and watch carefully for signs of rot in cucumbers lying on the ground.

Cucumber beetles can be a serious pest in many parts of the country, but they can be controlled by careful planning. Protect seedlings with cloches or row covers, especially when they are just appearing above the ground. Succession planting and interplanting should also limit the damage.

If you pinch out the tips of cucumber shoots after the sixth leaf, you will encourage the formation of fruiting side shoots but delay the production of cucumbers. Male flowers should be left on the plants of monoecious, or standard, varieties.

HARVESTING
Harvest slicers as soon as they are large enough to use; picklers should be four or five inches long. As a rule, the more cucumbers you pick, the more cucumbers the plants will produce. Pick gherkins when they are only two to three inches long.

PESTS AND DISEASES
The chief pests of this crop are cucumber beetles, squash vine borers, pickleworms, and whiteflies.

Diseases include bacterial wilt, cucumber mosaic virus, anthracnose, powdery mildew, downy mildew, and fusarium wilt.

GROWING CUCUMBERS INDOORS

The greenhouse is an ideal place to grow cucumbers, if you can provide a controlled environment that is warm and damp enough. If you sow the seeds early in the year, you will have to maintain a daytime temperature of at least 60°F for standard varieties and 70°F for gynoecious cucumbers; nighttime temperatures for all types should not dip below 50°F.

MAKING A START INDOORS

For an early crop, sow in late winter or early spring. Place two seeds in three-inch pots filled with seed-starting mix. Peat pots are ideal, since cucumbers resent root disturbance at transplanting time. Cover the pots with glass and paper and germinate the seeds at a temperature of 75°F.

Uncover the pots after germination, remove the weaker seedling, and grow the plants on in a minimum temperature of 60°F, or 70°F for all-female varieties, for at least the first month. To make a greenhouse trellis, fasten horizontal supporting wires at six-inch intervals, preferably across the end wall of the greenhouse, and one foot away from the glass.

When the seedlings have two true leaves (in addition to the smooth, elliptical seed leaves), transplant them into ten-inch pots filled with potting soil, one per pot, or into growing bags, two per bag. Water them in and stand the containers under the wires. Allow two and a half or three feet between plants. Fasten a cane behind each plant to support the stem.

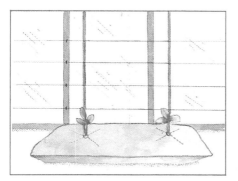

When planting indoor cucumbers, either in the greenhouse border or in containers, secure a cane to the wires behind each plant. This will support the main stem, while the wires take the weight of the fruit-bearing laterals.

TRAINING AND AFTERCARE

Pinch out the tip of each main shoot when it reaches the roof. Side shoots, or laterals, will then form, and it is these that will bear the fruit. Tie the laterals to the wires.

Pinch out the tips of laterals two leaves beyond the point where fruit forms. If a lateral shows no sign of fruiting, stop it at two feet. Remove any male flowers—the ones without the swelling of an embryo fruit—that happen to appear on all-female plants, and check the plants for signs of stress and disease.

Cucumbers do best in warm, humid conditions, so the growing medium must be kept moist at all times. Spraying the floor of the greenhouse will increase humidity, but whether you will be able to do this regularly

will depend on what other plants you are growing in the greenhouse. Continuously humid conditions are disastrous for tomatoes, for instance. Shade the plants from strong sunshine and apply a high-potash liquid fertilizer every ten to fourteen days when the fruit starts to develop.

HARVESTING

Cut the cucumbers as soon as they have reached the size typical for the variety. Picked too small, they are bland; left too long, the plant will stop producing.

PESTS AND DISEASES

As for outdoor cucumbers, opposite. Red spider mites can also be troublesome.

Once tiny cucumbers appear and start to grow on the laterals of greenhouse plants, pinch out the shoots just past the two leaves beyond the fruit. Feed the plants at least every two weeks from this stage on.

COLD FRAMES

To grow cucumbers in a cold frame, sow the seeds in midspring, and germinate them in heat as described above. Set one plant per frame in a raised mound of compost at the highest part. Pinch out the tip once the plant has six true leaves.

Shade the glass and open the cover about two inches on sunny days. Water the plants frequently, and spray the inside of the frame in hot weather.

Peg down the four best laterals, and direct each one to a corner of the frame. Remove all others. Pinch out their growing tips when they near the corners, or two leaves beyond the first fruit when it develops.

RECOMMENDED VARIETIES
Slicing cucumbers

'Marketmore 76' Dark green, glossy fruit averages six to nine inches. Plants are resistant to mildews, scab, and cucumber mosaic virus.

'Spacemaster' A bush variety with dark green, slender, crisp cucumbers.

'Sweet Success' An All-America Winner. Fruit is very long (twelve to fourteen inches), seedless, and crisp. Plants are disease resistant and prolific, parthenocarpic.

'Lemon' A pale yellow, apple-shaped cucumber, also good for pickling.

'Sweet Slice' A "burpless" variety with thin skin and no bitterness; disease tolerant.

'Poinsett' A standard variety that does especially well in the South.

'Early Triumph' An All-America Winner that is exceptionally hardy and disease resistant. Bush plants bear early.

Pickling cucumbers

'Bush Pickle' An early, very compact cucumber with four-inch fruit. Yields well.

'Peppi' The slightly tapered, elongated fruit is dark green. Early and compact.

'County Fair' A seedless, white-spined variety that has no bitterness gene.

'Salty' A gynoecious cucumber with blunt, cylindrical fruit.

Other varieties

'Burpless Hybrid' Ten-inch-long fruit is tasty and needs no peeling.

'Suyo Long' An oriental variety that bears very long, slender, dark green fruit.

'West India Gherkin' Very prolific.

'Armenian' Cucumbers grow to 3 feet long, but are best at 18 inches. Mild and sweet.

'Pot Luck Hybrid' A very dwarf cucumber: vines are eighteen inches long; fruits are seven inches long. Good for containers.

USING A GREENHOUSE, pages 12–13
SOWING UNDER GLASS, pages 38–39

WATERING AND MULCHING, pages 42–43
CUCUMBERS AND OTHER VEGETABLE FRUITS, pages 126–127

PESTS AND DISEASES, pages 172–175
CANNING, pages 228–229

The eggplant (*Solanum melongena*) is a tropical plant that originated in the Far East and was brought to the Mediterranean area sometime in the early Middle Ages. It is now becoming a favorite of American gardeners, perhaps because of its versatility in the kitchen.

The plants of this warmth-loving vegetable usually have a height and spread of about two feet, prickly leaves and stems, and attractive purple flowers. Most varieties bear black or purple fruit, but white, green, yellow, brown, and speckled varieties are also available. The size and shape of the eggplants vary, too, but the oval shape that gives them their name is most common.

Eggplants, being of tropical origin, require a long growing season with warm days and nights and plenty of sunshine. Cool, damp conditions do not suit them. If you live in the South or Southwest, you should have no trouble growing an impressive crop, and gardeners in most parts of the country can choose a variety that will do well outdoors. If you live in the far North or the Pacific Northwest, however, you might consider growing eggplants in a greenhouse, where you can give them the consistent warmth they need to bear prolifically.

Another possibility is to start the plants indoors and to transplant them to a cold frame or cloches for the first few weeks of their growing season, when nights, especially, are not reliably warm. Cloches are useful in all parts of the country to give the plants an earlier start. Eggplants must be sown indoors about two months before the soil warms up, so cloche protection can subtract about two weeks from the transplanting date. Similarly, a black plastic mulch will warm the soil for earlier transplanting.

Eggplants can also be grown in pots or growing bags on a sunny patio. However they are planted, though, they must have free-draining and well-manured soil in order to thrive. The best plan is to prepare the ground ahead of time by digging in plenty of well-rotted manure or compost; then, just before planting, add a little general fertilizer to each planting hole and mix it thoroughly with the soil.

MAKING A START
Whether you plan to grow the plants outdoors or in a greenhouse, sow the seeds in early spring in a temperature of 65° to 70°F. Set them singly in three-inch pots, and prepare one or two extra in case any fail to germinate. Cover the pots with glass and paper until the seedlings appear.

Grow the seedlings on in a temperature of around 60°F. Too much warmth will make them weak and spindly, but if they have too little, they will stop growing.

An alternative to starting your own plants from seed is to buy seedlings from garden centers, where they are usually available. Choose plants that are stocky and well supplied with healthy-looking leaves; these have strong root systems.

Planting outdoors
Harden the plants off during late spring by placing them in a cold frame. Gradually increase the amount of ventilation over a two-week period before transplanting them. Set the plants one and a half to two feet apart in rows; use the larger spacing if you are planting them in beds. Protect them from cold with cloches, and deter cutworms by placing a collar around the stem of each transplanted seedling.

Outdoor plants can also be grown in large pots or growing bags, which reduces the likelihood of disease. Wait until the risk of frost is over before planting. Stand pots one and a half feet apart. Plant three eggplants in a standard-size growing bag, and check frequently to see whether they need water.

Planting in a greenhouse
Prepare the soil as for outdoor plants, or use growing bags or eight-inch pots filled with sterilized potting soil.

Transplant in midspring if the greenhouse is heated. Wait for a week or two longer if the greenhouse is unheated, but meanwhile keep the plants in a warm place on the benches. Much depends on the weather, of course, and on prevailing night-time temperatures.

CARE OF THE CROP
Water the plants in, and subsequently insure that the soil does not dry out.

Pinch out the suckers of the plants when they are one foot high, which will encourage fruit-bearing shoots to form. Support the plants with stakes and string if they grow tall and bushy.

Apply a liquid high-potash fertilizer every two weeks once the first fruit starts to swell. Hosing the plants with water once or twice daily helps to suppress spider mites.

HARVESTING
Harvest the fruit when it has an even color and while it is still glossy. Once eggplants lose their shine they start to become tough and bitter. Cut the stems with scissors or clippers, and handle the fruit carefully. Eggplants will keep for up to two weeks after they are harvested.

To help greenhouse eggplants grow and ripen, allow only one to develop on each shoot. Remove other flowers and pinch out the tips of shoots at two or three leaves beyond the fruit that is left.

PESTS AND DISEASES
Flea beetles, spider mites, and Colorado potato beetles can be troublesome. Whiteflies are a problem in greenhouses.

Possible diseases are verticillium wilt, anthracnose, phomopsis blight, and tobacco mosaic virus.

RECOMMENDED VARIETIES
'Tycoon' An early-bearing oriental variety with elongated, dark-purple fruit.
'Dusky Hybrid' The oval, meaty black eggplants are delicately flavored. Plants bear early and prolifically, set fruit in adverse conditions, and resist viruses.
'Ichiban' A very heavy-bearing oriental type with long, slender, curving fruit.
'Agora' Semicylindrical fruit matures early.
'Easter Egg' Small, egg-shaped fruit is white when young, yellow at maturity; plants are small, productive, and early.

All peppers, including chiles, are species of the *Capsicum* genus, and they are among the most popular of garden plants because of their endless variety and wonderful flavor. There are red, yellow, and green bell or sweet peppers, as well as rare purple and white varieties. Hot peppers, or chiles, also come in a number of colors, and range in shape from small round cherry peppers to long, pencil-shaped cayenne varieties. In the kitchen, peppers can be used raw or cooked; they can be made into relishes, and some can also be dried.

Peppers are relatively easy to grow, as long as they are not subjected to cold and receive plenty of moisture and nutrients. They make decorative container plants, and will bear wherever there is plenty of sun. Rich, well-drained soil is ideal.

Set pepper plants between twelve and eighteen inches apart; chiles need less space than sweet peppers. Protect them from cold snaps with cloches or row covers, or plant them near a south-facing wall.

Spray container-grown peppers with water to aid moisture retention and to discourage pests such as red spider mites. Many pepper varieties are very ornamental and contribute color to a patio garden.

MAKING A START
Prepare the soil and sow the seeds as for eggplants, but be sure that the seedlings do not become constricted in their pots. Take care to harden them off gradually, so that they are never subjected to a drastic change in temperature.

Set the seedlings twelve to eighteen inches apart, depending on the variety. Plastic mulch, cloches, or row covers are valuable for transplants, but do not let them get too hot, or the flowers will drop.

CARE OF THE CROP
Once the plants are established, feed them with a handful of general fertilizer per plant or a mulch of well-rotted manure or compost. Water them well once a week, and support them with stakes if necessary.

Peppers are vulnerable to very high temperatures, which can cause the buds to drop, dry out the roots, and cause sunscald on the fruit. Protect the plants during hot, bright days by watering frequently and providing shade if possible.

HARVESTING
Start picking when the peppers are big enough to use; the plants will continue to produce fruit for several weeks. Bell peppers will turn red if left on the plant; these will have a sweeter taste and a higher proportion of vitamin C than the green ones.

PESTS AND DISEASES
Whiteflies, flea beetles, leaf miners, and Colorado potato beetles are possible pests.

Diseases include verticillium and fusarium wilt, leaf spot, and mosaic virus.

RECOMMENDED VARIETIES
Sweet peppers
'Ace' An early, prolific green pepper.
'Lady Bell' Deep, blocky green fruit has thick flesh and is good for stuffing.
'Jupiter' Plants produce well.
'Sweet Cherry' The small, green, buttonlike fruit is good for pickling or cooking.
'Sweet Chocolate' has rich brown skin and red flesh. Early; tolerates coolness.
'Sweet Banana' Long, pointed fruit.
'Gypsy Hybrid' An early yellow variety.
'Golden Bell' Fruit is blocky and four-lobed.
'Gold Crest' Productive, disease-resistant.

Chiles
'Hungarian Yellow Wax' Mild, elongated.
'Karlo' This is a good variety for northern areas. Fruit can be ground for paprika.
'Jalapeño' Dark green, thumb-sized peppers range from hot to very hot in flavor.
'Cayenne Long Thin' Very long pods.
'Thai Hot' Inch-long peppers are borne on ornamental bushes. Unique spicy flavor.

The pods of this tender plant (*Abelmoschus escutlentus*), also called gumbo, are popular in the South but are often considered an acquired taste elsewhere. It is worth sampling some before deciding whether to grow your own. Okra is a versatile vegetable: it can be added to stews, steamed and braised, fried in batter, or used to form the basis of dishes such as sweet and sour okra. A characteristic is the sticky "gum" okra exudes when cooked; hence the term *gumbo*.

Okra originated in tropical Africa and therefore does best in warm climates. However, like eggplants and peppers, it can be grown anywhere if it is protected from the cold. It grows from three to eight feet high, depending on whether you plant a dwarf or a tall variety. The taller varieties will need some form of support.

Pick the pods of okra before they exceed three or four inches in length. After this they are liable to become tough. Scissors or clippers are the best means of severing the stalks. Use the pods as soon as possible after picking, before they become limp. Do not refrigerate them.

MAKING A START AND AFTERCARE
The methods advised for sowing and growing eggplants also apply to okra, which does best in a clay soil.

HARVESTING
Be sure to pick the pods while they are still young and tender—no more than three or four inches long. Test for tenderness with your thumbnail. Cut them with scissors or a sharp knife; do not remove the caps.

RECOMMENDED VARIETIES
'Blondy' An All-America Winner. Lime-green pods; short, early, productive plants.
'Park's Candelabra' Tall plants; green ridged pods. Best on fertile soil.
'Emerald Green' Round, spineless pods.
'Red Okra' or 'Red River' Very ornamental, tall plants have red-tinged stems and leaves, maroon pods.

SOWING UNDER GLASS, pages 38–39
VEGETABLE FRUITS, pages 126–127

TOMATOES AND OTHER VEGETABLE FRUITS, page 128
PESTS AND DISEASES, pages 172–175

FREEZING VEGETABLES, pages 232–233

Tomatoes (*Lycopersicon esculentum*) rank high in any list of favorite garden crops. They are one of the most popular and most universally grown vegetables, despite their susceptibility to pests and diseases.

Tomatoes are versatile in their culinary use. They are one of the tastiest and most useful raw foods, and they are invaluable in sauces and in Mediterranean and Mexican cuisine. A surplus can easily be frozen as a purée or canned whole, and any unripe ones can be used to make green tomato chutney or chow-chow.

You can expect a yield of up to thirty pounds from each plant grown outdoors, depending on the variety and the growing method, and even more than this from plants grown in a greenhouse. The taste of all tomatoes is better when they are home grown and freshly picked, and home growing offers a much wider range of sizes, colors, and flavors than is ever found in the commercial product. The choice ranges from the cherry-sized fruits to beefsteak tomatoes that weigh one pound or more apiece. There are pink, yellow, and white varieties as well as plum- and pear-shaped ones. New kinds of tomato are introduced every year, and many are an improvement on the traditional choices.

Tomatoes are half-hardy plants, vulnerable to frost but well able to grow outdoors during the summer. They do best in a sunny position, except in very hot regions, where partial shade can be beneficial. Results will be poor during a damp, chilly summer, unless you choose one of the varieties specially bred to ripen quickly.

All tomatoes need a warm start so the seeds germinate successfully and the seed-

Determinate tomatoes, which need no pruning, ripen early but are limited in yield.

Indeterminate varieties are slightly more trouble but produce more tomatoes.

lings develop well. In a greenhouse, you can provide localized heat in a propagator or by placing the seed trays under a fluorescent light. In the home, a sunny windowsill can furnish the required warmth, but provide extra light with a fluorescent tube. From about midspring onward, the plants need little or no artificial warmth, so an unheated greenhouse is satisfactory.

Outdoors, you can grow tomatoes in the vegetable plot, in a flower border, or on the patio. In open ground they need fertile, well-drained soil enriched with rotted manure or compost. On a patio, use either growing bags or pots. You can choose either a determinate type, which is a limited, bush form, or an indeterminate type, which will continue growing until the plant dies. Obvi-

ously, the former is usually more suitable for those with restricted space, whereas the indeterminate varieties will bear well if left to sprawl in every direction.

You also have the option of training your tomato plants. Many gardeners find that restricting tomatoes to one or two stems, which they tie to stakes or trellises, protects the fruit and makes for easier harvesting. Others prefer to use cages, in which the tomatoes grow freely and support themselves, and still others plant their tomatoes in rows and simply let them grow.

You might also want to grow some tomatoes in your greenhouse, particularly during the fall and winter. Greenhouse tomatoes are usually trained, and they bear very well if given plenty of attention.

GROWING TOMATOES IN CONTAINERS

If you have a sunny patio or deck, it makes sense to grow tomatoes in pots or growing bags outdoors. Each plant requires a pot at least ten inches deep, or larger, filled with a good peat-based potting soil. Insert a stake in each pot and tie the growing plant to it at intervals with soft fabric or twine, allowing room for the stem to get wider. Later in the season, add a little more potting soil to cover the exposed roots, and feed the plants generously.

If you are using growing bags, plant three plants in each bag. To support them, make a trellis out of wood, or use one of the ready-made kinds. Outdoors, you must provide strong enough support to withstand winds.

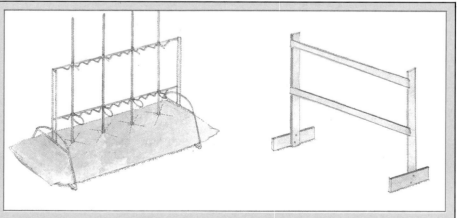

Tomatoes in growing bags outdoors require a frame to support the stems. You can buy ready-made trellises for the purpose.

Alternatively, it is not difficult to construct a homemade frame from pieces of scrap wood and two-by-fours. The support must be stable enough to withstand winds and eddies once the plants are fully grown.

GROWING TOMATOES OUTDOORS

Prepare the soil by digging in well-rotted manure or compost during the previous autumn; allow at least a bucketful to the square yard. Avoid growing tomatoes where potatoes, eggplants, peppers, or other members of the potato family were grown in the previous summer, since tomatoes are subject to the same pests and diseases as these other crops.

Plant outdoors only when there is no risk of spring frosts; it is safe to plant out three or four weeks earlier than this under cloches or in a cold frame. Sow the seeds approximately two months before the expected time of planting out, depending on the variety you are growing.

MAKING A START

Sow the seeds in a tray of seed-starting mix. After scattering them thinly, just cover them with more mix. Water them in with a fine spray, then cover them with glass and paper until they germinate.

If you do not have a greenhouse or a propagator, enclose the tray in a plastic bag and put it in a closet or some other warm, dark place. Check daily for signs of growth. Place the tray on a warm, well-lit window-sill as soon as the first shoots appear.

Prick the seedlings out individually into three-inch pots when the seed leaves have grown to at least twice their initial size. Hold each seedling by a leaf and ease it out of the starting mix with a pencil or small stick. Plant it in the middle of the pot with its leaves just clear of the surface—that is, deeper than it was previously.

Grow the plants on in gentle warmth. During good weather the sun may give sufficient heat and light by day, but a little artificial help will be needed at night, at least for the first few weeks, to prevent temperatures from falling too low and to provide the twelve hours of daily light that the seedlings need.

Move the plants to a cold frame for hardening off two weeks before planting out. At the same time, rake a dressing of general fertilizer into the planting site, at two ounces per square yard, and put cloches in position if these are to be used. Delay planting if there is any risk of frost, or if the soil temperature is below 50°F.

When planting, leave eighteen inches between trained plants and three feet between others. Water the plants in and set up stakes, trellises, or cages if you wish.

Avoid handling the stems when pricking out tomato seedlings into individual pots. If you plant them deeper than they were previously, they will form additional roots before they are moved to their final positions.

Removing suckers from the leaf axils on the main stem is a regular task when growing tomatoes on a stake or trellis. Wait until they are large enough to come away cleanly, but pinch them out before they are longer than about two inches.

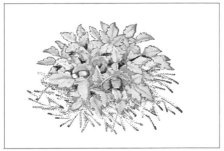

Lay either black plastic or a layer of straw beneath sprawling plants to help keep the fruit clean. Otherwise, any tomatoes close to the ground may lie directly on the soil, where they are prone to rot and vulnerable to damage by slugs and snails.

CARE OF THE CROP

If you are training your tomatoes to a stake or a trellis, tie the stems loosely to the support as they grow, and remove side shoots, or suckers, as they develop. These are shoots that grow between the leaf branches and the main stem; they are best removed when they are about one inch long. Pinch them out early in the day, when they are distended, so they come away cleanly. If you want to restrict the height of an indeterminate variety, pinch out the top when it has reached the appropriate height.

If you are growing your tomatoes in cages or simply in rows, you do not need to pinch out the suckers. It is a good idea to protect sprawling tomatoes with a mulch of black plastic or straw, however, and all tomatoes benefit from the addition of a thick organic mulch about a month after they are transplanted. A side dressing with a general

fertilizer is also a good idea; add a handful per plant when the first fruit begins to form, and another handful about a month later.

Some tomato diseases are caused by erratic supplies of water, so be careful to water the plants regularly and consistently. In dry or very hot weather, you may have to soak sandy soil as often as once a day; heavier ground should retain more moisture, and all soils will profit from mulching.

Mulching should also help protect the plants from blossom drop, which can occur in hot, dry weather, but you can help prevent this problem by placing your tomato crop in partial shade if you live in the South or Southwest. A similar strategy will help avoid sunscald as well.

HARVESTING

Harvest tomatoes when they are fully colored but still firm, or, if very high temperatures threaten, before they have colored completely. Pick the fruit as it ripens by twisting it upward while pressing with your thumb against the joint in the stalk. Do not pull the tomato away from its green calyx.

If unripe fruit remains on the plants in autumn, undo the ties, lay the plants flat, with straw beneath them, and cover them with cloches. Alternatively, uproot the plants and hang them indoors. They will continue to ripen.

Individual tomatoes will ripen best if stored in a cool, dark place along with an apple or two, which give off ethylene gas. Green tomatoes can be fried or pickled as well as made into chutney and other relishes, or they can be used to make pies or Mexican dishes.

GROWING TOMATOES IN A GREENHOUSE

Like other semitropical plants, tomatoes will grow very well in greenhouses, provided they are protected from temperature extremes and stagnant air. With adequate warmth—that is, a nighttime temperature of not less than 50°F—tomatoes can be harvested right through the year, though their growth is slower during the winter.

To grow tomatoes in an unheated greenhouse, sow seeds in early spring, which will produce fruit by midsummer, or in midsummer for a late-fall crop. If your summers are hot, be sure you can supply adequate shading and ventilation, and water the tomatoes often and well. To avoid problems with pests and diseases, plant greenhouse tomatoes in pots or growing bags.

MAKING A START

If you plan to use the greenhouse border (which is inadvisable if more than one or two crops of tomatoes have already been grown there), dig it well ahead of planting time and add plenty of well-rotted manure or compost. Rake in a dressing of general fertilizer, at two ounces per square yard, a week or two before planting, then give the soil a good soaking.

Plant when the young tomatoes are six to eight inches tall; set them one and a half feet apart, and plant them deep enough that their stems are able to develop new roots. If you use pots or growing bags, plant the tomatoes in the same way as described for outdoor tomatoes (see box on p.168). Water the plants in well, but do not insert stakes or a support frame.

RING CULTURE

This is a soilless method of growing tomatoes, which reduces the risk of soil-borne infection. Plant each tomato in a nine-inch bottomless container or "ring" filled with a vermiculite-peat mix or a ready-made soilless potting mix. Place the rings on a bed of coarse sand or gravel. Water the plants generously immediately after planting. After about ten days, start to water the sand or gravel itself; keep it constantly moist. Do not water the rings.

Once the fruit has begun to form, feed the plants with a high-potash liquid fertilizer once a week. Pinch out the suckers and stop the main stem.

CARE OF THE CROP

Support each plant with a vertical string; tie one end loosely around the stem just beneath the lowest true leaf and tie the other to a wire fastened to the greenhouse frame above the plants. Tie the upper end with a half-bow so that you can easily adjust the tension. Twist the plant's stem gently around the string.

Remove suckers when they are one inch long. Water the plants regularly, so that the soil never dries out—daily if necessary. Plants in growing bags or pots may need watering twice a day or even more.

Tomato plants like well-ventilated, airy conditions. Ventilate the greenhouse freely, and shade the glass during hot, bright weather. Spray the plants lightly with water on bright mornings; the extra humidity will help the fruit to set. Always water early so the leaves can dry by evening.

Feed the plants weekly with a high-potash liquid fertilizer once the fruit starts to develop. When the plants are two feet tall, cut off a few of the lower leaves to assist air circulation. Pinch out the top of the plant when it reaches the roof.

PESTS AND DISEASES

Tomato pests include cutworms, tomato hornworms, corn earworms, stinkbugs, nematodes, whiteflies, and spider mites.

Among diseases and disorders are blossom end rot, sunscald, late blight, fusarium wilt, verticillium wilt, curly top virus, tobacco mosaic virus, and early blight.

Support greenhouse plants by twisting the stems around string tied to the frame.

RECOMMENDED VARIETIES

Key
v resistant to verticillium wilt
f resistant to fusarium wilt
n resistant to root-knot nematodes
t resistant to tobacco mosaic virus

For slicing

'Burpee's Supersteak' Tall plants produce very large, flattened fruit. VFN
'Park's Whopper' An earlier, productive beefsteak type. VFNT
'Ultra Boy' Deep, globe-shaped tomatoes average more than a pound. VFN
'Celebrity' An All-America Winner. Round fruit averages 6 to 8 ounces. VFNT
'Pole King' A very tall variety that crops well; fruit has thick walls. VF
'Freedom' This variety produces well in poor weather and is easy to pick. VF
'Lady Luck' Plants are widely adapted; fruit is smooth and bright red. VFT
'Supersonic' A very productive variety with firm, meaty, slightly flattened fruit. VF
'White Beauty' Large, mild, ivory-colored tomatoes are good for salads and canning.
'Pink Girl' Slightly flattened, crack-resistant fruit is pink clear through. VF
'Lemon Boy' Large yellow fruit. VFN
'Burpee's Long Keeper' Golden-orange fruit keeps for 6 to 12 weeks.
'Nepal' A standard variety that bears 10- to 12-ounce fruit on tall plants.
'Delicious' set the world record for large, heavy tomatoes in 1974 and 1976.
'Jumbo' Good for greenhouses. VF

For containers

'Tiny Tim' An early cherry tomato; fruit is borne on 15-inch plants.
'Goldie' bears golden fruit on cascading vines that look nice in hanging baskets.
'Small Fry' This variety bears red cherry tomatoes on erect, two-foot-tall plants. VFN
'Red Robin' Fruit is one inch in diameter; plant takes 55 days to reach maturity.

For small fruit

'Sweet Chelsea' Supersweet, crack-resistant red fruit. VFT
'Sweet 100' Sweet, small, tender tomatoes.
'Sprint A' A good variety for short seasons.
'Subarctic Plenty' produces in 45 days.
'Pear' Red or yellow fruit is small and pear-shaped. Very prolific.
'Plum' Tomatoes are shaped like olives or plums. Available in red or yellow.

For cooking

'Roma' Elongated, thick-walled plum tomatoes have few seeds and compact vines. VF
'Bellstar' Dark red fruit is squarish and good for making juice as well as paste.

USING A GREENHOUSE, pages 12–13
SOWING SEEDS OUTDOORS, pages 36–37
SOWING UNDER GLASS, pages 38–39
TOMATOES AND OTHER VEGETABLE FRUITS, page 128
PESTS AND DISEASES, pages 172–175
FREEZING VEGETABLES, pages 232–233

MUSHROOMS

Although there are hundreds of different species of mushrooms growing wild, only a few species, notably *Agaricus bisporus albida*, are cultivated. White, cream, and brown varieties exist, of which the brown kind is most vigorous and disease resistant.

The cultivation of mushrooms bears no resemblance to that of any other vegetable in the food garden. Mushrooms are a fungus and obtain their nutrition in a completely different way from other crops. Cultivating mushrooms at home is an exciting process, though results can be unpredictable.

There are at least three ways to grow mushrooms. The easiest, if least adventurous, is to buy a commercial kit, as shown on the right. Results are reasonably reliable, as long as the pack is fresh. Most kits consist of a box of prepared compost that has already

been "spawned," or impregnated with the mushroom fungus. Provided you keep the compost at 50° to 55°F, and subsequently add the "casing" supplied with the kit to it, you can expect to start picking mushrooms within six weeks.

Mushroom kits (and spawn) are available from garden centers, nurseries, and seed suppliers. They offer a simple means of enjoying fresh mushrooms with a minimum of trouble. Instructions are provided.

The second method, which is something of a gamble, is to try growing mushrooms in the lawn. Though results are uncertain, this involves little trouble, unlike the third method—preparing your own mushroom compost and seeding it with spawn—which involves a fair amount of effort; the results are reasonably assured, however.

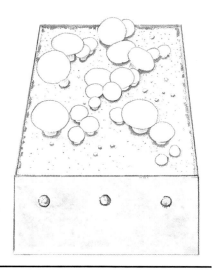

GROWING MUSHROOMS OUTDOORS
This method requires you to have a large enough area of lawn to devote a patch of it to mushroom growing; if mushrooms appear, this patch of grass will have to stay uncut for some time.

Choose an area of lawn that has not been treated with a hormone-based weedkiller. Pick a little-used spot so that no one will walk on the crop, if one appears.

In late summer or early fall, cut out and remove an area of turf about two inches deep. Loosen the base a little and work in some well-rotted horse manure before scattering some pelleted spawn on it, or else place separate small chunks of block spawn, about the size of a walnut, on it, ten to twelve inches apart. Then replace the turf.

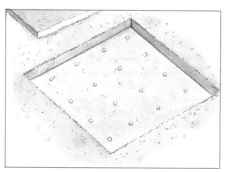

For an autumn crop of mushrooms outdoors, lift a shaded patch of turf and work some well-rotted manure into the soil beneath before placing the spawn. Replace the turf. Avoid using chemical weedkillers on this area.

Water the patch frequently. Avoid mowing from early fall onward, which is when the first mushrooms may appear.

HARVESTING
From spawning to picking takes about two months. The mushrooms will appear in flushes, every ten days or so, for about as long as they took to appear. They may be picked at the button stage or left until they open. Pick by twisting the mushrooms upward—do not just pull them out of the compost, or they will break.

Eat them with as little delay as possible.

GROWING MUSHROOMS INDOORS
Obtain a quantity of fresh horse manure containing plenty of straw and make a substantial heap; water it thoroughly if it is dry. Leave the heap for a week or two to heat up, then turn it weekly—outside to inside—until it decomposes into a dark, crumbly, pleasant-smelling mass.

Scoop some of this compost into containers about ten inches deep. Wooden boxes or cardboard boxes lined with plastic will serve the purpose. At first the temperature will rise, but after this check daily with a thermometer until it falls to 75°F. Once it does, introduce pieces of spawn at one-foot intervals, two inches deep, or else mix pelleted or grain spawn with the compost by scattering it on the surface. Place the boxes in a room or cellar that has a constant temperature of 50° to 55°F. Water lightly.

About ten days later, when the spawn

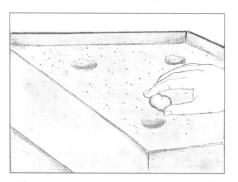

When growing mushrooms indoors, place the spawn in the prepared compost at one-foot intervals. Place the boxes out of direct sunlight in a room or cellar where the temperature remains fairly constant at 50° to 55°F.

has sent white threads through the compost, cover the surface with a layer of subsoil. This will trap warmth and moisture, but, being virtually sterile (unlike garden topsoil), it will not introduce spores of alien fungi. Keep this "casing" slightly moist by occasional spraying.

HARVESTING
Harvest the mushrooms in flushes, as they appear, as for mushrooms grown outdoors.

After picking, replace the casing each time by filling in holes left by the mushrooms. The used compost provides valuable humus for the garden.

MAKING AND USING GARDEN COMPOST, pages 30–31
TOMATOES AND OTHER VEGETABLE FRUITS, page 128

PESTS AND DISEASES OF VEGETABLES

There are several ways in which to cut down the risk of attacks from pests and diseases. These include nourishing the soil well, keeping it free of weeds, and planting your vegetables at the correct time and in the best weather conditions. (See also Pests and Diseases of Fruit, p.108.)

Chemical pesticides, both organic and inorganic (□), are described by their chemical names, not brand names. It is especially important to allow the correct period of time to elapse between the application of chemical pesticides and harvesting. Other remedies are denoted with a triangle (△).

APHIDS

Aphids, including greenflies, cluster on the leaves and stems of many vegetables and suck their sap, weakening the plants. They also spread disease. (See also root aphids.)
□ Among many commercial sprays are malathion, pyrethrum, rotenone, and insecticidal soap.

△ A hard spray of water may deter small colonies.

ASPARAGUS BEETLES

The adults and larvae of this damaging pest attack both the leaves and stems of plants from early summer onward, and can sometimes leave them bare.
□ Prompt treatment is essential. Use malathion, carbaryl, or rotenone.
△ Cut down the ferns and clean up the beds in late autumn.

Keep the garden free of trash.

JAPANESE BEETLES

These lovely iridescent beetles are very destructive; they feed on the leaves of beans, corn, asparagus, okra, and rhubarb as well as roses, and can fly fairly long distances. The larvae chew on the roots of grass in early summer.
□ To control adults, spray with carbaryl, malathion, or rotenone; two or three applications are best.

△ To control larvae, apply milky spore, a bacterial disease, to lawns; parasitic nematodes prevent damage to other roots. Beetles can be trapped.

LEAF MINERS

These tiny pests are the larvae of various species of flies and are particularly fond of leaf crops such as lettuce, spinach, beets, and Swiss chard. They tunnel within the leaves and are difficult to control after the eggs have been laid.
□ Spray plants with malathion, diazinon, or pyrethrum before the eggs have a chance to hatch.

△ Pick off and destroy any infested leaves. Protect plants from flies with floating row covers.

CABBAGE ROOT MAGGOTS

These destructive pests attack the roots of young brassicas and radishes, causing stunted plants that wilt easily.
□ Treat the soil before planting time with diazinon.
△ Simple deterrents to the fly that lays the eggs include using floating row covers or making mats: cut slits in small squares of carpet or tar paper and place one around each newly planted stem to cover the soil.

SQUASH BUGS

All vine crops, but particularly squash and pumpkins, are vulnerable to attacks by this insect, which sucks sap from the leaves. Affected plants wilt, turn dry, decline in vigor, and eventually become black.
□ Rotenone, malathion, and nicotine are effective sprays, and sabadilla dust will control adult beetles.
△ Trap squash bugs under planks or tar paper, and destroy eggs whenever you find them. Floating row covers provide some protection.

CATERPILLARS

The larvae of a number of moths and butterflies cause considerable damage to leafy crops. Cabbage loopers are one of the worst.
□ Spray or dust with *Bacillus thuringiensis* or rotenone.
△ Control moths with floating row covers or Trichogramma wasps.

MEXICAN BEAN BEETLES

These pests resemble ladybugs, to which they are related, but have sixteen spots on their backs. Both the adults and the spiny orangish larvae feed on leaves of most beans (soybeans are an exception).
□ Carbaryl, rotenone, malathion, and diazinon are effective sprays for adults. To deter larvae, dust bean rows with diatomaceous earth.
△ Prevent overwintering by cleaning up debris in the fall and by burning affected plants.

CUTWORMS

Fat brown, black, or variegated larvae chew stems of young plants at or below the soil line. The cutworms feed at night and curl up tightly when disturbed.
□ Spray with *Bacillus thuringiensis* or sprinkle wood ashes or diatomaceous earth around plants.
△ Make collars for seedlings from cardboard, tar paper, tuna fish cans, plastic bottles, etc. Push them at least a half inch into the soil. The only evidence that a cutworm has been at work will be the plant or seedling lying on its side.

FLEA BEETLES

Seedlings with holed leaves are under attack from these tiny, jumping insects.
□ Dust the seedlings with rotenone, pyrethrum, or diatomaceous earth.
△ Make a spray of garlic or hot peppers steeped in water, or protect plants with floating row covers.

TOMATO HORNWORMS

These big, fat green caterpillars with distinctive "horns" love all members of the potato family, including tomatoes, eggplants, potatoes, and peppers. They feed on both the leaves and the fruit.
□ Spray with malathion, or carbaryl, or apply *Bacillus thuringiensis* while the hornworm larvae are still small.
△ It is less dangerous, and relatively easy, to pick off the caterpillars by hand.

CUCUMBER BEETLES

These spotted or striped yellow-and-black beetles feed on the roots, vines, and leaves of all cucurbits, and spread bacterial wilt and mosaic virus from plant to plant.
□ When the beetles first appear, spray or dust with rotenone or carbaryl; repeat every week if necessary.
△ Protect transplanted seedlings with floating row covers or cloches. Parasitic nematodes can be useful in controling the larvae.

ONION MAGGOTS

Larvae burrowing into the bulbs of onions, shallots, and leeks cause wilting and discolored foliage and rotting bulbs.
□ Prevent by treating the soil or spraying young plants with diazinon. Dust with wood ashes or diatomaceous earth.
△ Remove and burn affected plants. Growing onions from sets reduces the risk since there is no thinning to attract the flies.

PEA AND BEAN WEEVILS

Pea weevils are a problem in western states; bean weevils infest dried beans.
□ Dust or spray plants with rotenone, malathion, or diazinon.
△ Protect dried peas and beans by drying them thoroughly before storage in airtight containers.

CORN EARWORMS

Striped caterpillars are green, pink, or dark brown and eat leaves, tassels, and kernels.
□ *Bacillus thuringiensis* is effective if applied early. Rotenone and carbaryl are possible sprays.
△ Use parasitic Trichogramma wasps, or trap earworms in pheromone (sex-lure) traps. Spray silks with mineral oil.

EUROPEAN CORN BORERS

Whitish larvae feed on stalks and ears, often leaving a telltale dust around bore holes.
□ Spray or dust with *Bacillus thuringiensis* every week or ten days. Carbaryl can also be used as a spray.
△ If you have a small crop, make slits in the stalks and remove the pests by hand.

COLORADO POTATO BEETLES

Potatoes, tomatoes, peppers, and eggplants are at risk from these small, yellow-and-black-striped beetles. The larvae are red and, like the adults, can destroy stems and leaves.
□ Rotenone, carbaryl, pyrethrum, and malathion are effective chemical controls if applied carefully and repeatedly.
△ Protection often deters Colorado potato beetles: a thick mulch or floating row covers will prevent over-wintering beetles from reaching plants.

RED SPIDER MITES

Most vegetables grown outdoors are at risk from these minute sap-sucking insects.
   In the greenhouse, red spider mites cause damage on tomatoes, cucumbers, and eggplants. They thrive in hot conditions.
□ Spray with insecticidal soap, a sulfur-based miticide, or dicofol.
△ Spray hard with cold water, or promote predatory mites and green lacewings.

ROOT APHIDS

These white, waxy insects live in the soil and feed on plant roots. Globe artichokes are among the plants that can be attacked. Examine the roots for signs if plants suddenly wilt and die.
□ Remove and dispose of affected plants; water the others with malathion or dimethoate.
△ Grow resistant varieties if root aphids are a problem.

SLUGS AND SNAILS

Many vegetables are at risk, but particularly leafy crops in the earlier stages of growth. Slugs and snails make holes in the leaves, but also eat tubers and roots. They leave slime trails and are most active in mild, damp weather.
□ See p.109 for suggested control measures.

ROOT-KNOT NEMATODES

These pests are microscopic, but the damage is severe to such crops as carrots, tomatoes, and spinach. The foliage and stems of affected plants become yellow and stunted.
□ Fumigate the soil before planting.
△ Plant resistant varieties, and be sure to add plenty of organic material to the soil. Manure tea can help, and rotating crops onto fresh land is essential.

SQUASH VINE BORERS

Cucumbers, melons, and pumpkins as well as all types of squash are susceptible to these fat white caterpillars, which burrow into the vines and cause the plants to wilt and die. Like other borers, these pests leave behind a sawdustlike frass.
□ During the egg-laying season, spray or dust vines with rotenone or diazinon.
△ Protection with row covers or cloches can be helpful. If you see wilted vines, slit them and remove the borers; the plants will recover, but may not bear particularly well.

WHITEFLIES

Whiteflies look like tiny moths when disturbed and damage many types of vegetables, including peppers, tomatoes, beans, squash, and lettuce.
□ Spray every five days for two weeks with insecticidal soap, ryania, rotenone, or pyrethrum.
△ Check all purchased plants before transplanting, as whiteflies thrive in greenhouses.

WIREWORMS

These slender orange grubs, about an inch long, are the larvae of the click beetle. They bore into roots and tubers of potatoes, corn, beets, and other plants and are especially troublesome in new gardens.
□ Dig newly cultivated land thoroughly, and apply diazinon before planting.

GROWING PLANTS NATURALLY, pages 19–21
PESTS AND DISEASES OF FRUITS, pages 108–111

ANTHRACNOSE

Patches and spots caused by a fungus appear on the leaves and fruit of beans, tomatoes, and cucumbers. Damage is variable, but in a damp summer plants may be destroyed.
□ Burn badly affected plants. Spray others with a fungicide or Bordeaux mixture.

BLOSSOM END ROT

A condition that occurs on tomatoes, peppers, and cucumbers that have been watered irregularly or lack calcium. The fruits have a dark, sunken patch on the side opposite the stalk.
△ Prevent by avoiding irregular watering and by mulching.

CROWN ROT

The name aptly describes this fungal infection of rhubarb, most prevalent on heavy, wet soils. Discolored leaves are often the first sign.
△ Dig up and burn affected plants. Replace with new ones elsewhere on the plot. Grow rhubarb on raised beds.

CUCUMBER MOSAIC VIRUS

A virus disease (see below) that affects cucumbers, pumpkins, squash, and peppers It causes mottling of the leaves and discolored and deformed fruit.
□ Spray against aphids, which may carry the virus. Destroy infected plants at the first symptoms.

ROOT ROT

Like stem rot, root rot is a fungal disease; it affects the roots of many plants, notably peas, and is most common in wet, heavy soils.
△ Improve drainage if necessary, and water only when the soil has dried out a bit.

PHOMOPSIS BLIGHT

Circular brown spots on leaves or fruit of eggplants indicate the presence of this fungus. Hot, humid weather contributes to the problem, which can eventually kill the eggplants.
□ Spray or dust with Bordeaux mixture or maneb, and burn infected plants.

BLOTCHY RIPENING

A disorder of greenhouse tomatoes and other vegetables that may be due to uneven watering, temperature, or feeding. Parts of the fruit are discolored and fail to ripen normally.
△ Give more attention to shading, ventilating, watering, and fertilizing.

BORON DEFICIENCY

Celery leaves become yellow and the stems develop cracks. The roots of turnips, rutabagas, and beets become discolored inside; beet leaves wilt and shrivel.
△ Apply borax to the soil at one ounce per twenty square yards. First mix it with dry sand for easier distribution.

DAMPING OFF

A fungal infection that causes seedlings to collapse. The seedlings are vulnerable when they are under stress from excessive moisture, overcrowding, or temperature extremes.
□ Dust seeds with captan or a copper-based fungicide.
△ Improve sowing techniques: always use clean containers and sterilized seed-starting mix. Do not water too heavily.

GRAY MOLD (BOTRYTIS)

A gray, furry mold appears on stems, leaves, and fruit. Most prevalent in still, damp conditions.
□ Dig up and dispose of badly affected plants. If spotted early, spray with benomyl or captan. After harvesting greenhouse crops, fumigate the soil. Give more attention to ventilation, watering, and warmth.

BLACK HEART

This disorder, which causes the leaves of celery to turn yellow and the hearts to blacken and rot, is caused by erratic or insufficient watering.
△ Water the plants regularly and thoroughly. If you suspect a calcium deficiency in your soil, add a fertilizer containing this mineral.

SEPTORIA BLIGHT

A fungal disease that first appears as yellow spots on celery or tomato leaves, then turns brownish-black and infects stalks. Cool, damp conditions foster the disease.
□ Spray or dust with Bordeaux mixture or a copper fungicide.
△ Plant tolerant varieties.

DOWNY MILDEW

Yellowing of the upper surfaces of leaves is combined with furry white or purple patches on the undersides. Damp weather favors the fungi responsible; young plants of brassicas and cucurbits are most at risk.
□ Spray with benomyl or a copper-based spray.
△ Avoid overcrowding and excessive dampness.

HALO BLIGHT

A seed-borne fungus disease that results in yellow-edged leaf spots and stunted growth in bush and pole snap beans.
△ Burn affected plants. Do not touch or move among plants in wet weather.

LEAF ROLL

Leaf roll in potatoes is caused by a virus that is spread by aphids. In tomatoes, it is more commonly the result of hot weather, dryness, or wet soil.
□ Control aphids as suggested on p.172. Protect tomatoes with shading, and water as necessary.

CLUB ROOT

A serious soil-borne fungal infection of brassicas. The roots become swollen and distorted, and the foliage yellows and wilts on warm days. Plants may eventually die. Especially common in poorly drained, acid soils.
□ Lime the soil thoroughly. Dip roots in benomyl.
△ Crop rotation is essential. Never grow brassicas in the same place more than once every three years.

STEM ROT

The base of the stems of affected plants (peas, beans, and tomatoes) first becomes discolored, then rots. The fungal spores responsible may persist in the soil.
□ Grow seedlings and container plants only in sterilized potting soil. If caught early, the disease can be controlled by watering with a copper compound such as copper carbonate or cuprous oxide.

LEAF SPOT

Spotting and browning of the leaves, and sometimes the stems, is due to fungal or bacterial infection. Tomatoes and peppers are the plants principally at risk, but many vegetables are vulnerable.
□ Spray with a fungicide such as benomyl.
△ Remove and burn diseased leaves. Do not handle wet plants, or you may spread the disease.

VERTICILLIUM WILT
This fungus infection is a serious hazard to members of the potato family, including tomatoes and peppers, and to okra. Leaves turn yellow, curl, and die, or they simply drop off the plant. The plant can live for some time, but will not produce well. The fungus can survive in the soil for twelve to fifteen years.
□ Treat the soil before planting with Bordeaux mixture or a copper-based fumigant.
△ Sow seeds in sterile potting mix, and plant resistant varieties. Rotate solanaceous crops. Dig up and burn infected plants.

POWDERY MILDEW
Beans, summer squash, and peas are particularly at risk from this fungal infection, which covers leaves and stems with a powdery coating.
□ Spray or dust with benomyl or copper.
△ Use a spray prepared from elderberry leaves.

ASPARAGUS RUST
A fungal infection that speckles the leaves and stems of asparagus with rust-colored spots and eventually kills the plant.
□ Spray with maneb after removing infected foliage.
△ Cut off and burn infected foliage. Plant resistant varieties, and restock if the trouble persists.

BACTERIAL WILT
A fairly common disease among cucurbits and melons, spread by cucumber beetles. The leaves and vines suddenly wilt and soon die.
□ Control the cucumber beetle (see p.173).
△ Plant resistant varieties. The fungus overwinters in the soil, so clean up carefully in the fall.

MAGNESIUM DEFICIENCY
The deficiency first shows in tomatoes as a yellowing of the lower leaves. This spreads upward and leaves turn brown. An excess of potash is often the cause.
□ Spray with a solution of magnesium sulfate: eight ounces in two and a half gallons of water, with added soft soap.

FUSARIUM WILT
Tomatoes, peppers, potatoes, cucumbers, squash, and peas wilt in hot weather, and the leaves turn yellow and curl. The fungus lives in the soil.
□ Apply copper carbonate to the soil before planting.
△ Plant resistant varieties. Burn infected plants.

BLACK ROT
A bacterial infection of brassicas, black rot begins with yellowing leaves and spreads to the heads of cabbages and Brussels sprouts.
□ Apply a copper-based fungicide to the soil.
△ Soak seeds in hot water before planting, and rotate crops as recommended. Burn any infected plants.

SCAB
Common scab of potatoes causes rough brown patches on the skin. It is disfiguring but does no great damage. It occurs most frequently on alkaline soils.
△ Scab is exacerbated by lime, so avoid planting in alkaline soil. Work in plenty of rotted organic matter and do not let the soil dry out. Plant on a four-inch layer of dry lawn clippings.

BROWN SPOT
Brown spot is a bacterial blight that affects lima and other shell beans. The small, red-brown spots appear on leaves and pods, especially in humid weather.
△ The best way to prevent disease of all kinds in beans is to avoid working among the plants when they are wet.

VIRUS DISEASES
Virus diseases are caused by microscopic organisms and are transmitted primarily by insects. Symptoms include discoloration, stunting, deformities, and wilting.
△ There is no cure. Dispose of affected plants. Buy resistant varieties, and control pests.

PETAL BLIGHT
Circular dark patches on the flower heads of globe artichokes may eventually lead to rotting.
□ Cut off and burn damaged heads. In future years, spray flower buds with maneb every two weeks until a month before harvest time.

SUNSCALD
Thin-skinned, discolored depressions may disfigure tomatoes and peppers exposed to excessive sunshine, whether in the greenhouse or outdoors.
△ Feed plants often to encourage leaf growth. Shade them if foliage is sparse.

CORN LEAF BLIGHT
A fungal disease prevalent in the East, this causes tan or greenish spots on the leaves of sweet corn. Hot, humid spring weather poses a hazard to young plants.
□ Spray or dust with Bordeaux mixture or maneb.
△ Plant tolerant varieties, and burn infected plants.

EARLY BLIGHT
Potatoes and tomatoes are susceptible to this fungus, which causes brown rings on leaves, spots on tubers, and leathery black spots on tomatoes.
□ Spray or dust with Bordeaux mixture, maneb, or a copper-based fungicide.
△ Plant certified seed potatoes.

WHITE MOLD
A fungal disease that attacks lettuce, beans, and cabbages. Infected plants develop wet spots and a cottonlike mold.
□ Dust or spray early in the season with maneb or Bordeaux mixture.
△ Rotate crops carefully. Dig up and burn any infected plants.

LATE BLIGHT
The principal fungal disease of potatoes, and sometimes tomatoes. Leaves develop brown patches and the edges curl. Before long the stem disintegrates and the infection spreads to the tubers.
□ Prevention provides the only real control. Spray or dust with a fungicide such as maneb or Bordeaux mixture. Repeat every two weeks during damp weather.

CORN SMUT
During hot summers this disease may infect sweet corn; it results in large "smut galls" full of fungal spores.
△ Cut off the growths before they burst and disperse the spores. Burn all the cornstalks. Plant tolerant varieties, and rotate the crop as recommended.

SPINACH BLIGHT
Caused by a virus that is spread by aphids, the leaves become increasingly discolored and distorted.
□ Spray to control the aphids (see p.172). Dig up and destroy affected plants.

ASTER YELLOWS
Carrots and lettuce are most affected; the disease is spread by leafhoppers. Carrots fail to develop and are covered with fine hairs. Lettuce leaves become yellow and do not form a head.
□ Control leafhoppers by careful weeding and use of pesticides.

WHIPTAIL
A lack of molybdenum causes the leaves of cauliflowers and broccoli to become narrow; heads fail to develop.
△ Spray several times with a foliar food containing molybdenum. Prevent a recurrence by watering with sodium molybdate dissolved in water.

GROWING PLANTS NATURALLY, pages 19–21
PESTS AND DISEASES OF FRUITS, pages 108–111

The
VEGETABLE COLOR
CATALOGUE II

Salad greens, even more than most other vegetables, must be home grown if you wish to enjoy them at their freshest and their best. Lettuce, spinach, and chicory are much better if they are eaten with all their flavor and crispness intact. By growing your own, you can also sample the more unusual leafy crops, such as rocket and corn salad, as well as the oriental vegetables and the less common herbs, which are seldom available in stores or supermarkets.

Although the color plates that follow are not intended to be totally comprehensive, they give an idea of the range and variety of salad greens, brassicas, onions, and herbs suitable for growing in the food garden.

The separate entries on pages 194–223 give specific details about sowing and individual cultivation requirements, as well as recommending varieties other than those selected for illustration.

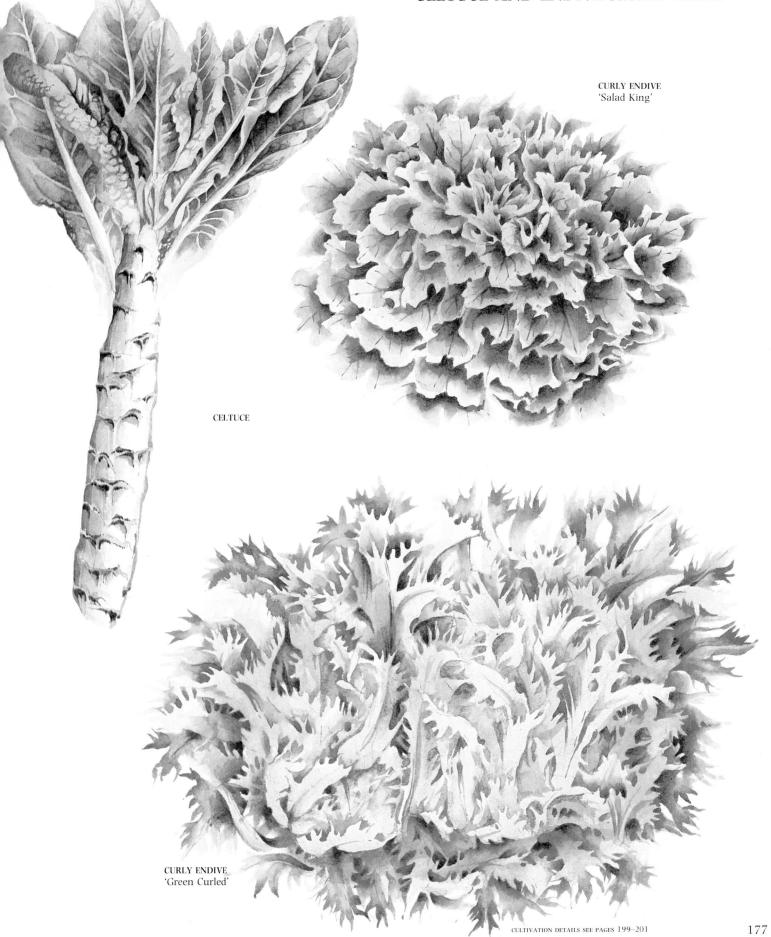

CURLY ENDIVE
'Salad King'

CELTUCE

CURLY ENDIVE
'Green Curled'

CULTIVATION DETAILS SEE PAGES 199–201

177

LETTUCE Selected varieties

CRISPHEAD LETTUCE
'Great Lakes'
'King Crown'

COS LETTUCE
'Winter Density'
'Valmaine'
'Green Towers'

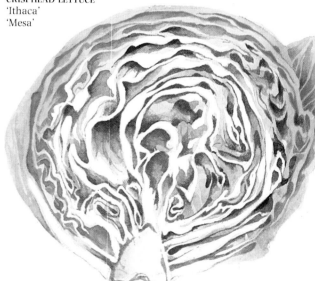

CRISPHEAD LETTUCE
'Ithaca'
'Mesa'

COS LETTUCE
'Little Gem'

RED HEADING LETTUCE
'Pirat'
'Rouge d'Hiver'

LOOSEHEAD LETTUCE
'Buttercrunch'
'Salad Bibb'
'Brune d'Hiver'

RED LEAF LETTUCE
'Red Salad Bowl'
'Red Sails'

GREEN LEAF LETTUCE
'Salad Bowl'
'Oakleaf'
'Green Ice'

CULTIVATION DETAILS SEE PAGES 194–195

SPINACH AND SALAD GREENS Selected varieties

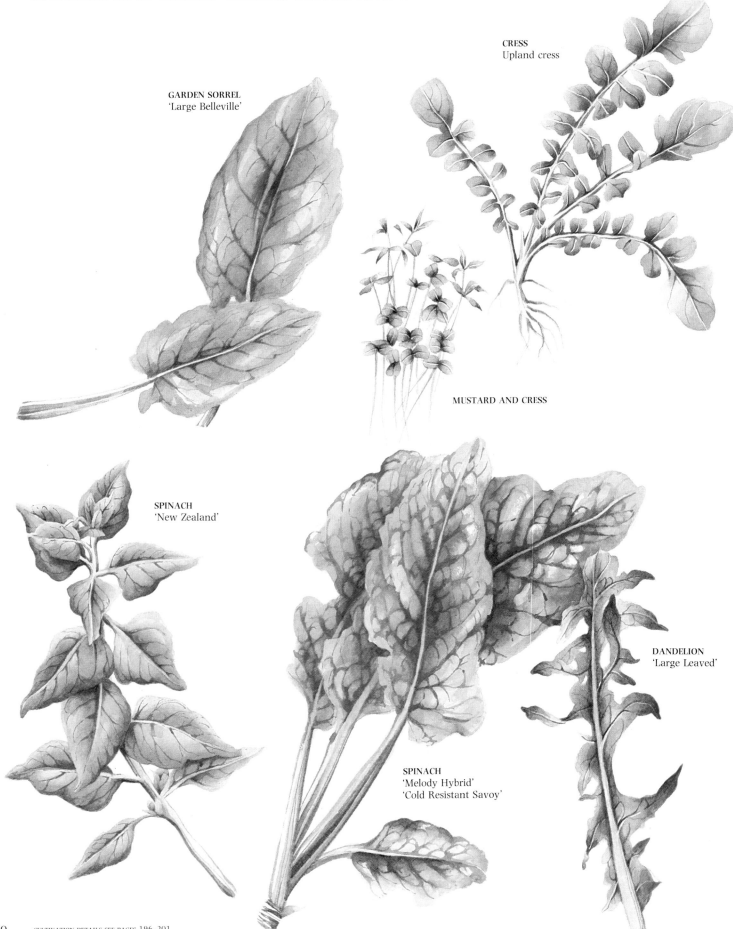

GARDEN SORREL
'Large Belleville'

CRESS
Upland cress

MUSTARD AND CRESS

SPINACH
'New Zealand'

SPINACH
'Melody Hybrid'
'Cold Resistant Savoy'

DANDELION
'Large Leaved'

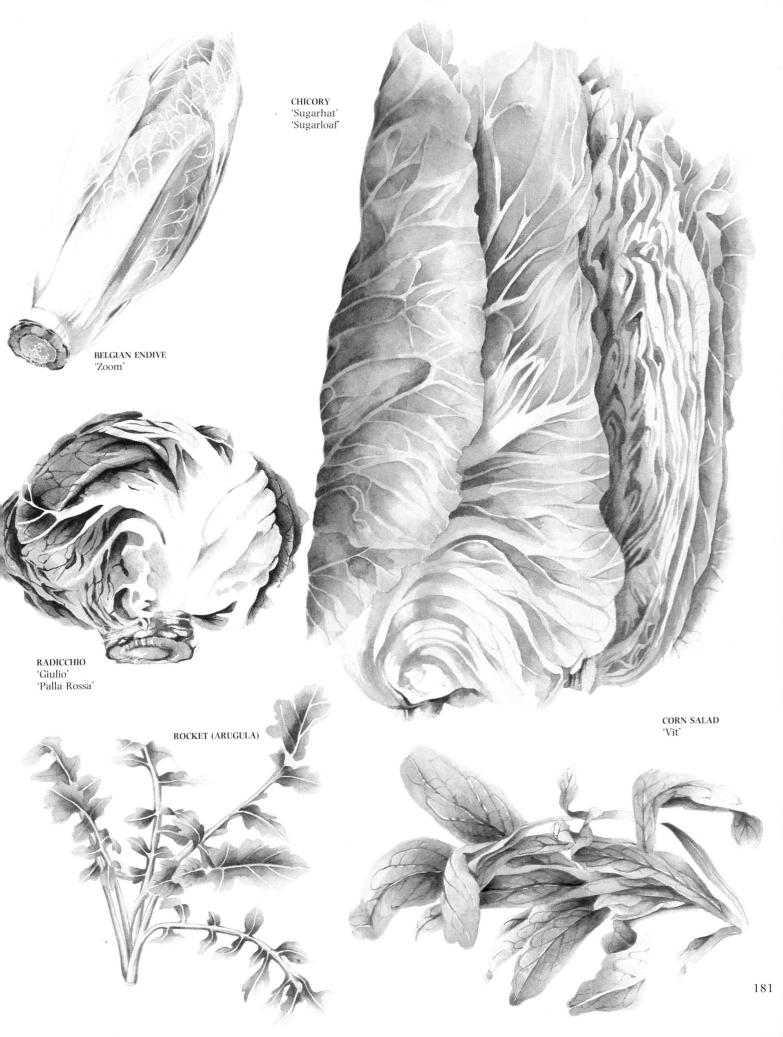

CHICORY
'Sugarhat'
'Sugarloaf'

BELGIAN ENDIVE
'Zoom'

RADICCHIO
'Giulio'
'Palla Rossa'

ROCKET (ARUGULA)

CORN SALAD
'Vit'

181

CABBAGES AND CHINESE VEGETABLES Selected varieties

MIDSEASON/LATE CABBAGE
'Bravo'
'Perfect Ball'

CABBAGE
'Early Jersey Wakefield'
'Treta'

COLLARDS
'Champion'

SAVOY CABBAGE
'Savoy King'
'Salarite'

RED CABBAGE
'Ruby Ball'

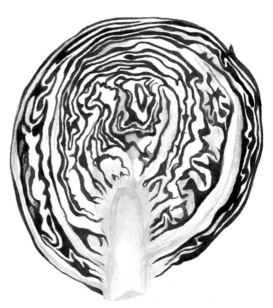

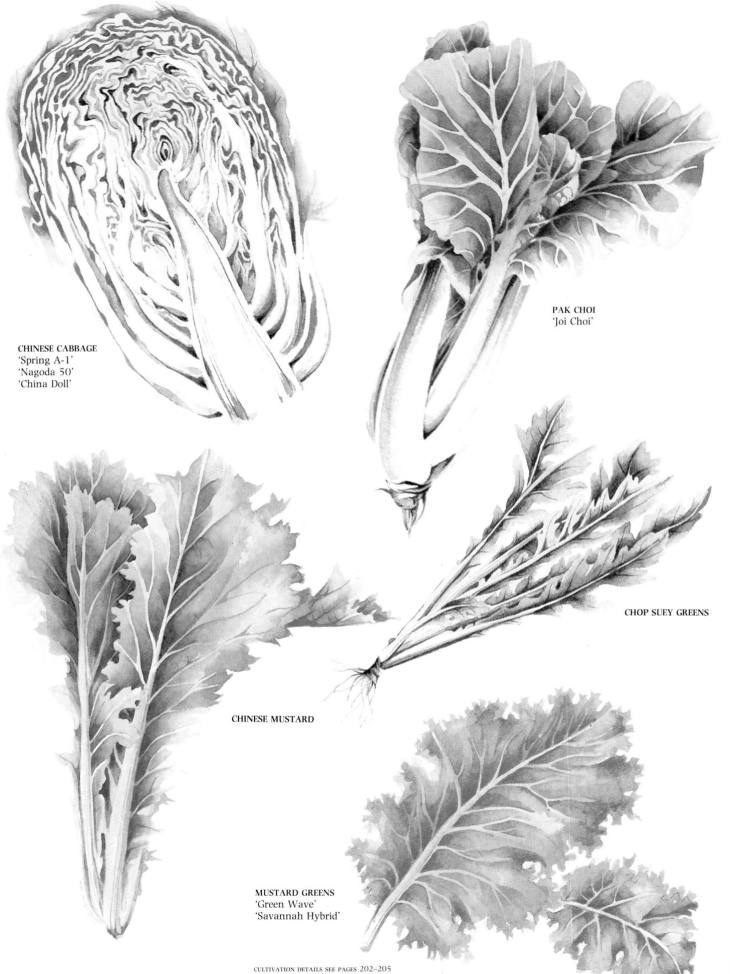

CHINESE CABBAGE
'Spring A-1'
'Nagoda 50'
'China Doll'

PAK CHOI
'Joi Choi'

CHOP SUEY GREENS

CHINESE MUSTARD

MUSTARD GREENS
'Green Wave'
'Savannah Hybrid'

CULTIVATION DETAILS SEE PAGES 202–205

BROCCOLI AND OTHER BRASSICAS Selected varieties

BRUSSELS SPROUT
'Prince Marvel'
'Captain Marvel'
'Jade Cross E'

WHITE CAULIFLOWER
'Snow Crown'
'White Knight'
'Dominant'
'White Contessa'

PURPLE CAULIFLOWER
'Violet Queen'
'Purple Cap'

BROCCOLI
'Emperor'
'Green Comet'
'Premium Crop'
'Citation'
'Green Goliath'

BROCCOLI RAAB (RAPINI)
'Raab'

KALE
'Spurt'
'Dwarf Siberian'

KALE
'Vates'

CULTIVATION DETAILS SEE PAGES 206–211

THE ONION FAMILY Selected varieties

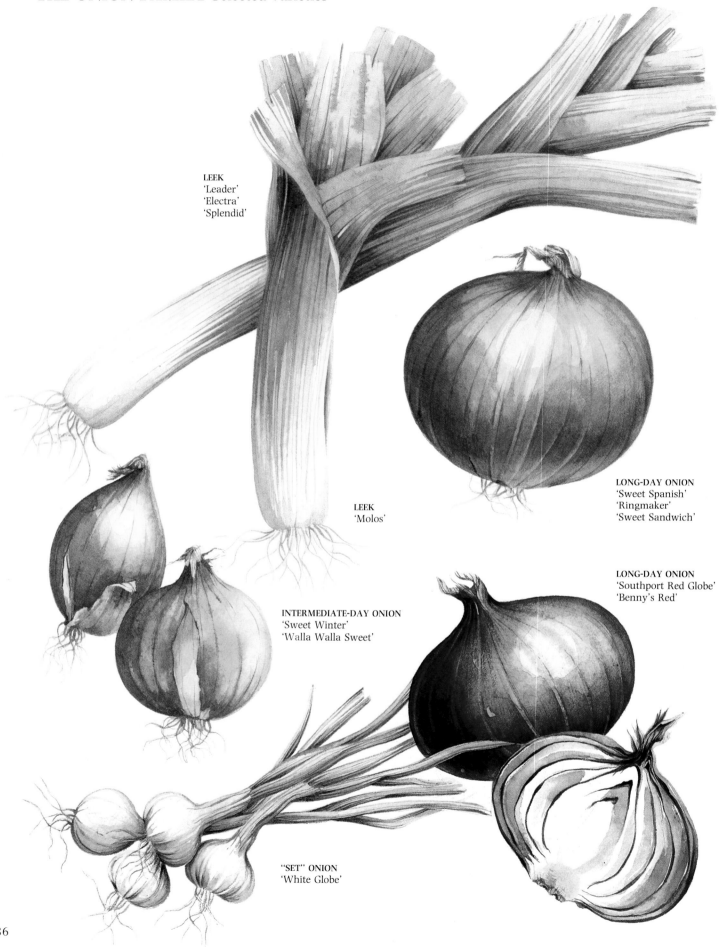

LEEK
'Leader'
'Electra'
'Splendid'

LEEK
'Molos'

LONG-DAY ONION
'Sweet Spanish'
'Ringmaker'
'Sweet Sandwich'

LONG-DAY ONION
'Southport Red Globe'
'Benny's Red'

INTERMEDIATE-DAY ONION
'Sweet Winter'
'Walla Walla Sweet'

"SET" ONION
'White Globe'

BUNCHING ONION
'Evergreen'
'Ishikura Long'
'Beltsville Bunching'

SHALLOT
'True French'
'Frogs' Legs'

"SET" ONION
'Stuttgarter'

RED GARLIC

GARLIC

SHORT-DAY ONION
White 'Bermuda'

FRESH GARLIC

CULTIVATION DETAILS SEE PAGES 213–216

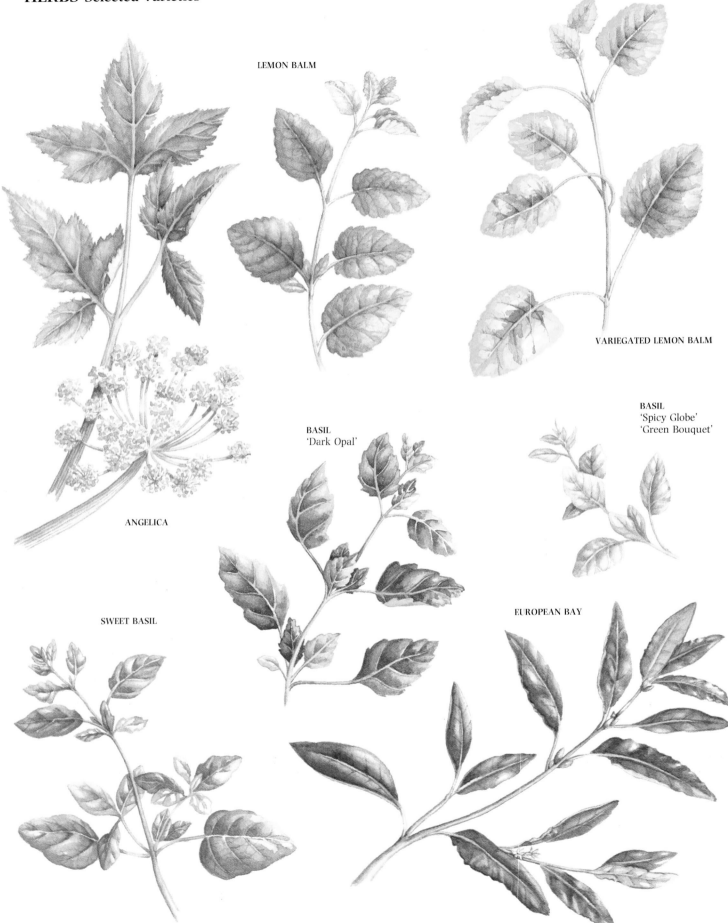

LEMON BALM

VARIEGATED LEMON BALM

BASIL
'Spicy Globe'
'Green Bouquet'

BASIL
'Dark Opal'

ANGELICA

EUROPEAN BAY

SWEET BASIL

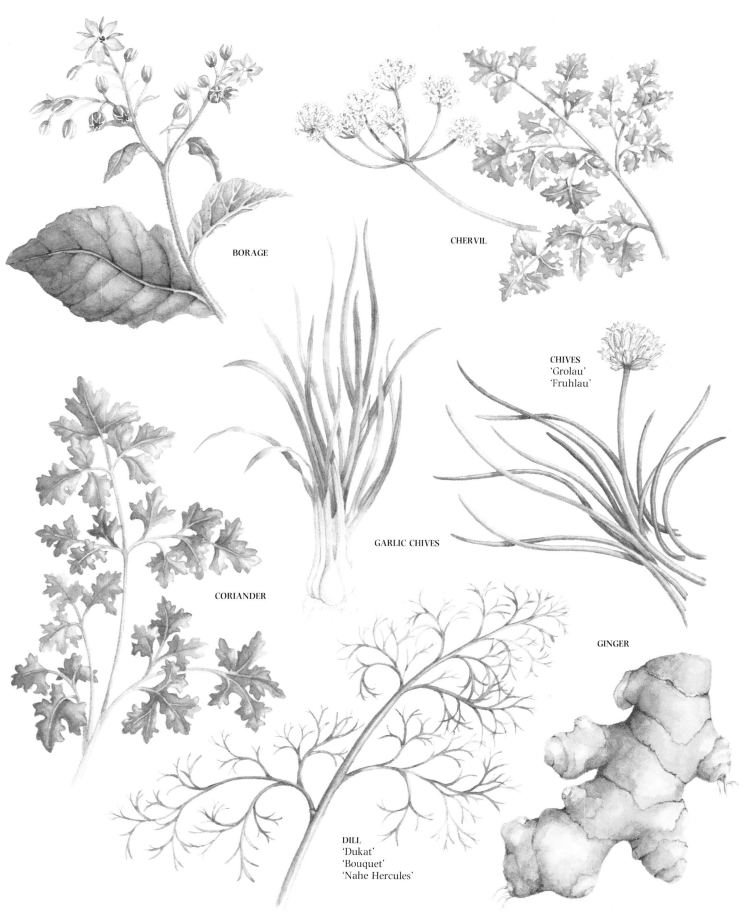

BORAGE

CHERVIL

CHIVES
'Grolau'
'Fruhlau'

GARLIC CHIVES

CORIANDER

GINGER

DILL
'Dukat'
'Bouquet'
'Nahe Hercules'

CULTIVATION DETAILS SEE PAGES 219–223

HERBS Selected varieties

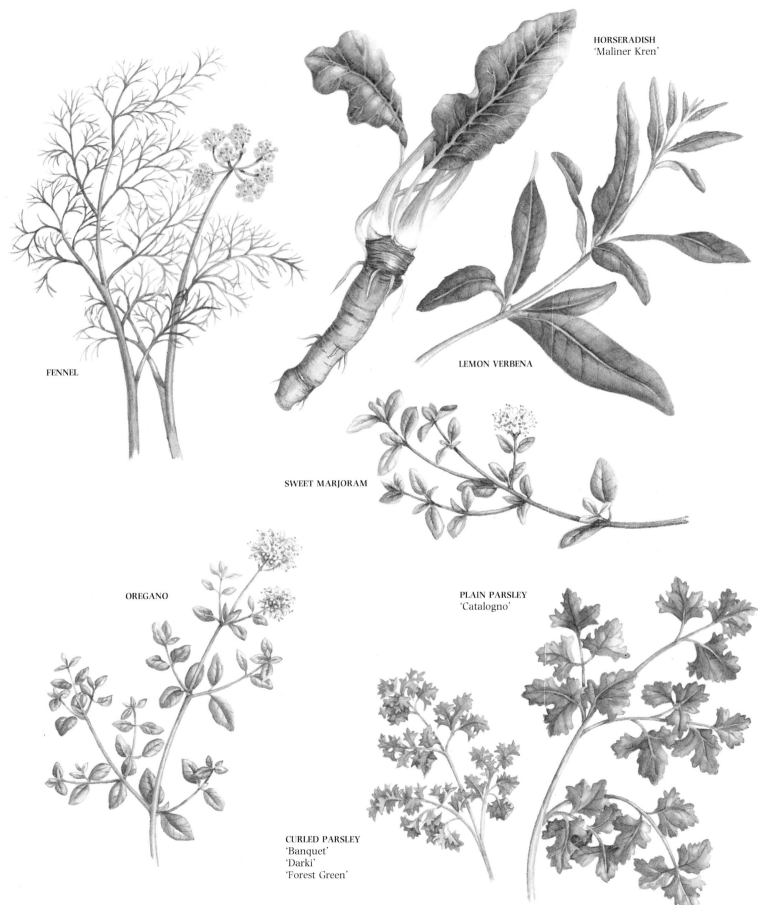

FENNEL

HORSERADISH
'Maliner Kren'

LEMON VERBENA

SWEET MARJORAM

OREGANO

PLAIN PARSLEY
'Catalogno'

CURLED PARSLEY
'Banquet'
'Darki'
'Forest Green'

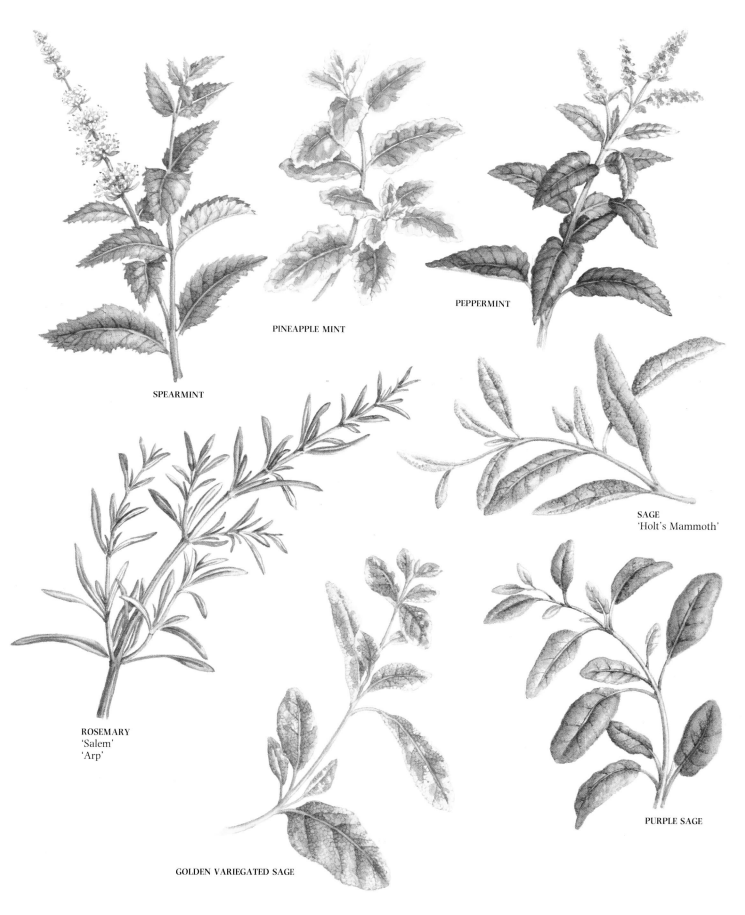

SPEARMINT

PINEAPPLE MINT

PEPPERMINT

SAGE
'Holt's Mammoth'

ROSEMARY
'Salem'
'Arp'

GOLDEN VARIEGATED SAGE

PURPLE SAGE

CULTIVATION DETAILS SEE PAGES 219–223

HERBS Selected varieties

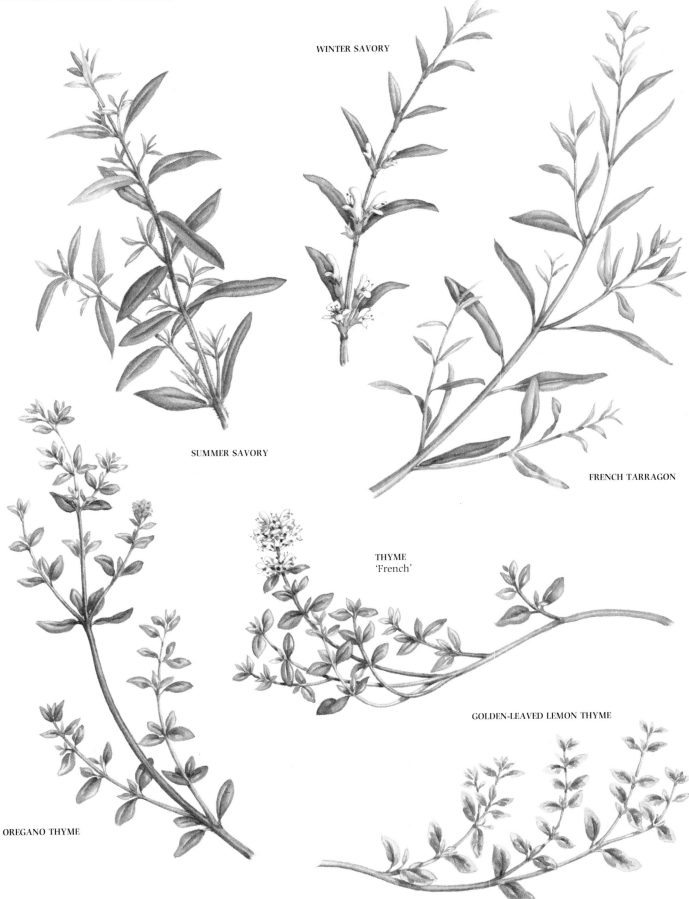

WINTER SAVORY

SUMMER SAVORY

FRENCH TARRAGON

THYME
'French'

GOLDEN-LEAVED LEMON THYME

OREGANO THYME

CULTIVATION DETAILS SEE PAGES 219–223

VEGETABLE GARDEN II

Leafy greens and herbs are the prettiest plants in any vegetable garden. They are elegant in shape and varied in the form and color of their foliage—leaves not only range through all shades of green but also come in purple, crimson, and yellow. Many herbs also offer the bonus of attractive flowers to add to their colorful and aromatic foliage.

Growing greens and herbs gives the gardener the opportunity to combine the best of traditional gardening practices with the best of the new species and varieties of plants now available. The idea of the herb garden goes back to medieval times, when herbs were grown primarily for medicinal purposes. Your herb garden, which might contain some of the most modern varieties of herbs, can easily be designed to reflect the ancient tradition of herb growing, and the pages devoted to herbs in the following section give some ideas as to how you might achieve this. If your space is limited, you might prefer to grow your herbs in containers; they respond well to this type of cultivation.

Both herbs and the more ornamental types of leafy salad greens also make attractive additions to the flower garden. For example, you might grow rosemary and bay among your shrubs, add thyme, French tarragon, sage, and lemon verbena to your herbaceous border, and edge beds and borders with chives, bush basil, red lettuce, or radicchio. Beds of annuals can comfortably contain borage, dill, coriander, and chervil.

Nowhere are the new additions to the vegetable garden more obvious than among the salad greens. As well as new types and colors of lettuce, you can try greens of European origin, such as escarole, endive, and radicchio, and modern varieties of lamb's lettuce,

dandelion, sorrel, and other established greens that have been rediscovered and become fashionable.

Other significant newcomers among salad greens are the oriental vegetables. Many garden centers and suppliers now offer seeds of these plants, many of which are brassicas. Most of them are easy to grow, but they should be included in your plans for crop rotation.

Chinese cabbage, pak choi, mustard greens, chop suey greens, and flowering mustards are among the most popular and available of the oriental vegetables. Some of them, including chop suey greens, are plants with attractive and edible flowers, which makes them especially versatile in the garden and in the kitchen.

Also included in the section that follows are the remaining brassicas—cabbages, cauliflowers, Brussels sprouts, broccoli, and kale—and the members of the onion family, which supply some of the elements essential to the culinary arts. These include onions themselves—both bulbing and salad types—and also leeks, garlic, and shallots. As with other families of food plants, new varieties of brassicas and onions and their close relations are appearing every year, with improvements in flavor and disease resistance.

When buying seeds or plants to grow in the herb or salad garden, you should remember that many herbs are sold by their generic name rather than a varietal name. So seeds of thyme, for instance, are labeled simply "Thyme" or "*Thymus*"; if you want a specific variety, you may have to shop carefully. Many of the new greens, because they have not yet been highly bred, are similarly sold by generic name, or simply by a common name such as "Mustard Spinach," though varieties are gradually appearing.

Lettuce is one of the most rewarding of home-grown salad vegetables, and there is now a wide variety of different types to choose from, many of which are not readily available in the supermarket.

Except in hot climates, home-grown lettuce can, at least in theory, be enjoyed right through the year, provided you have a greenhouse for the winter crop. In practice, year-round production calls for quite careful planning and management. Consistent results depend on a suitable site and soil, on the right choice of variety for the season, and on care and attention during the growing period to forestall any problems such as overcrowding, transplant shock, and dryness. Summer lettuce, in particular, is liable to bolt in reaction to any of these shortcomings. Early and late crops are

especially prone to fungus diseases, so it is important to choose varieties recommended for spring or fall planting.

As a rule, lettuce needs a sunny position. Partial shade is an advantage during the summer months. Shelter is valuable for early and overwintered crops. The soil needs to be free-draining and fertile, with plenty of organic matter to hold moisture. Good drainage is vital for winter and spring crops. A neutral or slightly acid soil (pH 6.5–7) is ideal.

Cloches, a cold frame, or a greenhouse can contribute to an extended growing season and continuity of supply. Lettuce transplants reasonably well, except during the summer, so you can start the earliest plants under glass while the vegetable plot is still too wet to work.

TYPES OF LETTUCE
Loosehead lettuce
Loosehead, or butterhead, lettuce is the widely grown type with smooth-edged leaves. This group includes fast-maturing varieties for spring sowing and extremely hardy kinds, such as 'Brune d'Hiver,' to sow outdoors during autumn for cutting in spring. There are also several varieties, such as the ever-popular 'Buttercrunch,' that are fairly heat resistant, and some that resist viral and fungal diseases.

Crisphead lettuce
Crispheads have firm, crisp leaves, often with crinkled edges. They grow a little more slowly than loosehead varieties, but are also slower to bolt. There are varieties that do well if planted in summer for a fall harvest, and others for sowing or planting under cloches or indoors in late winter.

Cos lettuce
Cos, or romaine, lettuce has an upright, slender form, with a crisp heart in the center of the elongated leaves. It is slower to mature than heading lettuce and needs very good soil.

Looseleaf lettuce
This type of lettuce produces masses of individual, tender leaves and no head. Instead of harvesting the whole plant, you can pick a number of leaves from several plants at a time. These varieties mature very quickly, and are good for gardens in the South and Southwest.

SOIL PREPARATION
It may not be necessary to earmark a special space for lettuce, since it is the ideal plant for catch cropping (using ground left empty between crops) and interplanting between slower-growing vegetables. The strategy should be to sow little and often, to insure constant supplies and to encourage the plants to grow rapidly.

If you do treat lettuce as a separate crop, include it in the legume section of your rotation, where the soil will have been enriched with plenty of manure. Dig this in during the previous fall, and afterward spread lime over the lettuce area if the soil is more acid than about pH 6.5.

Two weeks before sowing or planting out, rake in a dressing of general fertilizer at two

ounces per square yard. Supply another, similar dressing once the crop is growing well (though leave this until early spring in the case of winter lettuces).

SPACING
Whether sown directly or planted out, lettuce needs one foot between rows and a final spacing of three to sixteen inches between plants, depending on the ultimate size of the variety. The extremes are represented by miniature types such as 'Tom Thumb' and large crispheads like 'Great Lakes.' Most of the loosehead lettuces require an intermediate spacing.

Start thinning lettuce sown outdoors as soon as possible; if it is left too long, the quality of the lettuce will start to suffer.

MAKING A START
Lettuce germinates at surprisingly low temperatures, and it transplants reasonably well, which makes it possible to grow the crop almost all year round in northern gardens. The seeds can be sown where the plants are to grow or indoors for transplanting. Succession planting is recommended.

Sowing in place is best for leaf lettuce and for fall crops of crispheads, where transplanting can be risky. The main drawback is that germination can be poor if the weather conditions are unfavorable.

Indoor sowing gives good-quality plants and allows more flexibility over the timing: you can plant the seedlings out whenever space is available in the vegetable garden.

Plant most types of lettuce shallowly, especially when they have been started indoors, with the seed leaves just above soil level; plant cos types a little deeper.

For an early crop
Sow any type of lettuce in late winter or early spring, depending on the mildness of your district, for harvesting in late spring. Sow either directly in a cold frame or under cloches, or in flats in an unheated greenhouse, for transplanting a month or so later.

Harden off the seedlings, then transplant them at the correct spacings for the variety and type. Most lettuce will thrive if planted out a month or even six weeks before the last frost date, but cloches or row covers will protect the seedlings in harsh weather.

In the open
Sow directly between early spring and early summer, and thin the seedlings before they become overcrowded. You can transplant thinnings or use them in salads.

For a fall crop
A sowing made a week or two after midsummer will provide lettuce in the fall or

early winter. 'Iceberg' and other crisphead lettuces do particularly well if grown in cooler temperatures. Surplus thinnings can be moved to a cold frame. Cover the remainder with cloches if necessary.

For winter use
Some hardy varieties will stand the winter outdoors in mild areas. Sow the seeds in summer or early autumn. Covering them with cloches improves their quality.

Water the plants well when you set them out, then avoid watering during the winter months, since this heightens the risk of diseases. Thin to three inches in the fall, but leave the final spacing until spring.

Winter lettuce in a greenhouse
Provided you can maintain a minimum temperature of around 45°F, you can sow lettuce in flats in early autumn and subsequently plant in the greenhouse border to mature during winter.

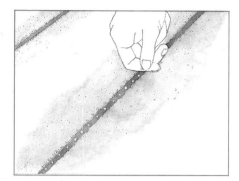

Well-spaced sowing prevents overcrowded seedlings and makes subsequent thinning a lot easier. The task is simplified by pelleted seeds, each of which is encased in a ball of soluble material.

Thin the seedlings in two stages: initially to two- or three-inch spacings; increase the gaps a little later as the plants develop. Progressive thinning insures that there are always plants in reserve if any of them fail to grow.

For the final thinning, alternate plants can be lifted with a trowel for planting elsewhere, until late spring. After this, warmer and drier weather makes them likely to bolt. Water the row first so that soil adheres to the roots. Lettuce should generally be transplanted when the plant has four or five true leaves.

CARE OF THE CROP
Water transplanted seedlings in well if the soil is at all dry. After this, keep them watered in dry weather, and hoe regularly.

HARVESTING
Lettuce remains fresh longest if it is gathered early in the morning. Pick head lettuces young, and pick the young leaves of looseleaf types. Cut through the stem of head lettuce with a sharp knife, just beneath the lowest leaves.

PESTS AND DISEASES
Potential pests include slugs, whiteflies, leaf miners, and earwigs.

Lettuce ailments include downy mildew, white mold, and aster yellows.

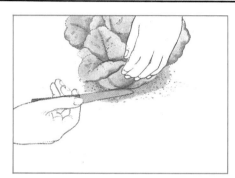

Harvest head lettuce by cutting through the stem with a sharp knife at ground level. Do this early in the day, and keep the lettuce in a cool place until eaten. Remove stumps from the soil as the row is cleared. Alternatively, pull up the whole plant and cut off the roots.

If cos lettuce seems reluctant to form a tight head, secure the leaves gently with string or a large elastic band. This will insure that the inner leaves, at least, become crisp and blanched.

LETTUCE LEAVES
If you are content with leaves rather than heads, there is a simple way to get a large output from a small area. Sow in closely spaced rows or broadcast seeds in beds and harvest the whole crop with scissors or a sharp knife.

Cos lettuce is best for this purpose. If you cut the plants about an inch above the ground, a second crop will grow. It will be ready for gathering a month or two later.

First make sure the ground is free of weeds. To broadcast, scatter the seeds very thinly over a square yard, then scuffle them gently into the surface. To sow in rows, make shallow furrows four inches apart, and sow sparingly. Thin to a final spacing of one inch.

RECOMMENDED VARIETIES
Loosehead varieties
'Buttercrunch' An All-America Winner. Dark green heads with buttery yellow centers.
'Salad Bibb' An early, slow-to-bolt type.
'Tania' Small, loose heads are soft and medium green. Good for fall harvests.
'Brune d'Hiver' A European lettuce that will overwinter with a good snow cover.
'Summer Boston' A heat-resistant type.
'Rougette du Midi' is a red butterhead variety; good in cool weather.
'Red Boston' Heads are tinged with red.
'Vasco' Very small 'Boston' type lettuce.
Crisphead varieties
'Ithaca' An early, dependable 'Iceberg' type.
'King Crown' Large, rather loose bright green heads; widely adapted.
'Mesa' has very large, compact heads.
'Pirat' Compact heads are green overlaid with dark red, with creamy yellow centers.
'Rosa' is a red-tinged 'Iceberg' type.
'Minetto' is good for small gardens; heads are small but very firm and crisp.
Cos varieties
'Winter Density' is a cos-butterhead cross that is very hardy.
'Valmaine' A standard cos type.
'Green Towers' Good for fall harvests.
'Little Gem' A compact romaine lettuce for close spacing. Slow to bolt.
Looseleaf varieties
'Salad Bowl' A popular, heat-resistant variety with wavy, lime-green leaves.
'Oakleaf' An old-fashioned lettuce.
'Green Ice' has exceptional flavor.
'Prizehead' Crisp, light green leaves are tinged with a reddish bronze color.
'Red Sails' A recent All-America Winner.
'Red Salad Bowl' turns deep red in cool weather. Heat resistant; slow to bolt.

SOWING SEEDS OUTDOORS, pages 36–37
SOWING UNDER GLASS, pages 38–39
SPACE-SAVING METHODS, pages 132–133
PESTS AND DISEASES, pages 172–175
LETTUCE, pages 178–179
195

Besides the true spinach (*Spinacea oleracea*), a variety of leafy vegetables, including New Zealand spinach and Swiss chard, are included under this heading. They resemble spinach and can be eaten raw or cooked in much the same way.

Spinach is a fast-growing annual that is fairly tricky to grow. The main danger is that it readily runs to seed in hot, dry conditions. You can sow spinach in late winter and early spring to provide a succession of tender leaves from late spring until the weather turns hot. Alternatively, you can sow the crop in late summer or early fall and harvest it in the autumn or possibly in the following spring. A late greenhouse crop is also a possibility.

The other leaf crops all remain in the ground for longer than spinach and must therefore be given a place in your crop rotation plan (see p.25). Perpetual spinach and Swiss chard are closely related; they are both hardy biennials and more tolerant than true spinach of hot, dry conditions. New Zealand spinach is a half-hardy annual that continues to grow all summer, even on the poorest soil; it produces mild-flavored leaves that have a spinach taste when they are cooked, although they taste different when eaten raw. Sorrel is a perennial herb whose leaves resemble those of spinach, although their flavor is quite different—sharper and rather lemony.

True spinach needs to be sown in really fertile soil, so that rapid growth is guaranteed. A heavy soil is more suitable than a light, sandy one; if you have light soil, you will have to enrich it with plenty of organic matter and manure. The pH should be about neutral. If spinach has ample moisture and nourishment, it will not bolt as readily when warm weather arrives.

Spinach sown in spring, especially the later sowings, should do well in partial shade. Spinach sown in the fall requires a sheltered site, fully open to the sun. It does not like cold, wet conditions.

SPRING CROPS: MAKING A START

Because spinach grows so quickly—it is usually ready to eat about six or seven weeks after planting—it is a good catch crop to grow on land that is vacant between a harvest in the late fall and a planting late in the following spring.

Prepare the soil by digging in plenty of well-rotted compost or manure, or add some general fertilizer at two ounces per square yard. Sow the seeds from early spring onward, as soon as the soil can be worked. Plant them a half-inch deep and about an inch apart in beds or rows; if you are planting in rows, make the furrows about one foot apart. It is best to sow little and often, in the same way as for lettuce, for a continuous crop.

CARE OF THE CROP

Thin the seedlings when they are large enough to be pulled out with your finger and thumb; they will be about an inch tall. Leave five or six inches between the remaining seedlings.

Water frequently, especially when dry conditions prevail and on light soil. To conserve moisture, mulch the plants with compost or rotted manure, and take care of any remaining weeds with a hoe.

Leaf miners are a real hazard to spinach in most parts of the country. These pests cannot be controlled with insecticides after the maggots have hatched, so watch for any eggs on the undersides of leaves and spray them immediately. Early crops should have less trouble with these pests.

Copious watering is essential during dry spells; otherwise the plants are likely to bolt prematurely. Frequent soaking with a hose will insure that the ground does not dry out, especially on light soil.

HARVESTING

When the leaves are large enough, start picking some from each plant. Do not pull them; instead, cut them or pinch them off. When hot weather threatens, cut off the whole plant close to the ground.

FALL AND WINTER CROPS

Prepare the soil as for the spring sowing. Plant seeds after the summer heat has passed; if you live in an area that has mild winters, continue planting until Thanksgiving or even later.

Harvest the plants six or eight weeks after they were planted for a fall crop. To overwinter spinach, plant late in the season and protect the plants from alternate freezing and thawing of the soil with a heavy mulch of leaves or straw and soil. Cloches will also provide some protection to fall and winter crops.

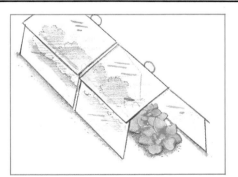

A covering of cloches makes all the difference to spinach in late fall. This will keep the plants growing more reliably during cold weather and will make the leaves more tender. Barn cloches are ideal for the purpose.

PESTS AND DISEASES

Besides the leaf miner, aphids and flea beetles can be troublesome.

Spinach can be infected by downy mildew and spinach blight.

RECOMMENDED VARIETIES

'Melody Hybrid' A recent All-America Winner. The plants are very productive and tolerate heat well; they are also disease resistant. Leaves are dark green, rounded, and flavorful.

'Skookum' An early, long-standing spinach with large, upright, semismooth leaves. Plants are mildew resistant.

'Cold Resistant Savoy' An excellent variety for overwintering, particularly where a snow cover will protect the plants. Leaves are crumpled and dark green; plants are slow to bolt in hot weather and are tolerant to spinach blight.

This low-growing, fleshy-leaved, trailing plant (*Tetragonia expansa*) is not a true spinach. It produces mild-flavored, spinach-like leaves and will grow on the poorest soil. It is half-hardy, however, and therefore vulnerable to frost. It can be sown outdoors during the spring, once it is safe to do so, or else sown indoors for planting out later. In mild regions of the South and West, it will grow as a perennial.

New Zealand spinach continues to grow right through the summer. Its main advantage is that it does not run to seed, even in hot weather, and in this respect it has an advantage over true spinach. Ideal conditions are provided by light soil that has been dug and manured during the previous fall.

MAKING A START
To start seeds indoors, sow them in a tray of seed-starting mix and germinate in gentle warmth—about 55°F—a little before midspring. Soak the seeds for a few hours first. Cover the tray with glass and paper until the seeds germinate.

When seedlings are large enough to handle, prick them out two inches apart. In late spring, move them to a cold frame for hardening off and dress the planting site with a balanced general fertilizer at two ounces per square yard.

Plant out when there is no further risk of frost; set the plants two feet apart in rows three feet apart.

To sow directly outdoors, allow three feet between the rows and sow two or three seeds every two feet. Later reduce the seedlings to a single strong plant in each planting position.

CARE OF THE CROP AND HARVESTING
Apply a second, similar amount of fertilizer when the plants are growing strongly. Encourage growth by watering in dry weather and by pinching out the tips of shoots as they develop.

Pick the young shoot tips, each bearing two or three leaves, frequently. The older leaves become tough.

There are no named varieties. The plants are usually free of pests and diseases.

This hardy biennial (*Beta vulgaris cicla*), sometimes called spinach beet, is a form of beet grown for its tender leaves rather than its roots. The leaves are used like spinach, though they are somewhat coarser in both texture and flavor. An abundant crop is produced on land liberally enriched with manure or compost during the previous autumn. This plant is useful over a longer period than true spinach is, and seldom runs to seed until its life cycle is completed late the following spring. It is related to but not the same as Swiss chard.

MAKING A START
Sow in midspring, after raking in some general fertilizer at two ounces per square yard two weeks before. Make the furrows fifteen inches apart and a half-inch deep. Sow the seeds thinly.

CARE OF THE CROP AND HARVESTING
Thin the seedlings to one-foot spacings. Once the plants are growing strongly, apply general fertilizer in the same amounts as before, and hoe this in around the plants. On poor soil, apply some high-nitrogen fertilizer to help to promote leaf growth. Water as often as necessary to prevent the soil from drying out.

Start picking the leaves before they become too large; take a few from the outside of each plant. Pick frequently, to encourage continuous cropping, and because the leaves become coarse if left to mature.

There are no named varieties. Pests and diseases are the same as those that affect spinach (see facing page).

SWISS CHARD
Swiss chard (*Beta vulgaris cicla*) is an easily grown member of the beet family that tolerates hot summer weather. The green leaves are cooked like spinach. Their thick white leaf stalks and the supporting stems are cooked and eaten like asparagus or stir-fried. An attractive form of this tall, vigorous plant, called rhubarb chard, has red stems and red-tinted foliage. It is handsome enough for any flower border.

Like perpetual spinach, Swiss chard is a hardy biennial, and it responds to the same treatment and spacings. Sow it from early spring through midsummer, and in the fall for winter crops in Zones 9 and 10. Pull the leaves, since cutting makes them bleed.

Garden sorrel (*Rumex acetosa*) is a common plant, sometimes found growing as a weed. But by removing the flowering stems of cultivated plants, you can induce them to produce a continuing supply of fresh, sharply flavored young leaves. Those picked in the wild, if you find them, are likely to become tough and dry once spring is over.

The young sorrel leaves, which have a delicious sharp, lemony flavor, can be used finely chopped in salads, preferably mixed with a blander leaf vegetable; the larger leaves can be cooked like spinach. Sorrel is also used as the basis for a number of soups and sauces.

In addition to the commonly cultivated plant, *Rumex acetosa*, which has narrow, arrow-shaped leaves, there is a species found principally in Europe, *Rumex scutatus*, or French sorrel. This has shield-shaped leaves, wider at the base, and a particularly acid flavor. Both are perennials and grown in the same way. Once established, sorrel is one of the first perennial plants to emerge in the spring.

MAKING A START
Choose a sunny situation and fertile, moisture-retentive soil. In dry soil the plants will be much less productive. Sow the seeds in midspring in a shallow furrow, and thin the seedlings to eight-inch spacings. Alternatively, sow them thinly in a windowbox or in a tub or large pot.

Keep the soil moist to insure steady growth. Pinch out the flowering heads when they appear.

Once they are large enough, take a few leaves per plant at each picking. They will freeze well if there is a surplus, and it is better to pick regularly than to leave the plants untouched for long periods.

To increase your stock, divide the roots in spring or autumn, and replant the pieces at once. It is a good idea to divide the plants every three years or so anyhow.

Sorrel, like many herbs, is seldom troubled by pests or diseases.

RECOMMENDED VARIETIES
'Large Belleville' is the only named variety you are likely to find; most often the plant is sold simply as "Garden Sorrel."

The diverse group of chicories (*Cichorium intybus*) includes two main kinds. The type generally classified as Witloof chicory or Belgian endive requires forcing during the winter to produce blanched, tightly packed shoots, called "chicons." Their somewhat bitter taste is modified by the blanching process. Though Witloof chicory is slightly more trouble to grow, it makes a welcome change for winter salads and can also be braised and eaten as a cooked vegetable.

The other type, leaf chicory, sometimes categorized under the varietal name 'Sugarloaf,' looks more like a giant cos lettuce, with densely packed, crisp leaves. It is gathered during autumn and early winter. Its quality is improved if it can be given winter protection in an unheated greenhouse or under cloches outdoors. The inner leaves are blanched naturally, and are sweeter than the outer ones. They are eaten raw or cooked like spinach.

In addition to these two kinds is a deep red or variegated chicory known as radicchio, which has a dramatic appearance. It starts off green but turns red when the weather becomes colder. Exposure to the cold also makes its taste less bitter. It can be left in the ground for winter use, or you can dig up the roots and force them like Witloof chicory; forcing turns them a pale pink color and produces milder, more tender shoots. Depending on the district in which radicchio is grown, it may need a covering of straw or cloches in the early winter, to extend its period of usefulness. Blanched or unblanched, it makes a crisp, tasty, and decorative salad vegetable.

Chicories are a good choice for salad greens, since they are available during the fall and winter, when lettuce and other salad crops are scarce. They can be grown easily and successfully in most climate zones, as they are fairly hardy and virtually free of pests and diseases. If you are short of space, you can even delay planting unblanched types until late fall.

None of the chicories is particularly fussy about soil, though they do best in fertile ground and an open, sunny situation. Ground manured for a previous crop is best for forcing varieties, which may otherwise develop forked roots, but nonforcing kinds will thrive in land dug and manured during the previous autumn. In both cases, apply a general fertilizer at one ounce per square yard two weeks before sowing.

When forcing chicory indoors, dig up the roots in batches, trim off most of the leaves, and then plant up to four roots in each nine-inch pot. Light garden soil will do, or use peat or potting soil.

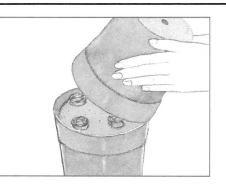

Cover the planted pot with another of similar size and stand it in a fairly warm room where the temperature is reasonably stable. Cover the drainage hole in the upper pot to exclude light.

Within a month the chicons should be three inches high and ready for eating. Cut them just above the base, and at once cover the pot again to encourage a second, smaller crop of young shoots.

WITLOOF CHICORY:
MAKING A START AND CARE

Sow seeds in late spring or early summer. Make the furrows a half-inch deep and one foot apart. When they are tall enough, thin the seedlings to six inches apart.

Keep the soil moist during dry weather. Add a general fertilizer at two ounces per square yard once the plants are growing strongly. Hoe regularly to keep weeds down, and remove any flower stalks in order to build up a strong root system.

FORCING INDOORS

Start digging up the roots in small batches from late fall onward; discard those that are small or forked. Cut off all but one inch of the leaves. Alternatively, dig them all up at the same time in late fall or early winter and place them in a shallow, marked trench in the ground (see p.44), covered with soil.

Force only a few roots at a time, to give a continuous supply of chicons during the winter. The roots will be about one foot long; trim the ends first, if necessary. Then stand three or four in a nine-inch pot, with damp soil or used potting soil packed between them. Invert a similar pot over the top and cover the drainage hole. Place the pots in total darkness in a moderately warm room, attic, or closet, or under the benches in a greenhouse, at a temperature of about 50° to 55°F. The shoots will take about three weeks to emerge from the soil.

Cut the chicons when they are about three or four inches high, just above their base. Dampen the soil and cover them again to encourage a second, smaller crop.

Those that cannot be eaten straight away should be wrapped in foil or kept in the refrigerator; they will become green and bitter if exposed to light.

FORCING OUTDOORS

This method is less trouble than the indoor method, and gives tighter chicons, but they take longer to develop. Its success depends on free-draining soil.

Cut off the leaves in fall, once the night temperatures are almost freezing; leave stumps of about one inch. Cover these with a four-inch layer of soil, then place cloches over the top. Start cutting once the blanched shoots appear; cut only a few at a time, since they deteriorate rapidly.

PESTS AND DISEASES

Chicory is seldom affected by disease, but may be attacked by slugs or cutworms.

RECOMMENDED VARIETIES

'Witloof' is the most widely used variety. 'Witloof Zoom,' an F_1 hybrid, is sometimes available.

LEAF CHICORY:
MAKING A START AND CARE
Sow seeds during late spring or early summer, in furrows a half-inch deep and one foot apart. The plants will need to stand about ten inches apart in the rows, so sow sparingly for subsequent thinning. Water well before sowing in hot weather.

The young green leaves, picked when they are two or three inches long, are quite mild and can be used in salads. Leave the remaining plants to form heads. Keep the plants hoed and watered. Add general fertilizer at two ounces per square yard once the crop is growing well.

HARVESTING
Start cutting the heads during the autumn. They are only moderately hardy, but should last well into the winter if covered with cloches before the onset of severe frosts.

RECOMMENDED VARIETIES
'Sugarhat' and 'Sugarloaf' are the two common varieties.

Cut through the stems of nonforcing chicories, such as 'Sugarloaf,' at soil level.

RADICCHIO
Sow and grow this beautiful chicory as for leaf kinds. From autumn onward, either cut and eat it as the heads mature, or else lift and force it.

Radicchio is reasonably winter hardy, though it will benefit from some protection. The main risk is from uneven soil temperatures. Mulch well to keep the ground from freezing, or, in the North, after it has frozen to prevent thawing. If you use a cold frame or greenhouse, keep it well ventilated.

RECOMMENDED VARIETIES
'Giulio' A burgundy-red radicchio for fall or winter harvest.
'Palla Rossa' An early variety for fall or early spring planting.
'Verona' will overwinter for a second crop in the spring.

Endive (*Cichorium endivia*) is often thought of as a type of lettuce, since it has much the same growing habits and uses, but in fact it belongs to the chicory family. Its flavor is more bitter than that of lettuce, and for this reason the plants are sometimes blanched for a period before being eaten to make them milder in flavor.

Endive, like chicory, is an excellent fall salad crop, since it is readily available at a time when lettuce is least plentiful. It can be grown during the summer, but it will not do well in hot weather, which turns the leaves bitter. It is less likely than lettuce to bolt, however. It is also relatively immune to pests and diseases.

For a winter crop it is best to grow the Batavian type of endive, or escarole. This is a tall plant, with broad, wavy-edged leaves.

MAKING A START
Sow curled varieties during the spring and late summer; the latest of these sowings will provide a fall crop. The hardy, broad-leaved escaroles can also be sown from spring onward, but it is a late-summer sowing that provides the winter harvest.

Give the seedbed a dressing of general fertilizer at two ounces per square yard about two weeks before sowing. Sow the seeds where the plants are to grow, making the furrows a half-inch deep and fifteen inches apart. Sow very thinly; water the furrows first in dry weather.

CARE OF THE CROP AND BLANCHING
Thin the seedlings of curled varieties to ten-inch spacings, and those of broad-leaved endives to fifteen-inch spacings. Make sure that the soil remains reasonably moist, or the plants may bolt. Apply a second, similar amount of fertilizer once the plants are growing strongly.

Crops for a winter harvest are best covered with cloches, in a mild region, or grown in a frame or in an unheated greenhouse.

It is mostly the curly-leaved endives that need blanching, since they are at their most bitter in hot weather. Escarole requires little blanching, since its central leaves are naturally crisp and pale.

If you wish to blanch the leaves, wait until the plants are mature and choose a time when the leaves are dry. Tie them loosely with soft string and cover each plant with a large, porous pot or some other light-proof container, with its drainage hole covered. Do not use a plastic pot, because the buildup of warmth inside causes disease. Blanch only two or three plants at a time, since they deteriorate soon after being exposed to the light.

The curled endive, a flat, lower-growing plant with frilled leaves, is less hardy and therefore more suited to summer and autumn crops. It also has a tendency to rot in damp, cold weather.

Endive is a vigorous but slow-growing crop; it lends itself to being cut successively if the roots are left in the ground after cutting. Both kinds need the same growing conditions as lettuce—that is, fertile, well-drained, but moisture-retentive soil and, as a rule, an open position. However, since endive has the tendency to run to seed in hot, dry conditions, spring-sown plants benefit from a little shade.

Grow endive in soil that was dug over and enriched with plenty of compost or manure during the previous autumn.

HARVESTING
Blanching takes a week or so during warm weather but up to three times as long during late autumn and winter. Cut through the stem of each plant with a sharp knife close to the soil surface, and use the endive at once.

PESTS AND DISEASES
Apart from slugs and snails, there are likely to be few problems.

RECOMMENDED VARIETIES
'Green Curled,' 'Ruffec,' and 'Salad King' are curled or fringed varieties suitable for blanching; harvest in the fall.
'Nuvol' is a self-blanching escarole that is less bitter than 'Batavian,' the standard garden variety.

Cover each tied plant with a flowerpot. Place a few pebbles beneath the rim to allow some ventilation, but cover the drainage hole to exclude light. Blanching is fastest in warm weather.

SOWING SEEDS OUTDOORS, pages 36–37
SOWING UNDER GLASS, pages 38–39

PESTS AND DISEASES, pages 172–175
CELTUCE AND ENDIVE, page 177

SPINACH AND SALAD GREENS, pages 180–181

199

In Britain, mustard and cress are almost always paired together as a quick-growing salad crop; they are equally useful in sandwiches and as a garnish. The two flavors complement each other well; however, there are advantages to growing the plants separately so that you can mix them, if you like, according to taste.

Garden cress (*Lepidium sativum*) has a peppery tang, and you will probably use a smaller quantity of it. White mustard (*Brassica hirta*), which is the kind usually grown, has a pungent, hot taste, but some people prefer to grow the milder-flavored black mustard (*Brassica nigra*). Cress germinates more slowly, so for a mixed crop maturing at the same time, sow cress three days earlier than mustard.

It is possible to grow mustard and cress in the garden, but more satisfactory, as a rule, to sow the seeds indoors. Outdoors, the low-growing plants become splashed with soil, although this is less likely under a cloche or in a cold frame.

SOWING OUTDOORS
Fine, light soil is needed; water it well before sowing. Sow at any time during the spring or late summer, though choose a shaded spot for warm-weather crops, as the cress might bolt. A cold frame is ideal.

Scatter the seeds closely over a small area, and press them into the surface with a short length of board. Cover with a cloche if the crop is planted in open ground, and leave one end uncovered. Do not allow the soil to dry out while the seeds germinate and the shoots develop.

SOWING INDOORS
Place several layers of blotting paper, paper towels, or cotton wool in a seed tray, or cover the bottom with peat or a peat-based potting soil. In each case make sure that the lining is thoroughly damp before scattering the seeds quite thickly. Press them down lightly, then cover the tray with glass and folded paper. In the winter, place the tray in a warm position near a radiator or elsewhere in the house, or place it in a heated greenhouse.

Uncover when the seeds germinate and place the tray in a well-lit position. Allow a few more days for the seedlings to become darker green and to expand fully. Keep the lining moist.

HARVESTING
Cut the crop with scissors when the stems are about two inches high. Outdoor sowings will give further crops.

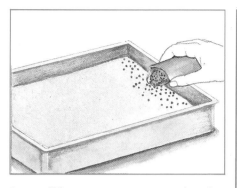

Layers of blotting paper or paper towels make a growing medium for mustard and cress, since the seedlings need only moisture during their brief lives. Place this in a seed tray or similar low-sided container.

Scatter the seeds fairly thickly over the dampened material. Remember to sow the cress three days before the mustard.

Cover each tray with a sheet of glass to conserve moisture and folded paper to exclude light. Turn the glass daily to prevent condensation from dripping onto the seeds. Remove as soon as they germinate.

Use scissors to harvest the mustard and cress when they have grown about two inches high. Discard the remains of indoor-grown plants. You can expect follow-up crops from outdoor sowings if you keep them watered.

Several kinds of cress are available, and all of them make good additions to salads. Garden cress (*Lepidium sativum*) is probably the most common; its light green, curly leaves are pleasantly pungent, and it can be grown from spring until winter in most of the country, and throughout the winter in mild southern and coastal regions.

Upland cress (*Barbarea praecox*) is a biennial that resembles a small dandelion. The peppery leaves are deeply lobed and dark green, and the plants do well in fall and early winter, when other greens are scarce.

As its name implies, watercress (*Nasturtium officinale*) is native to streams, and can be grown at home in cool, clear running water or in shaded, moist soil. The perennial plant produces thick, long-stemmed leaves that are good raw or in soups.

Most cresses are easy to grow and free of pests and diseases, though hot weather will cause them to bolt. In general, they require a rich soil that holds water well; they will thrive in partial shade, so they can be planted in awkward spots where other garden vegetables will not grow. Watercress is the exception: its roots must be kept constantly wet.

MAKING A START
For a summer crop, sow garden and upland cress in early spring; successive sowings will give you a continuing supply of garden cress until the weather turns hot. For a winter supply, sow upland cress in late summer and fall. Garden cress can be grown in pots indoors throughout the year, or outdoors in mild winters. Broadcast the seeds over a bed, or plant them a quarter-inch deep in rows nine inches apart.

To grow watercress in damp soil, sow seeds thickly in beds. Start plants in water by taking cuttings from supermarket watercress and anchoring them in a stream with a small stone or a piece of wood.

CARE OF THE CROP
Thin seedlings to eight-inch spacings when they are big enough; upland and watercress need more room than garden cress.

Keep the ground moist with frequent watering, and spray watercress with a fine mist every day. Protect late-season crops with cloches if necessary.

HARVESTING
Start picking leaves when the plants are big enough to produce more. To harvest watercress, cut off shoots when they are about six inches long.

PESTS AND DISEASES
Aphids and flea beetles are the only likely problems. Diseases are rare.

Rocket (*Eruca sativa*), or arugula, is another old-fashioned hardy annual which, like corn salad, is currently enjoying a revival of popularity as a salad ingredient. It is especially useful during the winter, when lettuce may be in short supply. Rocket leaves are sharply flavored: the young leaves are best, since the older ones have a hotter, more distinctly peppery taste. The attractive flowers can also be eaten.

Rocket grows best in cool conditions. Since it is fast-growing, it can be used for interplanting or catch cropping. If grown during the early winter months, it is best cloched to keep the leaves tender.

MAKING A START AND CARE
Prepare the soil as for corn salad and space the plants the same way. Sow in late summer or early autumn for a late crop, and during early spring for a late-spring crop. The plants bolt easily, so provide light shade and ample moisture.

CELTUCE
Celtuce (*Latuca sativa angustana*), also known as stem lettuce or asparagus lettuce, is an oriental lettuce with a swollen, edible stem. The young leaves can be eaten raw or cooked, and the stem is peeled and sliced and either eaten raw in salads or cooked like celery. The heart of the stem is crisp and crunchy, with a delicate taste.

Celtuce is grown like lettuce, and it usually needs a well-manured soil and plenty of moisture to do well. It makes a good autumn and winter crop from a late-summer sowing in mild southern and coastal regions.

Sow the seeds between early spring and early summer, in shallow furrows eighteen inches apart. Thin the seedlings when they are large enough to handle, to ten to twelve inches apart.

Water the plants well. Hoe regularly between the rows to prevent competition from weeds.

Pick the leaves once they are big enough to make a worthwhile harvest. The stems will be ready to eat about three months after sowing.

This hardy annual (*Valerianella locusta*), also known as lamb's lettuce, has been eaten for centuries. Like radicchio, it is currently enjoying a new popularity as an ingredient of *nouvelle cuisine* salads. The flowers are edible too. Corn salad is a good substitute for lettuce during winter. Cloches will help to maintain growth during the coldest months; they will also keep the leaves more tender and prevent them from becoming mud-splashed.

A sunny, sheltered position provides the best growing conditions. The soil needs to be well drained, and the plants will perform best if it has been enriched recently with plenty of well-rotted manure or compost.

MAKING A START
For a winter crop, sow during late summer or early autumn in furrows one inch deep and one foot apart. This spacing may be reduced to six inches when you are growing crops in beds. Thin the plants to four-inch spacings when they have three true leaves. Alternatively, sow or broadcast the seeds in the early spring.

CARE OF THE CROP
Water the plants generously for the first few weeks after sowing, and hoe frequently.

HARVESTING
Once there are enough leaves for a worthwhile picking—about three months after sowing—take a few of the largest leaves from each plant at a time. Wash them well, since they grow very near the ground.

RECOMMENDED VARIETIES
'Vit' is slow to bolt in warm weather. Most corn salad is sold under its generic name, however.

Pick a few leaves from corn salad plants often. Since they are quite small, this means that you must grow a number of plants in order to provide enough leaves for gathering at any one time.

Dandelion greens (*Taraxacum officinale*), blanched or green, make a pleasant addition to spring salads. They can also be cooked like spinach. They have a distinct, tart flavor, which is sweetened by blanching. Dandelion greens are at their best in spring, when the leaves are young and pale. After midsummer, they tend to become coarse and bitter; then they die back.

As every gardener knows, hardy perennial dandelions grow readily in most places. However, the leaves are more succulent on a rich soil. Rather than rely on weeds, sow one of the cultivated strains, which have larger, more tender leaves.

MAKING A START
Sow the seeds in late summer in furrows a half-inch deep and one foot apart. Thin them to a spacing of six to nine inches.

CARE OF THE CROP AND HARVESTING
When the plants mature in the following spring, cut off their flower heads. Blanch some plants in early spring, if you wish, by covering them with a large flowerpot. Alternatively, pick the leaves green in the spring and early summer months, and leave the plants to continue growing from year to year.

RECOMMENDED VARIETIES
Most cultivated dandelions are called '**Large Leaved**' or '**Thick Leaved.**'

SOWING SEEDS OUTDOORS, pages 36–37
SOWING UNDER GLASS, pages 38–39

PESTS AND DISEASES, pages 172–175
SPINACH AND SALAD GREENS, pages 180–181

CHICORY, pages 198–199

Cabbages (*Brassica oleracea capitata*) are the chief member of the brassica family and comprise several varieties. They come in various shapes—mainly round, conical, and looseleaf—and in a variety of colors: dark green, light green, white, and red, with pink, purple, or bluish variegations.

Until recently, cabbage had a poor culinary reputation, mainly because of its strong taste and smell and because it was habitually overcooked. But many of the newer varieties have a much more subtle flavor; provided you grow these and cook them so that they stay crisp, cabbage is first-rate. Red and white cabbages can also be pickled, or grated and used as coleslaw or a crisp winter salad vegetable.

All cabbages are hardy and easy to grow. The cultivation methods are broadly similar for all types. The planting times and spacings differ according to variety, however, and there are one or two other minor variations according to the season.

All cabbages need similar growing conditions. The ideal is an open site, where there is firm, fertile, free-draining soil that contains plenty of organic matter. If manure or compost was added for a previous crop, so much the better, and since cabbages follow nitrogen-rich legumes in the usual rotation, this is often the case. Otherwise, work in a moderate amount of well-rotted manure or compost some months before planting. Avoid freshly manured ground and loose, recently worked soil.

As a rule, sow the seeds in a separate seedbed or indoors, then set out the young plants in their final positions when they have four or five leaves. Fall cabbages may be sown in place if you prefer.

Spread lime over the soil surface following fall digging and before planting cabbages. This prevents the acid conditions that inhibit the growth of cabbages and other brassicas. It also helps to reduce the risk of club root disease, to which these plants are prone.

TYPES OF CABBAGE: WHEN TO SOW AND HARVEST

Various types of cabbage are suited to sowing and harvesting in particular seasons. By choosing varieties carefully, you should be able to have a continuing supply of cabbage for coleslaw and for cooking for much of the year.

Spring cabbage These early-maturing varieties form heads quickly once the worst of the winter weather is over, though they do not grow as large as the fall types. Like other cabbages, they will not tolerate summer heat, so it is important to get them into the ground early in the season.

Sow seeds indoors about two months before your last spring frost date, and prick them out into flats or pots when they have several true leaves. Begin to harden them off, preferably in a cold frame, about a month before the frost date. It is important to acclimatize them completely; otherwise they might tend to grow leggy. Protect them from hard frosts, if necessary, with cloches or row covers. Transplant them into their permanent site a week or two later. The heads, which average three or four pounds, will be ready to harvest about two and a half months after sowing—that is, a couple of weeks after the last spring frost.

Midseason cabbage Like spring cabbage, these varieties are started early in the season, but they stay in the ground longer, grow larger, and usually produce dense, round heads. Some Savoy cabbages, with crinkly leaves and a mild flavor, are midseason varieties.

Fall cabbage Late-season varieties are the cabbages most often seen in supermarkets during the winter, though those grown at home are far superior in flavor. They include most of the Savoy and red cabbages, as well as the large, very dense round cabbages that are best for sauerkraut.

Fall cabbage can be sown directly in rows or beds in summer; as long as the soil is kept moist and cool, they will thrive. Harvest the heads as late as possible—just before the hard frosts arrive—and keep them in a moist, cool place. If they are stored properly, some will keep for as long as four months.

MAKING A START

About two weeks before planting all types of cabbage, treat the planting site with a general fertilizer at two ounces per square yard. Firm the bed and rake it into a fine, crumbly tilth ready for planting.

When sowing fall cabbage in a seedbed, make the furrows a half-inch deep and six inches apart. Thin overcrowding seedlings to four or five inches apart.

Transplant young cabbage plants from the flats, pots, or seedbed in which they have been growing when they have four or five leaves. Use a dibber or a trowel to form planting holes; set each plant in its hole and then push the tool in again alongside to press soil against the roots. The spacings for different types are given below.

Water the plants in gently and mulch them generously to help them retain moisture and to keep the soil cool.

To sow fall cabbages directly where they are to grow, make furrows a half-inch deep and one foot apart. Sow thinly and later remove surplus seedlings to give a spacing between plants of eighteen to twenty-four inches, depending on the variety.

SPACINGS

Spring cabbage Transplant most varieties of spring cabbage to spacings of twelve to fifteen inches. If you are planting in rows, make them two and half feet apart.

Midseason cabbage Plant in rows that are two and a half to three feet apart, and leave fifteen inches between seedlings. Larger varieties may need more space: some require as much as two feet.

Fall cabbage Leave three feet between rows, and sow the seeds two inches apart. Thin seedlings to two-foot spacings when they are about four or five inches high.

A dibber is the best tool for planting cabbages of all types, since plants need to establish firm contact with the soil. Form a hole with the pointed end of the dibber, place the plant roots in the hole, and press the soil against them.

CARE OF THE CROP

After all types of cabbage have established their growth, feed them with some general fertilizer at two ounces per square yard. Hoe regularly to control weeds, but be careful not to damage the plants' roots.

It is a good idea to give cabbage a thick layer of straw, compost, or some other organic mulch to help the soil retain moisture. Spring cabbage in particular is apt to bolt if the soil temperature rises quickly in late spring or early summer. A thick mulch will also help suppress weeds and, depending on the material used, supply nutrients to the cabbage roots.

To avoid problems with cabbage root maggots, place mats around the stems of the plants just after transplanting (see p.172); these will also deter cutworms. Be

Cabbages need plenty of nitrogen to insure rapid, healthy growth. If given as part of a general fertilizer, apply half as a base dressing before sowing seeds and the remainder as a top dressing around the growing plants.

on the lookout for cabbageworms, which appear as white moths and can be controlled with regular applications of *Bacillus thuringiensis* (see p.21).

Splitting or cracking is a problem when cabbages are subject to too much water after their heads have formed. Dig a semicircle around each plant with your spade; this will sever some of the roots, thus limiting the plant's ability to take up moisture without harming its ability to survive.

HARVESTING

Start harvesting cabbage as soon as the heads have formed. Most spring varieties form heads of about three or four pounds; midseason and fall varieties are generally larger, averaging between five and eight pounds. The conical types produce very small but distinctly flavored heads, whereas many red and Savoy cabbages are best when they are about four pounds in size.

To harvest cabbage, cut through the thick stems with a sharp knife. Secondary heads may form after you have removed the central one. To increase the harvest, cut a cross about a half-inch deep in the top of the stump; the growth from each of the "stems" you have made can be eaten as greens.

Most cabbages are sweetest if they have

matured in cool weather, but although they can tolerate frost, they will not survive a heavy freeze. Therefore, it is best to cut all your fall cabbages when really cold weather is on the way and store them for winter use. One way to keep them is to place them in a pit in the ground and cover them with a thick coat of straw topped with plastic. This provides them with the moisture and the low temperatures they require, but they are vulnerable to mice, so you might want to place them in containers first.

PESTS AND DISEASES

Pests include aphids, cabbage root maggots, cabbageworms, and cabbage loopers.

Diseases include club root, downy mildew, white mold, and black rot.

Early cabbages can be planted close together in pairs. One plant of each pair can be harvested young; the plants that remain are left with sufficient space to grow into larger cabbages with heads. The cut stumps of cabbages will sprout again in a few weeks and provide you with an additional crop of greens.

RECOMMENDED VARIETIES

Spring varieties

'Early Jersey Wakefield' This early-maturing, conical cabbage has a mild flavor and crisp, tender leaves. Heads average two or three pounds.

'Treta' is similar to 'Early Jersey Wakefield,' but produces firmer, more uniform heads slightly earlier in the season.

'Golden Cross Hybrid' The tight, round heads have a creamy golden interior and form in two months. Plants are small, so they can be spaced fairly closely.

Midseason varieties

'Darkri Hybrid' is a fairly early cabbage with compact plants and firm, tender heads of extremely high quality.

'Stonehead Hybrid' An All-America Winner. Plants are small and resistant to fusarium yellows; heads are dense and have short cores.

'Roundup' The slightly flattened, very dense heads average three to six pounds.

'Tri Star Hybrid' cabbages have a nice flavor, particularly in coleslaw. The heads weigh six to eight pounds and do not brown in hot weather.

'Bravo' A disease-resistant variety that stands up well to adverse weather conditions. Heads are round and large.

'Perfect Ball' produces dense heads that keep well. Plants are disease resistant.

Fall varieties

'Zwann's Jumbo' The heads of this late-maturing variety are gigantic, pale green, firm, dense, and slightly flattened. A good choice for storage.

'Danish Ballhead' is an excellent cabbage for making sauerkraut. Heads have smooth, exposed tops, are very dense, and average nine pounds.

'Wisconsin All-Season' A good variety for

storage, with dense round heads.

Savoy varieties

'Spivoy' The plants are quite small, yet produce two-pound heads with dark bluish-green, crinkly leaves. Matures fairly early.

'Savoy King' is a fall cabbage rich in vitamins. The heads are large, round, and blue-green.

'Salarite' A midseason variety that has thick, juicy leaves. The heads are dense and butter-yellow in the interior.

Red varieties

'Ruby Ball' An All-America Winner. This very early variety can be grown in spring or fall. Heads weigh four or five pounds.

'Ruby Perfection Hybrid' yields well in midseason. Purplish-red heads average three or four pounds and are firm and uniform in size.

'Mammoth Red Rock' A fall cabbage that can reach seven pounds. Stores well.

SOWING SEEDS OUTDOORS, pages 36–37
PLANTING VEGETABLES, page 40

PESTS AND DISEASES, pages 172–175
CABBAGES AND CHINESE VEGETABLES, pages 182–183

STORING VEGETABLES, pages 226–227

203

Chinese cabbage (*Brassica pekinensis*) is a relative newcomer to the vegetable garden and has as much in common with lettuce as with ordinary cabbage. In appearance it resembles a giant cos lettuce; in the kitchen, it can be used raw in salads or stir-fried, braised, or simmered briefly.

Because they are brassicas, Chinese cabbages should take their place in the rotation of crops along with other members of the brassica family. Where they differ from other cabbages, apart from their milder flavor, is in their speedy growth and their marked disposition to bolt. Thus it is better to sow the seeds in summer than in spring, and to harvest the crop in the fall.

Because of the plant's tendency to bolt, it is better to sow plants in place than to move them from a seedbed. The inevitable stress of transplanting is a significant factor in inducing the production of flowers and seeds. However, some of the more recent F_1 hybrid varieties are bred to resist bolting, so these are the ones to choose.

To grow rapidly, Chinese cabbages need really fertile, moisture-retentive soil. You need to dig in an ample supply of organic matter, in the form of manure or compost, some months before sowing. If Chinese cabbages are grown as a follow-up to early potatoes, peas, or lettuce, supply a light dressing of well-rotted material.

Choose a part of the plot that gets a reasonable amount of sunshine, although shade for part of the day is an advantage in the summer months. Apply lime if the pH is much below 6.5.

About two weeks before sowing, rake general fertilizer into the site at three ounces per square yard.

MAKING A START

Sow around midsummer, or for a few weeks afterward. Make the furrows a half-inch deep and about eighteen inches apart, then water the soil thoroughly with a hose if the weather is warm and dry. Either sow the seeds very thinly and later thin the seedlings so that they are twelve to fifteen inches apart, or else place them in groups of three or four at the same distance. In this case, remove all but the strongest seedling.

If you want to grow Chinese cabbage in the spring, choose one of the bolt-resistant varieties and sow seeds indoors two or three months before the last spring frost date. Harden off and transplant the seedlings as for spring cabbage (see p.202). Growers in areas with mild winters may be able to succeed by sowing the seeds directly in the garden as soon as the soil can be worked.

Sow Chinese cabbages in groups to save seed. Soon after germination, remove all but the strongest seedling from each position and leave this to grow. Seedbed sowing is unwise, since transplanting encourages bolting.

CARE OF THE CROP

More than most vegetables, Chinese cabbage needs abundant moisture throughout the growing period. Dry soil means an inevitable check to its development.

Some time after thinning, and when the plants have started to grow strongly, supply two further dressings of general fertilizer, each at three ounces per square yard; leave an interval of two weeks between. Hoe each application in, and water generously.

Hoe regularly to prevent competition from weeds, and protect the crop from pests in the same way as you would protect other cabbages (see p.203).

Given good growing conditions, the cabbages will usually form solid heads without assistance. If the outer leaves seem floppy, however, it helps to tie the whole head, fairly loosely, with soft string.

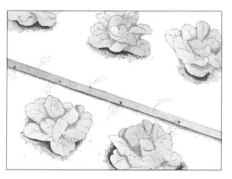

A drip hose that waters the soil rather than the leaves is ideal for Chinese cabbages. Plants need abundant moisture in order to insure steady growth and to minimize the risk that they will bolt.

HARVESTING

Chinese cabbage grows quickly and may be ready for picking as little as nine weeks after sowing. Cut the heads with a sharp knife as they mature during the autumn. The thick midrib makes good eating, along with the green part of each leaf.

Leave the stumps in the ground, and cover them with cloches for a secondary crop of tender greens. If there are still cabbages in the ground when frost threatens, harvest them, place them in plastic bags, and store them in the refrigerator.

PESTS AND DISEASES

The principal pests are cabbageworms, cabbage root maggots, aphids, flea beetles, and cabbage loopers.

Possible diseases include club root, downy mildew, black rot, white mold, and fusarium yellows.

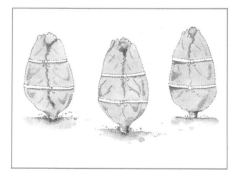

Chinese cabbages, like the tallest types of cos lettuce, may need securing with string during late summer. Secure in two places but keep the ties fairly loose. Take precautions against cabbageworms and other pests.

RECOMMENDED VARIETIES

'Spring A-1' This bolt-resistant variety is a good choice for spring crops. The heads are light green and cylindrical, and weigh three to four pounds.

'Nagoda 50' The barrel-shaped heads form very quickly in cool weather; can sometimes be harvested in less than two months.

'China Doll' is a slow-bolting, heat-resistant type bred for spring planting. The elongated heads have a creamy interior.

'W-R Super 90 Hybrid' A good variety for winter storage. Heads are firm and well formed; they average seven pounds. The plants are disease resistant.

'Jade Pagoda' is a vigorous hybrid that yields well. Heads are fairly firm, light green with yellow hearts.

OTHER ORIENTAL VEGETABLES

Oriental vegetables of all kinds are becoming popular in the West, and provide a change of taste and appearance from some more common crops. Their crisp texture and subtle, interesting flavors make them excellent for eating raw in salads or for light cooking, such as stir-frying.

CHOP SUEY GREENS

This edible species of annual chrysanthemum, also known as shungiku or garland chrysanthemum, is pretty enough for the flower border. It has yellow flowers and deeply cut, bright green, fleshy foliage. The flowers can be eaten fresh or dried, or added to soups and stir-fried dishes. The leaves have a distinctive, aromatic scent and a slightly pungent flavor. They are usually cooked lightly and often served mixed with other vegetables; they form a major ingredient of well-known dishes such as chop suey and sukiyaki.

Shungiku leaves can be ready for picking within two months or less from the time the seeds are sown. This speedy growth makes shungiku a good candidate for catch cropping and interplanting (see pp.132–133).

Any ordinary soil will do for chop suey greens, provided it contains plenty of organic matter and retains moisture well. Choose a sunny spot for early spring sowings but light shade for a summer-sown crop. Sow in the early spring or in midsummer in rows nine to twelve inches apart; thin the plants to four-inch spacings.

Keep the soil moist to promote rapid growth and insure the continued production of shoots and leaves, as well as to discourage bolting. The leaves are best when they are about five inches long and should be used right after harvesting.

Pinching out the tops of shungiku plants helps to stop them from flowering, and so prolongs the harvest of tender, mild leaves. Choose the youngest leaves for use in salads.

LEAFY CHINESE MUSTARDS

This group includes several hardy plants. **'Green-in-the-Snow'** (*Brassica juncea*) This hardy mustard grows up to twenty inches tall and has fairly coarse leaves with a sharp flavor; the young leaves can be shredded and eaten raw in salads, but the older ones should be cooked. They can taste distinctly hot when the plant is about to bolt.

'Tendergreen' mustard spinach (*Brassica rapa*) This fast-growing winter crop resembles spinach. The leaves are mild and the smaller ones can be used whole in salads; larger leaves need to be shredded before use. **Japanese greens 'Mizuna'** (*Brassica juncea japonica*) This plant has dark green, fernlike leaves and looks pretty in a flowerbed. It is low-growing (up to eight inches) and useful for interplanting between taller plants. Cut either individual leaves or the whole heads just above ground level; the plants will resprout several times.

Mustard greens (*Brassica juncea*) This useful autumn and winter crop is especially popular. The leaves have a slight peppery tang and may be used alone or with other greens. The small young leaves can be chopped and eaten raw in salads, and even the full-sized leaves remain tender. Continual picking encourages the production of new leaves.

There are both smooth-leaved and curly-leaved varieties of mustard greens. A dramatic-looking variety called 'Miike Purple' has huge leaves with striking purple veins.

You can sow the seeds in early spring for a late spring or early summer harvest, or in late summer or fall for a late crop. They have a tendency to bolt, however, if they are planted too late in spring.

For all these leafy mustards, the principal season of use is autumn and early winter; the main crop is sown around mid- or late summer. An early spring sowing is also worthwhile if you can spare cloches for frost protection. With rapid growth in mind, choose a spot that contains plenty of organic material. Light shade is best for a summer sowing, because the plants are generally quick to bolt.

Sow the seeds where they are to grow or transplant the seedlings from a seedbed. Allow one foot between rows, and thin the plants to a similar distance. 'Green-in-the-Snow' and 'Mizuna' require less space—thin the former to six to eight inches and the latter to nine inches apart.

Keep the plants well watered and hoe frequently to prevent competition from weeds. Take precautions against pests, especially while the plants are still young.

LEAFY CHINESE BRASSICAS

This is a blanket name for several hardy, quick-growing plants also known as Chinese celery. The best-known example is pak choi. The "celery" part of the name derives from the appearance of the stems, which are thick and pure white or light green.

The plants are compact, with bright green, rounded, glossy leaves. Both the leaves and the stems are succulent and mild. The center leaves are particularly good eaten raw, whereas the outer leaves can be used for stir-frying or braising. They are generally robust and relatively disease-free.

The soil conditions and cultivation requirements are broadly similar to those of the leafy mustards. Being smaller plants, however, the Chinese brassicas need a spacing between them of only nine inches in each direction.

Chinese brassicas grow rapidly and can be cut within five or six weeks of sowing. Though the leaves may be gathered individually, the stumps will resprout if the base of each stem is severed.

FLOWERING MUSTARDS

This group is grown chiefly for its edible flowers. Two main types are available: **Flowering Purple Pak Choi** This decorative, small-leaved brassica (*Brassica campestris purpurea*), also known as 'Hon Tsai Tai,' produces tasty flowering purple stalks. Both the young flowering stems and the leaves can be stir-fried or lightly braised.

'Hon Tsai Tai' needs a fertile, moisture-retaining soil. It is best used as a quick catch crop or interplanting since it takes up little space before flowering. Sow the seeds in spring for a summer crop, in cool areas, or in late summer for harvesting in early winter. It will survive a light frost, but for added safety can be overwintered in an unheated greenhouse or under cloches outdoors. Sow the seeds directly; transplant at, or thin to, fifteen-inch spacings. Keep the growing plants well watered.

Flowering Pak Choi This flowering mustard (*Brassica chinensis parachinensis*), known as 'Chinese Tsai Shim,' is less hardy than the purple-flowering type, but has thicker, more succulent shoots. Sow the seeds in spring for late summer and autumn salads. Grow it in the same way as 'Hon Tsai Tai,' but space the plants ten inches apart.

Brussels sprouts (*Brassica oleracea* var. *gemmifera*) are one of the most valuable of fall and winter vegetables. They are remarkably hardy and able to withstand all but the worst winter weather. By growing suitable varieties and protecting them in winter, you might be able to enjoy them from autumn right through until spring. If you grow your own Brussels sprouts, you can be sure of eating them at their best—as small, tightly formed "buttons," which taste far superior to the larger, loose sprouts usually found in supermarkets.

Nevertheless, Brussels sprouts have one major drawback. They occupy more space than most other crops and for a great part of the year. Set out in midsummer, they remain in place until at least the following winter. This disadvantage can be mini-mized by interplanting Brussels sprouts with faster-growing plants, such as rad-ishes, lettuce, or turnips. Another partial solution is to grow a compact variety, such as 'Captain Marvel,' which can be planted closer together.

There are both standard and F_1 hybrid varieties; the F_1 hybrids are noted for their heavy crops of uniform sprouts. These tend to mature over a relatively short period, whereas those on the standard varieties develop over a longer period and vary quite a lot in size and quality.

Brussels sprouts are reasonably easy to grow, provided that their basic needs are met. First, they are heavy feeders, and require really fertile soil to fulfill their potential. Choose a part of the plot that has been heavily manured; if you think it may lack organic matter, dig in some additional manure or compost before planting.

The ideal pH rating is 6.5, so spread lime over the dug ground during the winter if a soil test shows a significantly lower reading.

Brussels sprouts also require the ground in which they are planted to be firm. This is easier to achieve on a heavy soil than on a light, sandy one. If the ground is loose, the roots rock, which means that plants grow less well and may fail to form tight sprouts. Digging during the autumn gives the site six months to settle. At planting time, take care not to loosen more than the very top layer of soil. Choose a site open to the sun but sheltered from strong winds.

MAKING A START

Brussels sprouts are said to have the best flavor if they have been subjected to a few light frosts, so it is usual to grow them as a fall crop. Gardeners in the South and West, however, may raise a spring crop by sowing seeds directly in the plot as early in the year as possible and harvesting before the hot summer weather begins.

For the normal autumn harvest, sow the seeds in an uncovered seedbed or in flats or pots indoors four months before your first fall frost date. If you are growing more than one variety, sow them in batches, starting with the earliest, over a period of three or four weeks.

To start the plants indoors, sow seeds thinly in flats and transplant them to individual pots when they have two true leaves. Alternatively, place two seeds in each pot and remove the weaker seedling after they have germinated.

If you are not growing them under glass, sow the seeds thinly in furrows a half-inch deep and leave six inches between rows. Be sure to label different varieties accurately, since the seedlings will look almost identical once they have come up.

Soon after germination, thin the seed-lings to two- to three-inch spacings. If they are too close, they become spindly, and will not thrive after they are transplanted.

While the seedlings are growing, rake a dressing of general fertilizer lightly into the top inch of the planting site at three ounces per square yard.

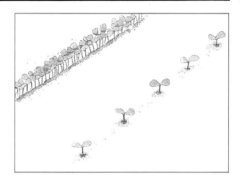

Seedlings of Brussels sprouts will grow spindly and tall if allowed to remain close together in the seedbed. Thin them to two or three inches apart as soon as they are large enough to handle, and while they are still at the seed-leaf stage of development.

PLANTING OUT

Move the plants to their final positions when they are about five inches high. Set them two and a half feet apart in each direction, or twenty inches in the case of compact varieties. Plant very firmly, with the aid of a dibber if you have one. Use the dibber to make the planting hole first, then press it down again beside the seedling to firm the soil against the plant.

Ideally, choose a wet day and transplant in the evening if possible. But if the soil is dry, water the plants in well. If planting is followed by a spell of hot, dry weather, rig up some form of temporary shading over the plants while they develop new roots. Tents made of newspaper will do, or you can use spun-bonded row covers.

If you have plans for interplanting, this is the time to sow other seeds between the Brussels sprouts plants.

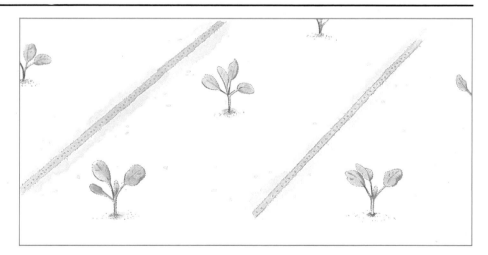

To save space, sow a quick-growing crop such as lettuce between newly planted Brussels sprouts. If sown between the rows or between individual plants in a row, it will mature and can be harvested before the Brussels sprouts have grown very large.

CARE OF THE CROP

Remove any shading once the leaves have ceased to be floppy. Keep the soil moist, however, until the plants are growing strongly. At this stage apply some fertilizer at the same rate as the first dressing, and then draw soil around the plants as a form of support. Apply a third and final dressing of fertilizer about a month later.

Hoe regularly to prevent weeds from becoming established. If the plot is exposed to the wind, secure each plant—especially the taller varieties—to a stake. Wind-rock will loosen the roots and damage the plants.

In the autumn, take off any yellow leaves and firm the soil around each plant.

Watch out for aphids and other pests and take immediate action if you see significant numbers of them.

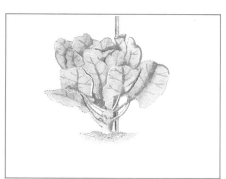

On an exposed site, Brussels sprouts need support to prevent damage from the wind, especially if they are growing in light soil. Insert stakes when the plants are half-grown, and secure the stems to these with string.

HARVESTING

Start picking sprouts at the bottom of each stem. Begin when the bottom ones are the size of a walnut, since the small, tight ones are crispest and have most flavor. Take a few from each plant by twisting them downward. Remember to remove any open sprouts that have not formed properly. Sprouts higher up the stem will increase in size to provide a succession of pickings.

Mature sprouts can be left on the plants for many weeks. Unless the weather turns warm, they will not deteriorate quickly. Once they have all been picked, the plant tops make surprisingly good eating.

Sprouts taste best after they have been sweetened by frost, but the plants will not survive in frozen ground. To insure a

The sprouts will form progressively on the stems, starting at the base. Pick them as they become large enough, taking a few from each plant at a time. As you do so, remove any sprouts that are poorly formed.

continuing harvest well into winter, mulch the soil heavily in early winter with straw or leaves, and place a cover of plastic over the rows or beds. Well-protected plants should continue to provide sprouts several weeks into the new year.

Dig up the stalks after the final harvest, since they harbor pests. Either chop them into small pieces and mix them into the compost heap, or burn them.

PESTS AND DISEASES

Pests are the same as for other brassicas: aphids, cabbage root maggots, cabbage-worms, cabbage loopers, and flea beetles.

Similarly, possible diseases of Brussels sprouts include club root, downy mildew, white mold, and black rot.

RECOMMENDED VARIETIES

'Prince Marvel' is a hybrid variety that produces medium-sized, firm sprouts that are uniform in size from the bottom to the top of the stem. Plants are vigorous and bear early in the season.

'Captain Marvel' An even earlier Brussels sprout; good for a spring crop. Plants are only two feet tall and disease tolerant.

'Jade Cross E' This hybrid variety produces large, tightly wrapped sprouts of uniform size and good flavor. The plants are very vigorous, and produce better if the tops are pinched out as the sprouts begin to mature.

'Long Island Improved' is a standard variety that matures about three weeks later than the hybrid types. The plants are tall and prolific; the sprouts have good flavor and freeze well.

SOWING SEEDS OUTDOORS, pages 36–37
PESTS AND DISEASES, pages 172–175

BROCCOLI AND OTHER BRASSICAS, 184–185

KALE AND COLLARDS

Kale (*Brassica oleracea acephala*) is one of the hardiest and least demanding of vegetables. After even a severe winter it will produce tender young shoots in the spring if it has been lightly protected. It is often grown to fill the midwinter gap when other winter vegetables are scarce. Kale is an ideal crop for cold, wet, northern climates, since it can withstand frost and needs a lot of moisture. It will also be productive in soils where other brassicas are less happy. Its crisp, curly leaves can be cooked or eaten raw.

Kale can take up a considerable amount of space in the vegetable garden, but mid-summer planting allows it to follow a crop harvested in early summer, such as spinach or peas. And for small gardens there are dwarf varieties that take up no more space than cabbages.

Two kinds of kale are commonly available: Siberian kale, which has plumelike, grayish-green leaves that are frilled at the edges, and Scotch kale, which has curlier, blue-green leaves. Collards, a standard crop in the South, are members of the same species as kale and are grown in much the same way; they can tolerate both heat and cold, but are slightly more finicky than kale about their growing conditions. Their leaves are smooth-edged and green, and are exceptionally high in vitamins and minerals.

All varieties of kale are highly ornamental, and make a good addition to a flowerbed or border. In fact, the red, white, and purple "flowering" kales are often grown simply for their color, though they too can be cooked or eaten raw.

Provided they have good drainage, kale and collards will grow in most soils. They need a reasonably open situation, however, and do best in moderately fertile ground. Land manured for a previous crop is ideal; if necessary, add lime to give a pH level of around 6.5. Like some other brassicas, these crops need firm soil, too, so avoid digging too close to planting time.

Kale and collards are usually sown directly outdoors, in early spring and again in midsummer. Gardeners in mild climate zones can sow both crops in late summer for a winter harvest.

MAKING A START
Sow kale directly in the garden as soon as the soil can be worked in spring, and continue sowing periodically from mid-spring to midsummer for several crops. Collards, which are a bit more tender, should be sown in midspring and again in mid- to late summer for a fall harvest.

About two weeks before planting, add general fertilizer to the site at the rate of three ounces per square yard. Make furrows for kale about two feet apart and for collards three feet apart, both a half-inch deep. Sow seeds thinly, and water the furrows if the weather is hot.

Once the seedlings are growing strongly, thin them to twelve- to eighteen-inch spacings, depending on the variety.

Frequent watering of kale may be needed if warm, dry weather coincides with the earlier stages of growth. It is important to keep young kale growing steadily. It will recover only slowly from any checks to its growth.

CARE OF THE CROP
About a month after planting collards, feed them with general fertilizer at about two ounces per square yard. Kale varieties should not need additional nutrients, but they will benefit from a heavy mulch before the soil has frozen in early winter. Straw and leaves are best for this purpose. Many varieties of kale are extremely hardy and will survive all but the worst winter conditions, especially if they are protected with a mulch, cloches, or row covers.

HARVESTING
Pick the young leaves of kale and collards from late summer on, but never take too many from one plant at a time. (The leaves will be sweeter in taste if they are refrigerated for a few days, or if they are picked after a few frosts.) Do not pick the terminal bud, or the plant will stop producing. When shoots develop in late winter and early spring, pick them when they have grown to at last finger length.

PESTS AND DISEASES
The most likely pests are aphids, flea beetles, and cabbageworms; cabbage root maggots are more likely to attack collards than either Siberian or Scotch kale.

Possible ailments are club root, downy mildew, white mold, and black rot.

Pick the leaves and young shoots of kale a few at a time. Never strip a plant of its foliage, or you may kill it. Harvest collards after the first fall frost, kale well into the winter.

RECOMMENDED VARIETIES
Kale
'Vates' A standard dwarf variety with curly, blue-green leaves. A taller variety, **'Winterbor,'** produces more leaves; both are moderately winter hardy.

'Spurt' A very hardy variety that produces tall, upright plants with tender stems and curly green leaves.

'Dwarf Siberian' This is a compact version of an old variety. The flat, gray-green leaves have frilled edges. Very cold hardy.

Collards
'Champion' A recent selection from 'Vates.' Short plants; broad, dark green leaves.

'Blue Max Hybrid' The upright, vigorous, short plants bear flavorful blue-green leaves in dense formations.

BROCCOLI

Broccoli (*Brassica oleracea italica*) is an increasingly popular crop, at least partly because it can be grown in both spring and fall for two crops. Although it prefers cool weather and will bolt in the hot summer sun, broccoli is relatively undemanding and will produce well anywhere in the country, provided you choose a suitable variety.

Broccoli raab (*Brassica rapa*), also known as rapini or turnip broccoli, is less well known but a valuable plant for greens and the tender, loosely formed flower heads. It is best sown in early spring for harvesting before the summer heat.

Both kinds of broccoli require a sunny site and a fertile soil with a pH around 6.5. If the soil was not heavily manured for a previous crop, dig in some well-rotted compost or manure. Add lime if necessary.

The **central heads of broccoli** are the first to form. Cut these before they run to seed to encourage side shoots to form. These side shoots will develop over a long period, often until the first frost puts an end to the growth of the plant.

The **secondary heads** of broccoli that form after the central head has been cut are smaller but may be quite numerous. Frequent cutting actually encourages more to form as the plant attempts to produce seed.

MAKING A START

The spring crop To grow broccoli successfully in northern climates, it is a good idea to start seeds indoors about a month and a half before the last spring frost date. Sow the seeds in flats or pots, and prick them out to individual containers when they are about an inch tall. Move them to a cold frame at least two weeks before planting, and set them into their permanent positions, eighteen inches apart in rows three feet apart, two weeks before the frost date. Protect them from hard freezes with cloches.

The fall crop For an autumn crop, sow broccoli seeds directly in the soil about three months before the first fall frost date. Make the furrows a half-inch deep and about two and half or three feet apart. Water the seeds in, and thin the seedlings when they have developed sufficiently; the spacing will vary depending on the variety. Be sure to keep the young plants well watered.

Broccoli raab Sow seeds directly in early spring, as soon as the ground can be worked (southern gardeners may be able to sow in late fall or winter). Treat the crop in the same way as summer-planted broccoli.

CARE OF THE CROP

Most broccoli needs to be watered generously if it is to grow quickly and form large heads. A mulch will help retain moisture, particularly for fall crops.

Feed broccoli plants a few weeks after they are established with two ounces of general fertilizer per square yard.

Broccoli raab is vulnerable to wind damage. If it is growing on an exposed site, draw soil around the stem to help provide extra anchorage. It may also be necessary to insert a stake beside each plant and secure the stem to it with string.

HARVESTING

Broccoli first develops a single, central head. If you cut this with a sharp knife when it is green and while the flower buds are still tightly closed, the head will have its best flavor and the plant will form side shoots with small heads. Frequent picking encourages the production of more side shoots; harvest them when their stems are four or five inches long.

Start picking the leaves and shoots of broccoli raab as soon as they are large enough to eat. The plants will continue to produce for at least a month.

PESTS AND DISEASES

Broccoli is subject to the same pests and diseases as kale and other brassicas (see opposite page). Cabbageworms are a particular hazard for crops sown in summer.

RECOMMENDED VARIETIES
Broccoli

'Emperor' Very vigorous plants bear reliable crops of dense heads six to eight inches in diameter. This variety does well in most parts of the country in both spring and fall, and is resistant to disease.

'Green Comet' is an extra-early hybrid good for spring planting. An All-America Winner. The heads are large, blue-green, and densely formed.

'Premium Crop' Also an All-America Winner. The eight- to nine-inch heads hold well without flowering.

'Citation' also holds well. The high-quality, blue-green heads are produced on large, vigorous plants that are disease resistant.

'Green Goliath' This is a good variety for several harvests of side shoots. The central heads mature gradually, so picking can extend over two months or more.

'Early Purple' This variety is a good choice for fall or winter harvesting in mild climates. The flower buds are deep purple.

Broccoli raab

'Raab' is the standard variety. The flower buds are picked with two or three inches of stem and cooked together with the leaves.

Cauliflowers (*Brassica oleracea botrytis*) are for vegetable growers who enjoy a challenge. Compared with most other brassicas, including cabbages and Brussels sprouts, they can prove decidedly temperamental. But successful cropping, measured by the gathering of evenly shaped, blemish-free heads, is within the reach of anyone prepared to take a little extra trouble. And the trouble is well worthwhile if you enjoy the crisp, nutty texture and distinctive taste of this vegetable. Cauliflower is also a versatile crop: it can be cooked and served in many different ways, or be eaten raw. The florets also freeze well.

Two essential requirements can make all the difference between success and failure when cultivating this crop. First is the soil, which has to be firm, fertile, and either neutral or only very slightly acid. It is worth taking a soil test, which should give a pH reading of 6.5 to 6.7—slightly more alkaline than for most brassicas. The soil must also contain ample organic matter, either left over from a previous crop or dug in before planting. The plot should be unshaded, although a little shelter is an advantage for plants that mature in early summer, when hot weather arrives.

The second essential is a growing routine that avoids all possible checks to development. The conditions likely to induce a setback include leaving seedlings too long before transplanting, lack of water at any stage of growth, and planting when it is too cold or too hot. Checks due to these or other causes often lead to undersized heads or heads that emerge from the leaves too soon.

MAKING A START

Seedbed sowings are made in the same way, whether in a cold frame or in the open. Make the furrows a half-inch deep with a space of six inches between rows. Sow the seeds very thinly and cover them with a layer of sifted soil or compost. Keep the cold frame closed until after germination, at least, unless it is very hot, then gradually supply a little ventilation.

Remove any surplus seedlings to give a spacing between plants of two to three inches. Water the seedbed carefully if a dry spell follows germination.

A week or two after the seedlings appear, apply general fertilizer to the planting site at three ounces per square yard. Rake this in gently so that you do not disturb the soil beneath the top inch or so.

It is best to transplant the seedlings before they grow too large, to avoid checks to growth. Move them when they are about five weeks old, or at about the five-leaf stage. Reject any seedlings that do not have a growing point. Water the seedlings during the previous evening and transplant them as quickly as possible, no deeper than in the seedbed. Use a dibber, if you have one, to make the holes and then to firm the soil against the roots; otherwise use a trowel. Water the plants in afterward.

Cloudy, damp weather is ideal, but the dehydrating effect of warm, dry weather can be reduced by erecting some temporary shading over the plants (see p.40).

Spacing varies according to the season in which the cauliflower will be harvested. As a general rule, the later the planting, the wider the space between plants can be. Leave twenty inches each way between spring cauliflowers and two feet between autumn cauliflowers. Purple cauliflower requires the same spacing as white. If you want to try to grow a winter cauliflower, leave slightly more space between plants—thirty inches is about right.

Sowing directly in rows or beds is especially worthwhile for autumn cauliflowers that would otherwise have to be moved from a seedbed in high summer. Apply a dressing of general fertilizer two weeks or so previously, at three ounces per square yard.

Make the furrows a half-inch deep and thirty inches apart. Water the furrows if the soil is dry, then sow the seeds in groups of three or four. When the seedlings are two inches tall, remove the surplus ones to leave the strongest plant at each spot.

TYPES OF CAULIFLOWER
Depending on your climate and soil conditions, you may want to grow one of the more unusual types of cauliflower, or plant cauliflower very early in the year for a spring harvest rather than the usual fall crop.

White cauliflower is usually sown in a seedbed, a cold frame, or flats and transplanted to its permanent site anytime from April until July, for a crop in late summer or fall. The heads will not form properly in hot weather, so it is important to pick a variety suitable for your growing season.

For a spring crop, sow the seeds indoors and prick them out into individual containers when they are two or three inches tall. Be sure to harden them off well before transplanting them into the garden, about a month before your last spring frost date.

Purple cauliflower is a less demanding crop than the white type; it is more tolerant of both heat and cold, and the heads, which turn green when cooked, do not have to be blanched. Because it requires a long growing season, plant purple cauliflower in early summer, for a harvest in late fall.

Winter cauliflower, also known as heading broccoli, is a popular European vegetable suitable for regions with mild winters and plenty of moisture, so it does well in the Pacific Northwest and on the California coast. Planted in summer or fall, it will bear firm white heads from early spring to summer, depending on the variety.

Seedlings started in the greenhouse provide an early spring crop of cauliflowers. Prick out the seedlings individually into peat pots, and keep them warm and well watered so that their growth is not checked. Harden the seedlings off before planting them out.

Seedlings grown outdoors in a seedbed need to be thinned at an early stage in their growth. Failure to do this will result in lanky plants that are likely to suffer from transplant shock when they are moved to their final positions.

CARE OF THE CROP

Be sure to keep the soil moist if a dry spell follows transplanting. Remove any shading material once the leaves have ceased to be limp. When the plants are growing strongly—about three weeks after transplanting—give the site a top dressing of general fertilizer at two ounces per square yard and scuffle it in.

Hoe regularly to prevent competition from weeds, or lay a thick mulch of hay, straw, or some other loose organic material. Black plastic is generally unsuitable, as it causes the soil to warm up too much. Continue watering as necessary, so that the bed gets at least two inches of water each month, either from a hose or from rainfall.

Draw soil around the stems in windy seasons for extra support—cauliflowers, like all brassicas, suffer from wind-rock.

When each head reaches tennis-ball size, bend about three of the outer leaves level with its top and tie them over it with string or a rubber band as protection. (This is unnecessary if the leaves are already turned over to cover the head.) The purpose is to blanch the heads—to prevent them from being turned yellow by the sun. In the case of winter- and spring-heading types, the covering helps to prevent damage due to rapid thawing of the heads after frost. Obviously, purple cauliflower does not need to be blanched.

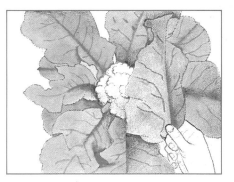

As the cauliflower heads develop, fold two or three leaves over them if they are not already covered by foliage. In late spring this will protect them from sun; in late fall, from rapid thawing following a frost.

HARVESTING

Harvest the heads of cauliflowers when they are firm; if they are left too long, the heads break up and flowers start to appear. If a complete row of cauliflowers appears to be maturing simultaneously, start to cut some of them before they attain full size. Heads picked in the morning, while they are still damp, last the longest, but do not gather any when they still have a light frost on them; wait until they dry.

Cauliflowers will keep for up to three weeks if they are placed in plastic bags and kept in the refrigerator. Alternatively, you can hang them upside down in a string bag, in a shed or in a cool place indoors.

Cauliflowers can be stored in a cool shed. If lifted complete with their roots, hung upside down, and sprayed occasionally with water, they will keep for two or three weeks.

PESTS AND DISEASES

The principal pests are cabbage loopers, cabbageworms, aphids, flea beetles, and cabbage root maggots.

The most likely diseases to affect cauliflower are club root, downy mildew, white mold, black rot, and whiptail.

RECOMMENDED VARIETIES
For spring and fall crops

'Snow Crown' This is an easy-to-grow hybrid with solid, medium-sized heads. It bears only fifty days after transplanting, so it is a good choice for a spring crop. An All-America Winner, it can also be planted in summer for an autumn harvest.
'White Knight' is slightly later than 'Snow Crown,' and the heads are a little larger. The leaves curl up to blanch the head naturally, and the heads do not color readily in hot or dry weather.
'Dominant' A particularly cold-hardy variety, ideal for a late planting on fertile soil. The leaves are abundant and easy to tie up; the heads are large and firm.
'White Contessa' bears pure white heads that average one pound in weight. The plants are moderately heat resistant, but do best in cool autumn conditions.

'Elgon' is a widely adaptable cauliflower that does well in both hot and cold weather. The plants are vigorous and yield plenty of firm, large heads.

Purple cauliflower
'Violet Queen' A hybrid variety that combines the qualities of cauliflower and broccoli. The plants take about three months to mature, and are best when grown for a fall harvest. The heads are good raw or cooked and freeze well (as do many cauliflower varieties).
'Purple Cap' bears heads that average six inches in diameter, although they are somewhat more uneven than white cauliflower.

Winter cauliflower
'Newton Seale' can be planted in June for a crop the following spring. It is hardy to Zone 6 and will produce large, exceptionally white heads that withstand frost.
'Snow's Winter White' A popular variety, also hardy to Zone 6. Heads are cold tolerant and easy to grow.

SOWING SEEDS OUTDOORS, pages 36–37
PLANTING VEGETABLES, page 40

PESTS AND DISEASES, pages 172–175
BROCCOLI AND OTHER BRASSICAS, 184–185

STORING VEGETABLES, pages 226–227

Leeks (*Allium porrum*) are one of the most versatile of autumn and winter vegetables, and deserve to be more popular than they are. They are members of the onion family but are both easier to grow and more dependable than most onions. Failure is unlikely, even in the coldest districts, since leeks can survive hard winters. They are also troubled by very few pests and diseases.

Leeks require a long, steady growing season and may occupy part of the vegetable plot or nearly a year. But space need not be a problem, despite their long occupation of the ground, since planting distances are closer than for some other winter vegetables, such as cabbages and Brussels sprouts.

Depending on the variety and on where you live, the harvest extends from early autumn until early spring. Northern gardeners can sow seeds in early spring for an autumn crop; southerners and those in mild coastal regions can sow directly in the garden in late summer for a winter or spring harvest.

Though not fussy about soil, leeks are most likely to thrive in fertile, well-worked ground that has not become compacted. Plenty of organic matter will help to insure good-sized stems. A pH rating of 6.5 to 7 (slightly acid to neutral) suits leeks best. The plants will grow best in a sunny spot.

It is a good idea to start leeks in a seedbed for subsequent transplanting. Apart from leaving the main site free a little longer, deep planting in a seedbed insures that the greatest possible length of stem is blanched and made edible.

MAKING A START

Sow seeds in a seedbed in early spring in the North or in the fall in mild regions, but be guided by soil temperature rather than the calendar. The seeds are unlikely to germinate until the soil starts to warm up, so you may have to sow them indoors in flats, under cloches, or in a cold frame.

Two weeks before sowing, rake general fertilizer into the seedbed at two ounces per square yard.

Make the furrows one inch deep and six inches apart. Sow very thinly, with the aim of growing seedlings spaced at least one inch apart. Thin the seedlings as necessary to achieve this.

Transplant the seedlings about two to three months after sowing, when they are about six to eight inches high. Rake general fertilizer into the site at four ounces per square yard two weeks beforehand. Water the planting site well the day before.

Use a dibber or the handle of a hoe to form holes about six inches deep—enough to take all but the top two inches of the plants. Leave one foot between the rows and six inches between plants.

Drop a plant into each hole and add some water: anchor the roots without drowning or floating the seedling. Do not replace any soil—this will crumble in gradually to blanch the stem.

CARE OF THE CROP

Little care is needed, beyond hoeing to suppress weeds and watering regularly.

Gradual hilling up will insure a maximum length of blanched stem, so draw soil around the developing stems from between the rows, using a hoe.

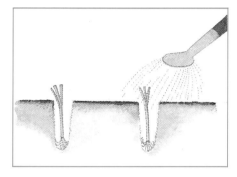

Before dropping the young leek plants into planting holes, cut off some of the floppy top growth and also trim the roots. Water the plants in, using a hose, so that some earth is washed over the roots.

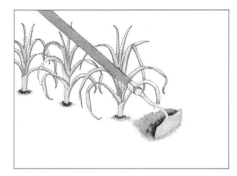

With the aim of increasing the length of the blanched stems, use a hoe to draw soil around them from the second half of summer onward. Leeks are slow-growing, but continue to develop until they are harvested.

HARVESTING

Start harvesting the leeks when the stems are about three or four inches thick, depending on the variety. Lift them carefully with a fork and take only as many as you require immediately; leeks will keep growing during the winter if they are mulched, but only slowly during the coldest months. Finish harvesting autumn varieties before the end of the year; they can be sliced and frozen, or store them in the refrigerator.

Any overwintered leeks that remain at spring planting time can be heeled in a small trench on a spare corner of the plot (see p.133) until they are needed. Harvest them before they run to seed.

PESTS AND DISEASES

Onion maggots and nematodes may prove troublesome, but seldom do.

Downy mildew is the most likely ailment.

Use a fork to ease leeks out of the soil; otherwise the stems are liable to break, It is helpful to carry a knife so that you can cut off the roots on the spot, together with the soil adhering to them.

RECOMMENDED VARIETIES

'Molos' Giant plants have long, thick white stems of superb quality.

'Leader' is a quick-growing variety with stems that are more slender than 'Molos.'

'Electra' A winter-hardy leek that does well in the North.

'Splendid' This variety is a good choice for spring planting in areas with cool summers.

'Nebraska' has long stems with little swelling at the base. For a fall harvest.

'King Richard' Stems are elegantly long and slender. Not cold hardy.

'Catalina' yields thick, heavy stems that overwinter well.

'Giant Musselburgh' An old standard. The leeks are short but very thick, and tolerate winter temperatures well.

'Broad London' A large, late-bearing variety with thick stems; good for overwintering.

No other vegetable plays a more important role in the kitchen than the onion (*Allium cepa*). It is an indispensable ingredient of countless cooked dishes. Onions are also easy to grow, and thanks to their excellent storage qualities, a vegetable plot can keep a family supplied with salad and cooking onions for most of the year.

There was once a period during midsummer when the winter-stored crop had finished and the current year's plants were still only half-grown. Today, however, the bunching varieties, which can be planted to mature at precisely this time, fill this gap.

Most other kinds of onions form bulbs, and are divided into two basic groups: long-day onions, which require a northern summer to form their bulbs, and short-day varieties, which do well in the South. The distinction is made according to the number of hours of daylight the onions need to develop their bulbs fully; the short-day varieties are able to mature quickly in the mild, short springs of southern regions, where the days do not lengthen appreciably as summer arrives, whereas the long-day types do better in cool areas where the summer days have fifteen or sixteen hours of light to offer. Onions also divide into other groups, some of which are described below.

BULBING ONIONS
In general, bulbing onions are considered to be either sweet onions, such as the well-known Vidalia and Walla Walla types, or storage onions, which are the kind usually found in supermarkets. Sweet onions often form very large, sweet bulbs, but they are fairly dependent on the ideal soil and climate conditions for which they have been bred to do their best. Storage onions, in contrast, grow well everywhere in the country except in the Deep South, and as their name implies, they keep well for several months if properly stored.

There are two quite different methods of growing bulb onions. One is by sowing seeds and the other is by planting sets: immature, grape-sized onion bulbs that are readily available from nurseries, garden centers, or through the mail. They are grown and harvested commercially during the season before they are sold.

Sets have a number of advantages and are probably the best choice unless you wish to grow very large bulbs or a particular variety that is available only as seed. They present few difficulties in growing, they are pest and disease resistant, and they mature ahead of seed-sown crops. They are certainly the better choice for gardeners living in regions where the summers tend to be short and wet. Bolting can be a hazard, but heat-treated sets seldom run to seed. The initial cost of sets is a little higher than for seed, but the difference is slight when weighed against the greater likelihood of a successful crop.

Seeds are a better choice than sets for the large-bulbed sweet onions, which grow bigger if given an extra-early start in the spring. They are also a good idea if you live in a mild region and want to grow onions during the fall and winter months for a late-spring harvest.

BUNCHING ONIONS
These straight, nonbulbing plants are used for their stems and are also known as scallions, spring onions, and green onions. Unlike immature bulbing onions, which are often used for the same purposes, true bunching onions do not form bulbs at all. Many varieties are perennial and will overwinter even in the most severe climates, but some mature very quickly and should be planted in the warmer months for a continuing harvest. They are almost always sold as seeds.

Bunching onions are most commonly used as a salad vegetable, but they are also useful in soups and stews and braised on their own or with peas. The green tops can be used as a garnish, much like chives.

PICKLING ONIONS
These small, delicately flavored bulbs, sometimes called pearl onions, are generally very white and have a nice sweet flavor. They are used in soups and stews, creamed, or cooked with other fresh vegetables such as peas and carrots—and of course they are the most common type for pickling. They are usually grown from seed and harvested during the summer.

Many gardeners grow standard onion varieties thickly planted in unfertilized soil to produce small onions for pickling, but varieties specially bred for the purpose are available from seed suppliers and nurseries.

SOIL AND POSITION
All onions do best in an open, sunny part of the plot, although overwintered crops can benefit from a little shelter. The ground needs to be well drained, and you must add some lime if a soil test gives a pH reading any lower than 6.5.

All types of onion need reasonably fertile soil, but seed-sown bulbing onions, in particular, require ample organic matter. Dig in a good amount of well-rotted compost or manure—one or two buckets to the square yard—during the previous autumn. This will give the ground time to settle and become firm. Firm soil is another requirement of onions; you may need to walk on it to achieve this.

Onion sets also respond to well-prepared soil, but they will give reasonable results with a less generous supply of well-rotted organic matter.

Bunching onions and pickling onions are less demanding than sweet and storage varieties. Averagely fertile soil will do, including ground manured for an earlier crop. But all onions need neutral or only slightly acid soil conditions.

It is important to plant onions in an area of the garden where weeds are nonexistent or can easily be controlled. Be sure to cultivate the plot thoroughly before planting, and remove any weeds as soon as they appear by hoeing or hand weeding.

Site your onion bed in an open, well-drained, and sunny place. In the fall dig over the soil and incorporate plenty of organic matter; add lime if the soil is acid. In early spring, add some general fertilizer and rake the soil to produce a fine tilth. Walk on the bed to firm it and rake again before planting.

BULBING ONIONS

From sets

Plant onion sets anytime between early spring and early summer, or in the fall if you live in a region with mild winters.

Give the bed a dressing of general fertilizer at three ounces per square yard two weeks before planting. Firm the soil. Leave one foot between rows and four inches between the bulbs. Simply push them into the soil, so that the tops are just visible. Then firm the soil around them again.

Birds have a habit of flicking newly planted sets out of the soil, so protect them with a humming line or with strands of black thread crisscrossed between pegs (see p.44). Keep the ground weed-free by frequent hoeing. Watering is necessary during the early stages and in hot, dry spells.

From spring-sown seeds

Sow the seeds during the first half of spring, once the ground has started to dry out and become warmer. Add general fertilizer at three ounces per square yard two weeks or so ahead of sowing. Make the furrows one foot apart and a half-inch deep. Sow thinly. Subsequently remove surplus seedlings to leave one plant every four inches.

Alternatively, sow the seeds under glass in the winter at one-inch spacings in trays or pans of seed-starting mix. Press the seeds into the surface and sift a little soil over the top, then water. Cover with glass and paper; remove these once the seeds germinate.

Harden the seedlings off and plant them out once the soil has started to warm up. Firm the bed and plant them six inches apart in rows one foot apart.

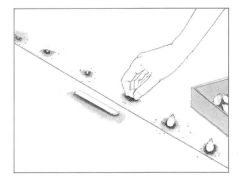

Plant onion sets so that most of the bulb is under the soil and only the tip remains visible. You will need a trowel for planting sets on firm soil, but if your soil is light and well cultivated, you should be able simply to press the sets into it.

From seeds sown in late summer

Onions suitable for sowing in late summer and autumn include some hardy bulbing varieties, including most short-day onions, and the bunching varieties that can be overwintered successfully. If you live in the South or in the mild coastal areas of the West, you should be able to grow bulb onions during the winter.

Sow the seeds during the last weeks of summer—at the very end in the mildest areas, but up to four weeks earlier in colder districts. Two weeks before sowing, enrich the bed with general fertilizer at the rate of four ounces per square yard.

Make the furrows, and water them, the evening before sowing; space them one foot apart. Sow thinly and subsequently thin the seedlings to one- to two-inch spacings. Keep the furrows moist during dry weather. Complete the thinning the following spring, to leave four inches between plants.

The alternative to sowing in rows is to prepare a raised bed in a sheltered part of the garden and to sow the seeds at closer spacings. Leave the seedlings unthinned over the winter, but thin them as soon as possible in the following spring.

Most onion varieties are fairly hardy, but if you have a garden that is cold or exposed to wind, protect summer-planted onions with cloches or a thick mulch of straw or hay from late autumn onward. Onions sown in the late summer are ready for harvesting beginning in the following spring and continuing into summer.

Bulbing onions grown from seed need thinning to provide the bulbs with sufficient space to develop. Do this in stages, and use the thinnings as spring onions. Do not overthin: small storage onions, which result from close spacing, store better than very large ones, and often have a better flavor.

BUNCHING ONIONS

For an early crop, sow in late winter in a cold frame or under cloches. Such an early sowing under cloches will succeed only on light, free-draining soil, and provided the soil has started to warm up. It is necessary to place the cloches in position two weeks or so before the seeds are sown in order to heat the soil adequately.

One alternative is to grow an extra-hardy variety that will stand the winter outdoors. In this case, sow in about midsummer if you live in a cold northern district, or two or three weeks later where conditions are more favorable. Or you can simply sow in spring for a summer/autumn crop.

At any season, rake in a dressing of general fertilizer at two ounces per square yard before sowing, and work the seedbed down to a fine tilth. Be sure that the area is completely free of weeds.

Make the furrows a half-inch deep and six to twelve inches apart. The narrower spacing is adequate for plants grown in a bed, but more working room will be needed between rows on an open plot. Sow very sparingly, so that you won't have any need to thin the seedlings any further until the first plants are pulled. The less thinning needed the better, since the smell given off by root disturbance during thinning attracts onion flies, whose maggots can cause considerable damage to the crop.

In cold northern states, cover overwintered onions with cloches from about midautumn onward, or mulch thickly with straw, leaves, or hay.

To blanch the stems of bunching onions, hill up the soil around them with a hoe. Keep the bed completely free of weeds by frequent shallow cultivation with a hoe or a pronged cultivator.

PICKLING ONIONS

Since only small bulbs are wanted, there is no need to manure the ground if it is already quite fertile. Prepare a fine seedbed. You can enrich it with a general fertilizer at two ounces per square yard two weeks before sowing, but this is not essential for these quick-growing bulbs.

Sow the seeds of pickling onions in spring, and sow them relatively thickly, so that their foliage soon keeps weeds to a minimum. Space the seeds no more than a half-inch apart, in rows that are a foot apart. Alternatively, sow them at the same distance in wide rows or bands about four or six inches across. If the onions grow quickly and seem to be crowding each other, thin a few and use the thinnings as scallions.

As with other onions, pickling varieties should be kept well watered early in their growing season.

CARE OF THE CROP

Hoe or hand-weed between onion plants to prevent competition from weeds. Water during prolonged dry weather, but stop watering as soon as the bulbs begin to ripen. Bulbing varieties will benefit from some additional feeding when they are beginning to swell. Add general fertilizer to the site at about two ounces per square yard; if you use a dry form, sprinkle it along the side of the row and then rake it in.

HARVESTING

Bulbing onions Gather onions once the necks have softened and the leaves have turned yellow and collapsed. Just before this process is complete, ease the bulbs gently upward with a fork to aid the ripening process. This is especially useful during a damp season, when you may also have to bend the onion tops over by hand or with a hoe to encourage early ripening.

Harvest the crop a week or two later by lifting each bulb carefully with a fork. Choose a dry day on which to do this. Brush the soil from the roots, then place the onions in a greenhouse, a shed, or an open-fronted shelter of some sort to finish drying and ripening. The larger the bulbs are, the longer this process will take—up to two weeks or more. The onions are ready for storing when the leaves are brittle. Remove any with thick necks, since they will not keep very well.

Store only sound, firm bulbs in net bags or, simplest of all, by forming braids (see p.232). If these are hung in a cool, dry, and reasonably frost-free place, you should still have onions the following spring. Inspect them frequently during the winter and remove any that have gone soft or show signs of mold.

Sweet onions can be kept in the same way as storage onions, but at best they will hold for only a few weeks.

Bunching onions Pull up the first salad onions when they are about six inches tall, or as soon as they seem worth eating. This should be about eight weeks after sowing, and at this stage there will be hardly any sign of a bulb. Leave others in the ground for up to twice as long, or harvest them in the spring after a fall planting.

PESTS AND DISEASES

Onion maggots may cause trouble. Possible ailments include downy mildew and rot.

RECOMMENDED VARIETIES

Sweet onions

'Granex' is a very popular short-day variety; it is planted to produce the famous Vidalia and Maui sweet onions. The bulbs sometimes reach five inches in diameter and are either flat or slightly tapered toward the root end. Stores poorly, however.

'Bermuda' This is the sweet onion usually available for sale in supermarkets. The bulbs are large, flat, flavorful, and rather soft. A short-day variety.

'Sweet Spanish' Both white and yellow types are available. The very large, sweet bulbs do well in the North, and new hybrid varieties keep fairly well.

'Ringmaker' is an early yellow hybrid sweet onion. A long-day variety.

'Southport Red Globe' Not quite as large as the Spanish onions, but this purple-skinned variety keeps better. Long-day.

'Benny's Red' Large bulbs have a bright red skin and pinkish-white flesh. Long-day.

'Sweet Sandwich' is a large, long-keeping yellow onion with round or top-shaped bulbs. Its pungency decreases with storage. Long-day.

'Torpedo' This spindle-shaped variety has purplish-red skin and a mild flavor. It can be overwintered, but tends to bolt. Spring planting in northern regions can yield one-pound bulbs.

'Owa' is a yellow 'Torpedo' variety; it keeps well and matures in 100 days.

'Sweet Winter' A variety bred for overwintering at the seedling stage. Good for northern gardens, it is extremely cold hardy and yields large, flat yellow bulbs the following summer.

'Walla Walla Sweet' Bred to do well in the Pacific Northwest. Large, exceptionally sweet onions overwinter in mild areas.

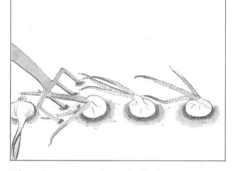

When they are nearly ready for harvesting, loosening bulbing onions with a fork helps to speed the process. This is especially useful during damp weather, when the foliage may take longer than usual to wither.

Greenhouse staging, or a bench in a well-ventilated shed, will provide ideal conditions for completing the ripening process. The stems and foliage must be completely dry before the crop is stored.

Storage onions

'Spartan Sleeper' is a good storage onion in most parts of the country. Bulbs have brown skin. Harvest in late summer.

'Copra' An early-maturing hybrid onion, with dark yellow skin and a chunky shape. Keeps extremely well.

'Buffalo' This very early variety is best in long-day areas. The bulbs are slightly flattened and have yellow skin.

'Tango' is a dark-red storage onion that has a mild flavor and slightly flattened bulbs.

'White Globe' Firm, smooth bulbs are pure white throughout. Keeps well.

'Improved Buccaneer' Round bronze bulbs average two inches in diameter. The plants produce dependably and keep well.

'Norstar' is a disease-resistant variety that produces early.

'Stuttgarter' is a variety that is usually sold in sets. The bulbs are small, flattened, and brown; they do not bolt if planted early.

'Golden Mosque' Another "set" variety. The bulbs are nearly round and yellow.

Bunching onions

'Evergreen' A very hardy white onion that produces slender scallions.

'Ishikura Long' is a moderately hardy type that sometimes reaches a foot in length. The stems are very thick and blanch well.

'Beltsville Bunching' The standard high-quality bunching onion for spring planting. The bulbs swell slightly, but the plants do well in hot, dry weather.

Pickling onions

'Crystal Wax Pickling PRR' These small white onions are globe-shaped and have almost no necks.

'Quicksilver' A standard white pickling variety; skins are thin and silvery.

SHALLOTS

Shallots (*Allium ascalonicum*) are used for pickling and as a milder, more subtle substitute for onions; they are one of the easiest crops to grow. Each offset planted in fall or early spring will sprout a cluster of six to twelve bulbs in just a few months.

There are pink- and yellow-skinned varieties of shallot and both types store extremely well—often for up to a year. Each year's crop provides bulbs for planting the following season. Make sure you start by purchasing certified virus-free sets.

Shallots need much the same growing conditions as onion sets—that is, an open position and well-worked, firm, and reasonably fertile soil that is either neutral or only slightly acid. Light soil is the best, if you can provide it.

GARLIC

Garlic (*Allium sativum*) is a member of the onion family grown for its unique pungent aroma and flavor. It is crushed or chopped to give a heightened flavor to almost any cooked dish. Garlic is indispensable in the modern kitchen and is an essential ingredient of Mediterranean and oriental cooking in particular. It is also said to have antiseptic properties and to work as an insect repellant and a cure for the common cold.

Each plant consists of about a dozen separate cloves. Home-grown garlic usually produces bigger, juicier, and more pungent cloves than those sold in supermarkets, so you may find that you need to grow only a few plants each year. An alternative to the ordinary kind is called elephant garlic; it has a very mild flavor and, as the name implies, large bulbs. It is best planted in the fall for a crop the following year.

Choose an open, sunny position and free-draining, fertile soil. Land manured for an earlier crop may be suitable, but dig in some more manure or compost before planting if you have any doubts about your soil's fertility. Spread lime if the soil is more than slightly acid—below pH 6.5. Raised beds are an asset if your soil is particularly heavy or does not drain well.

You can plant early in the spring, but it is usually better to plant during the autumn, if possible, since this gives more time for the bulbs to ripen during the following year. However, overwintering may not succeed on heavy, wet soil; under such conditions it is better to plant in late winter or early spring, but protect the bulbs from frost.

MAKING A START AND CARE

Plant in late fall or early spring, as soon as the soil will crumble. Choose medium-sized garlic cloves or shallot bulbs, and set them six inches apart in rows one foot apart, deep enough to bury all but their pointed tips, which should be facing up.

Water, if necessary, to keep the soil moist while the plants become established. Check after a few weeks to see whether any of the plants have been dislodged. Replant those that have as firmly as possible. Hoe regularly to keep down weeds.

Just before midsummer, draw some soil slightly away from the bulbs to help them ripen in the sun and air.

Plant shallots by digging a shallow hole with the tip of a trowel, then placing the bulb in this so that all but the tip is buried. Protect bulbs from birds until they have had time to anchor themselves with roots. This may take several weeks.

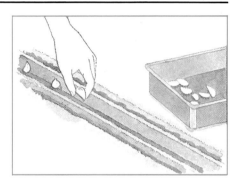

A continuous furrow, formed with a hoe and about one and a half inches deep, is a convenient way of planting garlic, and takes less time than making individual holes for each clove. Set cloves four inches apart, then cover with soil.

HARVESTING

Shallots The shriveling of the foliage in midsummer is a signal to dig up the bulbs with a fork and place them to dry in a well-ventilated place under cover. Once the leaves and stems are quite dead, split the bulbs into individual shallots and store these in net bags or braids in a cool, dry, frost-free place. You can also replant a few bulbs to provide next year's crop.

Garlic Dig up the plants with a fork during the second half of summer, after the foliage has turned yellow. Spread the bulbs to dry under cover, and hang them in bunches once the stems and leaves have withered. They can be braided like onions (see p.232), or you can use a few to start the next season's crop. Choose a cool, dry, frost-free place for storage—not the kitchen.

PESTS AND DISEASES

Garlic is rarely troubled by pests or diseases. Shallots may be affected by the problems of other onions (see p.215).

RECOMMENDED VARIETIES
Shallots

'True French' is a traditional European variety with pinkish cloves and a delicate flavor. 'Frogs' Legs' is a similar choice.
'Giant Red' Large, medium-red shallots.
'Gray' A yellow variety, with purplish flesh and a strong onion flavor.

Garlic

Most garlic is sold in sets under its generic name. It is possible to grow garlic from bulbs purchased in supermarkets or health-food stores, but those offered by seed companies are generally more reliable.

Shallot bulbs form in a tightly packed cluster around the single bulb originally planted. Dig up ripe bulbs, dry them under cover in a light, airy place, then break the clusters into individual bulbs before storing the crop.

PLANTING VEGETABLES, page 40
PESTS AND DISEASES, pages 172–175
THE ONION FAMILY, pages 186–187
ONIONS, pages 213–215

The seeds of many legumes and grains, if germinated and allowed to grow for a few days, produce sprouts that can be eaten when they are between half an inch and three inches long. These sprouted seeds deserve the increased popularity they are currently enjoying, since they are extremely quick and easy to grow. You can sprout seeds at any time of year, regardless of the space in your vegetable plot. Moreover, sprouts are highly nutritious, since they are rich in both protein and vitamins.

Sprouted seeds require minimum preparation before eating and are versatile in their culinary use. You can add them raw to mixed salads to give a crunchy texture, or they make a good addition to soups, stews, and various Chinese dishes. Mung beans (*Phaseolus mungo*) are the basis of much oriental cooking and are perhaps the best known of the sprouted seeds. The alfalfa sprouts that are commonly added to salads are another familiar edible seed sprout.

In fact, the sprouted seeds of most vegetables and grains are edible, and it is remarkable how such immature plants, only days old and grown without soil, can develop such distinctive flavor. One or two sprouts, notably those of tomatoes and potatoes, are actually harmful, however. Seeds from a farm or from seed packets may have been chemically treated, which may make them poisonous. For both these reasons, buy only approved types of seed sold especially for the purpose of sprouting by horticultural suppliers or health-food stores.

Remember also that since sprouted seeds develop so rapidly, they soon pass their peak of flavor and nutritional value. After this point they may become bitter. It is best to sprout small batches at intervals. The sprouts will keep for several days or up to two weeks in a sealed plastic bag in a refrigerator, provided they are rinsed daily with cold water to keep them fresh.

There are two principal methods of sprouting the seeds—one in a tray and the other in a jar—and results are reasonably assured with both of them, provided you follow a few simple rules. An average room temperature (between 55° and 70°F) is usually sufficient, but a short spell in a warm cupboard or closet will help one or two varieties and will also produce blanched shoots, which are whiter and crisper and in some cases have a better flavor than other sprouts (see p.218). Take care that the atmosphere is not too wet and warm, however, or the seeds will turn moldy. Rinsing the seeds in cold water—twice a day if possible—is essential to keep them fresh; otherwise they can become stagnant and develop a bitter taste.

Before starting with either method, rinse the seeds in a sieve under running water. Then cover them with tepid water and soak them for a few hours or overnight, until the seeds soften and swell up; the skins may begin to burst. Then rinse them again and let them drain.

SEED-SPROUTING KITS
There are now several types of seed-sprouting kits available from health-food stores and some garden centers. The most useful kind has several tiers so that you can sprout different kinds of seeds at the same time.

Most of the kits incorporate a method of pouring water in and out without removing the seeds, which makes rinsing quick and easy.

It is also possible to buy a plastic "sprouter cap" that fits most wide-mouthed preserving jars. The cap can be twisted into three positions, each with different-sized holes. The smallest-holed position is suitable for the smallest sprouted seeds, such as alfalfa. The middle position is for medium-sized seeds like mung beans, and the third, with the largest holes, is for rinsing off the hulls as the sprouted seeds grow.

SPROUTING IN A TRAY
This method is best for mung beans and lentils, which are eaten at an advanced stage of sprouting. Place a layer of doubled-over blotting paper, cotton wool, flannel, or several sheets of paper towels over the base of a waterproof tray. Dampen this layer thoroughly and distribute the seeds thickly in a single layer over it. Cover the tray with glass, aluminum foil, or a plastic bag and exclude all light until the seeds sprout. Keep the base moist by trickling in water at one end of the tray and pouring out any surplus at the other end. Do this daily.

For greener, unblanched shoots, move the tray to the light after the seeds have germinated. Either way, continue to keep the base moist while the shoots grow long enough to eat. Then cut them off the base with scissors.

Any shallow, waterproof tray that has been lined with absorbent material is suitable for sprouting seeds. To retain moisture and exclude light, cover the tray with glass and newspaper until the seeds have germinated.

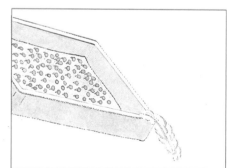

It is essential to keep the base moist until the sprouts are ready. To avoid disturbing the seeds, trickle water in at one end of the tray, and tilt it so that any not absorbed by the lining material runs out the other end.

SPROUTING IN A JAR

After soaking, pour a shallow layer (about a half-inch thick) of the damp seeds into a large glass jar, then cover the top with a circle of cotton or some other strong but porous material. Hold it in place securely with a rubber band.

Rest the jar on its side in a large bowl, and tilt it to drain off any surplus water. Place the bowl in the dark until the seeds sprout, then move them into the light if you would prefer green shoots.

Both before and after the seeds germinate, rinse and moisten them once or twice daily by half filling the jar with water and swirling the seeds gently. Drain the water out through the covering. To harvest the seeds, simply pull out the sprouts when they are long enough.

The jar method is an easy alternative to sprouting seeds in a tray or a purpose-made sprouter. Place a layer of soaked seeds in the bottom of the jar, cover the top with cloth, and secure it with an elastic band.

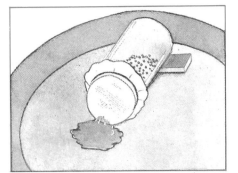

Drain off any surplus water by placing the jar on its side in a bowl, with its neck tilted down toward the cloth. Moisten the seeds with fresh water daily, and allow any surplus to drain away through the cloth as before.

TYPES OF SEED

Adzuki beans Grow in a tray or jar. Best blanched for eating when one inch long. Takes 4–5 days.

Alfalfa Grow in a jar. Excellent for salads, with a sweet garden-pea flavor. Eat when up to two inches long; let them turn green. Takes 1–3 days.

Mung beans Grow in a tray. Best eaten blanched when up to three inches long. Takes 3–8 days.

Fenugreek Grow in a warm place in a tray or jar. The spicy shoots are best eaten green when one inch long or up to three inches long. The curry flavor diminishes as sprouts get longer. Takes 3–5 days.

Wheat Grow in a warm place in a jar. Use blanched when only a half-inch long. Takes 4–5 days.

Buckwheat Grow in a jar or tray and harvest when between a half-inch and an inch long. Takes 2–4 days.

Chickpeas Grow in a jar and harvest when a half-inch long. Takes 3–4 days.

Lentils Grow in a jar and harvest when a half-inch to an inch long to eat raw or cooked. Takes 3–5 days.

Sunflower Grow in a jar and harvest after only two or three days when a half-inch long; otherwise the delicious shoots become too strong in taste. Takes 2–3 days.

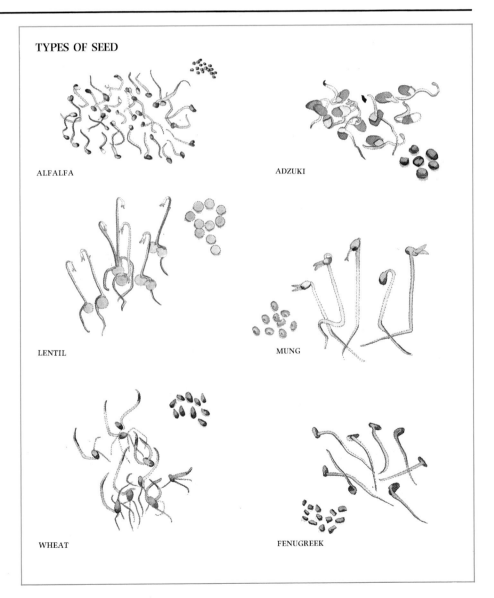

TYPES OF SEED

ALFALFA

ADZUKI

LENTIL

MUNG

WHEAT

FENUGREEK

It is well worth making space for a variety of herbs in any food garden. For the small space they occupy, herbs can have a considerable influence on the diversity and flavor of your cooking, and many are decorative (see Planting a Herb Garden, p.41).

This assortment of annual, biennial, and perennial plants will grow without fuss in almost any part of the garden that has free-draining soil. Some herbs, such as fennel and sage, are sufficiently ornamental to earn their place in the flower border. An alternative, especially where space is limited, is to cultivate a selection of herbs as pot plants. If you place the pots on the patio, the herbs will be handy for picking in any weather. Low-growing thyme, one of the least demanding herbs, will even grow in the spaces between paving slabs.

Most herbs die back in winter, except for evergreen perennials such as bay and rosemary. Some herbs, such as chervil and parsley, will grow throughout the winter, provided they have the protection of cloches, whereas others, like thyme, winter savory, and marjoram, will keep their leaves if they are grown in pots on a sunny indoor windowsill.

Although most herbs are all the better for being used fresh, many can be dried for winter use (see p.236). The common culinary herbs, such as basil, parsley, and chives, can also be frozen successfully.

You can start the majority of herbs from seed, or if you need only one or two plants, you can buy them from a garden center or nursery. Most perennials are easily propagated by division or by either tip cuttings of nonflowering shoots or heeled cuttings of semiripe wood (see p.41). The most suitable method of propagation is given under the individual entries that follow.

GROWING CONDITIONS

Most herbs like a sunny position and good drainage. Although the soil should be reasonably fertile, rich ground is seldom an advantage. Several herbs, including thyme, marjoram, winter savory, and sage, like a dryish position and develop more flavor and scent when grown in relatively poor soil. Others will tolerate light shade: these include chervil, angelica, and mint.

The practical purpose behind separating the plants in traditional patterned herb beds is to protect the weaker kinds from incursion by their more vigorous neighbors. Bear this in mind when devising your own planting scheme. Separation is particularly important for such invasive plants as mint and catnip. Prevent their roots from spreading, either by planting them in an old, bottomless bucket sunk up to its rim in the soil or by inserting vertical slates or a similar barrier around the plants. Alternatively, grow such herbs in a container.

GROWING HERBS IN CONTAINERS

Whether you choose pots or tubs, make sure there are drainage holes in the base before adding the potting soil. Use a soil-based mixture for perennial herbs and either a soil-based or a peat-based potting mixture for annuals.

Water the herbs frequently between spring and autumn during dry weather. Peat-based potting soil in particular should not be allowed to dry out or it will be difficult to saturate again.

Replant perennial plants in slightly larger pots each spring, or remove the upper three inches of potting soil and replace it with fresh material. Feed all plants with liquid fertilizer every two weeks during the spring and summer.

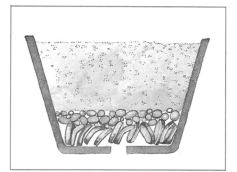

Most herbs like a free-draining soil, so be sure that the potting mixture in containers drains well. Place a layer of broken pots on the bottom, followed by a layer of gravel or small stones; then fill the pot or tub with good-quality potting soil.

There is no need to repot perennial herbs every year, provided the container is big enough. Simply remove the top three inches of soil and top-dress with fresh potting soil to the same level; do this annually.

SOWING SEEDS OUTDOORS, pages 36–37
GROWING HERBS, page 41

HERBS, pages 188–192
FREEZING AND DRYING HERBS, page 236

ANGELICA

This beautiful, hardy biennial herb (*Angelica archangelica*) grows tall (up to six feet high) and has bright green, serrated leaves that are smooth and glossy.

The young leaves and stems can be added sparingly to salads and to stewed fruits; both the leaves and the root can be used to flavor fish. The ridged, hollow stem can also be used as a candied decoration for cakes and cookies.

Sow seeds in midspring in shallow furrows, preferably in a rich, moist soil; sow them in groups of three or four about three feet apart. Harvest the leaves before the plant flowers, after which it loses its vigor. Dry them in the shade in order to preserve their color and scent. The seeds can be collected as soon as they ripen for planting out immediately.

BASIL

There are several varieties of this tender annual, which has a powerful, spicy flavor all its own. It is a valuable addition to salads, especially tomato salads, and can be used in cooked vegetable, meat, cheese, and tomato dishes. It is the basic ingredient of *pesto*, an Italian pasta sauce.

Sweet basil (*Ocimum basilicum*) has large, strongly flavored leaves and grows to about three feet high. There are also a beautiful purple-leaved variety, a lemon-scented variety, and several dwarf kinds. Bush basil, also known as Greek basil, is more compact and has small pointed leaves. It is a good choice for growing in a pot, and for bringing indoors during the winter.

Either sow under glass in gentle warmth during the first half of spring or outdoors in late spring. Space plants six to twelve inches apart, or plant them in individual pots.

Pinch out the tops to induce the plants to bush out, and pick the leaves as needed. Preserve by drying or freezing.

BORAGE

This easily grown annual (*Borago officinalis*) grows to a height of two or three feet. Its young leaves, when bruised or shredded, taste like cucumber and are used to flavor salads and drinks such as wine cup. The sweet-tasting blue flowers can also garnish salads or be candied and used for cake and cookie decoration.

Borage will grow in most types of soil. Sow the seeds where they are to grow, in spring for summer use and in summer for autumn use; sow them a half-inch deep and one foot apart, in groups of three. They will germinate rapidly. Thin to leave only the strongest seedling in each group.

LEMON BALM

The common name of this hardy perennial derives from the fragrance of its heart-shaped leaves when crushed. Lemon balm (*Melissa officinalis*) is easy to grow and is tolerant of most soils and of partial shade; it forms strong, bushy growth. There is also an attractive variegated variety.

The leaves provide a refreshing flavoring for summer drinks, including herb tea, and are a valuable addition to green and fruit salads as well as to cooked dishes. They may be used fresh or frozen in cooking; dry them to preserve their aroma.

Sow the seeds in a fine seedbed in midspring; later thin the seedlings to eighteen inches. Cut the plants back to near ground level in autumn, and cover the roots with straw if severe weather threatens. Propagate by division in spring or autumn.

BAY

This semihardy, slow-growing evergreen shrub (*Laurus nobilis*) will grow to fifteen feet or more if unchecked. With pruning, it can be kept to a more compact three feet. It is a good idea to grow a bay within the confines of a large pot or tub, especially in the North, where it must be moved indoors for the winter. The aromatic bay leaves are an essential ingredient of *bouquets garnis* and are used in many meat dishes and to flavor pâtés.

Buy a young, container-grown plant and set it in a sheltered spot. Pick the young leaves as needed; they are slightly bitter when fresh, but they sweeten as they dry.

Propagate by semiripe cuttings in late summer or early autumn.

CHERVIL

The finely cut leaves of this hardy annual (*Anthriscus cerefolium*) resemble parsley and give a delicate aniseed flavor to salads, sauces, and soups. Chervil is a fast-growing plant whose leaves remain green in winter; it does well when grown under cover, but bolts quickly in summer.

Sow in spring for summer use, or in late summer for potting up and growing indoors during the winter. Leave eight inches between plants. Keep the soil moist during dry weather to deter bolting.

Pick the leaves before the plants flower. They may be dried if you wish.

CHIVES

Chives (*Allium schoenoprasum*) are the smallest member of the onion family and are invaluable for giving a mild, oniony flavor to salads; they are also used to garnish soups and vegetable dishes, or they may be added to cold sauces. The plant is a hardy perennial and grows in clumps of narrow, hollow, spearlike leaves, up to one foot tall. Chives are easily grown and will thrive in either sun or partial shade; moisture is not essential.

Sow the seeds in place during the spring, and thin the seedlings to eight-inch spacings. In the first year, pinch off the round pink or purple flower heads before they open. Cut back the leaves periodically to encourage fresh growth.

Lift and divide the clumps every three years during spring or autumn. Plant them out in clumps of four or five, ten inches apart, preferably in rich soil.

DILL

Dill (*Anethum graveolens*) is a tall-growing hardy annual which reaches four feet in height. Its delicately flavored feathery leaves can be chopped in salads and are a particularly apt flavoring for fish. The seeds, and sometimes the stems, are used in pickling, especially of cucumbers.

Sow the seeds during spring or early summer, and later thin to leave nine inches between plants. Keep the plants well watered and weed-free. Start picking the foliage when the plants are about four inches high; they will resprout at least once. The leaves can be used fresh or dried.

Enclose the seedheads in paper bags to catch the ripe seeds, then hang them upside down under cover. Collect and store the seeds when they are quite dry.

GINGER

Ginger (*Zingiber officinalis*) is a tropical perennial that can be grown either in a heated greenhouse or in a container outdoors during the summer months, provided it is brought indoors for the winter. It is an essential flavoring in curries, pickles, and spiced meat, fish, rice, and vegetable dishes. It has a rich, pungent flavor.

Ginger is a root, which you can buy in some supermarkets or at health-food stores. When planted, it sends up lilylike fronds up to three feet high and produces a spike of yellow, purple-lipped flowers. At the end of the growing season it will have produced additional bulbs for culinary use. It can be used fresh or dried or can be preserved in syrup or vinegar.

CORIANDER

Both the seeds and the young leaves of this hardy annual (*Coriandrum sativum*) have culinary uses. The aromatic leaves give a spicy taste to soups, curries, and Mexican dishes (in Mexican cooking the herb is called *cilantro*), and the dried and ground seeds, used either whole or crushed, are a favorite, if not essential, ingredient of curries and of pickles.

Sow the seeds in spring and late summer and thin to a spacing of six inches. Germination is slow. The unripe seeds have a strange smell, which disappears once they are mature. Cut off the ripe seedheads and dry them thoroughly under cover. Rub the seeds out, then store them, either whole or ground into a powder.

FENNEL

This handsome perennial (*Foeniculum vulgare*) grows to five feet or more and is usually grown as an annual. Fennel bears a mass of feathery foliage—usually green, but there is a lovely bronzed variety—which gives a pronounced aniseed flavor to sauces served with fish, as well as to salads and soups. The aromatic seeds of fennel are used in pickling.

Sow groups of seeds eighteen inches apart during the spring and thin to the strongest single seedling. Gather the leaves and seedheads as for dill.

HORSERADISH

Although horseradish (*Amoracia rusticana*) is a hardy, long-lived perennial, it has a spreading, weedy habit that makes it advisable to dig up every part of the roots each year. They may be used raw or dried—but much of the flavor is lost during cooking. The traditional way to use horseradish is to grate or mince the roots and use them immediately to make horseradish sauce or cream for serving with meat.

To start growing horseradish, plant one-foot lengths of root, purchased from a nursery, at two-foot intervals and one foot deep during early spring. Harvest the roots during autumn; store them under cover in sand. Keep a few roots for replanting the following year.

HYSSOP

This hardy, partially evergreen perennial (*Hyssopus officinalis*) is of Mediterranean origin and has been used in cooking since Roman times. It has a bushy habit and can be used to form a low hedge. It has attractive shiny leaves and purple tubular spikes of flowers and grows up to three feet tall. The leaves have a pungent, minty, but rather bitter flavor, so use them sparingly. Their chief value is as a flavoring for soups, or to balance fatty meats or oily fish.

Sow seeds in a seedbed during the spring, and later plant out the seedlings at one-foot spacings in a light, well-drained soil. Set them a little closer to form a hedge, and cut off the growing tip of each plant. Use the leaves fresh or dried.

Hyssop plants should be renewed every three or four years; they may be propagated from tip cuttings.

MINT

Mint is a widely used and easily grown perennial herb, traditionally used in much Middle Eastern cooking and to make mint tea. There are several different species and hybrids, but the most familiar is spearmint or common mint (*Mentha spicata*). Other mints worth growing include apple or round-leaved mint (*Mentha rotundifolia*), peppermint (*Mentha x piperita*), and pineapple mint (*Mentha rotundifolia variegata*).

Mint is very hardy, and all species will grow almost anywhere; they prefer a semi-shaded position and damp conditions. To reduce their invasiveness, restrict them inside a buried bottomless bucket or similar container. Plant pieces of root two inches deep and about one foot apart during the spring and water well until they are established. Use the leaves fresh, dried, or frozen.

Propagate by lifting and dividing the roots during spring.

ROSEMARY

This semihardy evergreen herb (*Rosmarinus officinalis*) of Mediterranean origin grows into a bushy shrub some three feet tall, though it can be kept smaller by pruning and picking. There are also prostrate or creeping varieties that are less hardy. Rosemary has a strong, fragrant scent and taste and is widely used to flavor roast meat, stuffings, and sauces.

Rosemary likes a well-drained, fertile soil and a sunny, sheltered position. Sow the seeds in a bed outdoors, or in a pot, during spring. Thin the seedlings to four to six inches apart before planting out in early summer; allow two to three feet between plants. Rosemary can also be planted as a hedge in mild regions, in which case the plants should be spaced fifteen inches apart. Take semiripe cuttings during the summer months.

MARJORAM and OREGANO

These Mediterranean herbs are closely related members of the *Origanum* genus. The leaves of both may be used as a flavoring for meat, poultry, and pasta sauces.

Italian oregano (*Origanum onites*) is a compact, semihardy perennial that needs a warm, sheltered site. It may also be grown as a pot plant. Sow the slow-germinating seeds in spring and thin to one-foot spacings, or plant nursery-grown plants the same distance apart. Oregano may be propagated from cuttings.

Sweet marjoram (*Origanum majorana*), although naturally perennial, is not very hardy and may have to be treated as an annual. It has soft leaves and a sweeter flavor than oregano, and it grows twice as large, to two feet. Marjoram can either be started under glass in early spring or sown outdoors in midspring. Space the plants one foot apart.

PARSLEY

Parsley (*Petroselinum crispum*) is possibly the best-known culinary herb of all. Because it is a biennial, it runs to seed in its second year, so it is usually best grown as an annual. It needs moist conditions and a fertile soil, and is quite decorative.

Sow the seeds in spring for use during summer and autumn, and in summer to provide tender leaves during winter. Cover the plants with cloches in cold districts or during severe weather. Sow in shallow furrows where the plants are to grow, and thin the seedlings to about nine inches. Alternatively, sow in a pot and bring this indoors before winter. The seeds are slow to germinate, so keep the soil moist.

There are two main types of parsley: the kind with curly leaves, such as 'Banquet,' and the flat-leaved Italian variety, for example 'Catalogno.'

SAGE

Sage (*Salvia officinalis*) is a hardy evergreen perennial which grows to one or two feet high. The common sage has attractive gray-green leaves, but there are also purple- and golden-leaved forms. Sage is a good flavoring for many meats, especially veal and liver, and is used in the preparation of stuffings and in Italian cooking.

Sage prefers a well-drained, light soil and a sunny, sheltered position. Sow the seeds outdoors or in a cold frame during the spring, and later transplant the seedlings to allow one foot between plants.

Sage is fairly short-lived, so propagate new plants by dividing the older ones in spring or autumn every three years. Prune the shrubs back lightly in late summer. Use the leaves fresh or dried.

SAVORY

Both winter and summer savory have a fairly strong, spicy flavor that goes well with peas, beans, stuffings, and sauces.

Summer savory (*Satureja hortensis*) is a half-hardy annual with an erect, bushy form. Winter savory (*Satureja montana*) is a hardy perennial with evergreen leaves that has a more spreading habit.

Sow the seeds of either sort in midspring and later thin the plants to nine-inch spacings. The seeds germinate slowly. If they are transferred to pots in late summer, both types of savory can be grown on a windowsill indoors during the winter. Pick the leaves while they are young; the leaves of summer savory may be dried.

THYME

This aromatic Mediterranean herb (*Thymus* sp.) has small leaves and is extensively used in soups, stuffings, and many cooked dishes. The two most widely grown species are both hardy, dwarf, and evergreen.

Common or English thyme (*Thymus vulgaris*) is strongly flavored; lemon thyme (*Thymus x citriodorus*) has a more subtle aroma. There are beautiful variegated forms of both species.

All thymes are sun-loving and prefer a well-drained, fertile soil. Raise common thyme from a spring sowing outdoors, and transplant the seedlings to nine-inch spacings. Buy nursery-grown plants of lemon thyme in spring, and set them one foot apart. Renew the plants every three years or so; propagate them by division in spring. The leaves of all thymes may be dried.

Low-growing thymes will do well in crevices between paving stones, provided there is some soil beneath for their roots.

HERBS FOR A PURPOSE
Evergreen leaves
Bay
Rosemary
Sage

Basic culinary herbs
Mint
Sage
Thyme
Chives
Parsley
Basil

For pots and windowboxes
Basil
Borage
Chervil
Oregano and marjoram
Summer savory
Tarragon
Thyme

Bouquets garnis
Parsley (2–3 sprigs)
Marjoram (1 sprig)
Thyme (1 sprig)
Bay leaf

TARRAGON

This narrow-leaved, hardy perennial herb (*Artemisia dracunculus*) has a unique flavor, somewhat reminiscent of licorice. The leaves, which are a basic ingredient of *fines herbes*, are used in vinegar-making and to flavor chicken and other white meats, as well as in sauces and various cooked dishes. They may be dried or frozen.

The roots of the bushy plant are vulnerable to severe frost, so cover them with a layer of ashes, straw, or leaves if you live in a cold area. Restrict the roots in some way to prevent them from spreading.

Russian tarragon (*A. d. inodora*) has an inferior flavor to French tarragon (*A. d. sativa*); French tarragon is propagated only by cuttings, so seeds are usually of the Russian type.

LEMON VERBENA

This semihardy deciduous perennial shrub (*Aloysia triphylla*) can grow up to six feet tall. Its sweet, lemon-scented leaves can be used chopped in stuffings or to flavor fish and chicken as well as jams and jellies. It can also make a refreshing tea and is used to give fragrance to potpourris. Harvest the leaves at any time and store them in an airtight container; they will retain their flavor and scent for a long time.

Plant lemon verbena in a sunny position, though in a fairly dry, poor soil to keep its roots hardy. Cut the plant down after frost and cover its roots with straw or leaves until spring if you live in a mild district. Alternatively, overwinter it indoors in a pot.

STORING AND PRESERVING

If you store and preserve the bounty your food garden provides, you will be able to enjoy the tastes of summer all winter long, as well as the knowledge that nothing from your food garden has been allowed to go to waste.

The aim of all storage and preservation of fruits and vegetables is to prevent deterioriation after the crops have been harvested. If it is not preserved in some way, all food will decay sooner or later, but the time this takes can vary between hours and months.

As a rule, you should aim to harvest food for storing or preservation when it is young, full of flavor, and in prime condition. Vegetables are best harvested in the morning, and fruit should also be picked early in the day. If the weather is very hot, take a bucket of cold water with you, and plunge vegetables into it as soon as they are picked.

Storing and preserving food calls for considerable effort on the part of the gardener and/or the cook, but in some instances nature does provide a helping hand—in the form of vegetables and fruit that will last for at least part of the winter with only the minimum of assistance. Hardy roots such as parsnips and rutabagas and long-keeping apple varieties that need little more than a frost-free storage room are examples.

Most other crops need more careful attention if they are to keep well. Fruits such as pears should be individually wrapped before they are stored, as should the apple varieties that are more susceptible to decay. Beets, carrots, potatoes, onions, and other main crops also need protection if they are to last.

Of all the preserving methods commonly practiced, drying is one of the most ancient. It works successfully for many herbs and for certain fruits, though it is less well suited to preserving vegetables. By exposing the plant material to heat and by driving out most of the water it contains, drying makes it much more impervious to decay.

Fruits and vegetables preserved by canning keep well—often for well over a year. In the canning process, the food is heated and vacuum sealed. This insures that decay organisms are either killed or prevented from multiplying.

Freezing is the most popular method of preserving, and works not by killing bacteria and molds but by arresting their growth. There are very few crops that cannot be successfully frozen.

Though you will be aiming to pick vegetables and fruit for preserving when they are young and in the best possible condition, this is sometimes impracticable. You might find yourself, for instance, with a large crop of raspberries soaked by persistent rainfall, or a glut of overgrown zucchini on your return from vacationing. In situations such as these you need to improvise: you can freeze the raspberries as a purée, and cook the zucchini as part of a *ratatouille*, then freeze it.

Fruits and vegetables with a high water content, such as lettuce, melons, potatoes, and cucumbers, do not freeze successfully except as a purée or in soup. As the water in their cells turns to ice during the freezing process, the cells themselves—and thus the texture of the food—are destroyed.

Additional time-honored and appealing methods of preserving the home-grown harvest include pickling, in which vegetables are preserved in vinegar; salting; jam making; and crystallizing foods in sugar. You will find recipes for these in cookbooks and magazines.

Gentle handling is vital for fruit of all kinds, but especially for those that are to be stored for some time. Most fruit bruises easily, and even the slightest damage can reduce its storage life. Set aside for immediate consumption any fruit that shows signs of damage caused by pests or disease.

Freezing and canning are the only practical ways to keep berries and some tree fruits for eating during the winter (see pp.228–229 and pp.234–235). Some berries, such as strawberries and raspberries, deteriorate very rapidly after being picked. Others can be kept for varying lengths of time in a refrigerator (see below).

Some of the firm-fleshed tree fruits, notably apples and pears, can be stored in their natural state for winter use, though only a minority will keep in good condition until well into the new year. The particular variety is the critical factor, and their keeping qualities are noted in the descriptions of individual recommended varieties (see p.95 for apples and p.97 for pears). Apples and pears can also be cut up and dried, as can some other tree fruits.

STORING FRESH TREE FRUITS
Apples The best conditions for keeping apples in their natural state are a cool, dark, frost-free storage room where the atmosphere is fairly humid. If you have an unheated cellar, this is an ideal place.

Some apple growers wrap the fruit in special oiled paper or in tissue before storing it, but others do not. Wrapped apples probably keep slightly better than unwrapped ones, but wrapping makes it less easy to spot the first signs of rot.

Place the apples, wrapped or unwrapped, either in molded cardboard trays or in fruit boxes with extended corner posts to support the tray above (see p.91).
Pears Store pears as for apples (see p.97), though cardboard trays are less suitable for pears because of the shape of the fruit. Pick pears for storage before they are fully ripe and check frequently for signs of ripening, since most varieties remain in peak condition for only a brief period.
Peaches and nectarines The fruit will keep for up to a week in a refrigerator. It helps if the container is first lined with cotton wool. Peaches and nectarines also pass their peak quickly, so check them frequently.
Apricots Stored in a cool place, or in a refrigerator, apricots will remain in good condition for three weeks or more.
Cherries, plums, mulberries, and figs Eat these fruits as soon as possible after harvesting, or store them briefly in the refrigerator.
Quince Stored in a cool cellar or shed, these fruits will last for about two months. They can also be kept in a refrigerator.

STORING BERRIES
As a general rule, the storage life of berries is prolonged by cool conditions. Chill them as soon as possible, and pick the fruit early in the day, before it has had a chance to be warmed by the sun.
Strawberries Eat the ripe fruit within twelve hours of picking, or within two days if the fruit is placed in the refrigerator at once. If you pick strawberries while they are only two-thirds red, they will ripen in a refrigerator over a ten-day period.
Raspberries Pick these berries early in the day. Any that are not fully ripe will store for up to a week in a refrigerator, but fully ripe ones will last for only a couple of days.
Blueberries and cranberries These keep for a week or so at room temperature and for up to three times as long in a refrigerator.

Blackberries and hybrid berries Pick the berries while they are dry, if possible. If they are placed in a refrigerator, dry ones will keep for two or three days.
Currants Use currants as soon as possible after picking. They last a little longer if they are kept on the stalk, or "strig."
Gooseberries In the case of a temporary surplus, unpicked berries will keep without spoiling for much longer than other berries. This is more satisfactory than trying to keep the fruits once they have been picked.
Grapes Provided they are kept chilled in a refrigerator, undamaged fruits will remain sound for up to two months.
Kiwi fruits These fruits will store for about two weeks at room temperature, or for two or three months in a refrigerator. Other fruits nearby speed ripening, however.

DRYING
Dried fruits will keep for many months. This method works well for apples, pears, apricots, peaches, plums, and grapes. The fruit may be dried whole, halved, quartered, or sliced.

Lay the fruit on cheesecloth-covered wire cake racks or trays, with the cut surfaces uppermost. Dry them slowly in an oven at 120° to 150°F for several hours; keep the oven at the lowest temperature for the first hour so that the skins do not burst.

When the fruit is ready it should feel springy and soft; no moisture should come out when you press it. Cool the fruit at room temperature for twelve hours afterward, covered with a cloth. Then pack it in boxes lined with greaseproof or waxed paper and store in a dry, frost-free place.
Apples Peel, core, and cut them crosswise into slices a quarter-inch thick, and put them on skewers. Place in a cool oven with the door slightly ajar for four to six hours.
Pears Peel, core, and quarter, then drop the pieces into lightly salted water. Place on trays in a cool oven for four to six hours.
Apricots, peaches, and plums Place on trays and dry slowly in a cool oven with the door open. Once the skins begin to shrivel, raise the temperature to 150°F. Allow whole fruit two days to dry and halved fruit a day.
Grapes Use seedless grapes if possible. Wash and pat dry, and dry on trays in a cool oven for eight hours, gradually increasing the temperature to 150°F.

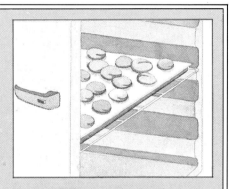

Plums and other stone fruit can be dried in a slow oven. Place the fruit in a single layer on a cheesecloth-covered tray; larger fruits are best halved and stoned first. Drying takes up to 48 hours, depending on the size and water content of the fruit. When it is ready, all the juices will have evaporated.

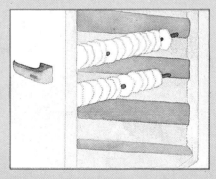

To dry apple rings, dip them in salted water to prevent them from discoloring, then pat them with absorbent paper to remove all excess water, place them on wooden skewers, and hang them in a slow oven. They should be thoroughly dry within six hours. Allow the rings to cool completely, then store them in airtight jars.

STORING VEGETABLES

Most vegetables keep better in the short term than berries do. Among the exceptions, however, are leafy vegetables such as lettuce and spinach, which should be eaten as soon as possible after gathering. Harvest them early in the day, while they are still cool and before they become dehydrated. If leafy vegetables or salad greens have to be kept for a while, place them in a refrigerator, then enclose them in a plastic bag once they have cooled off completely.

Harvest and handle with great care all vegetables that have to be kept for more than a few hours. Do not store any that are accidentally cut or bruised, or those showing signs of damage from pests or disease. Instead, use them right away.

STORING OUTDOORS

Some vegetable crops are sufficiently winter hardy to be left where they are growing until you need them. With certain qualifications, this applies to root vegetables such as carrots, beets, turnips, parsnips, and rutabagas as well as to leeks, celery, and celeriac. It is also applicable to Brussels sprouts, Savoy cabbages, and other brassicas that mature in winter.

The qualifying factors are mainly to do with soil and region. Root crops fare much better, and are easier to harvest, when they are left in light, free-draining soil instead of in sticky clay. Crops that will survive the winter in a relatively mild climate zone will suffer damage from hard frosts in an exposed northern garden.

If you have heavy soil, the best solution is to harvest root crops during late autumn or early winter and store them under cover. If your winter climate is risky, protect the plants with a thick layer of straw in early winter, and cover this in turn with netting pegged to the ground (see p.159). Except in the most severe weather, this will prevent the soil from freezing rock-hard, which would make harvesting impossible.

Under adverse climate conditions, select the hardiest varieties of brassicas or grow early-maturing varieties of vegetables that are suitable for freezing for winter use.

Always dig potatoes before winter and keep them in a frost-proof storage room.

STORING ROOT CROPS AND ONIONS

A safer means of storing root vegetables, provided you have the space, is in boxes in a ventilated shed or outbuilding. Place the roots in layers with slightly dampened peat moss or sand around them; take care not to include any damaged crops. When the weather is severe, place straw over and around the boxes for extra protection.

Store potatoes in paper or burlap sacks (not plastic, since they need to breathe). Be sure that their skins are completely dry first; the best way to do this is to dig up the tubers in the morning during a dry spell and leave them to dry on the surface of the soil for a few hours. Close the sacks and keep them in the dark in a frost-free, ventilated place. A generous packing of straw beneath, around, and over the bags is the best protection against possible frost. But never cover the sacks so thickly that you prevent a flow of air in and out.

Onions and garlic also need frost-free storage, but they should not be kept in the dark or they will start to sprout. Once they have been fully dried and ripened in a cool, dry place, either hang them in nylon or string net bags, or string them up by twisting their withered stems around a length of rope or thick string.

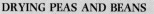

DRYING PEAS AND BEANS

Dried peas and beans are useful sources of protein. If you want to grow them for this purpose, choose appropriate varieties such as 'Jacobs Cattle Bean,' 'Soldier Bean,' or any of the varieties mentioned on p.136. Both southern peas and smooth-seeded garden peas are suitable for drying.

Simply leave the pods on the plant, provided the weather is dry, until they are withered and dry. In damp weather, pull up the plants and hang them in an airy, dry place. Shell them when the pods have withered, and leave the beans or peas spread out for a few days until they are completely dry. Store them in an airtight container.

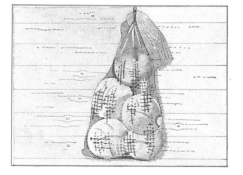

Peat moss is the ideal storage medium for carrots and other root crops; it should be slightly damp to prevent the crop from drying out. Store the roots in layers, with peat moss between each, in a frost-free place.

Burlap or paper sacks allow stored potatoes to breathe and permit the evaporation of moisture from around the crop. By contrast, moisture levels build up inside plastic sacks, which results in rotting. To protect the sacks from frost, stand them on straw, then pack more straw between and over them.

The solid heads of winter cabbages will keep for several months if placed in a net and hung in a cool but frost-free shed or cellar. Before you store the cabbages, cut each cleanly at the base and remove the outside leaves.

Tie onions to a rope by their stems and hang them in a light, dry, frost-free place. They should keep throughout the winter.

Canning offers a reliable means of preserving most kinds of fruit with its natural flavor, color, and texture intact. Canned fruit will keep well for one to two years, after which time the quality and nutritional value of the fruit will deteriorate, though it can still be eaten perfectly safely. Except in the case of tomatoes, canning is generally far less satisfactory for vegetables than freezing is. The most important requirements for successful canning are good-quality produce and rigid adherence to the rules of timing and hygiene.

WATER OR SYRUP?

Fruit can be satisfactorily canned in either water or syrup. The advantage of syrup is that it improves the color and the flavor of the fruit.

Prepare the syrup beforehand. Allow one pound of granulated sugar to every quart of water. Add the sugar to half the quantity of water, bring it slowly to the boil, stirring all the time, then let it boil fairly rapidly for one or two minutes.

Add the rest of the water. At the same time, when canning sweet fruit (pears, cherries, or strawberries), add two tablespoons of lemon juice to each quart of syrup; this will increase its acidity. Remove any scum from the surface before using the syrup for canning.

Cherries, small plums, peaches, and pears can be canned in a brandy syrup. Make a heavier syrup, allowing one pound of sugar to every pint of water. Add an equal quantity of brandy when the syrup is cool. Prick the fruit with a stainless steel fork so the syrup can permeate its flesh.

CANNING EQUIPMENT

You will need a large canner or very large cooking pan with a tight-fitting lid; it must be at least as deep as the jars, with space for a wire rack in the bottom, and should be big enough to hold at least three jars, allowing for a small space between them. Ready-made canners are useful, but they can be expensive.

Jars are available in a range of sizes and types; they come complete with tops and a supply of rubber seals. The widely used two-piece type has flat metal tops with an integral rubber ring, held in place by metal screw bands. Another popular kind has glass lids, separate rubber rings, and spring clip closures. The quart size is the most convenient, and the instructions here are based on this size.

Be sure that the rims of the jars are perfectly smooth and free from chips, or the closed jars will not remain airtight. Always check them carefully before use and fit fresh rubber seals and metal tops each time.

PREPARING THE FRUIT

In general, the small, firmer fruits, such as plums and apricots, can be canned more successfully than the softer berries, which lose their texture more easily.

Use only sound, ripe fruit for canning. The exception is gooseberries, which are better when slightly underripe. Remove the stalks and leaves of all fruit. It is better not to wash berries, though a quick rinse in cold water is sometimes necessary.

Wash stone fruit. Small plums and apricots may be canned whole, but large ones can be packed more closely if they are cut in half and the stones removed. Peel, halve, and stone peaches before canning.

Bulk quantities of the more common fruits, such as apples, can be preserved as canned pulp or purée (see below). This is also a good way to use up less-than-perfect fruit, such as windfalls, if you have a glut.

Choose small tomatoes for packing closely in the jars, or cut larger ones into halves or quarters. Preserve them in water or tomato juice. Alternatively, purée or juice them before you can them.

The preparation and timing for individual fruits are given in the chart opposite.

PACKING THE JARS

Wash the jars and tops carefully in hot water before filling; rinse and drain them, but leave them wet. Pack the fruit carefully and tightly; use the handle of a wooden spoon to help, but don't squash them.

As a rough guide, a quart jar will hold about two pounds of fruit. Pack in layers, or in concentric rings, and always leave a headspace of a half-inch or so; this allows air to escape during processing.

If your jars have separate rubber rings, soak them in warm water for about fifteen minutes. Dip them in boiling water immediately before putting them on the jars, to make them more supple.

For the water-bath method (see below), pour hot water or syrup gently over the contents of the jars, causing as few air bubbles as possible. Top up the jars to insure that the fruit is totally submerged.

Put the rubber seals and the tops in place. Secure the jars, but leave screw bands slightly loose, to allow air to escape during sterilization. Spring clips are designed to allow the steam to escape.

STERILIZATION
Water-bath method

It is necessary to insulate the jars from the hot base of the pan with a wire rack, a piece of wood, or a folded piece of cloth.

Pour enough water into the pan to reach the top of the jars and bring it to a boil. Carefully lower the jars into the pan, being sure to keep them from touching one another or the sides of the pan. Add enough boiling water to cover them completely.

Boil the jars for the times given in the chart opposite, but be sure to adjust for differences in size of the jars and altitude. Start counting when the water reaches a fast boil. Reduce the time by 10 percent if you are using pint jars; increase it by fifteen minutes for half-gallon jars. High altitudes require you to add one or two minutes for every thousand feet above sea level.

When the time is up, remove the jars and place them on wood, cloth, or paper; a cold surface might cause them to crack. Tighten the screw band of each jar, and leave the jars undisturbed for at least twelve hours.

Pressure canning

Pressure canning is the easiest method if you are canning a large quantity of fruit or vegetables. Simply follow the directions provided by the manufacturer. Times are noted in the chart opposite.

TESTING PROCESSED JARS

After twenty-four hours, the contents of the jars will have cooled completely and a vacuum should have formed. To find out whether the lids are securely sealed, remove the screw band or clip and lift the jar by its top. If it is airtight, the vacuum inside will hold it in place.

Wipe the jars, label them with the contents and the date, and store them in a cool, dark, well-ventilated place. A pantry or cellar is ideal.

To open canned fruit, stand the jar in hot water for a few minutes, then gently pry off the lid with the tip of a knife. Keep the opened jar covered in the refrigerator and use the contents within two or three days.

MAKING PULPS AND PURÉES

This is an economical way of preserving many fruits and some vegetables, such as tomatoes.

For pulps, simmer the prepared fruit in a little water until it is thoroughly cooked. Pour it into hot jars while it is boiling hot and seal them at once. Sterilize them by bringing the surrounding water up to boiling point and keeping it boiling for twenty minutes, or ten minutes in the case of tomato pulp. Remove the jars and allow them to cool, then check the seal.

To make a purée, blend and/or sieve the raw fruit or cooked pulp and sweeten and flavor or season it to taste. Sterilize in the same way as for pulps.

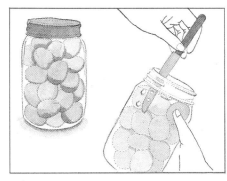

Release any trapped air bubbles from the jars after filling them with fruit. This helps to create a good seal. Tapping the sides may be sufficient; otherwise, insert a knife blade very gently down the side of the jar where the air is lodged.

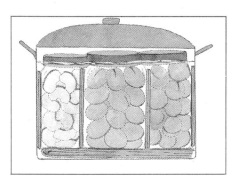

Place a piece of wood, a wire rack, a folded cloth, or even a layer of folded newspaper on the base of the pan beneath the jars. To reduce the risk of cracking, prevent the jars from touching each other by inserting a folded cloth between them.

A pair of nonslip tongs is invaluable for lifting jars out of the scalding water after they have been sterilized. Place them on a wooden surface, then tighten each of the lids.

CANNING TIMES

Accurate timing is critical for safe, long-term preservation. Figures are for quart jars. Check with your local agricultural extension agent for government guidelines; in general, allow an extra fifteen minutes for half-gallon jars, and reduce times by 10 percent for pint jars.

FRUIT	PREPARATION	WATER BATH	PRESSURE CANNING
Raspberries	Pick over, remove stalks.	15 minutes	1 lb./ 15 minutes
Blackberries and hybrid berries	Use only firm fruit.	15 minutes	1 lb./ 15 minutes
Gooseberries	Use underripe fruit; cut off stems with scissors.	15 minutes	1 lb./ 15 minutes
Currants	Remove stalks; rinse.	15 minutes	1 lb./ 15 minutes
Blueberries	Remove stalks.	10 minutes	1 lb./ 10 minutes
Cranberries	Remove stalks; pick over.	3 minutes	1 lb./ 3 minutes
Apples	Peel, core, and slice; immerse in water containing lemon juice to prevent browning. Rinse before packing.	20 minutes; applesauce needs only 15 minutes	1 lb./ 20 minutes
Dessert pears	Peel, halve, and core; immerse in water with lemon juice added. Rinse before packing.	25 minutes	1 lb./ 25 minutes
Cooking or unripe pears	Peel, halve, and core; immerse in water with lemon juice added. Tenderize in hot syrup.	30 minutes	1 lb./ 30 minutes
Quince	Peel, halve, and core; immerse in water with lemon juice added. Tenderize in hot syrup.	60 minutes	1 lb./ 60 minutes
Mulberries	Use only firm fruit.	15 minutes	1 lb./ 15 minutes
Figs	Remove stems and peel. Add $\frac{1}{2}$ tsp lemon juice to 1 quart syrup. Use equal quantities of fruit and syrup.	40 minutes	1 lb./ 40 minutes
Plums	Remove stalks, rinse, and wipe bloom from dark fruit. Halve and stone large fruit.	25 minutes	1 lb./ 25 minutes
Peaches	Blanch for 30 seconds; cool and remove skins. Halve and stone.	30 minutes	1 lb./ 30 minutes
Apricots	Remove stalks; rinse. Halve larger fruit by cutting round stone and twisting halves apart.	25 minutes	1 lb./ 25 minutes
Cherries	Remove stalks. Use whole or stone and add juice to syrup. Add $\frac{1}{2}$ tsp lemon juice to 1 quart syrup.	15 minutes	1 lb./ 15 minutes
Rhubarb	Remove leaves. Trim and cut stalks into short lengths. Soak overnight in hot syrup.	10 minutes	1 lb./ 10 minutes
Tomatoes	Choose firm tomatoes. Remove calyx, rinse, and halve or quarter if necessary. Heat before packing.	45 minutes; tomato juice needs 35 minutes	1 lb./ 45 minutes

Freezing is the best way to preserve home-grown fruits, vegetables, and many herbs for retention of their color, texture, and flavor. Freezing puts the organisms responsible for decay into a state of suspended animation, but their activities are resumed once the fruits or vegetables are thawed.

Virtually all home-grown fruits can be frozen, although some freeze more successfully than others. Pears, for example, lose their flavor when frozen, and the distinctive texture of fresh strawberries does not return once the frozen fruits are thawed.

The majority of vegetables also freeze satisfactorily. There are exceptions, however; these include leafy salad greens and others, such as cucumbers, with a high water content. In some instances, even these difficult types can be frozen if they are first cooked or made into a purée or a soup.

Successful freezing depends on following certain basic rules. Vegetables must first be blanched briefly in boiling water to halt the chemical processes going on inside them. If they are placed straight into the freezer without blanching, their flavor, appearance, and nutritional value will all suffer, because these processes will go on very slowly, even at subzero temperatures, and start up again as soon as the food is thawed.

Fruits do not need blanching, but some keep better if they are packed in sugar or syrup. Detailed instructions for individual vegetables and fruits are given in the charts on pp.232–233 and pp.234–235.

PICKING FOR FREEZING

Always freeze fruits and vegetables that are in peak condition. With vegetables, this means picking them while they are young and tender, and undamaged by pests and diseases, and with fruits before they become too ripe. In both cases, it means frequent, regular picking, preferably in small batches. Pick your crops daily if necessary to insure freshness and tenderness.

Processing small batches at a time is also necessary for the satisfactory operation of the freezer. The machine is able to cope with only a limited amount of unfrozen food in a day; as a rule, this should be no more than a tenth of its overall capacity.

Freeze garden produce as soon as possible after picking, before it can become dehydrated. Gather crops just before you plan to process them—ideally, early in the day.

Provided they are prepared well and frozen in peak condition, most fruits and vegetables will last for at least a year in the freezer without noticeable loss of quality. It makes sense to use them up within this period, and to adopt an annual pattern that corresponds to the growing and harvesting cycle of your crops.

PACKAGING

Efficient packaging is essential both to keep frozen foods in optimum condition and also to prevent smells and flavors from being transmitted from one type to another.

Plastic freezer bags, sold in several sizes, are one of the simplest forms of packaging. Always exclude as much air as possible from the bag (suck it out with a drinking straw), then seal the neck with a paper-covered wire twist.

Plastic or waxed boxes and tubs make convenient storage containers too, provided they have lids. Square or rectangular cartons make the most efficient use of space.

Clear labeling is essential; the label should record the contents, the approximate number of portions, and the date the food was put into the freezer. Use a pencil or a felt-tipped pen (not a ballpoint) to label packages and labels.

You may find it helpful to keep a record of everything you put into your freezer, and to note when you take foods out.

LOADING THE FREEZER

Place unfrozen foods in the coldest part of the freezer, where they will freeze with the least possible delay. Some freezers have a fast-freeze compartment for this purpose. Otherwise, turn the freezer to the coldest setting, then place the food on its bottom and along the sides. Most foods freeze solid within eight hours; turn the freezer down again after that.

When transferring foods after their initial freezing, place the packs in logical groups for easy retrieval, and help to cut down tedious searching with the aid of colored labels or stickers.

USING FROZEN FOODS

Allow frozen fruits to thaw quite gradually in a closed pack. Ideally, thaw them in the refrigerator for about six hours; this is especially important for fruits such as apples, which discolor quickly. Frozen fruits collapse rapidly and lose their texture if they are thawed in a warm place or left for too long once thawed. If you are in a hurry, you can thaw them (still in a covered container) for about three hours at average room temperature. Fruit that is to be cooked can be put into water or syrup while still frozen, and cooked at once.

By contrast, most vegetables are better cooked straight from the freezer, without giving them a chance to thaw.

Both vegetables and fruits should be eaten soon after being taken from the freezer. They will keep less long than fresh produce. Never refreeze any food that has been even partially thawed, except after thorough cooking.

Fruits spread out individually on a tray before dry freezing will remain separate even when packed together after they have frozen. Raspberries and strawberries are ideal for this method, and it works well for mushrooms, too. Fruits intended for eventual cooking are better packed and frozen together.

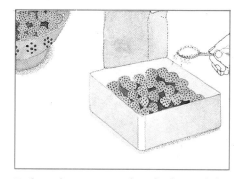

To freeze fruit in sugar, place the fruit and the sugar in layers in a rigid container. The thawed fruit will be soft and sweet, and suitable for use in a wide range of hot and cold desserts.

Rectangular containers make the best use of freezer space. To freeze puréed fruit, pour it into a plastic bag and place this in a square container. After the purée freezes, you can remove the bag and replace it in the freezer and reuse the container.

FREEZING FRUITS

Most fruits can be frozen sweetened or unsweetened, as you prefer. There are two principal methods of sweetening them for freezing: using dry sugar or a sugar syrup. The choice depends on the fruit and on its intended use.

UNSWEETENED FREEZING

This method suits most berries and is the least time-consuming. Dry-packed berries retain their shape better.

FREEZING IN SUGAR

The sugar method is suitable for fruits such as blueberries, currants, and gooseberries, as well as for cherries, but remember that sugar-frozen fruits are apt to go mushy when thawed. Use granulated sugar if possible, and allow approximately one pound of sugar to three pounds of fruit. Rigid containers are needed for this method. Layer the fruit and sugar alternately; start with fruit and finish with sugar.

FREEZING IN SUGAR SYRUP

Freezing in sugar syrup suits several stone fruits and also those that discolor easily, such as apples, peaches, plums, and apricots. It brings out the flavor of fruits such as figs, damson plums, grapes, and melons, and is a good method for fruits without much natural juice.

Allow about one quart of syrup for each three pounds of fruit. The proportion of granulated sugar to each quart of water is as follows:

Light syrup   8 ounces
Medium syrup   12 ounces
Heavy syrup   1 pound

Bring the sugar and water to the boil and boil steadily for about a minute, stirring all the time. Allow the syrup to cool. Add lemon juice at the rate of $1\frac{1}{2}$ tablespoons to each quart when freezing fruits such as apples or peaches, which are low in vitamin C and which thus discolor easily.

Place the fruit in rigid containers, and leave between a quarter-inch and a half-inch at the top to allow for expansion. Pour enough syrup over the fruit to cover it. If the fruit tends to float, place a little more in the container before fitting the lid. The syrup should come just to the top of the container.

POACHING

The skins of fruits such as apricots, plums, and peaches will harden during freezing unless they are removed or the fruit is poached. Halve and stone the fruit, then poach it in a heavy syrup (see above) for a few minutes. Allow it to cool, and then pack it into rigid containers. Alternatively, skin the fruit first.

PURÉES

Purées are a suitable form in which to freeze less-than-perfect fruit, but do not use any that are bruised or overripe.

FREEZING VEGETABLES

Most vegetables can be frozen satisfactorily and retain nearly all their natural flavor and appearance. The chief exceptions are those that contain a lot of water, such as leafy salad greens, radishes, asparagus, cucumbers, and some members of the squash family. Some vegetables, such as celery, tomatoes, and cabbage, can be frozen, but they will lose some of their texture and will be suitable only for use in cooked dishes, not in salads.

It is seldom worth bothering to freeze long-lasting, winter-hardy vegetables such as parsnips and leeks, since they are generally better left in the ground (see p.226).

The secret of successful vegetable freezing lies in blanching. For precise blanching times, see pages 232–233. Exceptions to the blanching rule are the one or two vegetables that require cooking before being placed in the freezer. Beets become rubbery if only blanched briefly. Tomatoes do not need blanching, but they do need skinning.

BLANCHING

Aim to complete the job as quickly as possible. Immerse the vegetables in boiling water and bring it back to the boil quickly. Aim to have the water boiling again within a minute of immersion. You will need a pan that holds about two and a half quarts. Blanch only small batches at a time (never more than one pound), and keep the pan on high heat for the required time.

You can use the same water, which may be lightly salted, for several batches. A wire basket makes it easy to immerse and remove vegetables. For peas and other small vegetables that can pass through the mesh, use cheesecloth bags, or line the basket with cheesecloth. Cover the pan during the blanching process.

Time the blanching very carefully. If the vegetables are blanched for too long, they will lose flavor and crispness. If they are blanched for too short a time, they will lose some of their nutritional value.

Immediately after blanching, cool the vegetables down as rapidly as possible in a bowl of cold water, preferably chilled with ice cubes. Chill them for the same length of time that they were blanched.

Once they are cooled right through, shake the vegetables in a colander and then quickly dry them on absorbent paper towels. Pack them in plastic bags or rigid containers. Exclude as much air as possible, seal the tops, and attach labels.

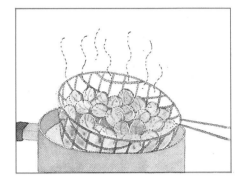

To blanch vegetables, always plunge them into water that is already boiling. Keep the heat turned up so that the water returns to the boil as quickly as possible. Blanch for the correct time—three or four minutes in the case of Brussels sprouts, depending on size.

Immediate cooling after blanching is important to prevent the vegetables from cooking and to help them keep their color. Lift the vegetables out of the water and immerse in cold water for two or three minutes. Iced water is ideal, or you can change the water once or twice during cooling.

Pack the cooled, drained, and dried vegetables into a plastic bag, then exclude as much air as possible by inserting a drinking straw through the neck, holding the plastic tight around it, and sucking out the air from inside. Seal the bag at once with a wire twist, label, and freeze.

FREEZING VEGETABLES, pages 232–233
FREEZING FRUITS, pages 234–235

VEGETABLE	PREPARATION	BLANCHING TIME	SERVING
Peas	Freeze only young peas. Shell, blanch, and cool. Pack in bags, or open-freeze, then pack. **Edible-podded peas** Wash whole pods. Trim, then blanch.	1 minute ½ minute	Cook for 5 minutes in boiling water. Cook for 7 minutes.
Shell beans	Shell small, young beans. Blanch, cool, then drain. Pack in bags, or open-freeze, then pack.	1½ minutes	Cook for 8 minutes in boiling water.
Snap beans	Trim. Leave whole or cut into one-inch pieces. Blanch, cool, then pack.	2 minutes	Cook in boiling water for 7 minutes (whole) or 5 minutes.
Runner beans	Trim. Cut in thick slices. Blanch, cool, and pack.	2 minutes	Cook for 7 minutes in boiling water.
Sweet corn	Avoid large, overripe cobs. Remove husks and silks, and slice off kernels if desired. Blanch, cool, drain, and pack.	4–6 minutes for cobs 3–5 minutes for kernels	Thaw cobs in fridge. Cook for 10 minutes in boiling water. Cook kernels for 5 minutes in boiling water.
Globe artichokes	Remove outer leaves and stalk. Cut out hairy choke, then wash and blanch. Add 1 tablespoon lemon juice to blanching water. Cool and drain upside down; pack.	6 minutes	Cook for 5 minutes in boiling water.
Asparagus	Remove woody portions and scales; wash well. Cut tips to 6 inches and blanch. Cool, drain, pack in rigid containers.	2–4 minutes	Cook for 5 minutes in boiling water.
Celery	Scrub and remove strings; cut into two-inch pieces. Blanch, cool, drain, and pack.	2 minutes	Braise or use in casseroles and soups.
Florence fennel	Wash and cut bulbs into pieces. Blanch and keep blanching water. Cool and drain. Pack in rigid containers with blanching water.	3 minutes	Simmer for 30 minutes in blanching water.
Jerusalem artichokes	Peel and slice. Soften in butter and cook in chicken stock. Purée and freeze.		Make into a soup with milk and cream, season.
Potatoes	**New** Peel and blanch. Drain and pack. **Old** Peel and dice or cut into French fries. Fry in clean fat for 4 minutes without browning. Cool and pack. Or peel and cook, then mash. Make into croquettes or duchess potatoes. Cook, then cool and pack in rigid containers.	4 minutes	Cook in boiling water until soft. Fry in deep fat. Thaw for 2 hours, then bake for 20 minutes in pre-heated oven at 350°F.
Carrots	Freeze only young, tender roots. Wash, peel, and leave whole or slice. Blanch, cool, drain, and pack.	3 minutes	Cook for 8 minutes in boiling water.
Parsnips	Trim and peel young roots. Dice or cut into quarters. Blanch, cool, drain, and pack.	2 minutes	Cook for 15 minutes in boiling water.
Rutabagas	Trim and peel. Dice or quarter. Blanch, cool, drain, and pack.	2 minutes	Cook for 15 minutes in boiling water.
Celeriac	Peel and dice or cut into thick slices. Blanch in water with 1 tablespoon lemon juice added. Cool, drain, and pack.	3 minutes	Cook for 10 minutes in boiling water.
Beets	Freeze only small young roots. Cook in boiling water until tender, then rub off skins. Pack in boxes, whole or sliced.		Thaw 2 hours, covered, in fridge. Drain and add dressing or reheat briefly in boiling water.
Salsify and scorzonera	Do not freeze well.		
Turnips	Peel, dice, and blanch small, young roots. Chop and blanch greens. Cool, drain, and pack.	2½ minutes for roots 2½ minutes for greens	Cook for 10 minutes in boiling water.
Kohlrabi	Use small, tender roots. Peel, dice, and blanch. Cool, drain, and pack.	2 minutes	Cook for 10 minutes in boiling water.

VEGETABLE	PREPARATION	BLANCHING TIME	SERVING
Winter squash and pumpkins	Cook until tender and purée. Cool and pack.		Thaw completely and use in soups, or heat and season.
Summer squash	Vegetable marrows must be peeled, seeded, and cooked until soft. Mash and freeze as a purée. Cut young squash and zucchini into half-inch slices. Blanch, cool, and pack.	1 minute	Reheat gently in butter. Fry in oil and butter.
Cucumbers	Do not freeze well.		
Eggplants	Use only tender, medium-sized eggplants. Peel and cut into one-inch slices. Blanch, chill and drain, then pack.	4 minutes	Thaw for 15 minutes and fry.
Peppers	Wash; remove stems, seeds, and membranes. Halve, dice, or slice, then blanch. Cool, drain, and pack.	2–3 minutes	Thaw for 1½ hours at room temperature, or add directly to sauces and stews.
Tomatoes	Wipe and freeze small fruits whole, without blanching. Or peel, chop, and cook for 5 minutes in their own juice. Cool and freeze. May also be puréed before freezing.		Fry, grill, or bake from frozen. Add to soups, sauces, and cooked dishes.
Mushrooms	Wipe and leave whole or slice. Blanch, or sauté in butter until soft.	4 minutes	Add frozen to dishes before cooking.
Lettuce	Does not freeze well, except as soup.		
Spinach, perpetual spinach, New Zealand spinach	Avoid older leaves with thick midribs. Remove stems from young leaves and wash. Blanch only a few leaves at a time, so they remain separate. Cool, drain, and press out excess moisture. Leave whole, chop, or purée; pack.	2 minutes	Cook from frozen for 7 minutes in butter.
Swiss chard	Freeze leaves and stems separately. Prepare and freeze leaves as for spinach. Blanch stems in water with 1 tablespoon lemon juice added. Cool, drain well, then pack in boxes or bags.	Leaves 2 minutes Stems 2 minutes	Cook leaves as for spinach. Cook stems for 7 minutes in boiling water.
Sorrel	Does not freeze well, except as a purée or soup.		
Chicory	Suitable only for cooking after freezing. Trim and wash; blanch in water with 1 tablespoon lemon juice added. Cool, drain, and press out excess water. Open-freeze, then pack in bags or boxes.	2 minutes	Thaw and cook gently in butter.
Brussels sprouts	Choose small, tight sprouts. Wash and trim. Blanch in water with a little vinegar added. Cool, drain, and pack.	3–4 minutes	Cook for 8 minutes in boiling water.
Cabbages	Crisp cabbages can be frozen. Wash, shred coarsely, and blanch. Cool, drain, and pack.	1½ minutes	Cook from frozen for 8 minutes in boiling water.
Kale and collards	Freeze only the youngest leaves and shoots, stripped from their stems. Blanch, cool, and drain. Chop, then pack.	1 minute	Cook for 8 minutes in boiling water.
Broccoli	Divide into florets and wash carefully; soak in salted water for 30 minutes. Length of blanching time depends on thickness of stalks. Cool, drain, and pack in rigid containers.	3–5 minutes	Cook for 7 minutes in boiling water.
Cauliflowers	Choose firm, compact heads. Divide into florets and wash. Blanch in water with 1 tablespoon lemon juice added. Cool, drain, and pack.	3 minutes	Cook for 8 minutes in boiling water.
Leeks	Will stand the winter outdoors. To freeze a surplus, trim and cut into rings; wash well. Blanch, cool and drain, then pack.	2 minutes	Use within 6 months. Thaw in container, then use in soups and cooked dishes.
Onions	Peel and chop or slice. Do not blanch. Overwrap to prevent the strong smell from spreading. Best stored as dry bulbs.		Thaw and use raw in salads, or add to cooked dishes.

FRUIT	PREPARATION	THAWING AND SERVING
Strawberries	Use ripe, firm fruits. UNSWEETENED Open-freeze first. Unsweetened berries retain their shape and texture best. DRY SUGAR Pack in layers with sugar in rigid container. SUGAR SYRUP Use a medium syrup. PURÉE Purée ripe fruit and sweeten to taste.	Thaw for 6 hours in fridge. Serve when barely thawed (*frappé*): strawberries deteriorate rapidly. Best used for mousses and ice creams.
Raspberries	UNSWEETENED Open-freeze on trays first. DRY SUGAR Pack in layers with sugar in rigid container. SUGAR SYRUP Use a light syrup. PURÉE Purée ripe fruit and sweeten to taste.	Thaw in fridge for 6 hours. Use fresh or in cooked desserts.
Blackberries	UNSWEETENED Open-freeze first. DRY SUGAR Pack in layers with sugar in rigid container. SUGAR SYRUP Use a heavy syrup. PURÉE Purée very ripe or less-than-perfect fruit and sweeten to taste.	Thaw in fridge for 6 hours. Use raw or cooked.
Loganberries and other hybrid berries	Prepare, freeze, and use as for blackberries.	
Gooseberries	Trim ripe fruits. UNSWEETENED Open-freeze, then pack in plastic bags. DRY SUGAR Pack in layers with sugar in rigid container. SUGAR SYRUP Use a medium syrup. PURÉE Cook to a pulp with a little water. Purée and sweeten to taste.	Cook from frozen or thaw in fridge for 6 hours to use in sauces, ice creams, mousses, and cooked pies and desserts.
Currants: red, white, and black	Strip from stems, wash, and drain. UNSWEETENED Open-freeze, then pack in bags or rigid containers. DRY SUGAR Pack in layers with sugar in rigid container. SUGAR SYRUP Use a medium syrup. PURÉE Cook black currants, then purée and sweeten to taste.	Cook while still frozen or thaw in fridge for 6 hours. Use for pies, mousses, and other desserts.
Blueberries	Wash and drain; crush slightly, since skins tend to toughen when frozen. UNSWEETENED Open-freeze, then pack in plastic bags. DRY SUGAR Pack in layers with sugar in rigid container. SUGAR SYRUP Use a heavy syrup.	Thaw in fridge for 6 hours. Best used in pies or other desserts.
Cranberries	Choose firm, glossy berries and wash and drain them. UNSWEETENED Open-freeze, then pack in bags. PURÉE Cook, purée, and sweeten to taste.	Cook in water and sugar while still frozen, or thaw purée in fridge for 6 hours.
Melons	Halve and remove seeds. Cut into cubes or scoop into balls. SUGAR SYRUP Toss in lemon juice and cover with a light syrup. Pack in rigid container.	Thaw in fridge for 6 hours; use while still slightly frosted. Use in fruit salads.
Kiwi fruits	Do not freeze well.	
Grapes	Freeze seedless grapes whole; others must be cut in half, skinned, and seeded. UNSWEETENED Freeze small seedless grapes whole. SUGAR SYRUP Use a light syrup for halved larger grapes.	Thaw in fridge for 6 hours. Use in fruit salads or pies.
Apples	Peel and core, then cut into thick slices. Drop at once into water containing 1 tablespoon lemon juice, then rinse. UNSWEETENED Blanch in boiling water for 1 minute, then cool and pack. DRY SUGAR Pack slices in layers with sugar in rigid container. SUGAR SYRUP Use a medium syrup. PURÉE Make this from windfalls or other damaged fruit, and with varieties that tend to go mushy when cooked. Cook with a little water and a little sugar until soft.	Cook from frozen for pies and other desserts. Use purée for sauces and puddings.

FRUIT	PREPARATION	THAWING AND SERVING
Pears	Not recommended for freezing unless peeled, quartered, cored, and cooked until tender in light syrup. Cool, then freeze pears and syrup together.	Thaw for 6 hours in fridge. Use in cooked desserts or mousses.
Quince	Peel and core, then cut into segments. Cook gently in a light syrup for 20 minutes. Cool, then pack slices and syrup in small, rigid containers.	Thaw for 6 hours in fridge. Use in small quantities with other fruits.
Mulberries	Freeze as for blackberries.	
Figs	Choose sweet, ripe figs; remove stems and avoid bruising. UNSWEETENED Open-freeze on trays, then pack in strong plastic bags. SUGAR SYRUP Use a light syrup, to which 1 tablespoon lemon juice has been added. Freeze peeled or unpeeled.	Thaw in fridge for 6 hours. Can be served as a dessert, in syrup.
Plums	Halve and remove the stones. Avoid varieties with tough skins, or scald for 1 minute in boiling water. Drop into water containing 1 tablespoon lemon juice. Drain and dry. UNSWEETENED Pack into rigid container. SUGAR SYRUP Use a light syrup.	Thaw in fridge for 6 hours, in closed pack. Use immediately, since the color is quickly lost.
Peaches and nectarines	Peel the fruit under cold running water. Halve and stone them, then dip them into water to which you have added 1 tablespoon lemon juice. Peaches discolor readily, so you need to work quickly. Leave in halves, or slice. DRY SUGAR Pack in layers with sugar in a rigid container. SUGAR SYRUP Use a light or medium syrup to which you have added 1½ tablespoons lemon juice to each quart of syrup. PURÉE Purée very ripe fruit and sweeten to taste. Add 1 tablespoon lemon juice to every pound of fruit.	Thaw in fridge for 6 hours. Use, nearly thawed, fresh or in cooked desserts.
Apricots	Peel, halve, and stone. Drop into water containing 1 tablespoon lemon juice. DRY SUGAR Pack halved fruit in layers with sugar in a rigid container. SUGAR SYRUP Peel the fruit, cut into slices, and cover with a medium syrup. PURÉE Purée very ripe stoned and sliced fruits. Sweeten to taste, and add lemon juice at 1 tablespoon per pound to prevent browning.	Thaw in covered container for 6 hours and use fresh or in cooked desserts.
Cherries	Chill in water for 1 hour to firm them, then remove the stones. UNSWEETENED Open-freeze, then pack in rigid container. Cherry juice remains liquid when frozen. DRY SUGAR Pack fruit in layers with sugar in rigid container. SUGAR SYRUP Use a medium syrup, to which you have added 1 tablespoon lemon juice, for sweet cherries. Use a heavy syrup, also with lemon juice added, for sour cherries.	Thaw in fridge for 6 hours and use uncooked or in pies or cooked desserts.
Rhubarb	Wash, trim, and cut the stalks into one-inch lengths. UNSWEETENED Blanch pieces in boiling water for 1 minute, then drain, cool, and pack. SUGAR SYRUP Use a medium or heavy syrup. PURÉE Cook to a pulp in a little water, then sweeten to taste.	Cook from frozen, or thaw purée in fridge for 6 hours.

All herbs are better for being freshly gathered, but there are several months of the year when picking is not possible for most species. Apart from evergreen herbs such as bay and rosemary, and any perennial or biennial herbs overwintered indoors in pots, from autumn onward it is necessary to rely on what you have preserved from the previous summer.

Herbs can be either dried or frozen for winter use; they will be unsuitable for use as a garnish, however. Remember that the flavor of dried herbs is usually more concentrated, and you need to use only half the quantity specified for fresh herbs in a recipe, except for rosemary and tarragon, which are used in equal quantities. Both methods of preservation are straightforward and easy to follow.

FREEZING HERBS
This means of preserving retains the flavor of herbs well, though they will become limp when they are thawed. Frozen herbs are best used within six months. The best results are obtained with young, tender stems and leaves which have been picked fairly early in the summer, before the plants come into flower. The most suitable herbs for freezing are the tender-leaved species such as basil, mint, chives, and parsley.

Freezing whole
Pick young shoots, or sprigs, and pack them in plastic bags. It is a good idea to place plastic bags in a rigid container afterward, to enable you to find them easily and to avoid undue crushing in the freezer.

It is essential to package frozen herbs in a really airtight fashion, to insure that their aroma does not permeate other foods in the freezer. Mint is especially penetrating. Seal plastic bags carefully, and reseal them well if you remove some of the contents and return the rest to the freezer.

Frozen herbs can be used to flavor foods without thawing; simply crumble them into the dish before cooking.

Freezing in water
This is a convenient way to freeze all kinds of leafy herbs. Strip the leaves from the stalks and chop them finely. Place a measured amount in each compartment of an ice-cube tray and top them up with water. Put the tray back into the freezer or the ice compartment of a refrigerator.

When the cubes are hard, empty them into a plastic container or freezer bag and seal tightly. Label the bag and place it in the freezer. Take several cubes out at a time and put them straight into the pan or dish with the ingredients they will flavor. If you are using the herbs for an omelette or some other dish in which you do not want extra water, thaw the cubes in a sieve.

DRYING HERBS
The leaves of herbs have maximum flavor and aroma when they are young and soft, before the flowers develop on the plant. This is the time to gather the leaves for drying; choose a warm, dry day, if possible, and pick them early in the morning.

Pull off any damaged or diseased leaves and tie up the sprigs in bunches. Strip larger-leaved herbs, such as sage and mint, from their stalks, then tie these together. There is no need to blanch herbs for drying, although immersing them for a few seconds in boiling water helps them to retain their color. Shake off excess moisture and dry them on paper towels.

Hang the bunches, leaves downward, to dry in a well-ventilated, dry, fairly warm place, such as a shed, a porch, or a room indoors. It is important to dry them in a dark place so that the color does not bleach out. If you wish, you can wrap them in cheesecloth or thin paper bags to keep the dust off. Drying will take between five and fourteen days, depending on the amount of warmth and humidity and the type of leaf.

Alternatively, spread the individual sprigs or leaves on a bench or tray, well spaced out. Place the tray on top of a radiator, in the oven, or in a warm cupboard. Turn the leaves every day or so to insure even drying. They will take only two or three days to dry out completely.

Although natural air drying is the best means of preserving herbs, you can also dry the leaves in an oven, set to the lowest temperature and with the door ajar. Place the blanched leaves on a covered tray and turn them after half an hour; they will be dry in an hour.

Whichever method you use, once the herbs are thoroughly dry and crisp enough to crumble when touched, remove the hard stalks and leaf midribs and keep the leaves as intact as possible. Store them, carefully labeled, in airtight jars in a cool place. Place glass jars in a dark cupboard. Crush the whole leaves just before use. Dried herbs will keep their flavor for about a year.

In addition to drying and storing herbs individually, you may want to make up a number of *bouquets garnis*, each consisting of three sprigs of parsley, a bay leaf, a sprig of marjoram, and a sprig of thyme—or any other combination. Tie the herbs together and dry them; leave them intact, but enclose each bunch in a small cheesecloth bag. Store the bags in an airtight jar.

If you wish to gather the seeds of herbs such as dill, fennel, and coriander, pick the flower heads when they are fully ripe and hang them upside down to dry in an airy place. Enclose them in a bag to catch the ripe seeds as they fall.

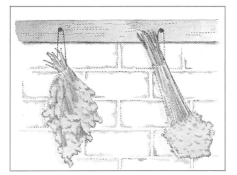

Small-leaved or feathery herbs, such as marjoram, fennel, and chervil, can be tied in bunches and hung upside down to dry in an airy place. Leaves of herbs such as sage and mint should be stripped from their stems and tied together by their leaf stalks.

When the herbs are thoroughly dry, strip the leaves off their stalks and store them in an airtight container such as a screw-top jar. Large leaves, such as sage, may need to be crumbled before storage, but small ones can be stored whole and crushed just before use.

Freezing finely chopped herbs in an ice-cube tray is a convenient method of preservation. Top them up with a little water before freezing, and simply drop the frozen cubes into the pan or dish when cooking. It is most convenient to freeze measured amounts, such as a teaspoonful or tablespoonful.

HERB, pages 219–223
FREEZING, pages 230–231

INDEX

INDEX

ADDRESSES OF SUPPLIERS

GENERAL SEED SUPPLIERS

Burpee Seed Co.
Warminster, PA 18974

Gurney's Seed and Nursery Co.
Yankton, SD 57079

Harris Moran Seed Co.
3670 Buffalo Road
Rochester, NY 14624

D. Landreth Seed Co.
180–188 West Ostend St.
Baltimore, MD 21230

Olds Seed Co.
P.O. Box 7790
Madison, WI 53707

Park Seed Co.
P.O. Box 31
Greenwood, SC 29646

Stokes Seeds
Box 548
Buffalo, NY 14240

Thompson & Morgan
P.O. Box 158
Jackson, NJ 08527

SPECIALTY SEED SUPPLIERS

Epicure Seeds Ltd.
P.O. Box 450
Brewster, NY 10509
(European seeds)

Gardenimport
P.O. Box 760
Thornhill, Ontario
CANADA L3T 4A5
(Seeds from England,
Catalogue $1)

Grace's Garden
10 Bay Street
Westport, CT 06880
(Giant vegetables,
Catalogue $1)

Herb Gathering Inc.
5742 Kenwood Ave.
Kansas City, MO 64110
(French vegetables,
Catalogue $2)

High Altitude Gardens
P.O. Box 4238
Ketchum, ID 83340

Le Jardin du Gourmet
P.O. Box 44
West Danville, VT 05873
(French seeds, shallots
Catalogue 50¢)

Johnny's Selected Seeds
Albion, ME 04910
(Short-season crops)

Le Marche Seeds Intl.
P.O. Box 566
Dixon, CA 95620
(Catalogue $2)

Native Seeds/SEARCH
3950 West New York Dr.
Tucson, AZ 85745
(Catalogue $1)

Nichols Garden Nursery
1190 North Pacific Hwy.
Albany, OR 97321
(Herbs, oriental
vegetables)

Pine Tree Garden Seeds
Rt. 100
New Gloucester, ME 04260

Plants of the Southwest
1812 Second St.
Santa Fe, NM 87501

Shepherd's Garden Seeds
7389 West Zayante Rd.
Felton, CA 95018
(Wide variety of foreign
seeds, Catalogue $1)

Sunrise Oriental Seed Co.
P.O. Box 10058
Elmwood, CT 06110
(Catalogue $1)

Vermont Bean Seed Co.
Garden Lane
Bomoseen, VT 05732

FRUITS, NUTS, AND BERRIES

Adams County Nursery, Inc.
P.O. Box 108
Aspers, PA 17304

Bear Creek Farms
P.O. Box 411
Northport, WA 99157
(Antique apples)

Edible Landscaping
Rt. 2, Box 343A
Afton, VA 22920
(Gooseberries, black
currants)

Emlong Nurseries, Inc.
Stevensville, MI 49127

**Henry Field's Seed &
Nursery**
Shenandoah, IA 51602

Dean Foster Nurseries, Inc.
P.O. Box 127
Hatford, MI 49057

Fowler Nurseries
525 Fowler Road
Newcastle, CA 95658

Johnson Nursery
Rt. 5
Elligay, GA 30540

Kelly Bros. Nurseries, Inc.
Dansville, NY 14437

Leuthardt Nurseries
Montauk Hwy., Box 666
East Moriches, NY 11940

Miller Nurseries
5060 West Lake Road
Canandaigua, NY 14424

Raintree Nursery
391 Butts Road
Morton, WA 98356

St Lawrence Nurseries
R.D. 2
Potsdam, NY 13676

Stark Brothers Nurseries
Louisiana, MO 63353

Vermont Fruit Tree Co.
Box 34
New Haven, VT 05472

Waynesboro Nurseries
Waynesboro, VA 22980